NO RIGHT TURN

NO RIGHT TURN

CONSERVATIVE POLITICS
IN A LIBERAL AMERICA

David T. Courtwright

HARVARD UNIVERSITY PRESS

Cambridge, Massachusetts

London, England

2010

Publication of this book has been supported through the generous provisions
of the Maurice and Lula Bradley Smith Memorial Fund.

Library of Congress Cataloging-in-Publication Data

Courtwright, David T., 1952–
No right turn : conservative politics in a liberal America / David T.
Courtwright.
    p.   cm.
Includes bibliographical references and index.
ISBN 978-0-674-04677-1 (alk. paper)
1. Conservatism—United States.   2. United States—Politics and
government—1945–1989.   3. United States—Politics and
government—1989–   4. Christianity and politics—United States.   5. United
States—Religion—1945–   I. Title.
    JC573.2.U6C68   2010
    320.520973—dc22   2010008321

To Andrew Courtwright and the memory of Bob Loftin

CONTENTS

NO RIGHT TURN

Richard Nixon liked to talk politics. Three weeks before the 1972 election he called up Chuck Colson, a political aide so attuned to the president that the two men often finished one another's sentences. The rest of the White House staff, Nixon told Colson, didn't understand the average voter. "The gut issue is amnesty, it's abortion, it's parochial aid to get to these people," he complained. "I mean, they're not appealed to by *revenue sharing*. Everybody wants me to go and make a big goddam speech about revenue sharing. Nobody gives a goddam."

"They really don't, Mr. President," Colson said. "You have to take issues that affect the person individually. First of all, you have 'Is the country safe?' That's the first thing people think of. The next thing after is it safe, is pride in the economy."

"Right."

"Then they begin to get to the issues like, 'Goddam, I don't want to be working hard and paying all this money to have . . .' "

"These welfare bums," Nixon interrupted.

"These welfare bums."

"Another thing is," Nixon said, 'I served, four and a half million of our kids served, and these bright intellectuals sent their kids off to Canada.' "

"Off to Canada, by God."

"To hell with them."

"That's exactly . . ."

"Oh, I know."

"And then," Colson said, "with some of the Catholic groups that we're winning, you get the parochial aid, and you get the abortion . . ."

"That's right."

"They're meaningful, basically, because . . ."

"You know what it all gets down to?" Nixon said. "It gets down to character, the national character. McGovern is for softening the character and I'm for toughening it up. And that's a big issue of this campaign."[1]

Nixon spoke a larger truth than he knew. The question of national character was an issue, not only in 1972, but in every presidential campaign from 1968 to 2008. It became the rallying cry of the counterrevolution against the legacies of the 1960s that transformed American politics. And it created problems for Democrats well beyond their McGovern miscue.

From the late 1960s Republican strategists sensed the potential for realignment. Democratic voters who had supported independent candidate George Wallace in 1968 were halfway out of the party. Defense, busing, crime, and welfare dependency might yet coax them into the Republican fold. Adviser Patrick Buchanan thought Nixon could meld blocs of historically hostile voters—eastern Republicans, southern Protestants, northern and western Catholics—into an unbeatable New Majority. If Nixon could raise his share of Catholic voters from 25 to 40 percent, he would gain more votes than if he went from 0 to 100 percent of Jewish voters. If he was going to give fifty Phantom jets to Israel when the Jews weren't going to support him anyway, why not at least help the Catholics bail out their school system?

Buchanan knew that southern Protestants disliked federal aid to northern parochial schools. But he sensed that American politics had reached the point where social conservatism counted for more than nativism. Anti-Catholicism, still potent in 1960 when John Kennedy squeaked into the White House, was a spent force. Two Catholics, Robert Kennedy and Eugene McCarthy, had run for the Democratic presidential nomination in 1968. Edmund Muskie, the son of Polish Catholic immigrants, had come close to the nomination in 1972. Another Catholic, Edward Kennedy, missed the prize when he drove off a Chappaquiddick bridge and left his blonde passenger to her fate. Character was decisive. Protestantism was not.

Yet the wrong religious *temperament* could alienate voters. Rank-and-file Catholics had shunned Eugene McCarthy in 1968, Buchanan thought, because he was a snobbish liberal who hobnobbed with peaceniks and radicals. Catholic working stiffs were "Dick Daley men." McGovern's softness on crime, abortion, pornography, and pot would make them Dick Nixon men. Already moving from their old ethnic neighborhoods into the suburbs, they were poised to move out of their old party, making common cause with morally conservative Protestants. "Working class types care about 'symbols,' such as Roosevelt's comparison of the Wall Street boys with the money-changers," Buchanan pointed out. Nixon could work the same populist magic with conservative social causes.

Which he did, winning every state but Massachusetts in the 1972 presidential election. Yet Nixon's coattails were short. Democrats still competed well on bread-and-butter issues. Liberals held sway in the Congress, the state capitols, the city halls, the courts, the bureaucracy, the media, and the universities. What Nixon had to do next, Buchanan argued, was lay siege to the liberal establishment. Appoint strict constructionists to check judicial activism. Fill jobs with political loyalists. Clean out the nest of vipers in public television. Gut the poverty programs, or at least send the research money to allies at Fordham and Brigham Young. Hammer the liberal media. Build a network of foundations to nurture conservative talent. The future beckoned. Nixon could be "the Republican FDR," the founder of a new political dynasty that would last well beyond his second term.[2]

Though the Watergate scandal would keep Nixon from realizing this ambition, Buchanan had glimpsed the future. In the 1980s and 1990s, the strategy of uniting religious, racial, and economic conservatives by attacking liberalism, moral root and institutional branch, made the Republicans the dominant national party, competitive in every region of the country. The strategy paved the way for the success of Ronald Reagan, the man who did become the Republican FDR, as well as George H. W. Bush, Newt Gingrich, George W. Bush, and Buchanan himself, still bashing liberals long after his boss boarded Marine One, spread his arms in a last salute, and departed the White House.

No Right Turn

This book describes the origins, politics, personalities, and outcome of the long national struggle over morality commonly called "the culture wars" or "the Culture War." (The plural evokes the many particular battles, the singular the underlying, epochal clash of worldviews.) Though its roots extend back to the Enlightenment, the Culture War only became politically consequential in the second half of the 1960s, when Republicans began using wedge issues like crime and permissiveness to pry blocs of morally conservative voters away from the Democratic Party, said to be controlled by the same liberal elite that dominated the press, schools, and judiciary. As best as I can tell, Daniel Patrick Moynihan first described the situation as a Culture War (*"Kulturkampf"*) in a 1970 memo to Nixon. I have made do with plain English to describe the era and the trend, the transformation and embitterment of politics by fundamental moral disputes that both parties, but especially the Republicans, exploited for their own ends. Those disputes did not end with the GOP's defeat in 2008. Like a hurricane downgraded to a tropical storm after making landfall, the Culture War has continued to disturb the nation's political weather. But that is the pundit's domain. My aim is to recreate the hurricane's path, and to show what happened to those caught in it.[3]

I also mean to solve a mystery. I found the culture warriors' motives and tactics easy to describe, but puzzled over the outcome of their struggle. For all their energy and political success, moral conservatives failed to win on their key issues, much less recapture the culture. They filled the airwaves with angry talk, the prisons with criminals, and the legislatures with Republicans. But they made little progress on abortion and school prayer, and lost ground on obscenity, gay rights, and legalized gambling. Popular culture kept getting raunchier. In protest-filled 1969, the televised Super Bowl entertainment consisted of the Florida A&M University Marching Band and a sideline interview with comedian Bob Hope. In placid 2004, with Republicans everywhere in power, Janet Jackson flashed her nipple ring during the halftime show. She was followed by a streaker with the name of an Internet gambling site emblazoned on his backside. What was going on?

This is a puzzle because revolutions and counterrevolutions driven by social and religious issues normally reshape cultures. Daily life changes, along with the faces in the palace. The theaters reopened after the English Restoration—and closed after the Iranian Revolution. The Republicans' Revolution of 1800 marked the end of the Federalists' gentlemanly cultural dominance as well as their hold on the presidency. The path from Thomas Jefferson to Andrew Jackson is easy to follow. The path from Richard Nixon to Janet Jackson is not. Somehow, the moral revolution of the 1960s became so entrenched that it defied the most determined attacks by its most politically successful enemies. They declared no truce, yet won no decisive victory. It was maddening. The more the liberals lost at the polls, the more their wicked works seemed to prosper. Why?

4

Answering that question required something more than the familiar definitions of liberalism and conservatism. Two distinct constellations of issues divided Americans and defined their domestic politics in the late twentieth century. The first involved moral questions like abortion, the second economic questions like taxation. Rather than being simply left or right, Americans evolved a politics in which it was possible to be morally left but economically right, or vice versa. Two major shifts, the moral one of the 1960s followed by the economic one of Reaganism, occurred within a single generation. By the 1990s American voters were more secular and permissive than their counterparts of the 1940s, but also more suspicious of the government's size and interference with market forces, at least when it involved something other than middle-class entitlements. Though seemingly opposed—the 1960s being more congenial to liberals, Reaganism to conservatives—these two revolutions of the self turned out to be mutually supportive, especially for baby boomers. The unfettered, high-tech capitalism and renewed prosperity of the 1980s and 1990s frustrated religious conservatives' efforts to reimpose traditional morality.[4]

The peculiarly American twist to this familiar story was the two-party system, which diminished the leverage of the resurgent religious voters. Unlike members of the religious parties in, say, Israel's Knesset, where the loss of a handful of seats could break a coalition, religious conservatives in America lacked institutional bargaining power. As Nixon foresaw, they had no practical alternative to the Republican Party once the Democratic Party made itself unavailable to them. The Republican strategy, said political scientist Earl Black, was to have the likes of Reverend Pat Robertson *on* the bus, not driving the bus. Once on board, religious conservatives found themselves seated well to the rear. From the late 1970s onward, Republicans made tax reduction and deregulation the core of their party's domestic program.[5]

The party's market wolves did not always feast at the expense of its religious lambs. Economic conservatives—the principled ones, anyway—had cause to be disappointed by free-spending Republicans. Yet, with three major domestic-policy exceptions—crime, drugs, and welfare—Republican politicians paid less attention to reactionary moral causes than to economic ones. The exceptions are important because they map America's racial and class fault lines. But when the object was something other than controlling the underclass, protecting the middle class, or disciplining the undeserving poor, moral conservatives usually stood at the back of the GOP line.

Many journalists and scholars have embraced the idea of a national "right turn" to describe political and social changes during the Culture War. A turning there was, but one full of switchbacks and dead ends, with resistance all along the way. A better metaphor would be the western front in 1914–1917. After a spectacular offensive and counteroffensive, the Great War bogged down into a stalemate, one that left the attackers in possession of much of the territory they had conquered. During the Culture War conservatives had the satisfaction of seeing liberals turned out of office, the top tax rates decline, and the Soviet Union collapse. But economic conservatives failed in their ultimate objective, to unravel the New Deal and bring federal spending under control. Moral conservatives failed in their ultimate objective, to wring permissiveness from the 1960s-saturated culture. Their counteroffensive failed to push the front back to Eisenhower, let alone to Hoover.

Republican politicians covered conservatism's strategic failures with optimistic slogans like "morning in America" and half-truths like "the Reagan Revolution." Confusing matters further, left-liberal activists seized on the myth of imminent conservative victory to rally their troops and fill their own war chests. But tactical alarmism did not mean that conservatives had won the Culture War. What they did win were enough battles to create a frustrating deadlock. That deadlock soured voters, imprisoned millions, drained the Treasury, stoked partisanship, stymied reform, and besmirched American democracy, or what was left of it in an age of media politics. There was something not right about Culture War politics, in all senses of the term.

Religious Temperaments

Behind its political façade, the Culture War was fundamentally a religious war, though not in the usual sense of combat between rival faiths. Battle lines formed within denominations. When, for example, Buchanan urged Nixon to go after Catholic voters, he meant the sort of Catholics who went on retreats, fought abortion in the state legislatures, and sent their kids to parochial schools. Though ethnic and often blue-collar, they respected the president's values. Nixon's name meant something to them. Liberal Catholics were hopeless, worse than the *Times* crowd. "There is a deep division in the Catholic community," Buchanan argued.

"We should be working the Catholic social conservatives—the clear majority."[6]

Historian Philip Greven gave a name to what Buchanan was describing. Greven said that all members of a religious group manifested *temperaments*, personal conceptions of God, self, sin, and duty that cut across denominational lines. Until the early nineteenth century, most Americans of European descent displayed one of three Protestant temperaments, Evangelical, Moderate, or Genteel. (He capitalized them to emphasize their common features, as I do.) The inner experience of the Evangelicals was one of self-suppression. They believed that humans were deeply flawed and that those who thought otherwise, and who satisfied themselves with earthly pleasures, were likely headed for hell. Evangelicals hoped to escape this fate because they had undergone a conversion rooted in the conviction of personal sinfulness and a resolve to subjugate their wills to God's. Moderates thought the self needed to be controlled rather than annihilated. They believed in sin, but not that everything worldly was sinful. Grace might come to an individual gradually, in the course of a restrained and dutiful life. The Genteel led a more self-indulgent existence. They took their state of grace for granted, confident that the church and sacraments would suffice for personal salvation. Raised by affectionate parents inclined to spare the rod, they had relaxed consciences, a benevolent conception of God, and a notion that church was a good place to catch up on gossip.[7]

The three Protestant temperaments formed a spectrum of attitudes toward the self, running from Genteel self-assertion on the left to Moderate self-control in the middle to Evangelical self-suppression on the right. These Protestant types persisted through the nineteenth and twentieth centuries, even as immigration made America a more diverse nation. The growing non-Protestant population evolved its own religious temperaments. Call these Devout, Observant, and Selective for the Catholics, and Orthodox, Conservative, and Reform for the Jews.

Devout Catholics involved themselves in numerous devotional practices, attended Mass daily, and confessed their sins weekly. The Observant were less involved in devotional practices, but attended Mass weekly and confessed at least once a year. The Selective graced their parish churches at Easter or Christmas and confessed rarely, if at all. Among Jews, the Orthodox punctiliously observed the Torah as God's binding Law. Conservative Jews minded the Law but worried less about pious comportment or avoiding Gentiles. Reform Jews regarded the Law as a product of human history, to be selectively obeyed while going about their affairs.

Then there were Americans who belonged to no church or synagogue and who professed no creed. They comprised a fourth, nonreligious category in which the self had become dominant. The nonreligious did not always think or act selfishly. Some embraced communitarian ideals and committed themselves to philanthropic sacrifice to alleviate suffering. But they acted out of a sense that whatever meaning or pleasure life holds was to be realized in this world, not in the next. They identified with no religion and often doubted or denied the existence of God. In 1957 the number of persons willing to admit such beliefs to pollsters was very small, 3 percent of the population. But their ranks expanded during the later 1960s and kept on growing, reaching 15 percent of the population in 2008. The typical nonbeliever was a highly educated male baby boomer living in a northeastern or west coast "blue state," though no region was without its skeptics and village atheists.[8]

"We do not see things as they are," one of Anaïs Nin's characters reflects, "we see them as we are." For the nonreligious, reality centered on the dominant self. Those of Genteel, Selective, or Reform temperament displayed more circumspect forms of self-assertion. Moderate, Observant, and Conservative believers showed more self-control, though not the self-suppression that marked the Evangelical, Devout, or Orthodox. The same spectrum ran through other faiths. There were apostate and progressive Muslims, as well as traditional and fundamentalist Muslims. There were ex-Mormons and "jack Mormons," as well as temple-endowed and zealous Mormons. For shorthand purposes, those most intent on reining in the self were on the "moral right" of a given faith tradition, those least intent on the "moral left."[9]

A philosopher would object to conflating the moral right and the religious right, or to using the terms interchangeably. After all, a person can arrive at a morally conservative position without appealing to supernatural belief. Two famous opponents of abortion, Bernard Nathanson and Nat Hentoff, were Jewish atheists when they decided, after careful reflection, that they could not justify killing the unborn. As a practical matter, though, most Americans (unless suffering through a philosophy essay exam) did not resort to formal ethical reasoning to settle moral questions, above all questions of sexual morality. Their views on these things hinged on their temperaments, the convictions about self, sin, and the world that were central to their identities. In Nathanson's case, pro-life conversion proved to be the first step in a spiritual journey that ended at the baptismal font.[10]

Religion shaped personal identity in other ways, such as separating in-groups from out-groups. Cuban-Americans who had not attended Mass in years still regarded their Catholicism as a mark of superiority to disciples of Santería. Jewish birth was hardly irrelevant to the social lives of nonreligious Jews. But religion's worldly uses should not obscure the psychological reality of belief, or its influence on behavior. "Religion is at the root of morality," as Buchanan put it, "and morality is the basis of law." Many secular intellectuals agreed with him. Marxists and Straussians both emphasized religion's moral influence, differing only as to its desirability. The Straussians regarded it as an indispensable source of moral guidance for the masses, if not for the elites who ruled them.[11]

Why did religious temperaments vary? Greven thought early upbringing determined religious outlook. Those who were raised by Evangelical parents, who had been severely disciplined as children, were more likely to submit to the Divine Parent later in life. They were also more likely to behave in puritanical and extremist ways, and to vent their suppressed anger against unholy outsiders, not to say their own bruised and welted offspring. Moderate parents who combined discipline with love and respect for autonomy produced even-tempered children who thought selfish impulses needed to be controlled, not annihilated. Genteel, indulgent parents got worldly, self-assertive children.[12]

George Lakoff, a linguist with a taste for politics, made a similar argument about unconscious worldviews. Liberals derived their outlooks from "Nurturant Parents," conservatives from "Strict Fathers." Moral preferences in politics reflected moral attitudes in families. Scratch a Clinton-impeachment supporter, find an authoritarian who thought naughty boys ought to be spanked. For Lakoff, the parent who let the baby cry through the night was more likely to be, and to raise, a moral conservative, other things being equal.[13]

Except that other things did not stay equal. Puberty, peers, and professors reshuffled childhood's deck, which was why religious parents worried about all three. Anything could happen. Alfred Kinsey and Hugh Hefner grew up in strict Methodist homes. *Penthouse* publisher Bob Guccione was an ex-seminarian. Madonna toed the line until she discovered boys. So did Andy Warhol, who finessed his homosexuality with a Devout to Selective Catholic switch. Conversely, Thomas Merton fathered an illegitimate child and flirted with communism before he converted to

Catholicism and became a Trappist monk. Temple Morgan was a blue-blooded Harvard student who fell under the spell of a Jesuit homilist named Leonard Feeney. In 1947 Morgan quit Harvard and embraced Rome, scandalizing Boston's Protestant establishment. The novelist Mary Gordon's father, another Harvard man, was a Jewish convert to Catholicism who came to admire Spanish dictator Francisco Franco and hate Protestants. Yet Mary Gordon herself became a Selective Catholic.[14]

Moral Right and Left

Though individuals could change their beliefs over a lifetime, they usually manifested a single temperament at any one point in time. Broadly speaking, the further they were to the right of a given faith, the more likely they were to believe in free will, sin, punishment, and absolute moral standards grounded in sacred scriptures. To violate these standards was to provoke God and to invite his punishment, as well as that of civil authorities. Moral rightists supported state action to suppress gambling, prostitution, obscenity, intoxication, sodomy, and abortion. Such legislation was both symbolic and instrumental in that it conferred official status on conservative norms and discouraged behavior that offended God and subverted family life.

For moral rightists, the patriarchal family was the basic unit of society. Strong families required clear gender roles, which doubled as firewalls against homosexuality and feminism. That was why gay Mormons, or Evangelical women who discovered feminism,went through hell. The churches they loved were unembarrassed about policing heterosexual norms or rebuking women who stepped outside of maternal roles. Threats to traditional roles were threats to the social order and to the idea of a divinely ordered cosmos, the psychological bedrock of all faith. God knew what He was doing when He made the world hierarchical and spelled out the rules. Individuals had to subordinate their desires to the wishes of familial, community, state, and other authorities, provided only that their orders did not countermand His Law.[15]

Psychologist Jonathan Haidt has compared our moral feelings to an audio equalizer with five sliding switches: caring, fairness, in-group loyalty, respect for authority, and purity. Moral rightists liked their music with all five tuned up. Moral leftists liked only the first two, caring and fairness. "Justice," as Abbie Hoffman put it, "is all you need." He meant social justice, not the policing of boundaries, deference, or sanctity. Moral leftists rejected the concept of absolute, let alone divinely inspired, moral standards. They opposed the prosecution of victimless crimes. Confronted with a prohibition, they asked, "Why not?"—the dying words, in fact, of psychedelic guru Timothy Leary. If unconvinced by a secular answer, moral leftists assumed the prohibition to be unjustified. That assumption rested on another assumption, that human beings were fundamentally good and, if liberated from arbitrary and oppressive authority, would flourish. "We regard men as infinitely precious," proclaimed the 1962 *Port Huron Statement* of the Students for a Democratic Society, "and possessed of unfulfilled capacities for reason, freedom, and love."[16]

And sex. Nowhere was the tendency of the moral leftists to challenge the old rules more apparent than with respect to sexual purity, the indispensable basis for sanctity in the Western religious tradition. They regarded sex as a legitimate pleasure, a means of growth and self-fulfillment, and, in some contexts, a vehicle of political expression. They did not regard it as necessarily linked to marriage or procreation, and hence opposed Judeo-Christian sexual ethics. "Let the bedroom be the last stronghold of individual initiative," journalist Richard Rovere wrote in his journal. "Masturbation, sodomy, fellation—let such as want them have them." More publicly, the novelist Philip Roth declared, "There are no sexual norms that an adult can take seriously."[17]

The further one was to the moral left, the more likely one's thinking was to be shaped by determinism and relativism. If individual beliefs about truth and morality were conditioned by historical, social, and cultural circumstances, there was good reason to be cautious about imposing any particular set of moral standards. Much energy went into unmasking moral claims, exposing assumptions thought to be natural and universal as myths of a dominant, coercive ideology. The denial of transcendent morality ran like a bright thread through feminist and sexual-minority literature. The same writers gave an activist edge to social constructionism, the ambitious intellectual movement that sought to overthrow existing conceptions of knowledge, empirical and religious. For social constructionists, the very idea of an autonomous individual thinker, let alone a free moral agent, was just another fairy tale.

Why those who believed all ideologies to be historically contingent should engage in so much "rights talk" for preferred causes was an apparent inconsistency, often noted by philosophers and intellectual historians.

One explanation is that moral leftists, rather than denying the existence of evil, tended to locate it in oppressive systems or privileged groups rather than in individuals. Thus fascism was evil, as was Stalinism, or segregation, or the bourgeoisie. Postmodernism notwithstanding, the moral left's dominant pattern of thinking remained progressive: Identify a social evil, analyze its causes, and use the knowledge to modify social arrangements to make the evil abate. The basic political assumption remained that of the Enlightenment. The educated vanguard could improve the world. Nor was this a purely secular impulse. The idea of targeting unjust social arrangements became entrenched in twentieth-century liberal religion, such as the Protestant Social Gospel movement, the Jewish Social Justice movement, and various liberation theologies.[18]

The deemphasis on personal sin and repentance drew the fire of religious traditionalists. Changing social and economic structures to create "a new man and a new world" was an illusion, Joseph Cardinal Ratzinger said in 1984. "It is precisely personal sin that is in reality at the root of unjust social structures." The only ones responsible for Wounded Knee, Pat Buchanan wrote, were the ones *at* Wounded Knee. Collective guilt was a liberal myth. Individual responsibility remained the moral right's irreducible bottom line. That was why most white Evangelicals supported the death penalty and denied that racial discrimination was systematic. If sinners would repent and embrace Jesus, they believed, people would make friends across racial lines.[19]

Nowhere were the differences between the moral left and right sharper than with respect to the existence, nature, and consequences of lust. Evangelicals took the matter so seriously, observed sociologist William Martin, that when they spoke of "immorality" without qualification they meant extramarital sex. No one, no matter how famous, escaped the obligation of continence. That was one reason why Evangelicals, white ones anyway, were reluctant to honor Martin Luther King Jr. with a national holiday. King devoted his life to the struggle for racial equality, a crusade that won him a Nobel Prize and the satisfaction of seeing the end of legal segregation. Yet he also drank to excess, told raunchy jokes, and indulged in numerous affairs, captured on FBI wiretap tapes with such unbecoming accompaniments as "I'm fucking for God!" and "I'm not a Negro tonight!" King wasn't an adulterer, one FBI official decided. He was a marathon adulterer. He was still at it in the Lorraine Motel, in the small hours of the night before his murder. He died with alcohol in his blood, fat in his liver, and a cigarette in his clenched hand.[20]

Those words are a litmus test. If they make you mad at King for be-having badly, you are likely on the moral right. If they make you mad at me for spilling the beans, you are likely on the moral left. King's allies certainly regarded his vices as peccadilloes, and hardly exceptional. "Everybody was out getting laid," recalled activist Michael Harrington, a disenchanted Catholic turned socialist and atheist. King's national sig-nificance stemmed from his leadership and courage, his willingness to put his life on the line. His dalliances were irrelevant.[21]

Senator Jesse Helms thought otherwise. He regarded King's adultery and communist associates as intertwined symbols of a society in spiritual crisis. In October 1983 he led a filibuster against a proposed national holiday to honor King. Many Americans thought the action petty and futile, but it played well with white religious conservatives, who helped secure Helms's reelection the following year. Though the King fight was about race, it also went deeper than race: Two decades later Helms would raise exactly the same moral objections when the name of Bill Clinton ("left-wing, undisciplined and ethically challenged") was men-tioned as a possible U.N. secretary-general. The rancor of the holiday debate—at one point Daniel Patrick Moynihan called Helms's FBI docu-mentation "a packet of filth" and threw it to the Senate floor, where he stomped on it with his size-twelve shoes—also illustrates a critical point made by sociologist James Davison Hunter. Culture War clashes were ugly and protracted because they involved different visions of the sacred. The politics of taxation lent themselves to compromise; the politics of sin did not. The habit of injecting patriotism into moral disputes—my way is the American way—simply added venom.[22]

The high psychological stakes of identity and moral propriety gave Culture War politics a trip-wire quality. Episodes like the 1990 suspen-sion of television commentator Andy Rooney, who made offhand re-marks offensive to blacks and gays, reminded everyone that words had become weapons that could discharge even without conscious intent. Liberal clergy enforced their own taboos. One, Howard Moody, ques-tioned whether "homophobes" should be ordained as ministers, or even counted as Christians. During the 1980s and 1990s, debates over openly gay clergy and other issues of sexual morality roiled the mainline churches, with the denominational leadership and some ministers assuming more progressive positions than their dwindling congregations. The Reverend J. Robert Williams, a gay Episcopal priest, went so far as to suggest that Mother Teresa would be a better person if she were sexually active.[23]

He succeeded only in stunning his audience. The what-next reaction of disaffected laity offers a final clue to the origins and bitterness of cultural warfare. What so exasperated traditionalists was the sense that immorality was being forced upon them. Their secular enemies, though a minority, had wormed their way into the seminaries, the media, the courts, and the schools. They had turned these institutions into siege engines, destroying the foundations of faith and coarsening the culture. A thousand reactionary sermons boiled down to a single plot: Demon-inspired enemies had seized the high institutional ground. Nor was this sense of conspiracy, betrayal, and secular aggression confined to the United States. It was, as Karen Armstrong observed, common to the world's fundamentalists and the source of what became, by the late 1970s, a global phenomenon. The relentless push of modernity had generated the hard shove of religious reaction, surprising secular elites who had supposed that religion was dead and that the future belonged to them.[24]

Religious conservatives had long attacked secular intellectuals for foisting humanism on the young and subverting the biblical foundations of faith by teaching higher criticism and godless evolution. What was different about the Culture War was that, by the late twentieth century, the crisis of faith had become more general and the targets of righteous ire more numerous. Though the contest was not quite even, religious conservatives still held some good cards. These included the growth of their own denominations, intrinsic organization and discipline, and the rise of popular illiberalism, with its related patriotic, racial, class, and gender anxieties. Jane Fonda bugged people. New Right leaders understood how to exploit these resentments and to mobilize voters across the social boundaries of faith. The foreign and domestic crises of liberalism in the 1960s and 1970s gave them their chance. Economic conservatives were as fed up as they were. They were more than willing to join forces. The ensuing alliance transformed the Republican Party and reshaped American politics. In the end, though, it delivered neither the full moral nor economic counterrevolutions that were the ultimate, and ultimately incompatible, aims of conservative reaction.

Economic Temperaments

Given the moral right's emphasis on individual responsibility, it might seem that religious conservatives were also likely to be economic conservatives. Yet most studies showed that race and class were better predictors of support for government assistance than religious belief. Wealthy Protestants may have been theologically liberal, yet they attended closely to their pocketbooks. Higher education translated into less fervent belief, but also more taxable income. By contrast, the smaller-than-average incomes of black Evangelicals and the larger-than-average families of Hasidic Jews disposed them to favor government assistance.[25]

Beyond self-interest lay the difficulty of interpreting scripture. The sacred texts contained injunctions about wealth and poverty, but lacked a detailed blueprint for a just political economy. "Render unto Caesar the things that are Caesar's" failed to specify a tax rate. "God helps those who help themselves," the verse most frequently quoted by Americans, had the disadvantage of not appearing in the Bible, scriptural illiteracy compounding the problem of scriptural ambiguity. (It came from Ben Franklin, author of America's true Book of Proverbs.) Jews, Christians, and Muslims all agreed that they should help the poor, but differed over the best means, which might entail anything from socialism to the capital and philanthropic investments made possible by the unhampered production of wealth.[26]

The simmering debate over the relationship between government and free enterprise, which came to a boil during the Great Depression, gave rise to a spectrum of economic temperaments. There were four general positions: those who embraced capitalism and resisted interference with market forces; those who accepted capitalism, provided that corporations behaved themselves and that the government could correct abuses (roughly, Theodore Roosevelt's New Nationalism); those who accepted capitalism, but only if the government provided continuous oversight and maintained key welfare programs (Franklin Roosevelt's New Deal and its embellishments); and those who rejected capitalism, favoring collective ownership and a comprehensive welfare state. If the central idea of modern liberalism, that government should build a fairer and more egalitarian society, ever commanded assent, it did so only in the abstract. When politicians specified the manner of fairness, the kind of equality, and the price in taxes and economic liberty, the consensus vanished.

Economic temperaments did not necessarily predict religious temperaments, or vice versa. William Jennings Bryan and Clarence Darrow were both economic progressives, yet clashed over the teaching of evolution in the 1925 Scopes trial. F. O. Matthiessen, a Yale Bonesman who won fame as a Harvard scholar, was an Anglican, a homosexual, and a socialist who refrained from joining the Communist Party only because of his unshakable belief in original sin. Alfred Kinsey, a champion of pansexual freedom who filmed himself masturbating with a rope cinched around his scrotum, was a pay-as-you-go fiscal conservative who voted Republican. Punk-rock guitarist Johnny Ramone worshiped Ronald Reagan. In 2005, biblically orthodox leaders of the National Association of Evangelicals joined heterodox environmentalists in calling for restrictions on carbon dioxide emissions. Genesis 2:15 commanded Adam to care for God's creation. If that meant alliance with the Sierra Club, then so be it.[27]

In geometry, intersecting lines make a plane. In late-twentieth-century politics, intersecting religious and economic temperaments made an ideological plane. Politics was a game with four corners and a center, played on what amounted to a square field. Libertarians who hated drug laws as much as they hated taxes were in the corner where the moral left met the economic right. "Statists" or "authoritarians" who wanted to punish drug users and robber barons were in the opposite corner, where the moral right met the economic left. "Left-liberals" were in the corner formed by the moral and economic left, "right-conservatives" in that formed by the moral and economic right. Those with centrist views on both sorts of issues were in the middle of the playing field and asssumed the role of swing voters in general elections.

Ideological planes, called Nolan charts, were well known to political scientists, who often used labels like "left-liberal" with precision. Yet everyday language seemed stuck on plain left and right. One reason was that politicians and journalists simply left the distinctions implicit. Newspaper readers told of "conservative" objections to a bill supporting embryonic stem-cell research understood the word to mean pro-life religious conservatives, not libertarians or biotech entrepreneurs. Liberal-conservative worked as a form of shorthand.

It also served as a political weapon. The revolt of left-liberal Democrats against the Vietnam War and their subsequent takeover of the party gave Republicans an opportunity to exploit dovishness. From Nixon on, they used "liberal" as a negative brand, uniting and energizing their patriotic and anticommunist coalition. Democrats were liberals. Liberals were weenies. Weenies would not protect America. Democrats rallied their troops with the menacing and equally amorphous "right wing." For epithets, lumping was better than splitting.

Another reason why the liberal-conservative distinction persisted was that, deep down, it had a real psychological basis. Conservative parents emphasized self-discipline, character, and success. The world was a tough

World's Smallest Political Quiz

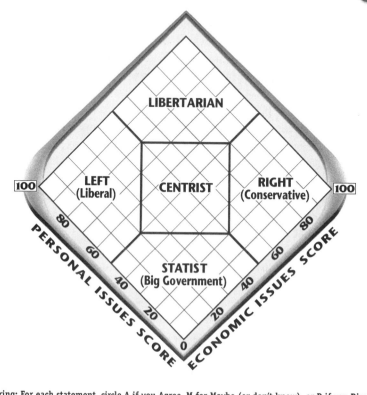

— Scoring: For each statement, circle A if you Agree, M for Maybe (or don't know), or D if you Disagree. —

How do you stand on
PERSONAL ISSUES?   20 10 0

- Government should not censor speech, press, media or Internet.   A   M   D
- Military service should be voluntary. There should be no draft.   A   M   D
- There should be no laws regarding sex between consenting adults.   A   M   D
- Repeal laws prohibiting adult possession and use of drugs.   A   M   D
- There should be no National ID card.   A   M   D

SCORING 20 for every A, 10 for every M, and 0 for every D: _____

How do you stand on
ECONOMIC ISSUES?   20 10 0

- End "corporate welfare." No government handouts to business.   A   M   D
- End government barriers to international free trade.   A   M   D
- Let people control their own retirement: privatize Social Security.   A   M   D
- Replace government welfare with private charity.   A   M   D
- Cut taxes and government spending by 50% or more.   A   M   D

SCORING 20 for every A, 10 for every M, and 0 for every D: _____

▶ FIND YOUR PLACE ON THE CHART

Mark your **PERSONAL** score on the lower-left scale; your **ECONOMIC** score on the lower- right. Then follow the grid lines until they meet at your political position. The Chart shows the political group that agrees with you most.

Advocates for Self-Government

269 Market Place Blvd., #106 ◆ Cartersville, GA 30121-2235
800-932-1776 ◆ Email: Quiz@TheAdvocates.org
Fax: 770-386-8373 ◆ Web: www.TheAdvocates.org

Figure 1   Quiz version of the Nolan chart. A moral conservative will have a low "personal issues" score, but not necessarily a high "economic issues" score. Conservatism, like liberalism, is divisible.

place. Your first job was to take care of yourself and your family. "Poverty is no crime in America," as Clare Boothe Luce wrote. "It is much worse." Conservatives, who thought hierarchically, saw poverty as a problem of backward races, classes, and subcultures as well as dissolute individuals. The street culture of poor, fatherless black men was, especially, the antithesis of their values. It was a fit object for control and punishment, rather than uplift—the preferred approach of Lakoff and other liberals who favored nurturing styles of parenting and governance. "Nurturance," retorted Bill O'Reilly, a teacher turned conservative broadcaster, was code for permissiveness. What worked was discipline and personal responsibility. Individuals wrestled with themselves for rectitude and with others for gain. Success or failure ordered the world. Inequality of outcome was natural, satisfying. The wicked and the feckless had it coming.[28]

The paradox of Culture War politics was that the psychological unity of the ascendant conservatives masked their sociological disunity. Liberals had their own inconsistencies, but none as great as the fact that the free market was not, and never had been, a morally conservative institution. Capitalism created not only winners and losers, but also wealth, temptations, intrusions, and distractions at odds with conservative religious values and moral self-discipline. The solution—to declare certain commercial activities and innovations off limits—would have clashed with corporate interests.

And it was corporate interests that shaped Republican policy. When disenchanted white Evangelicals left the Democratic Party and climbed aboard the GOP bus, they discovered that it was bound for Market Square rather than Church Street. Shared hatred of communism, pride in America, and belief in accountability made the company agreeable. Yet, in the end, it was still a detour. Whatever sins the moral revolution had visited upon America, libertarians like Ronald Reagan, David Stockman, and Rupert Murdoch were not the ones to purge them. By the 1980s, the Republican Party had become an uneasy coalition of natural social antagonists, a fact that became more apparent as the unifying Soviet threat receded.

Fortunately, there were still Democrats to hate. Having sorted out their own divisions, and committed themselves to civil rights and sexual freedom, the Democrats had become the Party of Enlightenment. That made it easier for Republican politicians to recruit the Enlightenment's traditionalist enemies and to keep their anger on boil against the liberals who had wrought such abrasive change. But this tactic could not conceal the cultural abrasiveness of capitalism itself, nor eliminate the gap between the objectives of the moral and economic right, however skillfully papered over with the rhetoric of personal responsibility. In a two-party system, the four-cornered question about moral and economic temperaments—which sides are you on?—inevitably translated into another, and more pointed, intraparty question: Who was using whom?

Economic and moral conservatives shared one other conviction in the second half of the twentieth century: They both thought liberals had hijacked American culture and government. The pressing task was to recapture them. In 1957, when interviewer Mike Wallace asked rising conservative star William F. Buckley Jr. what he was about, Buckley said he was an intellectual counterrevolutionary. He was out to overturn "the revised view of society" ushered in by Franklin Roosevelt. For conservatives of more narrowly moral concerns, the objective was to overturn the revised view of society ushered in by the 1960s. Speaking at the Religious Roundtable's 1980 National Affairs Briefing in Dallas, Baptist minister Adrian Rogers captured the prevailing nostalgia. What he wanted, he said, was "to get America back like it was when I was a boy."[1]

The determination to turn back the moral clock was the psychological wellspring of the moral counterrevolution that reshaped American politics. What Rogers was already doing in his own Southern Baptist Convention, wresting back political control from theological liberals, was what he and his allies planned to do in society as a whole: shrink the limits of the permissible. Two means presented themselves. These were a third party of reactionary platform, an option briefly pondered by New Right leaders in the 1970s, or an alliance with the Republican Party. Just as William Jennings Bryan's 1896 nomination brought the Populists back into the Democratic fold, Ronald Reagan's 1980 nomination provided a Republican vehicle for the religious right's counterrevolution. It was in fact Reagan, the personification of Rogers's boyhood America, who delivered the most memorable speech at the 1980 Dallas meeting. "This is a nonpartisan gathering, and so I know that you can't endorse me," he began, "but I only brought that up because I want you to know that I endorse you, and what you are doing." Seldom has an applause line worked so well.[2]

Reagan succeeded in his quest; the moral reactionaries mostly failed in theirs. But what was lost in that failure? What was America really like in the 1940s and early 1950s, when Adrian Rogers was growing up? What forces cracked the foundations of its once-formidable moral code? And what would late-twentieth-century America have looked like if conservatives had succeeded—as they assuredly did not—in dialing back the country's moral clock?

The Code

Prior to the 1960s, Americans publicly affirmed, even if they did not privately honor, the virtues of hard work, honesty, self-restraint, and loyalty to family and country. They admired self-reliance, though not self-aggrandizement. The first commandment in Minnesota, Garrison Keillor remembered, was "Don't Think You're Special Because You're Not." Those who were special, the WASP elite, were indoctrinated in the ethic of service to others. The Phillips Academy distilled the code to two words and put them on its seal. *Non sibi.* Not for self.[3]

Colloquial speech telescoped the code into a single word, "swell." "What a lousy word to mean so much," Ernest Hemingway complained to his editor Maxwell Perkins, upon whom he nevertheless bestowed the compliment. Once used to describe pride and arrogance, the word acquired a contrary, peculiarly American meaning of generosity and largeness of character. When Wilma, the girl next door in *The Best Years of Our Lives* (1946), married her sailor boyfriend who had lost both hands in the war, she lived up to her reputation as a "swell girl." She—they—had put the interests of others before their own.[4]

Swell girls were supposed to save it for their wedding nights. In March 1943, when pollsters asked whether young men having sex before marriage was "all right," "unfortunate," or "wicked," the responses were 14 percent all right, 42 percent unfortunate, and 37 percent wicked. For young women before marriage, the responses were 5 percent all right, 43 percent unfortunate, and 46 percent wicked—less a double standard than a double helping of disapproval. "Bad girls put out," Sally Belfrage wrote in her memoir of courtship in the 1950s. "A sexy virgin is what you have to be." She became a pregnant virgin when a swimmer from her West Point boyfriend made it through her panties. She wound up having an abortion. "Oh, baby, I'm so sorry," she thought, as the abortionist flushed the clotted remains down the toilet.[5]

The primary alternative for women in Belfrage's position was a speedy wedding. Births out of wedlock, though increasing, were still comparatively rare in the 1940s and 1950s. For the whole population, they numbered less than one birth in twenty and, among whites, only about one in fifty. But even shotgun marriages carried stigma, as Kathleen Birmingham discovered when she found herself pregnant. She and her boyfriend, Milton Babich, had grown up in West Allis, a Milwaukee suburb where people kept their cars polished and their sidewalks swept. Steadies since prom night, Kathleen and Milt were planning on marrying. Four kids seemed about right. When the necking escalated, their first got an early start. By Christmas 1948 Kathleen was sure. She told Milt. Then they balked. "The more we thought about it," she said, "the more we dreaded telling our folks. We'd disgrace them." They prepared to elope.

Pat Birmingham, Kathleen's sixteen-year-old sister, was a tease and a snoop. Milt feared that she had discovered Kathleen's condition and would reveal the shameful secret. When he warned Pat not to talk of it, she just laughed at him. He threatened her with a .22-caliber pistol. Giggling, she grabbed the barrel. He shot her twice. Six weeks later a fireboat crew found her weighted body in the Milwaukee River. When a jury promptly found Milton Babich guilty of first-degree murder, Kathleen, eight months pregnant, broke down sobbing. The judge asked him if he had anything to say. He stood up straight, like the honor student he was, and said, "I am not guilty of murder in the first degree, sir." The judge thought otherwise and added hard labor to the mandatory sentence of life in prison. John Bartlow Martin, a journalist who reflected on the case in his 1986 memoirs, called it the perfect contextual murder, inexplicable outside the sexual morality of the postwar middle class. "Such a crime is almost unimaginable today," he wrote. "One has to reread the Babich story to realize fully what is meant by the phrase 'the revolution in morals' of the 1960s and 1970s."[6]

That is exactly right. The Bastille of the old moral order was the taboo on sex outside marriage. By the time Martin revisited the tragedy, the sexual regime that branded Kathleen's pregnancy "illicit" had all but collapsed. It was done in by antibiotics for venereal disease, contraceptives, liberalized abortion laws, and a cultural shift toward personal fulfillment, gender equality, and permissiveness backed by the media, the courts, the schools, and Wall Street. There were big dogs in that fight, and the big dogs won. Two generations later high school girls like Kathleen did not necessarily wait for a steady, were more likely to take precautions, and, in the event that these failed, to end the pregnancy or to have the baby without marrying. Smiling principals handed them their diplomas as they waddled across the stage. If hypocrisy was the tribute vice paid to virtue, the toll became considerably less exacting after American society opened up in the 1960s and 1970s.

Nowhere was this more apparent than with respect to homosexuality. "When I grew up, being gay, being a sissy or anything like that, was verboten," said Richard Chamberlain, the actor who played television heartthrob Dr. Kildare. "I disliked myself intensely and feared this part of myself intensely and had to hide it." Coming out ended careers, or cut them off before they began. Soldiers discharged for homosexuality, the Veterans Administration ruled, could not claim benefits under the 1944 G.I. Bill of Rights. The price for discovery at Ohio State University in 1955 was parental notification and a letter of dismissal. Gay students found themselves in the campus chaplain's office, in a daze, their lives ripped apart, wondering what to do next.[7]

Female students faced another sort of deviance problem. They were expected to become wives and mothers, virtually the only approved social roles for young women in the postwar years. Half of all women were married by twenty, and those at university labored under the assumption that they soon would be. "We don't want any women here," the chairman of the Harvard English Department told Helen Vendler when she presented herself for graduate study. The future poetry critic left his office trembling. When Sandra Day O'Connor graduated third in the 1952 Stanford Law School class (first place went to future Chief Justice William Rehnquist, attending on the G.I. Bill), no private firm to which she applied offered her a job other than secretary.[8]

The stultifying effect of marital expectations on educated women inspired Betty Friedan, a Smith College graduate, to write *The Feminine Mystique* (1963). Rooted in the arid soil of suburban domesticity and the concealed subsoil of the author's radicalism and volatile personality—Friedan was not the swell type—the book awakened millions of women to the psychic limitations of homemaking. What often gets overlooked, though, is the constraining effect of marriage on the young *men* of Friedan's era. Favorable circumstances—an abundance of eligible brides, jobs that paid a living wage, rising real incomes—led them to marry in unprecedented numbers. It mattered that they went as fathers to the ball game rather than as bachelors to the pool hall. Crime and violent death rates dipped and stayed flat. Divorce rates did likewise, after a transient spike in 1945–1947 weeded out the improvident wartime marriages.[9]

Divorce was still enough of a taboo to stymie a political career. In 1961, when an allegation surfaced about John Kennedy's "other wife," ten congressmen requested the supposed smoking-gun genealogy from the Library of Congress. There was nothing to the rumor. Kennedy's adultery was another matter. But it went unreported by a press corps disinclined to lower its professional tone, lose its access, or undermine the legitimacy of the government, then in high repute. Discreet philandering could be overlooked to avoid scandal and spare the family. But politicians who left their wives and children were fair game, especially if, like presidential hopeful William O. Douglas, they remarried blonde divorcées many years their junior. "You don't have to marry 'em, just sleep with 'em," Democratic fixer Tommy Corcoran yelled at the impulsive Douglas.[10]

The family boom helped propel church membership to record levels during the 1950s. Worshipers wearing coats, ties, hats, and white gloves packed the cushioned pews. Religion was a mark of respectability. Without it, discovered Belfrage, the odd-duck daughter of English atheists, "you are really out of it." Americans regarded religious belief as integral to both the political and the moral order. "Our form of government," President-Elect Eisenhower said in 1952, "has no sense unless it is founded in a deeply felt religious faith, and I don't care what it is. With us of course it is the Judeo-Christian concept but it must be a religion that all men are created equal."[11]

All men, not all behaviors. With some exceptions, the churches supported the remnants of the Victorian- and Progressive-era laws against vice. Though once-taboo cigarettes had become ubiquitous and prohibitionists had retreated to dry rural strongholds, the bans on pornography, prostitution, gambling, and illicit drug use were prosecuted with sufficient vigor to keep these vices underground. Anthony Comstock (1844–1915) and other purity crusaders of his generation had stressed the public character of commercial vice, whose very openness ensnared the innocent and scandalized the respectable. Better to drive it out of sight. Make the pornographers show their grainy stag films on improvised screens, or peddle their dirty postcards from subway lockers. Charles Bamberger, forty-three years with the New York Society for the Suppression of Vice, readily conceded that enforcement never shut down the pornography business. But it "kept the odor from becoming too redolent" and the small-timers away from big money.[12]

These words fairly describe most vice-control efforts in the 1940s and 1950s. Middle-class Americans were no longer as keen on outlawing sin as they had been in the Victorian era, yet they acknowledged a policeable boundary. Hollywood had its Production Code, the Post Office its inspectors. Montgomery Ward had to hold up 300,000 catalogs and mark "not available" by four advertised books on sex and marriage before the Post Office allowed it to finish its fall 1944 mailing. Magazines deemed obscene lost second-class mailing privileges, which amounted to a death sentence. "The trick," remembered Martin, who turned out fact-based crime stories, "was to write right up to the edge of the obscene and stop."[13]

That one word, "stop," sums up what Rogers meant when he evoked the moral repose of his childhood. It wasn't that people were good. As a Baptist, he didn't believe that for a second. But they at least lived in a society in which authorities said no and people internalized the consistent moral and patriotic message of religious and political institutions. The default value was trust, whether in neighbors or the government. A thumb got you a ride. Security systems were for banks. President Truman took his Sunday morning constitutional in downtown Washington. "Like to look in merchants' windows," the ex-haberdasher confided in his 1947 diary. Then he strolled back to the White House and worked on the State of the Union address.[14]

Two groups, Norman Mailer wrote in a famous 1957 essay, made a point of defying conventional morality. These groups were Negro men whose economically futureless lives left them little choice but to live in the existential present, and the alienated "white Negro" hipsters upon whom they bestowed their subcultural dowry of jazz and kicks. Hipsters were "philosophical psychopaths" who preferred jive and pot and libertine sex to death by conformity. Numbering at most 100,000, working odd jobs or not at all, they comprised a subversive underworld whose with-it language and free ways fascinated adolescents. "I first read *On the Road* in high school in Omaha," said actor Nick Nolte. "I remember thinking, 'You mean you can do that? Pick up and go?' It seemed incredible to me."[15]

Sniffing the rising breeze of civil rights, Mailer thought that Hip might grow into a popular movement whose libidinous energies would "rebound against the antisexual foundation of every organized power in America, and bring into the air such animosities, antipathies, and new conflicts of interest that the mean empty hypocrisies of mass conformity will no longer work. A time of violence, new hysteria, confusion and rebellion will then be likely to replace the time of conformity." In the end, he predicted, Hip would be absorbed into the culture, becoming another colorful thread in the tapestry of American life. The alternative was that even liberals would face up to its social implications and recoil. In fact, both things happened. The yin of indignation chased the yang of cooptation. Hip became the golden thorn in the American flesh, commercially invaluable yet permanently irritating. Even Allen Ginsberg, the king of beat poets, wound up pitching Gap jeans.[16]

Few other than Mailer saw this in 1957. The prevailing mood was one of consensus, a cliché that, for all its exceptions, captured the narrow range of mass opinion in the 1950s. Most Americans remained conformist, patriotic, and trusting in government. Eisenhower, who confided to his brother that rich reactionaries intent on abolishing the New Deal were "negligible" in number and "stupid," proved to be a caretaker of the welfare state. Disenchanted Taft Republicans found consolation in the pages of Buckley's *National Review,* whose contributors revitalized conservatism by attacking its common enemies. These were the communists, statists, and secularists who threatened national security, economic freedom, and traditional morality. To keep things palatable, Buckley excluded the paranoids and haters and added splashes of erudition and wit. Still, his "fusionist" conservatism remained a contrarian movement during the 1950s. Most business and labor leaders accepted Ike's informal pact. Corporations offered high wages and selective benefits, filling gaps in the New and Fair Deals, while the government managed the economy and stimulated investment.[17]

This arrangement yielded rising incomes and sustained profits. The shape of the postwar welfare state, points out historian William Berman, depended less on class conflict than on the values of social harmony, underwritten by the nation's global hegemony. There were plenty of other people's resources to go around. Civil rights excepted, domestic-policy fights were over degree, not kind. Neither party challenged the ethic of self-restraint and family stability. The Democratic Party of Chicago journalist Mike Royko's boyhood had the same base, "hard-working, two-fisted family men," in the 1950s that it had in the Depression. The difference was that more of them lived in their own brick bungalows rather than in rented flats above candy stores and corner saloons.[18]

Protestant, Catholic, Jew

No man embraced the code more enthusiastically than Richard Daley, Chicago's powerful mayor. Daley, as Royko observed, was a small-town boy raised in a big city. Chicago neighborhoods remained ethnic villages, self-contained and pedestrian. Residents walked to the store, the theater, the parish church. Royko grew up on the Polish Northwest Side, Daley in Irish Bridgeport. Anyone could tell the difference, even with eyes closed, "by the odors of the food stores and the open kitchen windows, the sound of the foreign or familiar language, and by whether a stranger hit you in the head with a rock." There were hatreds in Daley's America, and deep ones at that. But they involved race, ethnicity, religion, and WASP privilege rather than moral disputes. That was the contradiction, or maybe the genius, of the social order: one acknowledged public code, many separate subsocieties. The big story of the next forty years was the unraveling of the moral consensus *and* the weakening of the old racial, ethnic, and denominational antagonisms, paving the way for a more fluid social system of lifestyle preferences and a more polarized political system of alliances among those of similar religious and economic temperaments.[19]

Sociologists distinguish between primary relationships that are personal and intimate, like friendship and marriage, and secondary relationships that are formal and transactional, like tipping. For a minority group to be fully assimilated, its members must develop both primary and secondary relationships across ethnic lines. Adopting the dominant culture's speech, dress, and political norms is not enough. While shared wartime sacrifices won for Poles, Italians, Jews, and other recent European immigrant groups tacit recognition as American (some historians add "white") citizens, their postwar communities remained socially distant.[20]

The surest sign of distance was the rarity of intermarriage. In 1900, 99 percent of New Haven's Jews married other Jews; in 1950, 96 percent. Sally Belfrage, a blue-eyed blonde who dated Jewish boys, few others being available at the Bronx High School of Science, encountered "a running mother tantrum on the theme: Get that shiksa out of my life." WASP parents cast Italians in a similar role. One Midwesterner beat his daughter for seeing an Italian boy, whom he regarded as the "same as a Negro." In 1900, 98 percent of New Haven's Italians had married other Italians; in 1950, it was still 77 percent. When they and other Catholics married out of their national group they overwhelmingly wed other European Catholics, an ethnically if not religiously "mixed marriage" that raised eyebrows and prompted the occasional elopement. Those who married Protestants faced far worse. George Herbert Walker, the Catholic grandfather and namesake of the first President Bush, was promptly disinherited when he wed a Presbyterian beauty named Lucretia Wear.[21]

In every faith, the most zealous were the most vigilant against outsiders. Leonard Feeney, the Jesuit dynamo who converted Temple Morgan, insisted that salvation was impossible outside the Church. He damned Protestants and double-damned Jews. That was too much, at least in postwar Boston. In 1949 the Jesuits tossed him out of the order, and in 1953 the Holy Office threw him out of the Church. None of this deterred Feeney and his lay followers, the Slaves of the Immaculate Heart of Mary. They vilified liberals, protested the opening of a Catholic chapel at mostly Jewish Brandeis University, and even interrupted a Notre Dame football game. In 1958 Feeney and a hundred Slaves hived off to establish a rural monastery with no newspapers, radios, or televisions, and with separate quarters for women and men. This was boundary maintenance with a vengeance.[22]

America's ultimate taboo, though, was interracial marriage, illegal in twenty-nine states in 1950 and aberrant everywhere else. Martin Luther King Jr. discovered just how aberrant while studying for his divinity degree at Crozer Theological Seminary. A dapper ladies' man called "Tweed," after his suits, King had fallen in love with a white woman whose mother worked at the school. He spoke of marrying her, but friends told him she would ruin his pastoral career in the black community and God only knew what would happen in the white. They were right. The vast majority of whites, 96 percent of those polled in 1958, disapproved of interracial marriages.[23]

White Protestants held the institutional high ground. "Careers were not simply open to talent," remembered columnist Joseph Alsop, "careers were open to talent with the right kind of origins and the right kind of names." This did not include, before the war, Jewish names. In 1940 only 7 of Yale University's 167 full professors were Jewish. All of them were in the graduate schools, none in Yale College. As late as 1958 Jews could not marry in Harvard's white-steepled Memorial Church unless a Protestant minister presided over the service. Most country clubs had quotas, and most were overwhelmingly Christian or Jewish. Club managers could tell them apart by glancing at the tabs. The Christians spent more on liquor, the Jews on food.[24]

One solution to blocked mobility was a name change. Army officer Jacob Rudnitsky, told he'd never advance past captain with a name like that, became Jacob Rudd. He made lieutenant colonel and passed on the abbreviation to his son, future Weatherman Mark Rudd. Catholics had to be careful, too. Thirty-two-year-old Rosemary Woods could pass, but she nevertheless breathed a sigh of relief when newly elected Senator Richard Nixon neglected to ask her religion before hiring her as his personal secretary. Salvatore Lombino, who began writing in the Navy during the war, changed his name to gain traction with publishers. He had great success as Evan Hunter and later as Ed McBain.[25]

Other writers had great success with anti-Catholic books. Paul Blanshard's *American Freedom and Catholic Power* (1949), which stressed Catholicism's threat to democracy, sold 240,000 copies in its first edition. Protestants still gathered to hear supposed ex-nuns reveal the horrors of the convent. Real nuns rose daily to prayer, meditation, Mass, and chores before beginning their unsalaried jobs as teachers. Phonics doubled as catechism: "S—short I—N. Sin is what makes God unhappy." So did unshined shoes, whose owners stayed after school. Tim Russert, a student at Buffalo's Canisius High School, once asked the prefect of discipline for mercy. "Russert," Father John Sturm replied, "mercy is for God. I deliver justice."[26]

The ultimate terror was supernatural. Pat Buchanan's father held his son's hand above a match flame to give him a taste of hell. The Jesuits spelled out the sins of impurity that would send him there. Joseph Califano Jr., another Jesuit product, had to "leave room for the Holy Ghost" during the slow dances. When Rudolph Giuliani's classmates kicked up the tempo with "Wake Up Little Susie," one of the Christian Brothers smashed the record. Fifties Catholicism, said novelist Robert Stone, was about death trumping sex. Dead people had a future in the Church. Fornicators did not. With its self-obliterating spirituality and mile-wide streak of prudery, the Church provided the base of Mailer's "antisexual foundation." The stone that had been rejected had become the cornerstone.[27]

The Catholic hierarchy was far more unembarrassed and tough-minded in publicly opposing sin than the mainline Protestant clergy whose Victorian forebears had enacted the vice laws. The Motion Picture Production Code was a Catholic creation, and it was mainly fear of Catholic boycott that backed it up. Though criminal abortion was a lucrative business, few journalists described it frankly, and those who did made sure to state the Church's categorical opposition to avoid "beefs from the Catholics." Contraception was another minefield, especially in states with large Catholic populations. Prescott Bush, father and grandfather of presidents, lost his first bid for a Senate seat from Connecticut when broadcaster Walter Winchell reported that he had supported the American Birth Control League.[28]

Church leaders attacked subversion with the same zeal that they showed for suppressing vice. "Communism is *Un-American*," thundered Cardinal Spellman. Catholicism was not. Catholic priests cheered Joe Mc-Carthy, blessed fighter jets bound for Korean combat. Catholic thinkers like Buckley brought intellectual rigor to the crusade. Catholic activists like Phyllis Schlafly spread their ideas among grassroots anticommunists. No postwar political movement was more popular. How, then, was one to explain the persistence of anti-Catholicism in Cold War America?[29]

John Courtney Murray, a tall, courtly Jesuit adept at blending history and theology, gave the question a subtle answer. There were really two sorts of nativism. The first held that America was a Protestant nation, that Catholics were anti-Protestant, and, therefore, that Catholics were anti-American. Suspicion of Catholics was, in one sense, natural among conservative Protestants. Like all people concerned with salvation, they took theological differences seriously—as did Murray, who held Catholicism to be superior to other faiths. Anti-Catholicism also had its cruder side, such as the myth of riflemen drilling in church basements, next to the tunnels the Vatican spies used.

Murray was less concerned with folk prejudice than with the second strand of nativism, as exemplified by Blanshard. This strain was naturalist rather than Protestant. It held that America was a democratic nation; democracy must be predicated on a naturalist or secularist philosophy; the Church rejected such philosophies; therefore, the Church was anti-American. Blanshard, an atheist committed to socialism, eugenics, and sexual freedom (territory he explored outside his own marriage), did not care about papal indulgences. He cared about the Church's influence on issues like contraception. So did other sexual progressives, who peppered their writings with anti-Catholicism.

Murray saw the American Church caught between the old Protestant right and the rising moral left. To avoid being whipsawed, he urged the Vatican to abandon its opposition to religiously pluralistic democracy. The thoughtful Protestant theist, he wrote, understood that naturalism was his enemy and the Church his ally against it. "However, he is definitely not willing to be friends with a Church that seems to him to be the political enemy of 'the American way of life,' with which Protestantism has historically identified itself." Though more than a few Italian cardinals objected, Murray's pluralist views finally triumphed in *Dignitatis Humanae* (1965), the Second Vatican Council's declaration on religious freedom.[30]

Saint Yellow-Hair

The story of Clare Boothe Luce's conversion to Catholicism, a national sensation in 1946, illustrates how seriously Protestant–Catholic differences were taken in postwar America, and how those differences could yet be strategically subordinated in the face of a more compelling secular threat. The illegitimate daughter of a gold-digging mother, Clare Luce used her looks, wit, and pen to win fame as a courtesan, journalist, and playwright, batting out three Broadway hits in as many years. A youthful feminist who had voted for Roosevelt in 1932, she became a Republican after marrying Henry Luce in 1935. Harry, as he was known, was the son of Presbyterian missionaries, a "sincere American bourgeois square" devoted to God, the GOP, and his growing magazine empire. Besotted, grasping at what he thought was his last chance for worldly happiness, Harry left his wife and young children to set up court with Clare. John Billings, *Time*'s managing editor, saw things differently. "She's just a yellow-haired bitch who is spending his money like water."[31]

Harry Luce's fortune survived; his infatuation did not. Over the next five years guilt for leaving his family and resentment of his new wife's demanding ways reduced the marriage to a sexless shell, despite Clare's futile coquetry. He pursued other mistresses, she other interests, first as a war correspondent and then, in 1942, as a successful Republican congressional candidate. Attacking Roosevelt's military and foreign policies, and skewering his party for its hypocritical failure to end lynching, she emerged as a high-profile Republican establishment liberal who hated the Soviet Union and its works.[32]

That was not a bad place to be in the mid-1940s for a rising politician with a famous name and a model's bones. But beneath her confident façade, Clare Luce was melting down. Sexually and emotionally abused as a child, she suffered from a condition that would today probably be diagnosed as borderline personality disorder. Borderlines are haunted by chronic fear of abandonment, instability of identity and mood, feelings of worthlessness and emptiness, suicidal thoughts, self-destructive behavior, and chaotic relationships, caused by idealizing people one day and paranoically demonizing them the next.[33]

Clare kept her demons at bay by compulsively striving for success. High society, the stage, country houses, and politics kept her busy and temporarily satisfied her need for attention. Then something so catastrophic happened that she was plunged into unremitting depression and

Figure 2 Clare and Harry Luce honeymooning in Cuba, winter of 1935–1936. She was one of America's most talented and envied women, he one of its wealthiest and most influential men. Her insecurities and his regrets made the marriage miserable.

despair. On January 11, 1944, Ann Brokaw, Clare's only child by a previous marriage, was returning to Stanford University when a refugee language teacher, a bad driver with worse brakes who was late for class, plowed into her car. Ann flew out the passenger door, hit a tree, and died when the spinning car crushed her against it. Clare, who had breakfasted with Ann just an hour before, was devastated. Horribly, absurdly, her own daughter had joined the mangled innocents she had seen in the rubble of war. "Were they sleeping," she asked herself, "or were they rotting?"[34]

Finding no peace, and no consolation in her loveless, childless marriage—she was infertile now, and haunted by the memory of a youthful abortion and several miscarriages—the most envied woman in America hit bottom in a New York City hotel room one night in autumn 1945. "I tasted at long last the *real* meaning of meaninglessness: it is to believe that one is crawling to extinction, unloved, unlovable and unloving in the same kind of world." In tears, she knelt and recited the Our Father, the one prayer she knew by heart. Something stronger was needed now.

She opened a letter from Edward Wiatrak, a Jesuit missionary who had been patiently fishing for her soul. Had she, Father Wiatrak asked in his letter, read St. Augustine's *Confessions?* Taking the cue, Luce dialed his rectory, then hung up. She felt ridiculous calling a *Catholic* priest. But she had tried everything else, and so she picked up the receiver again, only to discover that the hotel operator had not broken the connection. "Father," she said when Wiatrak answered. "I am not in trouble. But my mind is in trouble." "We know," he said. "This is the call we have been praying for." The pronoun had a literal meaning. Wiatrak had hooked a big catch, but it would take more than a Polish football-player-turned-priest to reel her in. He made an appointment for her to see Monsignor Fulton Sheen.[35]

Sheen was a Louvain-trained theologian who won fame as a Catholic apologist. He had a knack for performance and a piercing gaze, softened by a disarming smile and Irish wit. "Hearing nuns' confessions," he once said, "is like being stoned to death with popcorn." He sensed that Clare's would be another matter. "Listen," she said, waving her manicured finger under his nose, "if God is good, why did He take my daughter?"

"In order that you might be here in the faith," Sheen said.

"Is that why you invited me to dinner?" she demanded.

"That is the reason."

Over the next several months of instruction, Sheen took every punch she threw. The night he broached hell, she argued against its existence for an hour and fifteen minutes. He heard her out and replied in kind. In the end, Clare's emotional need weighed more in the scale of conversion than Sheen's apologetics. She became a Catholic, she said, because she felt personally responsible for her sins, and she wanted to get rid of them. When Sheen asked her whom she would like to hear her confession, she said "someone who has seen the rise and fall of empires."[36]

In early 1946 Luce announced that she would not seek reelection to Congress and, a short time later, that she had joined the Catholic Church.

Thousands of people wrote her letters. Catholic opinion hovered between joy and triumphalism, Protestant opinion between guarded approval and abhorrence. Many Protestants were glad of her change of heart, though troubled by her implicit derogation of their faith. Why should Rome be the true north of the convert's compass? Less sympathetic correspondents charged her with superstition and treachery: "Now that you have become an idol worshiper, who owes allegiance to an Italian pope, I would suggest that you take the veil as soon as possible so that decent Americans can forget your antics."[37]

Luce kept her secretaries busy replying to the stacked mail. She was now in the convert-making business herself. In the spring of 1947 she published an account of her conversion in *McCall's,* a popular women's magazine. Updating St. Augustine, she told of a gaudy life unfulfilled by the Genteel Episcopal faith in which she had been schooled. Her first husband, she remembered, "attended church faithfully on Sundays, except on rainy days, in good golfing weather, in the summer, when traveling or when ill of the colds to which he was very susceptible." None of this offered much consolation for the world's brimming cup of death and madness. Catholicism did, though, shrewdly, she stressed its core message of submission to a loving God who had sent His only Son to redeem mankind. There was no point in raking up Counter-Reformation embers. What united true Christians was their understanding that selfishness was the soul's illness and Jesus Christ its cure. The great chasm in American society was not that separating Protestants and Catholics, but that separating Christians and unbelievers. Luce sensed, with a clarity born of her own conversion, the outline of the coming Culture War: that Americans of conservative religious temperament would have to make common cause across denominational lines to oppose the secular juggernaut.[38]

Luce named their common enemy—the Enlightenment in the guise of intellectually fashionable isms. She had flirted with all of the isms, from Marxism to Freudianism, and found them as wanting as her beaux. The worst was communism, a fanatical secular faith that, perversely, destroyed people for their supposed class sins rather than for the personal sins that were the actual cause of human grief. Spiritually, Luce suggested, it was not that far a step from the basement of Lubyanka prison to the corridors of liberal power. Contemporary liberalism had elevated the rights of self-expression over those of property. A person could believe what he wanted, vote how he wanted, and pretty much do what he wanted, yet might be made to sacrifice income and economic freedom for

Figure 3 "Two magazines are competing for exclusive serial rights if we convert" was Bill Mauldin's caption for this 1947 cartoon. It satirized the hullabaloo over Clare Luce's 1946 conversion to Catholicism, which she defended in a popular magazine series the following year.

the security of others. Social betterment, not God's Law, measured the world. Therein lay liberalism's flaw. Its metaphysics pushed people toward materialism, relativism, and agnosticism, while its economic doctrine set them on the slippery slope of socialism—a doctrine, as she later put it, "workable only in heaven, where it isn't needed, and in hell, where they've got it."[39]

Luce became, if only in her own mind, the cardinal of Catholic converts, right down to her floor-length crimson cape. In the coming years, however, her faith cooled as she became disenchanted with the Church's views on women, contraception, and pampered bishops, Sheen among them. What drove her was her quest to escape neurotic self-preoccupation. She found temporary solace in LSD. Taking 100 micrograms after Holy Communion pushed the limits of Catholic orthodoxy in 1961, but serenity is where you find it. Luce kept looking for causes in which to lose herself, with the curious result that, by the time she died in 1987, she was a pro-ERA, pro-pill, pro-life, pro-nuke Catholic feminist hawk. As much layered as contradictory, her many conversions marked the political strata of a long and singularly restless life.[40]

One conviction, however, only strengthened with time. That was her belief that all liberalism was left-liberalism, that it was socialistic and atheistic gradualism flying the colors of pragmatism. "Moscow and Rome, all else fellow travelers of the two," she wrote in 1949. Belief was either "Man centered" or "God centered." Postwar liberals doubted that their choices came down to Moscow or Rome, but did admit the tension between humanism and faith. "I am intolerant even of the idea of spirituality," Richard Rovere wrote privately. "It bugs me." The growing suspicion that liberalism was the smiling cousin of godless communism animated the legion of moral reactionaries who flocked to the banners of Buckley, Goldwater, and Reagan, the very men to whom Luce attached the drifting boat of her personality during her lioness-in-winter years.[41]

When Did the Moral Revolution Begin?

If secularism and liberalism lay behind the revolution in personal morality, when, exactly, did that revolution occur? Clare Luce thought it well advanced by the early 1960s. In her youth, she wrote, people accepted the truth of the Ten Commandments, regardless of whether they kept them; by the 1960s, most Americans felt free to disregard them, except for thou shalt not kill. Though few historians have put the matter so boldly, they have agreed that the moral revolution began well before the 1960s. Victorianism was like a heavily armored battleship slowly foundering under sustained attack. The first hits registered in the 1910s and

1920s, when modernism and consumerism took hold and new norms of liberated sexuality, exemplified by the flapper and the matinee idol, challenged Victorian ideals of continence. The 1920s had its own culture war, fought largely within the Protestant camp, pitting fundamentalists against modernists, the country against the city, and the Ku Klux Klan against local miscreants and tipplers. The modern, the urban, and the wet prevailed. In 1933 Repeal struck Victorianism amidships, opening a hole near its waterline. Prohibition's triumphant enemies, who included vice entrepreneurs, the wealthy who wanted taxes shifted from their incomes, libertarians, and acid-penned skeptics like H. L. Mencken, continued to press for moral liberalization.[42]

World War II, which introduced millions to barracks life, landed another blow. Soldiers smoked and cursed; condom makers prospered; poker games ran nonstop. Lawrence, Kansas, home of the world's largest solid rocket propellant plant, added twenty-six new downtown bars. In Evansville, Indiana, hillbilly women drove rivets during the day and prowled the bars at night, tricked out in lipstick and mink stoles. Money did things to people. True, money also made the marriage boom possible, and marriage applied the behavioral brakes. But all the young couples and full obstetrics wards proved only a temporary departure from longer-term trends, such as women's increasing marriage ages and declining fertility, which marked a historic shift in gender roles and sexual behavior.[43]

Social history is a stream. There were signs of turbulence—Kinsey, Frederick's of Hollywood, Hugh Hefner, *Mad Magazine*, the Beats, Lenny Bruce—before the water turned white in the 1960s. Many postwar trends—the rising rate of premarital sex, the popularity of psychotherapy and humanistic psychology, the disease concept of alcoholism, the spread of Sunday commerce—pointed to moral liberalization. It did not take a sociologist to read self-assertiveness in the cars, with their toothy chrome grills and tailfins that could emasculate King Kong. That said, the decisive historical change, which historian John Burnham called the inversion of Victorian mores, by which public *opposition* to vices became increasingly deviant, rather than the vices themselves, was not yet complete at the end of the 1950s. The battleship, on fire and taking on water, was still afloat, its colors tattered but unstruck. Then the tempo of the attack suddenly increased, and it broke up and sank. This was what contemporaries meant when they spoke of a moral or sexual revolution. It was the acceleration that they sensed, the rapid, decisive culmination of events already underway. The divorce rate increased as much in six years, 1964 through 1969, as it had in the previous forty-four.[44]

Historical custom assigns a symbolic beginning to revolutions, even those that have been brewing for years. When was the 1776 or 1789 of the moral revolution? The question is a variant of a more familiar one, when did the 1960s begin? "The sixties began in 1954," answered Weatherman-turned-law-professor Bernardine Dohrn, "and the real news is that they're not over yet." That is a defensible claim on both ends. In 1954 the Supreme Court held segregated schools inherently unequal, the Senate held Joe McCarthy accountable, and Elvis Presley launched his recording career. Then again, Liberace dominated the television ratings that year, and Billy Graham made the cover of *Time,* accusing finger pointed straight at the reader. Chuck Berry and Rosa Parks made big entrances in 1955; James Dean made his and exited in a Porsche Spyder. In 1958 Eisenhower's fading popularity and a sour economy translated into big gains for industrial-state liberals. They had momentum and a target, the disparity between private plenty and public neglect indicted in John Kenneth Galbraith's bestseller, *The Affluent Society.* Another popular choice is 1963, a year of civil rights showdowns, the first stirrings of Beatlemania, and the collective trauma of John Kennedy's murder—on the same day as the quieter deaths of Christian apologist C. S. Lewis and psychedelic pioneer Aldous Huxley, who floated to oblivion on a cloud of LSD.[45]

But perhaps the best answer is that the 1960s began in 1960. If the essence of the revolution was the unraveling of the warp of moral taboos and of the woof of creedal distinctions, then two events that year, the commercial introduction of the birth-control pill and Kennedy's election, loom large in hindsight. Like the airplane, the pill was an invention long pursued by determined visionaries and perfected only after trial and error. At least a half million women were experimentally taking Enovid "off label," as a contraceptive, before the FDA officially authorized its use for that purpose in May 1960. Five years later, six million American women had prescriptions. By century's end, four out of every five women born after the war had used oral contraceptives sometime during their reproductive years.

It is easy to understand why. For all the talk of sexual realism in fiction, Richard Rovere complained in 1949, no writer ever said anything about fishing around the bureau drawer for contraceptives, or the trip to the bathroom when it was all over. Twice it looked as if Rovere's wife,

Eleanor, had become pregnant, despite their precautions and fear of penury. At one point *he* began experiencing menstrual symptoms, sympathetically anticipating the sign of danger passed. The pill made worries about leaks irrelevant and spontaneity possible. After 1960 domestic condom sales fell sharply. By 1968 oral contraceptive users outnumbered condom users two-to-one. Writing in 1973, Blanshard called the condom a relic of sex's dark ages, which the pill had flooded with the light of erotic possibility. "Perhaps some future historian will hail it as our century's greatest contribution to happiness—and also to the dissolution of Christian monogamy."[46]

Or any sort of monogamy. By the early 1970s, the pill and other advanced forms of contraception were also widely available to unmarried women and increasingly backstopped by legal abortion. This freed sexually active women to pursue education and careers, postponing marriage or avoiding it altogether. The chief social prop of abstinence, the fear of out-of-wedlock pregnancy, had been kicked aside. "Chastity became a purely moral decision," sociologist Robert Nisbet observed, and an increasingly less popular one at that. Unmarried cohabitation, once confined to the lower classes, became a feature of middle-class life, as couples met, lived together, and then, if it suited them, tied the knot.[47]

If improved contraception separated intercourse from procreation, why did birth rates for unmarried women rise steadily during the 1970s and 1980s? Under the old moral code, couples who engaged in premarital intercourse did so with the understanding that they would marry should pregnancy result. Milton Babich and Kathleen Birmingham knew what they had to do. Their tragedy lay in trying to hide the inevitable. Less sensitive sorts broke the news and got on with it. "There wasn't no choice," shrugged a San Francisco man. "So I married her." But contraception and abortion did mean choices, and tempted men to shift responsibility. If their pregnant lovers used contraception erratically, or refused an abortion, that was their affair. Shotgun marriage rates fell. Out-of-wedlock births rose, a process that became self-sustaining as illegitimacy became more common and less stigmatized, even chic in liberated circles.[48]

All that lay in the future. At the time, in 1960, the pill's selling point was family planning, an objective that enjoyed wide support among elites concerned with population control. These included prominent lay Catholics like Buckley and John Rock, the outspoken Harvard obstetrician who had helped develop the pill. Clare Luce was scathing. "The Church's rhythm method is a fearful weasel," she informed John Courtney Murray. "If sex is *solely* for the purposes of procreation, then coitus in periods of known infertility is *just* as wrong as contraceptive methods." Luce was happy to have the Church draw the line at abortion and sterilization, but prayed the pill would be ruled in bounds.[49]

That was a reasonable hope. By 1960 more than a third of Catholic couples of childbearing age had used or were using artificial contraception, which created enormous personal and pastoral difficulties. The Second Vatican Council (1962–1965) opened the Church to the winds of change, and the majority of experts on a special pontifical commission recommended modifying the ban. Rome had grudgingly accommodated itself to other revolutions. Contraception seemed a comma away from joining science, nationalism, industrialization, and democracy.

Yet, in another way, the firm "no" of *Humane Vitae* (1968) was unsurprising. The Church had reacted to contraceptive encroachments in the 1930s and 1940s by becoming more, not less, explicit in its condemnation. The unfolding sexual revolution hardly encouraged liberalization. How could any genital act, including homosexuality, be declared unnatural if sex was unyoked from procreation? The intertwined contraceptive and feminist movements threatened traditional Catholicism, which was hostile to the erotic, suspicious of self-assertion, and subtly dependent on large families whose surplus children filled the seminaries and convents. Contraception's long-term consequences were anyone's guess. Separated from motherhood and marriage, Cardinal Ratzinger said, sex was "a kind of drifting mine." Best to keep the mine tethered.[50]

The birth-control decision released the floodwaters of Selective Catholicism and decisively weakened the American Church as a bastion of the old sexual morality. When millions of parishioners saw the Church abandoning the Latin Mass and meatless Fridays, but clinging to the contraceptive ban, they launched a silent Reformation, remaining Catholic on their own terms. "I don't confess that I take the pill, because I don't believe it is a sin," said a New Jersey woman with four children. If conscience overruled the Magisterium, then the Church was becoming Protestant. Alternatively, if contraception was a habitual mortal sin, there wasn't much point in honoring its other requirements. Mass attendance dropped. Lines outside the confessional disappeared. Confessors twiddled their thumbs, or had second thoughts themselves. One in ten active priests quit between 1966 and 1971. Others fell back on "don't ask, don't tell, don't preach." Catholicism became an institutional amalgam of Judaism: Reform congregations led by an Orthodox hierarchy with a Conservative clergy maneuvering between the two. No faction was happy with the situation, which Ratzinger frankly called a crisis of Church authority and which he inherited in 2005 when he became Pope Benedict XVI.[51]

The Catholic hierarchy—any hierarchy—would have found strict morality easier to maintain under conditions of social isolation. But even as the showdown over contraception was building, ghetto Catholicism was dissolving. Freeways and white flight emptied out the old ethnic neighborhoods and their echoing marble churches. The other key event of 1960, John Kennedy's presidential election, symbolized and accelerated Catholic assimilation.

Kennedy knew his religion would work both for and against him. He hoped to take advantage of the disproportionate concentration of white Protestants in the southern states, where loyalty to the Democratic Party might offset anti-Catholic sentiment, keeping the South's electoral votes in his column. Then, in the North, where ethnic groups were concentrated, the combined Catholic, black, and Jewish votes would deliver large states like Illinois and New York. "The Jews will be for me," he predicted. "If a Catholic can't make it, no Jew can make it. They know that."[52]

The strategy succeeded, though only just. Protestants told pollsters they would not hold his religion against him, but this was often a polite evasion. Journalist John Bartlow Martin, working as a Kennedy advance man, got a different story from local politicians and cabbies. They told him the Catholic issue was Kennedy's biggest liability. It dogged him from Indiana's Klan country to California's Central Valley, where Bible-Belt transplants clung to old hatreds. In the South, where white Evangelicals disliked the party's liberal platform as much as Kennedy's faith, things were even trickier. Two conservative religious forces, the rising one of temperamental reaction and the declining but still potent one of sectarian suspicion, intersected in the region, leaving Kennedy in their political crosshairs.[53]

At the other end of the spectrum, liberal Protestants worried about both the church–state issue and whether Kennedy was a doctrinaire anti-communist. He had never repudiated Joe McCarthy, his brother Robert had worked for the red-baiting senator, and his sisters Patricia and Jean had actually dated the man. Protestant opposition offset Kennedy's advantages in money, television savvy, and organization. His advisers thought he would win with at least 53 percent of the popular vote. He squeaked by with 49.7 to Vice President Richard Nixon's 49.6. Had he not tapped Lyndon Johnson as his running mate, counting on the powerful Texas senator to help him hang on to part of the South, Kennedy might well have lost the campaign.[54]

Kennedy also helped himself by addressing the Catholic issue forthrightly. He pledged rigid church–state separation and then delivered on the promise. As president, he refused to support federal aid for parochial schools or to officially receive Vatican diplomats. Kennedy, said Billy Graham, "turned out to be a Baptist president." Actually, he was an ultra-Selective Catholic who once told Clare Luce that she was foolish to strap the cross to her back and journalist-friend Ben Bradlee that he was "all for people solving their problems by abortion." But we know what Graham meant. The scrupulous religious neutrality of the Kennedy administration weakened anti-Catholicism, at least in presidential politics. Even Blanshard, who was invited to the White House, went away impressed. By the end of Kennedy's administration no one could assume that any Catholic politician—or, for that matter, any Catholic—would automatically do Rome's bidding.[55]

Billy Graham, who had opposed Kennedy but who quietly patched things up with the White House after the election, found his own relationship with the Church changing. In the late 1950s many priests warned parishioners to stay away from Graham's revival meetings. By 1964 Richard Cardinal Cushing was urging Catholic youth to attend, saying Graham's message was "one of Christ crucified, and no Catholic can do anything but become a better Catholic from hearing him." In 1977 Graham held a crusade in the Notre Dame football stadium; four years later he was warmly received by Pope John Paul II. By the 1990s Graham could count on dioceses and parishes actively promoting his rallies. "I think that the evaporation of hostility is one of the biggest untold stories of modern times," said Graham biographer Grant Wacker. "You only have to go back to the 1960s to see how dramatic the shift has been."[56]

So dramatic, in fact, that interfaith cooperation became commonplace on a range of sensitive issues, from school prayer to abortion. Clare Luce and John Courtney Murray were right: Religious conservatives found their most reliable cultural allies across traditionally hostile

Figure 4   John F. Kennedy shakes hands with Father Richard J. Casey after Mass on Inauguration Day, 1961. As president, though, Kennedy kept his relations with the Church at a cool distance.

denominational lines. What they had not foreseen, though, was how that alliance would broaden, under professional political guidance, to include racial and economic conservatives, who had reasons of their own to be unhappy with the decade of change ushered in by John Kennedy's election.

3

OVERCOME

After Joe Kennedy polished off his second lobster, he adjourned to the living room of Harry Luce's Waldorf apartment to watch his son accept the 1960 Democratic nomination. Joe had decided not to stay in Los Angeles for the speech, but had flown back to New York and dropped in on *Time*'s editor-in-chief. Though Luce was a Republican, the men were old friends. Joe's liquor ads had helped Harry's magazines weather the Depression.

As Harry waited for the televised coverage to begin, his journalistic instincts took over. He began to probe. He assumed, he said, that Jack Kennedy would adopt a liberal domestic policy. Joe began swearing. No son of *his* could possibly be a liberal.

"I told Joe to hush," Luce wrote later. "It was in the nature of politics that in order to win, a Democratic candidate for the Presidency had to take a liberal position (while, of course, retaining the automatic support of the solid South) and that we would not hold that against him. 'But,' I said, 'If Jack shows any signs of going soft on Communism—then we would clobber him.'"

"Well," Joe said, "you don't have to worry about that."[1]

Six months later, on the occasion of his inauguration, John Kennedy pledged the nation to "bear any burden" against its totalitarian foe. In May 1961 he launched a race to the moon to shore up America's Cold War prestige. In June 1963, standing on the balcony of the Rathaus Schöneberg, he declared himself and all free men to be proud citizens of Berlin. Few doubted his sincerity. His problem was to convince zealous anticommunists that his cautious, sometimes halting moves on the Cold War's global chessboard matched his rhetoric. "Goddamit, these people turn out more mail than anybody," an exasperated Kennedy told Richard Rovere in March 1962. "I've had more letters about Katanga"—a mineral-rich breakaway province in the Congo whose fate keenly interested the John Birch Society—"than about anything else."[2]

Cue Ball

Kennedy's liberalism (notwithstanding his father's denial, John Kennedy was a liberal, though of the business-friendly variety) presented the opposite political problem. In domestic policy, he had to be careful that his deeds did not get too far out in front of his rhetoric. Nowhere was this truer than in the area of civil rights. The abolition of the southern caste system and the elevation of blacks to full citizenship was the most pressing domestic issue facing the nation.

It was, in fact, old business, left over from the sectional struggles of the nineteenth century. The North had prevailed in the long conflict over slavery expansion and in the ensuing civil war spawned by preemptive secession. But a third struggle, the political and paramilitary conflicts over the status of freedmen, had ended with Southerners in possession of the field. Northern ambivalence about blacks and federal power, together with southern resistance, had defeated all attempts to permanently recast race relations. Slavery had always been about more than labor. It had been about racial control. On that point white Southerners would not yield.

By 1900 slavery had given way to Jim Crow, a system of deferential etiquette, strict segregation, and disfranchisement sustained by custom, law, and terror. Blacks still worked the fields as sharecroppers, but struggled as the price of cotton and other staples fell. Women took jobs as domestics, though black men who drifted to towns and cities had trouble finding work. They settled into what one historian called a counter-Victorian life of erratic labor, casual sex, absent fatherhood, vice, and hot-tempered violence that prefigured the urban underclass of the later twentieth century and that inspired repression in the guise of alcohol and cocaine prohibitions, vagrancy arrests, convict labor, and lynchings for sexual offenses.[3]

Millions of blacks voted with their feet. By 1960 four in ten resided outside the South. Those who remained lived under a segregation regime little changed from that of the turn of the century. The Warren Court's mid-1950s efforts to end separate and unequal schools had succeeded mainly in stirring the Massive Resistance pot, killing off southern racial moderates instead of Jim Crow. In New Orleans, double-chinned matrons screamed obscenities at black schoolgirls, warming up for any white parents who dared bring their children to the same school. Southern delegates arrived at the 1960 Democratic convention sporting "Never" lapel pins.[4]

Kennedy and his advisers favored legal equality for blacks. As liberals, they were heirs to the progressive tradition of bringing marginal groups into the American mainstream. As cold warriors, they were sensitive to the need to deny the communists a potent propaganda issue. As Democrats, they were mindful of black voters. Two weeks before the 1960 election, when Martin Luther King Jr. was sentenced to hard labor in a Georgia prison for a traffic misdemeanor, John Kennedy called King's pregnant wife, Coretta, and pledged his assistance. The next day Robert Kennedy, John's brother and campaign manager, called the judge handling the case. King was released, John Kennedy got the credit, and Reverend Martin Luther King Sr. announced that he was switching his vote from Nixon. He had intended to oppose Kennedy on religious grounds. "Imagine Martin Luther King having a bigot for a father," Kennedy mused. "Well, we all have fathers, don't we?"[5]

The best politicians are the ones who give people hope, or at least give them hope without spending too much political capital. But there are limits to symbolic placation, especially after electoral success brings pressure for action. In Kennedy's case, action meant sustained Justice Department efforts to enforce existing civil rights laws and protect nonviolent protesters against segregationists of the sort who favored white socks, hair oil, and tire irons. It also meant issuing new executive orders and legislative proposals to end public discrimination, secure voting rights, and provide educational and economic opportunities necessary for achieving full equality. In none of these areas did the administration move forcefully or consistently until 1963. Even then, Robert Kennedy feared that King was maintaining ties to communist advisers. He authorized FBI wiretaps, inadvertently providing J. Edgar Hoover the opportunity to escalate his campaign against King from passive-aggressive opposition to sexual leaks and blackmail.

The reasons for the Kennedy brothers' caution are not hard to find. They were afraid of antagonizing white Southerners, on whom their reelection hopes hinged. During the campaign Kennedy staffers had soft-pedaled the Coretta Scott King episode in the white press, while playing it up in pamphlets for black churchgoers. This was classic "dog-whistle politics," mobilizing base voters without alerting the opposition. But the

Kennedys knew that concrete measures would generate an electoral backlash and further frustrate relations with Congress, dominated by long-serving southern committee chairmen. Their willingness to join with Republicans to block or water down progressive legislation, the most basic fact of national politics since the New Deal unraveled in the late 1930s, had stymied the administration. Kennedy could get action on business measures like investment tax credits, but so fundamental a liberal reform as health insurance for the elderly remained tantalizingly shy of a majority. A strong civil rights bill might deepen congressional antagonism and prolong the deadlock.

Events forced Kennedy's hand. By 1963 King and other civil rights leaders were angling to make their local picketing campaigns national news. They succeeded in Birmingham, Alabama, a raw industrial city whose pugnacious police chief, Eugene "Bull" Connor, could be counted on to repress dissent. That April King inaugurated a black boycott of downtown businesses and began to organize demonstrations, ending in time for news crews to process the film for the nightly broadcasts. The demonstrations climaxed in early May when black children, their elders' ranks thinned by mass arrests, confronted paddy wagons, police dogs, and monitor guns. A. G. Gaston, the city's wealthiest black businessman, was on the phone when he glanced outside his window. "They've turned the fire hoses on a little black girl," he gasped. "And they're rolling that girl right down the middle of the street."

The wire photos and news footage produced what psychologists call a "hot cognition," not unlike that of a coughing smoker who finds blood in his sputum. Procrastination was no longer an option. When a brokered truce in Birmingham was shattered by terror bombings and riots, Kennedy decided to act. He told his staff to begin drafting new civil rights legislation. On June 11, he used another spectacle, Governor George Wallace's schoolhouse-door stand against the enrollment of two black students at the University of Alabama, as the occasion to announce his program. Striking a chord of prudence, unity, and justice, Kennedy called civil rights a fundamental moral issue. "It is as old as the Scriptures and is as clear as the American Constitution," he told his television audience. "The heart of the question is whether all Americans are to be afforded equal rights and equal opportunities, whether we are going to treat our fellow Americans as we want to be treated."[6]

When Kennedy equated black equality with biblical morality, he pleased religious liberals. Yet millions of white Evangelicals opposed civil rights and found scriptural justification for doing so. Integration, they believed, would lead to miscegenation, violating the Creator's scheme of separate races. Blacks and whites could share spiritual kinship, but not one another's beds. Liberal clergy who marched for integration were in league with the Antichrist, if not sexual sinners themselves. Spent condoms were said to litter the campsites of the 1965 Selma-to-Montgomery marches. Those actually present only recalled red ants and mud, but the details are almost beside the point. Stripped to its essentials, the intra-Protestant struggle over civil rights became another battle over modernism. On one side stood progressives who denounced racial segregation as heresy or, as a jailed King put it, "the invention of a god gone mad." On the other stood traditionalists who refused to substitute "a social Gospel for the Blood-purchased Gospel of Christ." The Catholic Church, more cosmopolitan and concerned with social justice, had less trouble with the issue. Individual Catholics were another matter. More than a few greeted King's 1966 Chicago freedom marches with rocks, cherry bombs, and jeers.[7]

The crisis was particularly acute for conservative clergy in liberalizing Protestant denominations. In 1963 Reverend James P. Dees, fourteen years an Episcopal priest in North Carolina, decided he had had enough of disregard for the Bible, appeasement of communists, and alliance with worldly reformers bent on "a mongrelized society." Saying his church had left him, rather than the other way around, he established the Anglican Orthodox Church with its own seminary, priests, and missionaries. The breakaway church prospered over the next dozen years, as Dees used stories of nude interracial baptisms to solicit members and donations. Apostasy had its uses. So did disasters. God spoke when a tornado struck a Georgia town "harboring" a gay Episcopal newsletter. For Dees, the road from civil rights ended in Sodom.[8]

Historians who despise everything that James Dees stood for fully agree that the civil rights movement gave impetus to a broader social and moral revolution. The struggle for black equality was one of history's well-struck cue balls, transferring its energy to the waiting rack of liberation movements that exploded across the political table in the late 1960s and early 1970s. Its successes inspired advocates of rights for women, homosexuals, Chicanos, Indians, children, the disabled, tenants, welfare recipients, and long-hairs who wanted to let their freak flags fly. The surprise hit movie of 1969, *Easy Rider*, linked the rebellions of the 1960s in the story of two white Negroes on panhead Harleys, dispatched by shotgun-toting rednecks. Only liberated women were missing from the film, and they did not stay off the screen for long. Feminists followed the civil rights movement's example of challenging stereotypes. "When evaluating a general statement about women," Gloria Steinem told senators during the 1970 hearings on the Equal Rights Amendment (ERA), "it might be valuable to substitute 'black people' for 'women'—just to test the prejudice at work." Advocates for the disabled adopted similar rhetoric and added an antiwelfare sweetener: Disability-rights legislation would enable people to be self-supporting. The campaign ultimately bore fruit in the 1990 Americans with Disabilities Act, passed by large majorities and signed by George H. W. Bush, a Republican president not otherwise inclined toward litigious policies.[9]

The civil rights struggle provided more than inspiration. It bequeathed to other movements a cadre of experienced activists, including virtually the entire leadership of the New Left. Those who had not personally marched against segregation could sift the movement for tactics to mobilize their own aggrieved constituencies. King's life became, in the years after his 1968 murder, a casebook for direct nonviolent action. The book, however, was open to everyone. To the dismay of many civil rights veterans, it would be cited by Randall Terry and Ralph Reed and other conservative activists determined to attract recruits to the cause of moral counterrevolution.

The Warren Court

One of the counterrevolution's earliest and most important targets was the Warren Court, whose decisions laid the constitutional foundation for the rights revolutions. There was some irony in this confrontation. The man who gave his name to the Court was a former prosecutor who had lost his own father in an unsolved murder—certainly not a background predictive of decisions favoring criminals. Nor did Earl Warren's religious beliefs necessarily square with the decisions banning school prayer. Warren was a soft Moderate, a monogamous prude, and sometime Baptist churchgoer who read his bedside Bible attentively, adding the Talmud as a further guide to law and morality. A person devoid of religion, he said, was "almost a lost soul."

Almost. Warren had his worldly side and was, or became, a liberal activist. A Republican, he had come of age in the Progressive era, and believed that government could create a better and more just society. A likable, gregarious man, the sort who read the sports pages first, he was a political natural who grew increasingly confident in the exercise of power. When Eisenhower appointed him to the Court in 1953 ("the biggest damn fool thing I ever did," as Eisenhower later reflected), Warren was in his third term as the most successful governor in California's history. He would transfer his executive energy and can-do spirit to the Supreme Court.[10]

Like John Kennedy, Warren discovered that there were political limits to what he could accomplish. The 1954 and 1955 school desegregation decisions and the 1957 *Mallory* case, in which a confessed black rapist under sentence of death was released because he had not been promptly arraigned by D.C. police, angered southern and conservative congressmen. So did rulings protecting the rights of accused communists, prompting the introduction of more than a hundred retaliatory bills during the first congressional session of 1957. Matters came to a head in the summer of 1958, when the Senate came within one vote of enacting legislation to restrict the Court's jurisdiction. Only frantic maneuvering by Majority Leader Lyndon Johnson, whose presidential hopes depended on keeping his party's liberals happy, prevented its passage.[11]

As in the Court-packing crisis of 1937, the justices got the message. With Felix Frankfurter leading the retreat, the Court marked time on domestic-security, race, and other rights issues for the next three years. The four core liberals—Warren, William Douglas, William Brennan, and Hugo Black—lacked a reliable majority. That changed in 1962, when the seventy-nine-year-old Frankfurter, worn down by his fight against the *Baker* v. *Carr* reapportionment decision, suffered a stroke at his desk. When he was carried out of the Supreme Court building, he complained that his shoes were being left behind. Kennedy filled them with his trusted secretary of labor, Arthur J. Goldberg.

Goldberg's appointment gave the Court a fifth liberal or, more precisely, left-liberal vote. Ever since the 1937 showdown over New Deal legislation, the Court had acceded to federal management of the economy. Now a majority of justices, self-consciously allied with the ascendant progressive forces in the executive and legislative branches and national media, were determined to carve out new constitutional guarantees for individuals. Each of these guarantees inspired fresh lines of litigation, as activists and their clients seized the precedents to advance their causes outside less amenable legislative channels. Indeed, the volume of lawsuits itself soon became an issue, with moral and economic conservatives blaming "the litigation explosion" on an unholy alliance of liberal elites, money-hungry lawyers, and irresponsible clients, who salted the taxpayers' wounds by using legal-service funds to pursue their claims.[12]

If the Warren Court acted the role of legal sorcerer's apprentice, its wand was the doctrine of "incorporation," which applied protections in the federal Bill of Rights to the states through the Fourteenth Amendment. Rather, it selectively applied these rights, the liberal majority being less keen on keeping and bearing arms than on free expression and privacy guarantees. Contrary Supreme Court rulings were simply overturned. The Warren Court dispatched forty-five such precedents, only one of which was more liberal than its own decision. (All previous Courts together had done so only eighty-eight times, and not necessarily in a liberal direction.) Most of the overruling came in the 1962 through 1968 terms, the activist period people recall when they hear the words "Warren Court."[13]

During those years the Court loosened everything from libel constraints on the press to residency requirements for welfare recipients. It had already begun dismantling the creaking Victorian system of censorship, ruling in 1957 that censors had to consider a work's overall literary merit rather than the mere presence of objectionable passages. James Joyce and D. H. Lawrence raised few eyebrows. But then, between 1963 and 1967, the Court handed down a series of rulings that extended access to unabashedly erotic materials. By the time Warren retired, in 1969, adults could legally purchase all but hard-core pornography, and that was lurking offstage.

Religious conservatives found the 1962 and 1963 decisions banning official prayers and devotional Bible readings in public schools to be just as appalling. "They put Negroes in the school and now they've driven God out," fumed Alabama Representative George Andrews. Cardinal Spellman, kibitzing from the parochial sidelines, condemned the attack on "Godly tradition"—another signal of Protestant–Catholic concordance in the face of the common secular enemy. No other issue before the Court generated more widespread outrage, or angry mail, than school prayer.

The rights of accused criminals were not far behind. The public accepted lawyers for indigent defendants; that seemed fair play. But reversing the convictions of guilty criminals because they had not had counsel present when they confessed or because the arresting officer had failed to provide adequate warnings of their rights (which warnings the Court proceeded to spell out for all states) was too much for Americans worried about lawlessness and federal intrusion. "Support Your Local Police" bumper stickers sprouted alongside "Impeach Earl Warren."

Warren stood his ground. He had a square-shooting prosecutor's disdain for lazy cops who relied too heavily on confessions. He knew the deck could be stacked against defendants, especially in high-profile cases. He had even argued that the Dallas police's running commentary on Kennedy's assassination, which had mixed false information with avowals of Lee Harvey Oswald's guilt, had compromised the possibility of an impartial jury trial—a trial made unnecessary only by the supreme incompetence of allowing the prime suspect to be murdered in their custody.

Good reasons can be trumped by bad examples, the worst of which was Danny Escobedo. After the Court overturned his murder conviction, in 1964, Escobedo was rearrested for robbery, heroin trafficking, molesting his thirteen-year-old stepdaughter, and shooting a man in the face, among other offenses. "You are a career criminal," said the last judge who sentenced him, on federal weapons charges. He certainly looked the part when his mug shot made the cover of *Time*. With crime rates surging, the need for police professionalism was not the lesson most people took from Escobedo's life. By 1968 more than six Americans in ten thought the Supreme Court too lenient on criminals. That was close to the same proportion who voted that year for Richard Nixon or George Wallace, both of whom attacked the Court. "If you walk out of this hotel tonight and someone knocks you on the head," Wallace sneered in his stump speech, "he'll be out of jail before you're out of the hospital, and on Monday morning they'll try the policeman instead of the criminal."[14]

Rural voters with little reason to fear muggers had other reasons to resent the Court. Its one-man, one-vote decisions, notably *Reynolds v. Sims* (1964), had ended the malapportionment that had sustained their power in state legislatures and the U.S. House of Representatives. Faced with rotten boroughs like those in Florida and California, whose senate districts contained anywhere from thousands to millions of residents, the Court transferred power from a rural elite it saw as both backward and unfairly privileged to better-educated urban and suburban voters. Lucas Powe Jr., a Warren Court scholar who clerked for Justice Douglas, thought it all boiled down to who and whom. The who was a cosmopolitan and temporarily unimpeded activist judicial majority that "demanded national liberal values be adopted in outlying areas of the United States." The whom, the most distant outliers of the ascendant liberal culture, were rural white Southerners of conservative racial and religious beliefs and old-school Catholics. These same groups formed the backbone of the moral counterrevolution, set to escalate after seven justices of the succeeding Burger Court took a relatively uncontroversial 1965 decision assuring married couples' access to contraceptives and made it, in *Roe* v. *Wade* (1973), the basis for legalizing abortion throughout the nation.[15]

The Court's decisions on race, obscenity, school prayer, criminal justice, and sexual privacy transformed American politics by mobilizing angry moral conservatives, fostering new alliances among cultural outliers, and nationalizing the struggle over morality, once the domain of state legislators and local officials who decided what students recited in home room and which films showed at the Rialto. If activist judges had arrogated such powers to themselves, the only practical response was to elect presidents pledged to appointing justices of a restrained character. The days when a William O. Douglas could breeze through his Senate Judiciary Committee hearing in five minutes were over. The Culture War that spread in the wake of the 1954–1973 decisions became, in its constitutional dimension, a struggle to pack the Court by other means. Nowhere would that objective become clearer, and yet more frustrated, than with respect to abortion.

Liberal Tide

When historians explain the outpouring of liberal legislation in 1964 and 1965, they cite three kinds of causes, those of structure, agency, and contingency. The liberals could not have triumphed if the economy had not been prosperous and Americans anxious that their country should keep moving forward in an ideologically competitive world. The liberals would not have triumphed had not specific individuals, notably King and Johnson, seized the opportunities for change. And the liberals might not have triumphed, or triumphed when they did, had it not been for Kennedy's murder. Had he lived, King confided, civil rights legislation would have sunk back in a morass of delay and compromise. Kennedy's death meant real support for a real bill. Swift passage, Johnson reminded Congress on November 27, would be the best possible memorial to the slain president.[16]

Eventually, the assassination came back to haunt the liberals, especially after the Vietnam War turned sour and the Warren Commission investigation unraveled into a lengthening skein of conspiracy theories.

Johnson himself never accepted the conclusion that Oswald had acted alone. He suspected that Fidel Castro had recruited the Marxist sympathizer, knowing the U.S. government "had been operating a damned Murder Inc. in the Caribbean." But the first substantial charges of cover-up and conspiracy did not begin surfacing until 1966, and by then Johnson had been elected president in his own right, finished off Jim Crow, and launched an ambitious expansion of the welfare state. "I had to take the dead man's program and turn it into a martyr's cause," he later said. "That way Kennedy would live on forever and so would I."[17]

One by one, Johnson maneuvered Kennedy's tax-cut stimulus, civil rights bill, and embryonic antipoverty program through Congress. If it took a few water projects and judicial appointments to grease the wheels, fine. Johnson had his sights on something grander. "The Great Society rests on abundance and liberty for all," he told the University of Michigan's 1964 graduating class. "It demands an end to poverty and racial injustice, to which we are totally committed in our time." Twenty-nine times the crowd interrupted Johnson with applause. On the return trip, he was flying higher than Air Force One.[18]

Johnson's opponent in the 1964 election, Senator Barry Goldwater, was the most important losing presidential candidate in postwar history. His champions credited him with putting the country on the high road to Reaganism. His critics charged him with putting it on the low road to intractable division. Everyone found him colorful. Enthusiast by nature, westerner by birth, pilot by training, Goldwater liked ham radios, Indian lore, and liberty, in whose defense, he said, extremism was no vice. He disliked unions, bureaucracies, red tape, meddling judges, and federal appropriations, save for damming the Colorado River and combating world communism.[19]

Like Johnson, Goldwater benefited from a shocking turn of fortune. In 1963 Republican front-runner Nelson Rockefeller married his recently divorced lover, Margaretta "Happy" Murphy. She had surrendered custody of her four children to secure her divorce, adding the aggravating circumstance of home-wrecking to the primal offense of wife-dumping. "Rockefeller queered the pitch," wrote Harry Luce, reflecting, perhaps, his own unhappy experience of blonde divorcées. Soviet Premier Nikita Khrushchev chimed in, denouncing "parasitic capitalists who live a life of luxury, drinking, carousing, and changing wives." Goldwater surged ahead of Rockefeller in the polls. With the help of grassroots activists, the junior senator from Arizona held on through a bumpy primary ride, securing enough delegates for a first-ballot nomination at a memorably contentious convention.[20]

Goldwater's electoral base was anything but homogeneous. He inherited the Taft wing of the party, the golf-tanned Roosevelt haters disenchanted by Eisenhower's "dime-store New Deal" and alarmed by Johnson's plans to turn it into Macy's. He appealed to middle-class strivers in suburban Sunbelt counties, religious conservatives upset by secularism and subversion, and southern segregationists, mostly lifelong Democrats whom Johnson predicted would desert the party in 1964. And he had the cranks. Cartoonist Bill Mauldin drew Goldwater's supporters as a fruitcake chorus: a tennis-shoed Bircher, an umbrella-toting bluenose, a Strangelovian general, a geeky libertarian, and a backwoods hick, all singing "We Shall Overcome." What really held Goldwater's coalition together was its enemies, communists abroad and godless interfering race-mixing liberals at home.[21]

Not that Goldwater was godly. The assimilated son of a dapper Jewish merchant who married a mannish Episcopalian nurse twelve years his junior, Goldwater was not devout and never pretended to be. Johnson, a sentimental and not entirely insincere Christian, was far more at home in church. He made sure everyone saw the Secret Service men drop folding money in the collection plate, but otherwise his pleasure in worshipful company was unfeigned. Not so Goldwater's. He did not even get points for his paternity among Jewish voters, who went four to one against him in 1964.[22]

Goldwater's true scripture was the Tenth Amendment: "The powers not delegated to the United States by the Constitution, nor prohibited by it to the States, are reserved to the States respectively, or to the people." He opposed the civil rights bill because it threatened unconstitutional federal interference with private property. It was the owner's motel and, besides, laws couldn't make people like one another. He later, and consistently, opposed attempts to police consensual sex on the same ground of personal freedom. What Moral Majority founder Jerry Falwell really needed, Goldwater said, was "a swift kick in the ass."[23]

How could a half-Jewish libertarian whose wife had helped found Phoenix's Planned Parenthood clinic excite white Evangelicals in 1964? The puzzle is worth pondering. Over the next three decades a string of not particularly religious Republican presidential candidates worked Goldwater's trick again and again. Religious voters could embrace a Nixon or a Reagan as one of their own if they frosted the cake of patriotism and personal responsibility with a thin icing of divinity. Goldwater's solution was to call for a constitutional amendment restoring school prayer and to decry the rising damp of obscenity, immorality, and lawlessness. With a hard line on communism and applause lines like that, it mattered little how much time Lyndon Johnson spent in church.[24]

Johnson nearly ran the table anyway. He left Goldwater only Arizona, a five-state slice of Dixie, and fewer than four popular votes in ten. Goldwater supporters blamed Kennedy's assassination. Dallas tainted all forms of extremism, took the wind out of their candidate's sails, and let Johnson run as the candidate of consensus and continuity. The *National Review* had all but thrown in the towel by October. "Three Presidents in twelve months is the kind of thing they go for in the banana republics, or the Balkans; not in America."[25]

In fact, Goldwater had his chances. Johnson had nothing of Eisenhower's dignity or Kennedy's style and was dogged by charges of corruption. Blue-collar voters feared integration and black job competition. "I am *much* less optimistic than most people I talk to," John Bartlow Martin wrote in his campaign journal. He thought Goldwater could win if he connected the haters and malcontents with the regular GOP. He even looked presidential. He seemed calmer than Johnson on television, helped along, Martin suspected, by tranquilizers before airtime. All he had to do was "seem increasingly reasonable, if he can."[26]

He could not. Goldwater's opposition to mandatory Social Security and talk about the possible use of tactical nuclear weapons allowed Democrats to paint him as a reactionary and a kook. "Zioncheck could beat him," Johnson confided to reporters, evoking howls of sympathetic laughter. Marion Zioncheck was a mentally unbalanced New Deal congressman who had killed himself by leaping from his Seattle office window. When the soundness of the man became the issue, rather than the soundness of his ideas, it was over. John Updike, no dove, shuddered when a beautiful inamorata confided in bed that she was going to vote for Goldwater. Adultery was one thing in Updike's circles; Goldwater was beyond the pale.[27]

Goldwater entered history as a watershed candidate because he demonstrated two important truths. The first was that a conservative coalition of diverse priorities and varied religious temperaments could, when united behind a charismatic candidate and animated by a spirit of principled militancy, capture a major party. The second was that, to win national elections, fusionist conservatives had to learn to exploit backlash while avoiding extremist talk and third-rail entitlement programs. Martin's insight, that a telegenic Republican could deftly harness popular resentments, was confirmed two years later when an ex-Hollywood actor became governor of the nation's largest state. Reagan stuck to a common-sense conservative script. "He believed basically what Barry believed," said campaign strategist Stuart Spencer. "He said a lot of things that Barry said, but he said them differently. He said them in a soft way, in a more forgiving way. Style was the difference."[28]

The other problem with the Oswald-got-Goldwater theory is that liberal congressional candidates also ran strongly in 1964, suggesting voters had more on their minds than stability. Every one of the fifty-nine representatives rated most liberal won reelection. Sixteen of the fifty-six rated most conservative lost their seats. The more conservative the congressman, the more likely his defeat. Half of the northern representatives who had voted against the civil rights bill lost, but not one who voted in favor. The Democrats gained thirty-seven seats in the House and two in the Senate, giving Johnson the most lopsided congressional majorities since Roosevelt's historic 1936 victory.[29]

Johnson used this majority to increase federal aid to education, create Medicare, and set up a federal–state scheme to pay medical bills for welfare recipients, poor children, the disabled, and elderly persons needing long-term care. Medicaid excluded the general run of the adult working poor, but they might qualify for job training, food stamps, and other poverty programs. When club-wielding police and marauding toughs turned the campaign to register black voters in Selma, Alabama, into a bloody stalemate, Johnson seized the occasion to introduce yet another landmark law. The 1965 Voting Rights Act outlawed electoral practices that were racially discriminatory in intent or impact, and made the U.S. attorney general the registrar of last resort.

In Johnson's mind, all of these measures were linked. The real issue, he said in a March 15 address to Congress, was whether blacks would become citizens in every sense, whether all Americans would "overcome the crippling legacy of bigotry and injustice." He paused a beat for effect. "And we *shall* overcome." Members of Congress and Supreme Court justices—four were in attendance, Warren among them—rose in ovation. Then Johnson reprised the line, pledging to overcome poverty, ignorance, and disease, the common enemies that knew no bounds of race or class. The greatness of America, he said, was that it could offer everyone hope of a fuller life.[30]

It was Johnson's most famous speech and the most coherent expression of the liberal dream by any postwar president. Johnson aimed to uplift and incorporate all Americans into a single national community whose problems would be managed by a progressive national state led by a dynamic president. Everything about the man—his own youthful poverty, his experience teaching Mexican children, his political formation during the New Deal, his bottomless hunger for approval and recognition—pushed in the same direction. He was America's hospitable Big Daddy, and he welcomed more to the table. In 1965 he signed legislation abolishing national-origin quotas on immigration and raising the annual limit. Latin American and Asian immigration surged.[31]

Goldwater supporters despaired. Richard Viguerie could not look at the front page of the *Washington Post* for six months after the election. Liberals rejoiced. Johnson had taken the spirit of liberal nurturance and given it legislative flesh. Not that his intentions were purely altruistic. In private, he complained that half the black teens living in slums couldn't pass an Army physical. "Their IQ is too low, or their health is too low, or they don't know how to wash their teeth or shave," he told John McCone, the ex-CIA director who headed the Watts riot commission. "Bob McNamara thinks they ought to be pulling a bunch of them in and letting them do some of the fighting along with others, but they don't." Unless white boys were going to do all the soldiering, the ghettos had to go.[32]

Reform for the sake of the draft pool seems an odd civil rights argument. But in some ways it was the best card in Johnson's hand. Johnson knew, as did King, that civil rights and poverty programs carried national security weight. They made the country stronger, impervious to Soviet propaganda. Johnson could sell his domestic agenda if he wrapped it in the flag of preparedness while demonstrating, as had Kennedy, his determination to stop communism.[33]

Hence the Vietnam War. The great lesson of Johnson's senatorial career had been the power of anticommunism. He had seen Nixon's pinkbaiting destroy the career of Helen Gahagan Douglas, a rising House Democrat who happened also to be Johnson's lover. He had watched Joe McCarthy rake Harry Truman and Secretary of State Dean Acheson over the coals of Red China. During the 1960 campaign, he had led his spittle-covered wife through a right-wing Dallas crowd waving "Lyndon is a Judas" placards. All that would be as nothing if a communist takeover in South Vietnam started the regional dominoes toppling, one country and one disastrous headline at a time, in the middle of a big liberal domestic push. The dim prospect of winning the war simply made Johnson's dilemma more exquisite. "If I left the woman I really loved—the Great Society—in order to get involved with that bitch of a war on the other side of the world, then I would lose everything at home . . . ," he said later. "But if I left that war and let the Communists take over South Vietnam, then I would be seen as a coward and my nation would be seen as an appeaser. . . ." That was too much for the proud Texan, a man who once unzipped himself before his secretary of the interior and demanded to know, "Has Ho Chi Minh got anything like that?"[34]

Actually, he did. Johnson's war abroad ended in defeat. His war at home ended in half-victory. Universal welfare programs did reduce poverty—for the aged. Over the next decade Medicare and expanded Social Security benefits slashed the elderly poverty rate, long the nation's highest by age group. By 1975 a retiree was only slightly more likely to be poor than the general population, and less likely than those under eighteen. Yet, despite the growth of the black middle class, Johnson's targeted programs did not end poverty or behavioral problems among the black urban poor. Measured by declining labor force participation and the rise in fatherless, welfare-dependent households, the plight of the ghetto underclass worsened in the decade after the war on poverty was declared.[35]

Social scientists fingered several suspects. Chief among them were intractable racism, the legacy of slavery, the loss of accessible jobs paying a living wage, the rise of a self-defeating culture of poverty, the unfortunate timing of the sexual and drug revolutions, and "assortive mating." This last had, according to the genes-are-destiny school, produced a subcaste of low-intelligence blacks, as impervious to betterment in a service economy as the emerging and separately unequal underclass of low-intelligence whites. Though none of these explanations excluded any other, the debate immediately became polarized. It became, in fact, a culture war in miniature, reflecting temperamental preferences for who or what got the blame.

The same finger-pointing surfaced in the postmortems of Johnson's poverty programs. Critics found evidence of middle-class rake-offs, poor coordination, insufficient generosity, or, alternatively, perverse generosity that allowed the poor to shun work and marry the state instead of providing for their own children. Even those who thought targeted programs useful conceded that they clashed with federal transportation and housing policies. Ghetto isolation worsened as whites abandoned cities to commute with cheap gas on federally funded highways from suburban houses financed with subsidized mortgages and tax breaks. Seizing the civil rights moment, white homeowners evoked the principles of color-blind meritocracy and free association to defend their good suburban fortune: no Jim Crow here. They similarly opposed busing for school integration, the liberal policy that most clearly threatened their subsidized "secession of the successful." Republican politicians, scenting votes, quickly followed suit.[36]

If anything helped the urban poor, it was Johnson's war in Vietnam. With so many young men in khaki or college, and the Pentagon spending freely, employers were panting to hire. In 1968, when unemployment dipped to 3.4 percent, General Motors plant managers posted signs asking workers, black veterans among them, to please bring in their friends. But the blue-collar job market slackened as the war wound down. Worse news followed during the 1970s, as signs of long-term deindustrialization became unmistakable.[37]

Beyond the economic reality lay a political one: Much of the public thought Johnson's antipoverty programs unnecessary or undeserved. When Roosevelt had launched his New Deal, the country was in crisis, and crisis justified action. In the mid-1960s the economy was humming. Voters distinguished between legitimate programs of a universal character (everyone gets old and sick) and illegitimate programs targeted at, well, the illegitimate. The universal programs, such as Medicare and Social Security—technically, insurance programs to which workers contributed—were politically "white," deserved, popular, and uncuttable. The targeted programs, such as AFDC welfare payments to single mothers, were "black," suspect, unpopular with the Democrats' working-class constituency, and, as events proved, cuttable indeed.[38]

If it was bad for the poor to be undeserving, it was worse for them to be ungrateful. In August 1965, less than a week after Johnson signed the Voting Rights Act, Los Angeles's Watts neighborhood erupted. Onlookers watched black looters carry sofas from burning furniture stores, then rush back in to grab the matching chairs. Four days of looting, arson, and sniping left thirty-four dead. Riots scarred more than 100 American cities over the next three years, claiming 225 lives. The cost in ill-will was just as high. "This looting in the race riots? They should tell the schvartzes they will shoot to kill," said a Jewish patent attorney. He was, of all things, a former student of the radical lawyer William Kunstler.[39]

A new breed of black nationalists, men partial to sunglasses, leather jackets, and Kool cigarettes, egged on the rioters. "If America don't come around, we going to burn it down . . . ," H. Rap Brown told a crowd in Cambridge, Maryland. "The streets are yours. Take 'em." Brown wanted liberation of black communities, not integration with the white man. "Separate but equal," he said, "is cool with me." History turned on a dime in the 1960s. Almost overnight, King's dream of a color-blind society had given way to chants of Black Power, Johnson's Great Society to burning cities. "How is it possible after all we've accomplished?" the stunned president asked after Watts. "How could it be? Is the world topsy-turvy?"[40]

A Bad Elizabethan Drama

That question was on the minds of many voters in November 1966. They gave an answer not to Johnson's liking. Republicans picked up three seats in the Senate and forty-seven in the House, where the old southern-Republican alliance was again in a position to block liberal legislation. The Republicans gained eight governorships, including California. Reagan romped home with a million votes to spare. Nationally, eight in ten voters said racial problems were uppermost in their minds.[41]

That would change in 1967, as the shadow of war lengthened. At bottom, Vietnam was an elective war of disappointing outcome and mounting casualties. Like Korea before and Iraq after, it provoked opposition from hawks impatient to win and get out, and doves who just wanted to get out. Both camps despised the strategy of protracted escalation, or what Johnson called "going up old Ho Chi Minh's leg an inch at a time." Dump Johnson talk spread among liberals. Antiwar radicals stepped up their protests. When Cardinal Spellman died, in early December 1967—the same week Eugene McCarthy announced he was challenging the president in four primaries—Johnson had to attend the funeral under armed guard, riding to St. Patrick's Cathedral through streets blue with police. Four months later, on Sunday night, March 31, 1968, Johnson told a stunned nation that, in the interests of unity and peace, he would neither seek nor accept the 1968 Democratic presidential nomination. Network commentators were, for once, at a loss for words. Their viewers were not. Phone usage hit all-time highs. White House callers could not get through for an hour.[42]

The different patterns of Vietnam dissent represented different temperaments. Moral conservatives, who loathed communism as state atheism, and economic conservatives, who despised it as totalitarian socialism, supported containment. If they dissented, it was over whether a half-war was the wisest way to fight, or whether a half-country was the wisest place to make a stand. "It was like a semi-erection for the American people," said Johnson adviser Harry McPherson. "It was completely unsatisfactory." Sixty percent of those who voted for Eugene McCarthy in the March 1968 New Hampshire primary were hawks who were fed up with Johnson. Many were unaware of McCarthy's dovish views. "He chased all those communists out the State Department," explained one elderly voter, "so I think we can give him a chance."[43]

Those on the moral and economic left, temperamentally less hostile to communism, turned on Johnson for very different reasons. The candidate of peace and prosperity had, on thin pretext, committed American troops and firepower to support an unpopular minority regime in a distant civil war, with no stop-loss order for blood or treasure. Martin Luther King Jr. held his uneasy peace until April 1967, then spoke out from America's most visible liberal pulpit, New York's Riverside Church. The war, he said, had plunged an eviscerating trocar into the nation's belly, sucking out the resources promised to the poor. Johnson reddened with anger when aides brought him the news.[44]

Yet King had only thought Vietnam a terrible, remediable error. New Left radicals were convinced that Vietnam had been no mistake, but a sinister manifestation of the imperialism and racism lurking behind liberalism's beneficent mask. They, too, felt betrayed. In 1964 Students for a Democratic Society (SDS) had gone "Part of the Way with LBJ." In 1968 SDS called for a boycott of the elections and organized mass protests to besiege the ruling class. The threat might have passed for a joke had not the intervening years transformed SDS from a handful of intellectuals with a mimeograph machine into a seething cauldron of protest.[45]

Bill Ayers, a leader of the SDS Weatherman faction, likened the war to turning a corner and discovering a man you trusted assaulting a stranger. Dismay may have been the right feeling, but action was the right response. College men felt the added lash of guilt. Nearly two in three male high school graduates had entered college in 1968, many to avoid the draft. They knew that others were dying in their place. "All we ever talked about at Yale then was school, sex, and the war in Vietnam, and not always in that order," admitted Mark Soler, one of George W. Bush's classmates. Trust in government plummeted among the young, in uniform and out.[46]

Older Americans also had their doubts. The Tet Offensive struck every major city in South Vietnam in January 1968. Yet the majority, fearful of demoralizing American soldiers, abhorred public protest. Worse that students should wave Viet Cong flags while attending school at taxpayer expense. Third-party candidate George Wallace made sure the spotlight caught his long-haired hecklers, whom he invited to come forward so he could autograph their sandals. Professors who advocated communist victory in Vietnam could take their souvenir in the form of a promised federal indictment.[47]

Wallace rallies were political camp meetings. Fiddlers fiddled and preachers preached while costumed cowgirls worked the crowd for small bills. Then the candidate appeared, shot a crisp salute, and launched into a practiced diatribe against the agitators and anarchists and the sissy britches who were letting them ruin the country. "I'm sick and tired of . . ." hit the audience where it lived. Before long the shouting, whistling partisans were stepping all over Wallace's lines. The atmosphere was telepathic. "He was saying what was on their minds, saying it like it is, saying it the way they said it to each other in the bars," wrote Teddy White, awed by Wallace's performance in Cicero. Young Karl Rove, who watched the show at the Mormon Tabernacle, never forgot the reaction when Wallace defied any protester to lie down in front of *his* car. "The crowd just roared in hatred," Rove said. "And it astonished me."[48]

Wallace stood for more than hate. He was an authoritarian populist, anti-intellectual and pro-working man, hard moral rightist and soft economic leftist. He had built highways and clinics in Alabama, increased pensions and unemployment compensation. He ran as a friend of labor. Outside the South, his natural supporter was the blue-collar Democrat who despised hippies, blockbusters, and welfare mothers of the sort who demanded that Korvette's department store send their bills to the welfare agency. "You see that," said one New Yorker, "and you want to go out and strangle someone." Wallace promised that, should his third-party candidacy deadlock the election, he would release his electoral votes to any rival who would punish advocates of enemy victory, eliminate federal poverty programs, curtail foreign aid, stand up for law and order, end civil rights legislation, name conservative justices, and return control of "domestic institutions" to the states.[49]

In January 1960, when John Kennedy had announced his candidacy, Americans thought the primary danger came from without, from communist expansion. In March 1968, when Robert Kennedy belatedly announced his candidacy, Americans were increasingly convinced that the danger came from within, from the crisis of order and morality. The reaction against

Figure 5 Photographer Jim Marshall captured a patriotic counter-demonstrator outside Berkeley's Wheeler Auditorium in October 1965. Despite the war's growing unpopularity, antiwar street activists were the most despised group in the country by the late 1960s.

domestic liberalism, itemized by Wallace's promises, posed a huge problem for Robert Kennedy. His record since his 1964 election to the Senate was, if anything, more liberal than Johnson's. He wanted to end the war and refocus the nation's energies on racial justice, for Chicanos and Indians as well as black Americans. Still, as he entered the remaining primaries, trying to convince party bosses that he was their best hope, he had the unique advantage of being a Kennedy. He had inherited his brother's political organization and charismatic authority. The most Catholic of the four sons, as well as the most radical, he had also inherited the clan's tendency to divide the world into with-us and against-us. "Bob always cut," wrote John Bartlow Martin, who rejoined the Kennedy team. "He pushed buttons no one else pushed; he aroused wild enthusiasm and love and equally wild hate." And like no white candidate before or since, he commanded the loyalties of minorities and the disaffected young. His problem was how to hold on to Democrats disaffected *by* minorities and the young.[50]

Kennedy had a past as a cold warrior and a mafia buster. Use that past, his advisers told him. Use it in the make-or-break Indiana primary. Hoosiers were sick of the war and sick of rioters. Tell them that you will tolerate neither racial violence nor racial injustice. Tell them that you were once the nation's top cop. Kennedy nodded. "I can go pretty far in that direction," he said. In 1967, two months after he broke with LBJ over Vietnam, Kennedy had co-sponsored a bill to *increase* penalties for desecrating the flag. He knew his base was safe. He could cut his hair and talk law and order with Kokomo auto workers and still win nine-tenths of the black vote, which was what he got in Indiana. Enough whites joined them to give Kennedy a momentum-shifting win.[51]

Martin wanted to repeat the tactic in California. He suggested that the candidate put in an appearance at McCarthy-friendly Berkeley. Californians didn't like Berkeley students. Campus hotheads booing Kennedy would be political gold. So would footage of another California disaster, a scowling Nixon telling the press "you won't have Nixon to kick around any more" after he lost the 1962 gubernatorial election. Looking ahead to the fall election, Martin suggested that Kennedy run Nixon's pout over and over, followed by "Would you trust this man with the Presidency of the United States?"

Martin's memo outlining post-California strategy was in Robert Kennedy's breast pocket when, after delivering his on-to-Chicago victory speech, he exited the Ambassador Hotel ballroom through the kitchen pantry. His assassin, Sirhan Sirhan, put a bullet in his head and two more in his body. Sirens filled the Los Angeles night. "The whole thing, the whole last few years," wrote a disbelieving Martin, "seems a little like a bad Elizabethan drama, where the curtain comes down on a stage filled with dead bodies."[52]

Nixon by a Nose

One of the enduring myths of American history is that Robert Kennedy was the last politician capable of national reconciliation, of ending the divisive war abroad and racial strife at home. Arthur Schlesinger Jr., the presidential historian and Kennedy family intimate, thought he would have brought back the enchantment of the early 1960s, restoring a sense of idealistic national purpose. Bill Clinton claimed him as the first New Democrat, a man who intuited that progressive politics in America required blending novel policies with traditional values. "If he had become President," Clinton wrote, "America's journey through the rest of the twentieth century would have been very different." No Sirhan, no Culture War.[53]

This is nostalgic bunk. At best, Robert Kennedy papered over the Democrats' widening temperamental gap. News reports to the contrary, he never had that much pull with blue-collar voters. In Indiana, he ran behind in 59 out of 70 white precincts in Gary, offsetting the lost votes with heavy minority turnout—a pattern that became central to Democratic politics over the next half century. Had Kennedy lined up the tricky combination shot of nomination, a prospect that even his ally George McGovern doubted, he was hardly assured of the presidency. Democrats who had supported Adlai Stevenson, the witty Democratic standardbearer in the 1952 and 1956 elections, were lukewarm to Kennedy. They preferred McCarthy, as did college-educated whites generally. McCarthy embarrassed Kennedy by winning the primary in mostly white Oregon, and ran ahead of him in the California suburbs. Kennedy's bid for a justice-with-order coalition of minorities and Wallace supporters struck most Democratic politicians as somewhere between delusional and duplicitous. His political project, grafting an expansive, antiwar liberalism onto a socially conservative base, was equally untested and doubtful. When McGovern tried the same thing four years later, he got nowhere. Granted, McGovern lacked Kennedy's charisma. Yet so did Jimmy Carter, who won in 1976 by tacking away from left-liberalism.[54]

To doubt that Robert Kennedy could have saved the Roosevelt coalition is not to dismiss his murder as irrelevant. Had he lived but lost the nomination, Kennedy might still have used his leverage to nudge the eventual nominee, Vice President Hubert Humphrey, toward a negotiated peace position. Had a compromise peace plank dampened the antiwar protests at the Chicago convention that August, the Democrats might have held on to the White House in November. Had Kennedy joined Humphrey on a unity ticket, their chances would have been even better. Running mate or no, Humphrey expected that Kennedy would support him in the end, both men being "essentially straight-line liberal Democrats." As it was, Chicago ruined Humphrey's chances. The last thing he needed was enraged delegates screaming insults or Daley's blue-helmeted police drawing their night sticks and charging obscenity-chanting demonstrators. The whole world watched the disaster. Few observers gave Humphrey a chance of surviving it.[55]

Of all those to speculate on the consequences of Robert Kennedy's murder that eventful summer, the most important was Earl Warren. He felt sure that Nixon would now win the presidency. At seventy-seven, the chief justice wanted Johnson to name his successor before Nixon, whom he despised, had the chance. That June, he announced his intention to resign. Johnson picked Abe Fortas, his loyal friend and adviser, to replace Warren. He nominated another crony, federal appeals court judge Homer Thornberry, to take Fortas's seat. Johnson thought adding a Texas Democrat to the Court would placate southern conservatives.

In ordinary circumstances it would have. But too much bile had built up behind Fortas's record. With Nixon privately encouraging him, Michigan's Robert Griffin led the Republican attack. Griffin pounded the Judiciary Committee table and said it was time the Senate asserted its power. South Carolina's Strom Thurmond, who had switched from Democrat to Republican in 1964, seized on the crime issue. "Mallory, Mallory, I want that word to ring in your ears—Mallory," he chided Fortas. That Fortas had not actually been on the Court when it had overturned the conviction of the black rapist did nothing to stop the tirade. Thurmond also made sure that his colleagues and the press attended private screenings of the movies Fortas's supposedly decisive vote had loosed on the world. (Yale Law School cheekily selected one of them as the main feature of its "Fortas Film Festival" later that year.) In effect, one judge was pilloried for the collective sins of left-liberal activism, much as Robert Bork would be for his conservative views nearly two decades later. When Fortas's nomination came before the full Senate, his supporters could muster only forty-five votes against the fatal filibuster.[56]

Warren's hunch about a Nixon victory proved correct. Humphrey ran defiantly as a liberal, only to finish with nearly 12 million fewer votes than Johnson in 1964. That drop was both absolutely and proportionately greater than the 5.6 million votes the economic crisis cost Herbert Hoover between 1928 and 1932. Most ominously, only 35 percent of whites chose the Humphrey–Muskie ticket. The backlash did lasting damage to their party. In 1964, 27 percent of Americans called themselves "strong Democrats." That figure fell to 20 percent in 1968, then 15 percent in 1972. The overcomers had been overcome.[57]

Though not by much: Nixon won with just 43.4 percent of the popular vote to Humphrey's 42.7. Humphrey closed as northern labor came back to him. "They know which side their bread is buttered on," a local party official told me, explaining the world to a kid working in his first campaign. Martin, who gamely supported Humphrey after Robert Kennedy's assassination, thought 10 million dollars in September and a clean break over Vietnam would have put his man over the top. "We gave Nixon pause," he reflected as the eventful year drew to a close. "He can't go too far right now. He has no mandate."[58]

The president-elect well understood the narrowness of his election. And he did not, as Martin hoped, venture too far to the right on domestic policy. But Nixon also sensed something else, that he had found a decisive issue in national moral character. Over the next four years he exploited it so skillfully that no ambiguity attended his next electoral victory.

4

"The real dividing line in recent American history," said historian Christopher Lasch, "is the line between those who lived through the 1960s and those who didn't. All of us who experienced the 60s, that profound upheaval after which nothing was ever the same again, were unavoidably marked for life." Others have compared the experience to living through the Civil War, with the nation unraveling in the five awful months from King's April 1968 murder to the August convention riots. "We couldn't imagine the American people turning on the American people," said Chicago policeman Joe Pecoraro, "and I guess since then it has been going on."[1]

Bill Clinton, who watched the Chicago riots on a Shreveport hotel television, thought the crisis marked the precise point where American politics turned from the practical business of bettering lives into zero-sum psychic warfare. "The kids and their supporters saw the mayor and the cops as authoritarian, ignorant, violent bigots. The mayor and his largely blue-collar ethnic police force saw the kids as foul-mouthed, immoral, unpatriotic, soft, upper-class kids who were too spoiled to respect authority, too selfish to appreciate what it takes to hold a society together, too cowardly to serve in Vietnam." The only winners in this family feud were reactionaries who, rebounding with terrific force from the 1960s, proved themselves more resourceful in marshalling resentment to achieve power—and more determined to hang on to power once they had it.[2]

Perhaps because the enemies of the 1960s had him personally in their sights, Clinton blurred the distinction between political assertiveness and cultural reconquest. A world in which Daley's own son and mayoral heir, Richard M. Daley, would climb into an aqua-colored 1956 Thunderbird to help launch the city's annual Gay and Lesbian Pride Parade was not one of reactionary triumph. Clinton was right, though, that Chicago crystallized the sense of belonging to one side or the other. Yippie provocateurs

Jerry Rubin and Abbie Hoffman, who promised joint-rolling contests and nude grope-ins for peace, had made sure to rub the nation's nose in the counterculture. Straights saw more than antiwar protesters. They saw reckless kids grasping at anarchic freedom. The police saw red:

> *Police operator:* 1814, get a wagon over at 1436. We've got an injured hippie.
> *Voice:* 1436 North Wells?
> *Operator:* North Wells.

Five other units chimed in:

> That's no emergency.
> Let him take a bus.
> Kick the fucker.
> Knock his teeth out.
> Throw him in the wastepaper basket.[3]

Yale law professor Charles Reich tried to put a progressive historical frame around the conflict. In his 1970 best-seller, *The Greening of America*, Reich argued that America had passed from preindustrial individualism to consumer conformism to an emergent third stage of liberated "lifestyles" evident in its bell-bottomed youth. The coinage stuck, minus the hyphen. So did Reich's idea that the 1960s had unleashed something bigger than civil rights and antiwar protest. Disenchanted young people had rejected the repressive code at the very heart of their elders' world. "Start doing what you want to do," Reich wrote in his memoirs. "Stop doing what you don't want to do." Virtually every cultural critic who followed him put the fashion for self-assertion at the center of the decade's legacy. If the 1930s had marked a breakthrough for the economic left, the 1960s signaled a comparable breakthrough for the moral left, which seized cultural ground from discredited religious and political institutions.[4]

The World According to Nixon

The temperamental logic of *The Greening of America* came into sharper focus six years later when Reich revealed that he was a long-repressed homosexual who had, in his early forties, decided to forego tenure in New Haven for gay life in San Francisco. No such revelation was required to understand why Richard Nixon, who clung to everything Reich rejected, should see only menace in the counterculture. Nixon had been schooled in

Whittier, California, a Quaker town whose citizens viewed government assistance with deep suspicion. When Nixon's older brother Harold contracted tuberculosis, the family doctor urged prompt admission to the public sanitarium. The facility was excellent, the cost minimal. Hannah and Frank Nixon spurned his advice. For five years they skimped and borrowed to provide private treatment in a futile attempt to save their son's life. "Both my mother and father were almost fierce in their adherence to what is now depreciatingly referred to as puritan ethics," Nixon later wrote. "Not only were they deeply religious, but they carried their principles over into their lives in other respects and particularly in an insistence that to 'accept help from the government,' no matter how difficult our own circumstances were, was simply wrong from a moral standpoint."[5]

Here was Lakoff's ideal conservative type, the striver whose strict upbringing left him with an indivisible sense of personal responsibility. Nixon didn't need charisma to win votes, Clare Luce observed, because he so was perfectly attuned to Square America. His tastes (football, Mantovani, John Ford) were its tastes, his prejudices (blacks, idlers, snobs) were its prejudices. When Nixon groused about welfare bums, he meant it. The contempt in his voice was unmistakable and is preserved like a fly in amber in the White House tapes.[6]

Those tapes preserve something else—the vindictive preoccupations of a deceitful loner, haunted by insecurity and filled with punishing rage. The strangest fact about this very strange man was that he was a tormented introvert who rose to the top of an extrovert's profession. With a hot-tempered father and an emotionally distant mother, Nixon had early sought security in the role of wary grind. As a child he had answered to two nicknames, "Dick" and "Gloomy Gus." Law school added a third, "Iron Butt," for his legendary study hours. Life became a lonely struggle for survival in a loveless world. It offered one consolation, the transmuting ambition born of the insults and snubs. "If your anger is deep enough and strong enough," Nixon told aide Ken Clawson, "you learn that you can change those attitudes by excellence, personal gut performance while those who have everything are sitting on their fat butts." Another aide, Bryce Harlow, got the man in a sentence: "Richard Nixon went up the walls of life with his claws."[7]

They were sharp claws. Nixon possessed a keen intelligence, a knack for performance, and a prodigious memory. As president he could recite verbatim the fence-whitewashing episode from *Tom Sawyer* that he had learned in grade school. His problem was that of every narcissist:

Achievement brought no respite. Once he had reached the top, he still had to live with his ulcers and his demons. He fled them, not in the sleep denied by chronic insomnia, but in the waking dream of omnipotence and grand achievement. He'd show them. He'd tidy up the nation's messes, restore its prestige, enter its history as a great statesman. That he sometimes succeeded, that he thought outside the box more often and more creatively than any other postwar president, adds fascination and sympathy to his essentially tragic story.[8]

At the heart of Nixon's tragedy lay his inability to distinguish between his political enemies and America's enemies. Publicly, Nixon had campaigned to bring the nation together. Privately, he railed against the elite that scorned him. The educated, society's natural leaders, had lost their guts, Nixon told his staff. They drank too much, they parroted fashionable talk. They knocked the system and boo-hooed about the blacks, who were hopeless anyway. The Jews had the wettest hankies. A few tough ones, like Henry Kissinger, knew the score. The rest were pathetic. The pot legalizers? All Jews. The vacant Jewish seat on the Supreme Court? Oh, he'd fill it—sometime after he died. The scheming bastards already had the bureaucracy, the media, the arts, the campuses. Permissiveness and defeatism had spread everywhere, even to the clergy. No wonder the churches were emptying out. Now the Catholics were starting down the same damn road. And look at the schools, filled with nihilism and dope. Most of the kids would be better off if they got out from behind their desks and did some honest work.[9]

Nixon saw himself as the leader of a band of tough-minded intellectuals who could achieve power and reverse the national decline by making common cause with the white working class. What hard-hats and beauticians lacked in learning they made up for with an uncorrupted moral sense. The same applied to the Hispanics. "They do have some concept of the manly life, at least," Nixon told John Ehrlichman, his chief domestic-policy adviser. "They don't live like a bunch of dogs, which the Negroes do." The nominally Protestant Nixon was all for priests knocking some sense into their charges. He never lost his conviction that religious belief was indispensable for public order. He trusted, and was trusted by, voters of morally conservative temperament. They embraced him as one of their own, despite the peculiarity of his youthful Quakerism and the vagueness of his adult beliefs. Nixon lived what Clare Luce foresaw: temperament supplanting creed in politics. He thought this way himself. When he railed against "the Jews," Nixon meant left-liberal Jews, not the Orthodox.[10]

Nixon was discreet about where he did his railing. When Billy Graham privately complained that Jews were behind pornography, that their grip on the media had to be broken, Nixon immediately agreed. "Boy, I can't ever say that," he admitted. "But I believe it." Nixon often held his tongue. Everyone knew that public schooling was lousy, he complained to Ehrlichman. The thing was, you couldn't say so, or you'd provoke the education establishment. "We'll praise them—pat them on the ass. A demagogue could make a lot of votes on this issue—we've got to live with them."[11]

Fake Right

It was a revealing piece of hypocrisy. Given his right-conservative temperament, Nixon would have preferred a domestic policy aimed at reducing taxes, bureaucracy, union influence, crime, vice, spending, and the supply of money. That he did none of these things consistently, that he presided over an erratically liberal domestic policy, was due to a fateful combination of circumstances. Nixon was the first elected president in 120 years to assume office with the opposition party controlling both houses of Congress. Democrats commanded Capitol Hill, their bureaucratic allies the granite-clad buildings that ran like outworks beneath it. To call Nixon paranoid, Chief of Staff Bob Haldeman observed, was to ignore very real enemies throughout the government, the press, and the establishment. They could block any reactionary policy shift.[12]

Not that domestic legislation was Nixon's primary concern. He could use his executive authority to keep faith on key issues. He would nominate judges who were conservative on crime. He would cast his attorney general, John Mitchell, as a "helluva crime-fighter," Dick Tracy with a pipe. He would propose bills halting busing to achieve racial balance, softening the blow with more money for inner-city schools. He would pursue peace with honor in Vietnam, the doves be damned. "North Vietnam cannot defeat or humiliate the United States. Only Americans can do that," he told 80 million television viewers on November 3, 1969. The silent-majority address, the most important of his presidency, gave Nixon a bump in the polls and time for a fateful gamble. He thought he could prevail in peace negotiations by building up South Vietnam, intimidating North Vietnam, and getting the divided Soviets and Chinese to back off their client. As in poker and football, two obsessions that shaped Nixon's worldview, what counted was the gutsy call at the right time. Foreign-policy decisions made or broke presidencies. Domestic mistakes were fixable. Congress could tinker with the details. The Kremlin was less forgiving.[13]

What mattered about domestic policy was its political impact. Nixon's grand objective, realignment, required more than moral and racial appeals. Blue-collar workers wanted workplace protections and more generous retirement benefits; Nixon gave them both. Though he privately regarded environmentalism as a radical stalking horse, he coopted the public's growing anxiety over pollution with measures like the 1970 Environmental Protection Act. Free-market orthodoxy never stood between him and votes. In August 1971, anxious to address the trade deficit and inflation before an election year, he ended the direct convertibility of the dollar to gold, decreed a surcharge on imports, and imposed a temporary freeze on wages, profits, and prices. Hotel managers who wanted to change their pay-toilet locks from a dime to a quarter were told to wait. "The conservatives got the rhetoric and the liberals got the government," complained Howard Phillips, a budget hawk who walked out of the Republican Party in 1974. Far from dismantling the Great Society, Nixon had expanded it. Allocations for social spending were 60 percent higher in Nixon's last fiscal year than in Johnson's.[14]

If spending generates votes, so does anger. But after the polls close, anger is best reduced to a low simmer. As president, Nixon avoided overt demagoguery. He wanted to be like Dwight Eisenhower or Charles de Gaulle, not George Wallace. Let someone else confront the hecklers. He would content himself with nods to God and country. He wore a flag lapel pin, appeared with Billy Graham, tut-tutted New York State's liberal abortion law, and attended Sunday services in the East Room with a carefully selected mix of VIPs and POW wives. Colson invited Evangelical leaders to the White House, showed them around the West Wing, then casually suggested that they drop by the Oval Office. Nixon reeled them in with a few well-rehearsed words and a pair of gold-plated presidential cuff links. They practically bowed on the way out.[15]

Nixon landed bigger fish on the presidential yacht, over chateaubriand and vintage Bordeaux in the main salon. Briefed by Colson, he made sure to display his knowledge of the religious issues that concerned his guest. At intervals Nixon would interrupt the conversation to say, "Chuck, I want this done. This man is right. You order the attorney general to take care of that tomorrow morning." It was not all an act. "The president meant what he said, and we even thought some of the things might be accomplished," Colson allowed. "But whatever else happened, that religious leader was convinced that Richard Nixon was on his side." Politics, Colson saw, was about how "people in power use power to keep themselves in power." Sympathetic or not, politicians worked special-interest groups for everything they could get. Nixon simply worked harder than the rest.[16]

He also worked more subtly. He exploited "the Social Issue"—street crime, race riots, defiant kids, and permissiveness—through deft gestures. He even ordered the removal of *Portnoy's Complaint*, Philip Roth's comedic novel of sexual obsession, from the White House library and then leaked the news that he had done so. But he mostly refrained from overt attacks on welfare queens and newsroom lefties. That was why the tapes were so scurrilous: Nixon was venting in private what he could not express in public. He was letting his hair down with the boys—only the boys, Nixon's prejudices fully extending to women. Kissinger went so far as to call the White House atmosphere "slightly homosexual," though intensely homosocial would be more accurate. Yet Nixon supported the ERA and sought a conservative female Supreme Court nominee, rubbing his hands over the prospect of Senate liberals taking their law-and-order pill with a sugar-coating of feminism. He really was Tricky Dick.[17]

If Nixon thought placatory gestures wiser than demagoguery, he was happy to have others go after his enemies. That role fell to Spiro T. Agnew. The vice president was a one-man composite of the New Majority, an ambitious small-time attorney who had surrendered his Greek name, church, and immigrant father's party to become "Ted" Agnew, Episcopalian, Republican, and, in 1966, governor of Maryland. Winning office as a racial moderate, Agnew hardened his position in 1968, rebuking black militants and the civil rights leaders who tolerated them. Nixon put him on the ticket to appeal to southern and border-state voters tempted by Wallace. In office, Agnew used the lecture circuit to skewer media snobs, "sociological soreheads," and "cicerones of self-hate." He was good copy and, by 1969, the third most admired man in America, behind Nixon and Billy Graham. Yet, by a three-to-one margin, Americans did not want Agnew to become president. Pat Buchanan drew the obvious moral. Agnew's insults had taken a toll on liberal Democrats, but at the price of his own electability. The last thing Nixon needed to do was to wade into that sort of fight. Mind you, don't *stop* the fight. Just stay above it.[18]

The catch was that few surrogates were available to Nixon outside his administration. The problem with your silent majority, Moynihan told Nixon in 1970, was that it was silent. Adversarial elites controlled information flow and opinion formation. "You may have more troops," Moynihan observed, "but the other side has more fire-power." So Nixon did what any outgunned insurgent with mass support would do. He fell back on guerrilla warfare, tactics matched to his taste for stealth and misdirection. When Edith Efron published a book critical of television news' left-liberal slant, the president told Colson to buy up as many copies as necessary to make it a best-seller. But when the capers turned felonious, the tracks led to the White House. By attempting to conceal them, Nixon turned the political scandal of the 1972 burglary of the Democrat's Watergate headquarters into a constitutional crisis, giving his enemies the chance to bring him down.[19]

Moynihan always regretted Watergate and the mentality of unrelenting political warfare from which it grew. Moynihan was a veteran of the Kennedy and Johnson administrations who had had second thoughts about liberal prescriptions for urban ills and had gone to work advising the new president. Nixon had done good things, he insisted, and might have done more had not his political side overcome his presidential one. Moynihan never doubted that enlightened policy could transform lives. Or save them, his first government project being automotive safety. But the eponymous 1965 Moynihan Report, which grounded the ghetto's culture of poverty in family instability, and its author's habit of criticizing improvident welfare schemes, won him no left-liberal friends. Moynihan never recanted or lost sight of the importance of fathers. His own father, an alcoholic, had abandoned his family during the Depression. Moynihan had shined shoes in Times Square and unloaded freight for 78 cents an hour, before finishing college on the G.I. Bill. But in diagnosing black fatherlessness as a social pathology, if only for the cure of Great Society medicine, Moynihan had "blamed the victim," the gravest of heresies against the new dispensation of militant racial pride.

Moynihan's trip to the political doghouse endeared him to Nixon, who had felt the same lash of liberal scorn, and to a rising generation of Jewish neoconservatives worried about license at home and totalitarianism abroad. (Change your name to "Goynihan," teased *New York Times* correspondent Max Frankel, when an Arab newspaper misidentified Moynihan as a Jew.) Yet his relationships with conservatives of any variety were always fraught. At bottom he was a Catholic social democrat with a streak of pessimism. He would have made a good liberal pope, being anticommunist, pro-labor, communitarian, and sympathetically skep-

Figure 6   Pat Buchanan, who wrote many of Spiro Agnew's speeches, called the vice president "the bayonet of the Republican Party." Cartoonist Edmund Valtman cast him as the hatchet man. "The assassin's dilemma," joked Nixon's aides, "if they kill Nixon, they get Agnew."

tical about the run of humanity. "For most persons it would be exceedingly painful to live in a world where you get what is coming to you," he told Nixon. The president shared the sentiment, if not the regret.[20]

Moynihan tried to steer Nixon on a vital-center course. He advised him to wind up the war, maintain employment, and reform welfare. Agnew scared him. He thought Agnew made the administration look duplicitous and risked further dividing the country. When Nixon discovered Arthur Jensen's controversial work on race and intelligence, Moynihan sounded a four-bell alarm. It was one thing to discuss the matter privately in the White House, he advised Nixon. But "in the bowels of Christ I plead with you not to let the Vice President say anything." He had made the same point in a famous leaked memo calling for a period of "benign neglect" in race relations, quiet progress being preferable to pot-banging.[21]

Though the phrase landed Moynihan back in the soup, he was at least consistent in the matter of demagoguery. The world was like his mother's bar, a place better off if the troublemakers kept their yaps shut. That they felt no compunction to do so, or to refrain from cross-sniping at him during his ensuing senatorial career, made Moynihan the Culture War's most paradoxical figure, the serial insider as perpetual outsider, never fully at ease in anyone's camp. Journalist Robert Novak judged him a latter-day Henry Clay, the most talented politician of his generation never to become president. Novak thought Moynihan's number-one problem was that he couldn't figure out whose political bed he belonged in: Witness his service in Nixon's cabinet. His number-two problem was more common in Washington: "He drank too much."[22]

Nixon respected Moynihan and heard him out. He was disinclined, however, to alter the domestic game plan. He would keep faking Big Ted Agnew around right end while he carried the ball up the middle. Rather than running straight ahead, he zigged left and then zagged right. He backed off the Everglades Jetport, pleasing environmentalists, but defied them on the Supersonic Transport. He cut funding at the Corporation for Public Broadcasting, but increased it at the National Endowments for the Humanities and Arts—with strings to keep the money from *avant-gardists*. He opposed busing students to achieve racial balance, but supported the "Philadelphia Plan," which set minority hiring goals for contractors on federally financed construction projects. Nixon believed in black progress through black jobs. Work was what worked, if anything would. But he also relished the prospect of driving another wedge into the Democratic coalition by setting civil rights activists and white union members against one another. "Only Nixon could go to Philadelphia," as one labor historian tartly put it.[23]

What looked like ideological confusion, then, was often stutter-stepping to keep opponents off balance. Nixon could pick his way up the domestic middle for the same reason he could make an opening to China: His anticommunist credentials were in impeccable order. When Buchanan fired off a memo complaining that the zig-zagging was alienating conservatives, the president replied, "You overlook RN's consistent hard line on foreign policy." The same logic that had trapped Johnson in Vietnam, dead communists as *bona fides,* worked for Nixon during his long withdrawal. Hanging tough abroad covered a multitude of sins at home.[24]

Cops and Docs

Better, though, if Nixon could frame his zigs in a way that avoided raising conservative hackles. Float the dollar, but avoid talk of "devaluation," which connoted weakness. "Richard Nixon at times seemed to believe there was no national issue that was not susceptible to public-relations treatment," Ehrlichman decided. He had perfected what others had begun: the media presidency based on news management and image manipulation. He had been adept at moral camouflage since his Whittier College days, when he won the student presidency by promising dances on the Quaker campus. Chaperoned dancers would be better off, he argued, than on their own in wicked Los Angeles.[25]

It all came down to packaging. When Ehrlichman wrote, "Our welfare reform effort has been a good zig, without damage to the Social Issue, with promise of strong blue-collar appeal," Nixon replied cautiously. "This *may* be questionable politically unless *more* emphasis on work," he scribbled in the margin. He was referring to the Family Assistance Plan, a Moynihan-hatched guaranteed income scheme made palatable by a work requirement. "The total, total emphasis of our welfare reform support now should be work," Nixon later told Ehrlichman and Haldeman, "and not the fact that we're going to put more of these little Negro bastards on welfare rolls at twenty-four hundred dollars a family." Otherwise, he said, the bill would never pass. More importantly, there would be hell to pay politically.[26]

The Family Assistance Plan died in a cross fire between Senate liberals who pronounced it insufficiently generous and conservatives who smelled another subsidy for layabouts. Nixon had better luck with the 1970 Controlled Substances Act, a major drug-policy reform to which he imparted a rightward spin. In the 1980s, after Congress amended the law in draconian fashion, no spin would be necessary. But Nixon and his advisers had to exercise considerable public relations ingenuity with the original legislation, which was anything but a simple get-tough law.

At the beginning of the 1960s, illicit drug use remained rare outside bohemian and ghetto neighborhoods. The big drug on campus was Purple Death, a grape drink laced with pot-luck booze, ladled out of a washtub. By 1965, though, marijuana was becoming a fixture at schools like Michigan. Even frat boys lit up. Marijuana surfaced in suburban high schools in 1967–1968, and harder drugs after that. No social class was immune. Eighty-three percent of the Harvard/Radcliffe class of 1970 reported using marijuana at some point in their lives, 43 percent psychedelics. The 1960s attitude toward acid, remembered Animals lead singer Eric Burdon, was "you're letting your generation down if you don't try this."[27]

The Army had its own generation gap. Thirty-five percent of the troops arriving in Vietnam in 1969 were already marijuana smokers. In-country they could buy joints in cigarette packs, pre-rolled and soaked in opium. Cheap heroin hit big in 1970. Officers visiting firebases heard empty plastic vials crunching underfoot. Though much GI drug use was sporadic—unwinding after combat, partying during R & R—the situation was still unprecedented and alarming. So was the condition of the ghettos. In some Harlem neighborhoods a third of the permanent residents were said to be addicted, not counting the junkies catting in abandoned buildings or small-fry glue sniffers.[28]

Nixon viewed drug abuse as social rot, lethal in a competitive world. He wanted to act fast, and he needed to act systematically. Federal drug control was antiquated, deriving its authority from a patchwork of laws and court rulings from the days of corked paregoric bottles. Simply "scheduling" the flood of novel drugs to determine their degree of regulation required a new administrative system. Plans to overhaul federal drug laws had begun late in the Johnson administration. Nixon incorporated them in a reform bill he sent to Congress in July 1969. For good measure, Nixon announced that the Justice Department was drafting a compatible model law for state governments. Forty-four states adopted it before the decade was out.

Nixon's legislative message gave rhetorical priority to law enforcement. He had long favored strict punishment, especially for traffickers. In the 1950s Congress had twice increased mandatory minimum sentences for violating drug laws, with many states following suit. Nixon was still pushing that nostrum in his 1962 California gubernatorial campaign, when he called for executing traffickers with multiple convictions. But by then legal and medical thinking about the problem had taken a therapeutic turn. Professional opinion held addiction to be a disease, something to be prevented or treated rather than simply punished. Judges should sentence those convicted of small purchases or sales in a flexible way, with rehabilitation the ultimate goal.

The final versions of the 1970 legislation did just this. Health, Education, and Welfare officials and congressional Democrats tacked on funding for public health approaches and eliminated mandatory minimum sentences, save for professional criminals engaged in continuous conspiracies. First-time marijuana possession, previously a felony requiring two-to-ten years in prison, became a misdemeanor punishable by no more than a one-year term—or none, judges being free to grant probation. Judicial discretion, explained a Republican congressman from Texas, would translate into more appropriate sentences and more respect for the law. The congressman's name was George H. W. Bush.[29]

Ehrlichman was still worried, however. Flexible sentences could make the administration look soft. Get out an explanation fast, he told aides, and make it something that newspaper readers could swallow with their coffee. The trick was to bury the reform lead. "This bill is tough," announced John Ingersoll, director of the Bureau of Narcotics and Dangerous Drugs. "But it is also fair." It contained "harsh sentences" for major traffickers, which was where he wanted to focus anyway. The bill also had attractive enforcement provisions, such as 300 new agents and "no-knock" search warrants. Readers could well imagine rookie narcs kicking in their first doors. Nixon himself appeared, hands casually in pockets, at a drug-sniffing-dog demonstration on the White House lawn. Applied to hybrid reforms like the 1970 drug legislation, public relations became a simple matter of cherry picking: Stress whatever appealed to the base; downplay the rest.[30]

With crime still rising and military heroin use still in the headlines, Nixon declared a national drug emergency in June 1971. But this was to be a big-tent drug war, just as the 1970 bill had been a big-tent reform. Nixon proposed a White House drug office and unprecedented treatment and research funding, which Congress approved without a single "nay" vote. Vietnam added bipartisan urgency and a measure of sympathy.

Drafted kids sent to fight overseas merited special consideration and help.[31]

That same June Nixon named Jerry Jaffe to head the new Special Action Office for Drug Abuse Prevention. The bespectacled Jewish psychiatrist showed up at the White House in a rumpled suit, psychedelic tie, and Elvis sideburns. But he was no mistake. Nixon knew that Jaffe meant more drug treatment, specifically more methadone. Aides Jeffrey Donfeld and Egil "Bud" Krogh had become convinced that methadone maintenance cut crime, and had in turn convinced Ehrlichman and Nixon. "At least a move from heroin methadone, that's a wonderful move," Nixon told Daley when he visited the Oval Office. Why not try it in Chicago?[32]

Thus American drug policy entered its therapeutic golden age of 1971 to 1973. Yet Nixon, mindful to balance his zigs with zags, defied advice to decriminalize marijuana. He held fast to the domino theory of drugs. "It's marijuana, then it's speed, then it's LSD, then it's heroin," he told Daley—this in the same conversation in which he endorsed methadone. Nixon knew, as did Daley, that marijuana smokers were his cultural enemies, flipping the bird in his direction every time they fired up a joint. Methadone was about street crime. Marijuana was about youthful defiance and seemed a good place to draw a line in the political sand.[33]

Nor did Nixon give up on locking away drug traffickers. Judges may not like mandatory minimums, he said. But the people did. "Who cares about the Jaffe stuff, the treating of the addicts?" he told Haldeman. Mothers worried about protecting their kids from pushers. Tough drug enforcement was middle-class insurance and good politics. Reluctantly, pragmatically, Nixon had invited the docs into his drug war. But he kept the spotlight on the cops. In early 1972 he set up the Office of Drug Abuse Law Enforcement to coordinate federal and local sweeps against street dealers. He named Commissioner of Customs Myles Ambrose, a Republican inclined to power suits and striped ties, as its head. Jaffe's star fell as Ambrose's rose.[34]

It fell further in early 1973 when Nelson Rockefeller, governor of New York and erstwhile champion of the therapeutic approach, called for mandatory life sentences for drug traffickers. Addicts were like an invading army, Rockefeller said. They wiped out entire neighborhoods, they threatened society itself. "This has to stop," he announced during his State of the State address. "This . . . is . . . going . . . to . . . stop." Two-thirds of New Yorkers agreed with him. Rockefeller the horn-rimmed liberal had failed to secure the Republican nomination in three previous tries. Perhaps Rocky the stern father would have better luck in 1976.[35]

Nixon thought so. "Rocky can ride the thing for all it's worth," he told Haldeman and Ehrlichman. He wanted to ride along. For all he had done on narcotics, the right wing was still "killing us on the thing." The obvious move was stricter federal sentencing. In March 1973 Nixon proposed minimum five-year terms for convicted heroin traffickers. Big fish with prior drug felonies were to serve life without parole. He again buried the lead, scarcely mentioning that two-thirds of his proposed drug budget targeted treatment, prevention, and research. He knew that the public would remember his indictment of permissiveness, not his budget numbers.[36]

Nixon never got his heroin legislation. Like many of the other course corrections he plotted for his second term, this one was overtaken by the Watergate crisis. He fumbled the ball, so to speak, just when he was finally ready to cut back to the right. The wave of scandals also changed Rockefeller's fortunes. In 1974 he became vice president, the second named under the Twenty-fifth Amendment. The first, Gerald Ford, had replaced the bribery-tainted Agnew as vice president in late 1973. When Ford replaced the Watergate-tainted Nixon as president the following summer, he named Rockefeller to serve as vice president in his stead. In September 1975 Rockefeller nearly ascended the final rung when two different assassins tried to shoot Ford. The first, an addled Charles Manson groupie, pointed her .45-caliber pistol straight at the president but failed to rack a round into the firing chamber.

That same fall Ford pressured Rockefeller into announcing that he would not run for vice president in 1976. With the New Right on the warpath and a Reagan challenge looming, Ford needed someone more congenial to conservatives. He ultimately picked Senator Robert Dole. Rockefeller was left to pursue other ambitions. In 1979 he died of a heart attack in the company of his mistress, in a townhouse across the street from his beloved Museum of Modern Art. The stripes of drug policy, it turned out, were easier to change than those of temperament.

Fire on the Right

Though Goldwater Republicans worried about a Rockefeller revival— Goldwater himself, back in the Senate, had voted against Rockefeller's vice presidential nomination—he was not the biggest problem their movement faced. In hindsight, the biggest problem was the legacy of Nixon's canny posturing. "Buchanan," the president told his speech writer, "you have to give the nuts 20 percent of what they want." Those words distill four decades of Culture War politics. Nixon blazed a trail of tokenism through the political thicket of counterrevolution. His successors mostly followed it. Right-conservatives grew increasingly frustrated. Having nominated one of their own in 1964, having apparently elected one of their own in 1968, having *surely* elected one of their own in 1980, they never got a Republican administration that governed in a consistently conservative fashion, moral or, for that matter, economic. Nixon was the first in a long line of White House disappointments.[37]

This disappointment did not become apparent immediately. In 1969 and 1970, when Nixon was nominating law-and-order judges and defying antiwar protesters, conservatives held their fire. By January 1971, however, Buchanan detected signs of alienation. They don't like your domestic legislation, he warned Nixon, and they don't like you using them. "One of the constant complaints heard is that RN 'takes the conservatives for granted; he doesn't think we have anywhere to go,'" Buchanan explained. "They feel that they are the dominant force in the Republican Party; yet, the President seems sensitive to them only at election times; they feel themselves to be the 'niggers of the Nixon Administration.'" The dramatic events of the next eight months—Nixon's announcement that he would travel to Beijing, the imposition of wage and price controls, the plans for negotiating strategic arms limitations despite unilateral cuts in defense spending, and the seating of Communist China in the United Nations—brought open rebellion. "Does Nixon eat with chopsticks?" asked a Kansas Republican. *National Review*'s publisher, William Rusher, said it felt like being in a rain of shit.[38]

Rusher was part of a cabal of conservative activists and publishers, the Manhattan Twelve, who resolved that July to "suspend support" for the president. The circumlocution was chosen to placate the group's ambivalent but indispensable leader, William F. Buckley Jr. As *National Review* editor and high priest of fusionist conservatism, Buckley was the one intellectual who posed a real threat to the administration. But Buckley only meant to bluff Nixon to the right, not to so undermine him that the Democrats regained the White House. Buckley reluctantly supported a Republican primary challenge by John Ashbrook, an Ohio representative who called Nixon a liberal wolf in conservative clothing. When Ashbrook faired poorly in New Hampshire, taking less than 10 percent of

Figure 7 Richard Nixon, December 1971. Despite expanding social programs and improving relations with communist powers, Nixon calculated that he could retain conservative support through religious and patriotic gestures (like his flag lapel pin) and high-profile moves against crime, drugs, and busing. "If Republican politicians quote Reagan," conservative journalist David Frum later wrote, "their political operatives study Nixon."

the vote, Buckley pulled back. The emergence of George McGovern as the likely Democratic standard-bearer meant that it was time to circle the wagons. Barry Goldwater was of the same mind. Stick with Nixon, he told a disgruntled constituent. He gave us four good justices and a righteous vice president.[39]

Rusher held out. He refused to support Nixon in 1972, arguing that the conservative movement would prosper in opposition. A liberal like McGovern in the White House would push mainstream voters to the right. The events of the next four years did, in a roundabout way, vindicate his judgment. The slow torture of Watergate, the related collapse of Nixon's second-term plans to trim the Great Society, Ford's selection of Nelson Rockefeller and support for the ERA and abortion rights, communist victories in Southeast Asia, stagflation, Reagan's failure to win the 1976 GOP nomination, and the election of Jimmy Carter, seen as McGovern in a cardigan—these disasters were the crucible in which the New Right was formed. Its mood was rebellious. Some activists, notably Rusher and Richard Viguerie, contemplated bolting the Republicans to form an independent right-conservative party. Viguerie likened the GOP to a disabled tank blocking a bridge. To get your troops across, you first had to push it into the water. As it happened, the 1978 election gains and the 1980 Reagan nomination got the tank moving again. Third-party talk ceased. The conservative aim shifted to securing control of the party and purging it of its liberal and moderate elements.[40]

In 1972, though, most conservatives stuck with Nixon. Three things snuffed out the rebellion. The first was the boomlet brought about by Nixon's economic moves. The pipers of easy money, devaluation, and price controls would have to be paid, but not until after the election. The second was the May 15, 1972, shooting of George Wallace. Arthur Bremer, who did not neglect to load his pistol, crippled Wallace with a bullet to the spine. Wallace had been campaigning in the Democratic primaries, winning the blue-collar Democrats whom Nixon had hoped to attract. A Democratic nomination was unlikely, but Wallace might again run as an independent. In 1968 he had won nearly 10 million votes, and he looked to be running stronger in the 1972 primaries. Camped to the right of Nixon on busing and crime, there was no doubt whose column Wallace's votes would come from in the general election. "Main key for us," Haldeman wrote, "is to keep this a two-way race." Wallace's paralysis ensured that it remained so. Then, in the third and decisive development of 1972, insurgent left-liberal Democrats nominated their own champion, South Dakota Senator George McGovern.[41]

Everything else being "new" in the long 1960s, the insurgents called themselves practitioners of the New Politics. Like their counterparts on the New Right, they sought to recapture their party in the name of a rising populist coalition. Their coalition was one of the moral and economic left, combining the antiwar and civil rights movements, feminists, environmentalists, and welfare-rights organizers. Its activists were young, well educated, secular or religiously liberal, committed to social democracy and broadening individual rights. They were the purest expression yet of what Clare Luce had called the central tendency of modern liberalism, the expansion of personal freedom at the expense of economic freedom.

Their first goal was to reform the Democratic Party, whose elders had nominated Hubert Humphrey in 1968 without his having entered, let alone won, a single primary. Had Humphrey become president, he would have controlled any rules revisions, whose study was promised as a sop to the party's antiwar wing at the 1968 convention. But Humphrey's defeat, and the party's disarray, gave reformers their chance. Paradoxically, the rules changes of the next three years made the party's nomination process both more and less democratic. The percentage of delegates directly elected through caucuses and primaries (82 percent in 1972, compared to 43 percent in 1968) nearly doubled. But the same reform undercut state and local party barons who had picked delegates attuned to working-class constituents. White-collar groups, who had long set the Republican agenda, now set the Democratic. The New Deal tent collapsed at its center pole. Power shifted from the decaying machines and unions to affluent reformers and their minority allies, sundering liberalism's once-broad class base. Hard hats were out; degrees and dashikis were in. Rhodes Scholar Bill Clinton, prototype New Politics comer, turned up at a September 1969 Martha's Vineyard strategy meeting with hair that reminded one observer of an afro.[42]

The change was obvious at the 1972 convention. Three in ten McGovern delegates were under thirty. Four in ten held postgraduate degrees. More than seven in ten called themselves liberals. Eight in ten had never held elected office. Nearly nine in ten had never before served as delegates. One delegate, rising to announce his state's vote, began with the words, "Mr. Chairman, New York—the first state to boycott lettuce . . ." In the California delegation gay activists chanted, "Two, four, six, eight, we don't overpopulate."[43]

Democratic veterans winced. McGovern headquarters resembled a dorm full of barefoot kids taping up signs. Writer Michael Novak remembered trying to find out why Slovak factory workers in Joliet, Illinois, turned a cold shoulder to Sargent Shriver, the eventual 1972 Democratic vice presidential candidate. (The first, Thomas Eagleton, was forced to withdraw after revelations of past electroshock treatments for depression, a fiasco that made McGovern look like a bungling amateur.) Novak found his answer when he met with the party's miniskirted "advance person," who sported a pro-abortion button on the collar of her see-through blouse. It wasn't just the clash of sexual politics, he thought. It was the clash of classes. Republicans sensed it too and pounced. One of his best campaign jokes, Agnew told Nixon, was that Shriver's father had eight hungry mouths to feed: his wife, his son, and six polo ponies.[44]

Buchanan saw the situation as the mirror image of 1964. The Democrats had staged a convention of the heart, not of the head. In McGovern, they had embraced a candidate vulnerable to charges of extremism. Like Johnson, Nixon was a known quantity—not popular, but known. The trick was to shift the focus to McGovern, making him the symbol of spinelessness, countercultural excess, and the radical takeover of his party. The trick worked. Asked what they first thought of when they heard McGovern's name, white voters over thirty-five gave such replies as "hippies," "welfare," and "too lenient." "Weakness," said one, "that sums him up."[45]

George McGovern was not a weak man. He was a decorated bomber pilot who had built his postwar life on the foundations of thrift, hard work, and an enduring marriage. He had grown up in a religious household so strict that he was unsure whether his parents, had they still been alive in 1972, would have voted for him. One of many liberal senators who had turned against the war, he became the favorite only after Edward Kennedy disgraced himself, the supercilious Eugene McCarthy spoiled his chances, and Edmund Muskie stumbled in the early primaries. (Muskie got a shove from Nixon's operatives, who fabricated such chimeras as "Democrats for Muskie and Busing.") When Bremer shot Wallace, the road to nomination was open.[46]

The road to the presidency was not. McGovern's big issue, Vietnam, was fading. The Democratic platform, a catalogue of rights for everyone from welfare recipients to those who preferred alternative "lifestyles and private habits," played to Nixon's strength. Nixon's cultural politics were as potent as ever, and, with Wallace gone, he had busing and crime to himself. Churchgoing southern whites, mostly registered Democrats, gave Nixon 86 percent of their votes. Overall, he won nearly 61 percent of the popular vote, the last and most significant way in which 1972 reversed the results of 1964. Buckley officially pronounced the conservative revolt at an end. By an act of "jacobinical fury, self-hatred, and whimsy," the Democrats had nominated McGovern and united the right.[47]

But Nixon's victory was tainted. Before the election, reporters Bob Woodward and Carl Bernstein had learned enough to report that the Watergate break-in was part of a long-standing White House campaign of espionage and sabotage. Their guide to Nixon's political netherworld was no less than the deputy director of the FBI, W. Mark Felt. His confirmations and leads helped them to map the conspiracy and keep the story alive until it erupted into a full-blown scandal and televised investigation the following spring. Charles Reich, watching in New Haven, penned a cheery May Day letter to William O. Douglas: At last voters would see their law-and-order president as a lawless phony. Robert Bork, Reich's Yale colleague and the Nixon administration's new solicitor general, arrived in Washington that June "in a period of explosions." He got hit by one himself when, following the resignations of two of his own superiors, he carried out Nixon's order to fire special prosecutor Archibald Cox in the "Saturday Night Massacre" of October 20, 1973.[48]

Cox's offense had been to demand greater access to Nixon's taped conversations, whose contested, grudging, and edited release became the decisive ground over which the Watergate battle raged for the next nine months. The last redoubt fell in July 1974 when the Supreme Court unanimously ruled that the president had to hand over the subpoenaed tapes. These included fatal confirmation that the president and his inner circle had tried to derail the FBI's investigation of the break-in on spurious national security grounds. Just as damaging politically was the revelation of Nixon's profane and duplicitous character. Billy Graham wept when he read the transcripts. Pat Robertson called on Nixon to repent. Goldwater told him that he was sick of the lying and that the Congress was bound to remove him. On August 6 Nixon began outlining his resignation speech. He was going with dignity, he told Alexander Haig, his new chief of staff, and Ron Ziegler, his long-suffering press secretary. Then he paused and said, "Well, I screwed it up good, real good, didn't I?"[49]

Kansas

He had, and the GOP as well. After the 1974 elections Democrats controlled more than two-thirds of the House and more than 60 percent of the Senate. In 1976 Ford lost his own presidential bid when his controversial pardon of Nixon, intended to end the Watergate scab-picking, tipped the balance of a close race against him. Yet historians have found Watergate less than an unqualified liberal victory. At bottom liberalism depended on public confidence in the federal government, which was unusually high in the wake of the New Deal, World War II, and the prosperous years that followed. But Watergate finished what Vietnam had begun, the erosion of trust in national institutions and leaders. The train of revelations that followed, among them CIA plots to murder heads of state and FBI spying on civil rights figures, proved liberals no strangers to the abuse of power. And Nixon's exile to San Clemente did nothing to end the backlash against the cultural ambitions of 1960s liberalism.[50]

It is true that backlash politics, with the exception of the ERA ratification fight, moved off center stage in 1974 and 1975. The campuses were quiet again. The only students who raised eyebrows were the streakers. The economy, beset by inflation, lost jobs, and a slumping Dow, was uppermost in Americans' minds. Gerald Ford, struggling with the deficit, aimed his legislative vetoes at spending, not personal behavior. Ford himself was an affable, hard-working square, Nixon minus the demons. But his brief presidency fell in the post-pill, pre-AIDS sweet spot of the sexual revolution. Novelist John Updike caught the irony when he titled one of his bed-hoppers *Memories of the Ford Administration.*[51]

If moral issues no longer figured as prominently in Washington politics, they still played an important role in local and state races. That was especially true after January 22, 1973, when the Supreme Court put its match to the fuse of the abortion-rights controversy. The first big explosion came in Kansas, where a physician named Bill Roy challenged Republican veteran Bob Dole for his Senate seat.

Bill Roy was an unlikely cultural combatant. An Illinois farm boy, he had grown up knowing no Jews, few Catholics, and only a handful of Democrats, identifiable because the Roosevelt administration had blessed them with postal jobs. A self-starter who lost his father at fifteen, Roy got through college in two years and enrolled in medical school. He delivered babies on Chicago's South Side and saw women admitted to the Detroit Receiving Hospital after botched abortions. A stint in the Air Force reinforced his distaste for militarism. But he was not yet political. He had a booming obstetrical practice in Topeka and a large family of his own. In 1960 he voted for Nixon. He thought Kennedy's missile-gap issue was phony.

Four years later Bill Roy voted for Johnson, and four years after that for Humphrey. Roy had seen black men humiliated by police; he had inoculated black children in schools whose doors hung from hinges. After King's murder he and his wife, Jane Roy, attended a black church to show solidarity. He visited white churches to deliver lay sermons on racial justice. Someone poured acid on his car. Roy was undeterred. In 1970 he finished a law degree after years of squeezing courses into his obstetrical schedule. Jane Roy attended with him, matching Phyllis Schlafly's feat of earning her law degree while raising six children. Something about the emotions of the 1960s, hope and anger, lit a fire under people. Nixon's refusal to end the war stoked it. Roy was attending a medical meeting when he read about Kent State. That tore it. The condo in Vail could wait. He withdrew his savings, switched his party affiliation, and filed to run for the House.

Kansans rarely sent Democrats to Washington. Yet "Dr. Bill Roy for Congress" had a nice logic. He and his partners had delivered 20,000 babies in the Topeka area. Every time he went to a coffee, he ran into patients or their relatives and friends. Black, Hispanic, Junior League: Babies were the common denominator. Roy discovered that, while voters disliked long-hairs from the University of Kansas, they listened when a clean-cut obstetrician told them Vietnam was tearing families apart. He won handily. He landed a spot on the Commerce Committee. He looked forward to shaping the universal health care he was sure was coming. He planned a twenty-year career in Congress. He pinched himself. If anyone lived the liberal dream in the early 1970s, it was Bill Roy.[52]

The dream died in 1974 when Roy challenged Republican Senator Bob Dole, who was up for reelection. Dole had taken a very different path to Capitol Hill. His upbringing bore an uncanny resemblance to Nixon's, down to a sick brother and worker-bee parents who took care of their own. But the young striver from Russell, Kansas, had physical gifts of which the awkward Nixon could only dream. Dole played end on his football team and became a track star. His athletic career ended in 1945, when a German machine gunner spotted him on the Italian front. After three years of harrowing rehabilitation, he still had to clutch a pen to control the splayed fingers of his mangled right arm.

Dole married his occupational therapist. He learned to knot his tie with one hand, studied law, and, in 1952, won election as Russell County Attorney. He arrived at the Court House early and did his private legal work in the evening, careful to charge farmers little or nothing to fill out their tax returns. If Nixon's political gift was strategic, Dole's was tactical. "Well, I didn't grow up with all the advantages," he would tell small-town voters. "Had to work . . ." Dole did not need to finish his sentences to make them understand he was one of them.[53]

Politics became Dole's life. He gained the U.S. House in 1960 and the Senate in 1968. He ran as a small-government conservative, aiming his caustic one-liners at LBJ's Great Society. A Nixon loyalist, he was going places, until his 1972 divorce and ill-starred service as Republican national chairman during the Watergate break-in made him vulnerable. "It was a tough, tough time for Republicans," Dole later said. "I thought I was going to lose that race." Kansas Democrats scented blood. When Governor Robert Docking declined to run, they turned to Bill Roy as their natural candidate.

Roy ran as Mr. Clean, much as Jimmy Carter would two years later. By August Dole's campaign was in disarray, and he was trailing badly in the polls. Dole started to throw anything at the wall, trying to find something that would stick. One charge that did stick was his accusation, made in the last minute of a debate at the Kansas State Fair, that Roy favored abortion on demand. Roy, caught off guard, fumbled for a response.

Though Dole exaggerated Roy's position, the issue had undeniable legitimacy. At first undecided what to do about *Roe,* Dole had finally come out for a constitutional amendment to ban abortion. Roy opposed all such amendments. He had once had a woman, a divorced mother and private secretary to a bank president, fall on her knees in his office and beg him to name an abortionist who would not kill her. He had written in favor of allowing abortion before twenty weeks of gestation and had helped secure passage of Kansas's relatively liberal abortion law. Under that law he had personally performed a handful of abortions, whose medical necessity had been certified by two other physicians. Several involved psychiatric patients: Topeka was the home of the Menninger Clinic. He and his obstetrical partners "never felt we were dirty, or unlawful, or unchristian, or anything else, to do them under these circumstances."

The pickets at Roy's speeches begged to differ. Skull-and-cross-bones ads appeared in small newspapers. Fliers with fetuses in garbage bags and pro-choice quotations from Roy appeared under windshield wipers on cars in church parking lots. Dole continued to raise the abortion issue in public appearances, though he always denied orchestrating the anti-abortion campaign. "We had some crazy people on the right showing these fetuses in jars, . . . running ads that I never approved: 'Save a life, vote Dole,' or something. Crazy things like that."

Dole's authorized attack ads did stick to conventional themes. They charged Roy with voting "like a big-city eastern liberal" and of slinging mud at Russell's finest. They did not mention abortion. But they did not have to. Dole's verbal jabs—ask Bill Roy about those abortions he performed—had aroused a sleeping giant, powerful though not yet well coordinated. "There was a base out there that really responded," Dole reflected. He thought abortion a "big factor" in his narrow, come-from-behind victory, though he was not certain it was decisive.

Roy was certain. In some Catholic precincts he was off fifty votes from his previous tallies, in a race decided by fewer than two votes per precinct. "I would have beaten Bob Dole by 50,000 votes without the abortion issue," Roy said. He came to see what had happened in 1974 as a parable, one in which the well-intentioned amateur discovers that the hardened professional will pick up any club to save his political life. Roy went back to delivering babies. Dole went back to Washington. In 1976 he became the Republican vice presidential nominee, in 1984 the Senate majority leader, and in 1996 the Republican presidential nominee.[54]

On one thing both men did agree: Their 1974 contest put abortion on the national political map. The club was plainly there for others to wield. Yet picking it up always entailed a risk. Swung too wildly, it could alienate moderate voters whose votes had to be added to those of the religious conservatives to secure Republican victory. Dole's own presidential aspirations would be vastly complicated by this problem. For the rest of his career he voted pro-life and talked pro-life, citing the 1974 campaign as proof of his commitment. Religious conservatives knew, however, that Dole was a pragmatist who cut deals. They did not trust him. And he did not trust them. He needed their votes but could not allow himself to be pulled into their orbit.

The person who best understood Dole's predicament turned out to be Nixon. After Watergate, he had engineered a comeback of his own, securing a place in national politics as a venerable kibitzer. The man simply refused to quit. He continued to advise Republican politicians, especially Dole, whom he regarded as a protégé and an alter ego through whom he could vicariously recapture the White House. Before his death in 1994, Nixon bequeathed to Dole a "game plan" for winning the presidency. Hang tough on the budget and taxes. Temper your conservatism with compassion on health and welfare issues. And do it on television. No one paid attention to print media any more. With the religious right, Nixon advised, "Follow Reagan's strategy. Reagan was not one of them but he was able to get their support." The trick was to remember that "they need you more than you need them." Be friendly to Pat Robertson and his ilk, but never let them have the appearance of veto power. "Support them when they are right but oppose them when they are off on one of their extreme kooky issues."[55]

With his cynicism and fascination with politics undiminished by age, Nixon saw that his old maxim still applied. Give the nuts 20 percent of what they wanted. But mind which 20 percent, and be careful how you do it.

5

CHEERLEADERS FOR THE REV

"The central conservative truth is that it is culture, not politics, that determines the success of society," said Daniel Patrick Moynihan. "The central liberal truth is that politics can change a culture and save it from itself." Nixon demonstrated another truth, that *politicians* could succeed by seeming to save society, while the culture went its merry way. In a media-driven consumer society premised on self-assertion, Nixon and other prophets of moral revival faced a dilemma. If they ventured beyond gestures, they ran afoul of majority inclinations and vested interests. The big, rule-proving exception, the imprisonment of millions of street criminals and drug abusers over the next thirty years, occurred at the point where racial backlash was strongest and where there were no countervailing financial interests. Indeed, billions could be made by servicing the expanded penal system. A realist who cared only for winning, Nixon dealt successfully with the dilemma, even though his tokenism and equivocal reformism often ran against his deepest policy instincts. No wonder he had trouble sleeping.[1]

Historians who regard Nixon as the era's central political figure point to his perfection of televised image politics which, joined to the siege engine of the permanent campaign, finally breached the walls of liberalism, already weakened from within. But his career also prefigured the moral counterrevolution's fate, that of political victory followed by mounting cultural frustration. Two workaholic Republicans and a born-again Baptist served as presidents during the 1970s. Yet by virtually any measure— abortion, divorce, extramarital births, teenage sex, cohabitation, crime rates, sitcom jiggles, pornography, drug and alcohol consumption—the moral revolution accelerated during the "Me Decade." If the 1960s were the Friday night of American history, the 1970s were the Saturday night when the party really got going. On the hustings, politicians deplored the solipsistic turn. In power, none dared refloat the battleship of Victorianism, sunk deep in shark-infested waters. The basic pattern of Culture War politics was bait and switch.

Boomers

Yet electoral calculation is too slender a plot line to bear the whole weight of the story. Understanding why the moral revolution had legs, despite the political success of its enemies, requires another look at the underlying social changes. The most important changes were in the lives of the baby boomers and in the marketing strategies that revolved around them.

Convention defines "baby boomers" as those Americans born during the high-fertility years from 1946 to 1964. The beginning date has never made much sense. The fertility rise actually commenced in the early 1940s, when the economy perked up and servicemen rushed to the altar. The war babies who followed figured prominently in the upheavals of the 1960s. Most of the key figures of the New Left were born before 1946, as were Stokely Carmichael and Rap Brown, not to say Bob Dylan, Jimi Hendrix, Janis Joplin, Jim Morrison, and all four of the Beatles. (Elvis Presley, born in 1935, belonged to the previous generation by birth and culture: He said "sir" in his movies.) The boom, then, began in 1940. By the time it had run its course, at the end of 1964, close to 96 million Americans had been born, more people than lived in the entire country when the boomers' grandparents had elected Woodrow Wilson president.

The population, which had been getting older, began to get younger. In 1970 half of all Americans were twenty-eight or under, the lowest median age since the 1930 census. Warren Court or no, the presence of so many teens and young adults was bound to inflate the rates of drug and alcohol abuse, violent death, and crime. And new marriages were bound to feel the strain. Boomers, particularly the later ones, faced a lifetime of stiffer competition for everything from selective college admissions to good jobs. This inescapable rivalry meant that many would be less successful and upwardly mobile than their parents. Lowered expectations undermined boomers' willingness to get and stay married, if not their contraceptively enhanced enthusiasm for sex. As women entered the workforce to support themselves or maintain family income, the new economic realities put wind in the political mainsails of feminism, equal pay for equal work and reproductive freedom.[2]

If the baby boom was a necessary cause for the moral changes of the 1960s, it was not necessarily a sufficient one. We know this because World War I and the early 1920s had produced another bumper crop of babies. While these children had grown up to cause their own crime and unemployment ripples in the 1930s, they had not rejected the values of their parents. On the contrary, they became part of the "Greatest Generation," steeled by adversity and triumphant against totalitarianism, who had raised their families and built a mighty economy. Why, then, were their own children more self-centered? Why were their children less likely to feel that the Ten Commandments applied personally to them? Why, in 1940, did 20 percent of American men and just 11 percent of women agree that "I am an important person," while 62 percent of men and 66 percent of women affirmed that bold claim in 1990? And how, if devout, self-denying parents tend to produce devout, self-denying children, could such a shift occur within one generation?[3]

First, not all boomers rebelled. Those whom sociologist Wade Clark Roof called "Loyalists" remained steadfastly patriotic, morally conservative, and active members of their parents' churches. But they were a minority. Fifty-eight percent of baby boomers raised in self-described religious households, exposed to the full flowering of the national religious revival in the 1950s, nevertheless quit churchgoing altogether during at least part of their adolescent or young adult years. Eighty-four percent of Jewish boomers fell into the "Dropout" category, as did 60 percent of mainline Protestants, 57 percent of Catholics, and 54 percent of Evangelicals. The more involved in the counterculture and the more sexually permissive they were, the more likely boomers were to become, and remain, unchurched. Boomer "Returnees" who drifted back to churchgoing typically had more moderate social views and, often, children of their own. But as adults they saw religion differently, as an adjunct to the quest for personal meaning. "That's why they shop around to find a congregation that 'feels comfortable.' . . . ," Roof wrote in 1992. "Returnees are more inclined than Loyalists to say they go not out of duty or obligation, but 'if you feel it meets your needs.'" Guilt was out. Praise bands were in.[4]

Roof found that the most educated were the least religious, an important clue to the boomers' leftward shift in religious temperament. The boomers became the most educated generation in American history. By 1982, adults had completed an average of four more years of formal schooling than adults in 1940, and were four times more likely to have graduated from college. Adult Jews, a sixth of whom possessed post-graduate degrees by 1977, had both the highest level of education and the highest rates of religious nonobservance. Granted, Jews had other reasons for embracing Enlightenment values. They could flourish in what political scientist Charles Liebman made bold to call a "Judaized" society of free thought, religious estrangement, and church–state separation, yet maintain group identity with the help of a revitalized Zionism, a unifying civil religion the worldliest Jew might embrace. Yet the correlation between higher education and nonobservance held for Catholics and Protestants as well as Jews. The more prestigious and less parochial the college, the greater the likelihood that students would lose their faith. Exposure to scientific scholarship mattered.[5]

Education's effects went beyond Darwin. The boomers were the first generation in which prolonged adolescence was the norm. Their grand-parents had gone to grade school and then to work. Their parents, if they were lucky, to high school and then to work. College was for the rich or, after World War II, veterans. Yet 84 percent of the boomers completed high school, and nearly half went on to college. Whatever learning schools provided, they doubled as adolescent holding pens, incubators for a self-conscious youth culture simultaneously nourished by the media. The cafeteria was the place where kids retold *Laugh-In* gags and pondered, over soggy cheeseburgers, the lyrics of "Louie Louie."

Colleges offered advanced work in the counterculture along with generous helpings of antirepressive theory. The works of Paul Goodman, Herbert Marcuse, and other Freudian revisionists lined the campus bookstore, along with the no-less-liberated handbooks of second-wave feminism. *Our Bodies, Ourselves,* which debuted in 1970 in stapled newsprint and sold 4 million copies before the century was out, explained everything from abortion to orgasm. What was not available on campus could be purchased in the town square. "Books that the Bohemians of my generation smuggled in from Paris," Michael Harrington mused in 1970, "are now to be found in the corner drugstore."[6]

Harrington sensed something else, that media executives were spinning the straw of youthful insurgency into gold. The boomers represented a rising market of unprecedented size and affluence, softened up by an unprecedented barrage of television. By the time the last boomers graduated from high school, in the early 1980s, they had averaged more time in front of television than in the classroom. Television *was* their cultural classroom, their finishing school of consumption. Its million commercials drummed in a powerful lesson: that the right purchases solved all problems and satisfied all desires. Clairol made of materialism a jingle: "If I have only one life to live, let me live it as a blonde." Bottle blonde to punk Blondie was an easy marketing step. Attractively packaged, the counterculture moved merchandise.[7]

But Madison Avenue's real discovery was that youthfulness and nonconformity were saleable concepts as important as the nonconformist youth market itself. Make Volkswagens hip and everyone, over-thirty types included, could buy them without feeling unfashionable. "The countercultural style has become a permanent fixture on the American scene, impervious to the angriest assaults of cultural and political conservatives, because it so conveniently and efficiently transforms the myriad petty tyrannies of economic life—all the complaints about conformity, oppression, bureaucracy, meaninglessness, and the disappearance of individualism that became virtually a national obsession during the 1950s—into rationales for consuming," was how historian Thomas Frank described the trend. Long after the boomers had cleaned out their stashes, the domesticated counterculture flourished as hip consumerism. Hip-hop and grunge and other passing storms of youthful transgression replenished the aquifer of cooptable cool beneath the suburb-fruited plain.[8]

Critics also noticed the ways in which journalists promoted the youthful counterculture. Agnew scoffed at the "mediamorphosis" by which "hoodlums and lawbreakers . . . emerge simply as 'kids' who are 'trying to tell us something, if we would only listen.'" Both sides understood that television had become the indispensable force multiplier. By 1970 America was a society where, if it was not on television, it did not matter. Or it did not happen: Organizers at Yale canceled protests in the absence of television cameras, the *New Haven Register* not answering to their purposes. (The *New York Times* was another matter, its stories reliably setting the agenda for network news.) Journalists like NBC's John Chancellor defended their coverage, claiming that by 1968 antiwar protest had simply become too big to ignore. That was true. But in covering it the networks also broadcast the identity-shaping message of progressive youth versus corrupt age. "There's a struggle going on in the world today between young people and between those old, menopausal men who run this country," Jerry Rubin lectured television news crews during the Chicago convention protests. "And it's a struggle about what the future of this country is about."[9]

Others sensed, in the drama of Chicago, a more primal truth about the socialization of the rebellious young. It was not schooling that had spoiled them, or advertising, or rock and roll, or television. It was their parents who, acting on the advice of a psychoanalytically trained pediatrician named Benjamin Spock, had introduced permissiveness into their infant lives. Spock got the blame because Spock sold. The two books most often found in postwar homes were the Bible and Spock's *Baby and Child Care,* the latter being, in the judgment of historian Paula Fass, "far more likely to be read and followed."[10]

Spock preached the Freudian equivalent of the Genteel temperament: healthy, neurosis-free children raised by confident, empathic parents who relied on encouragement and gentle correction rather than regular punishment. Even Spock's index entries ("Bedtime—keeping it happy") read like haikus against rigidity. He acknowledged the need for enforcing limits, making the point more explicitly in later editions of his book. But he plainly preferred nurture, in the double sense of nurture over nature and nurturing parents over authoritarian parents. Look at the kids and cops in the streets of Chicago, wrote activist David Obst, and anyone could tell whose parents had read Spock and whose had not. That Spock was himself an outspoken critic of the war strengthened the link between his counsel and boomer rebelliousness.[11]

Yet Spock's own mother had been a snowy-haired will-breaker so quick to detect naughtiness that he suspected her of X-ray vision. Unable to follow his own advice, Spock had been similarly strict and formal with his two sons, who laughed, a little bitterly, at charges of their famous father's permissiveness. There are other reasons to question the Spock-spoiled-a-generation thesis. *Baby and Child Care* was, after all, but one installment in a long line of easy-does-it best-sellers dating back to John Locke's *Some Thoughts Concerning Education* (1693). The Western tide had been running against patriarchy, Calvinism, parental tyranny, and physical coercion since the Enlightenment, as better-educated parents lavished more attention and affection on a deliberately smaller number of children. Spock's book rode this long ideological wave.[12]

The year Spock published, 1946, also marked the beginning of an era of unparalleled education and affluence. These were forces of known secularizing and liberalizing influence, regardless of who wrote the baby books. William O'Brien, a plain-spoken Catholic priest who worked with boomer drug abusers, thought the real key was their parents' experiences. Children of the Depression, they decided they were going to give their own children the things they had never had. That impulse, carried too far, had fostered emotional infantilism. Maturity required accepting and mastering challenges, which challenges he made sure his therapeutic community belatedly supplied.[13]

Conservative social critics offered countless variations on this theme. Whether rooted in boomer overindulgence or underclass neglect, defective self-control led to defective social order. Only by changing incentives, as in welfare work requirements or stricter sentencing, could individuals be made to face the consequences of their actions. That they *deserved* to face those consequences was the emotional link between moral and economic conservatives. That bond, together with their outspoken fear of communism and often unspoken doubts about blacks, formed the common ground of conservatism in the 1970s. When Reagan wrapped those sentiments in can-do individualism and patriotism, he attracted a youth following of his own as boomers entered their tax-paying, child-raising, and crime-fearing years.

Radicals

Rather than asking what forces shaped the character of a generation, many writers have addressed a narrower question, what shaped the character of its radical element? That element was never large, no more than one college student in nine in 1970. Yet the hated war gave the radicals credibility with reformist students and faculty, and access to the national media. By the spring of 1970, with an assist from Nixon's Cambodia invasion, they had so stirred the pot that Americans ranked campus unrest as the nation's most important problem. No public institution of any size was immune. When historian Stephen Ambrose accepted a chair at remote Kansas State University, he was surprised to find organized groups of civil rights and antiwar activists, including forty hardy souls who heckled Nixon from the back of the auditorium during the annual Landon Lecture. Ambrose added his own catcalls when the president accused campus bombers of "contempt for human life." Here's a fine one, Ambrose thought, to be lecturing us on bombing.[14]

If radicalism was a campus phenomenon, it was also a heavily Jewish one. A majority of the steering committee of the 1964 Berkeley Free Speech Movement was Jewish; likewise the membership of the influential SDS chapters at Michigan and Columbia. "It's hard to remember the names of non-Jewish Columbia SDS'ers," Mark Rudd wrote four decades later. "It was as much a Jewish fraternity as Sammie." Three of the four protesters killed at Kent State University in May 1970 were Jews. Nationally, 23 percent of Jewish students polled that year called themselves "far left," compared to 4 percent of Protestant and 2 percent of Catholic students. Like their Gentile counterparts, the Jews who joined SDS came mainly from affluent, child-centered, and liberal households. Growing up in the darkening shadow of the camps and the bomb, they had learned to value equality and take political ideas seriously, including the socialist and antiauthoritarian traditions their ancestors had brought from Eastern Europe. Accustomed to getting their way as children, they also found themselves, from 1965 on, not getting their way from elders who professed their values. Liberal rhetoric seemed a polite cover for materialism and careerism. At worst it was a pretext for imperial war.[15]

The reactions to liberal hypocrisy ranged from kvetching to lighting up the ROTC building. Though violent protests fed the national backlash, they had the opposite effect within radical organizations. David Obst thought it all came down to a simple rule: the wilder, the cooler. The cooler you were, the more often you got laid. "Guys were very much into cashing in their political clout, sleeping with everything female that wiggled," remembered antiwar activist Cynthia Wills. SDS organizer Mark Rudd scored so often he fell asleep at night counting women instead of sheep. Todd Gitlin, himself an SDS president, thought more than testosterone was involved. A third to half of the early leadership "came from visibly broken or unstable families," an exceptionally high number for children of the 1940s. Few hesitated to slip out of a strike committee meeting for a toss or a toke. The revolution stumbled along to the beat of two drummers: Marx, who preached change by organizing the masses, and Thoreau (updated by Ginsberg and Leary), who preached change by transforming individual consciousness. At best, the pursuit of both dreams produced tension; at worst, it produced disaster. Always it produced anger among outsiders who saw only the reckless hedonism of the impious young.[16]

Consider the life of Susan Stern, born in 1943. Stern's father, David Tanenbaum, was a wealthy Jewish businessman with a violent temper and a taste for manipulation. Following his inevitable divorce, he managed to gain custody of nine-year-old Susan and her younger brother, Roger. He proceeded to bully and abuse Susan, who came to abhor his touch and smell. But he also obsessively loved and spoiled her, grooming her to be "my princess, my princess." He provided her with Caribbean cruises, riding lessons, country club meals, and a lavish wedding after she graduated from Syracuse University in 1965.[17]

The bride he gave away was a mess. Insecure, haunted by fear of abandonment, and suffering swings of mood and opinion, she clung to the dream of becoming a writer and of starting a new life with her husband, Robby Stern. They met in a literature class in the fall of 1964. Tall and ambitious, he was easy to cast in the role of white knight, the one who would carry her away from her miserable past. But Robby had other ideas about his purpose in life. In 1938, his parents had made a harrowing escape from Nazi Germany. The experience, and the loss of his own mother in the Holocaust, had left Robby's father, Fred Stern, wary of government power. He kept to his textile business in Charlotte, North Carolina. He told Robby to keep his head down, get ahead, and avoid pushing too hard on controversial issues. Robby, who had a knack for organizing, thought otherwise. He enrolled at Syracuse to get out of the South. He immediately entered campus politics and worked to end athletic competition with schools that fielded segregated teams. He attended his first antiwar meeting in 1964, read the radical sociologist C. Wright Mills, and cultivated activist friends.[18]

Robby and his circle shaped Susan's own growing political discontent, especially after the fall of 1965, when she spent a chaotic term teaching sixth grade in a Syracuse ghetto school. Dismissed for her unorthodox methods and failure to keep order, Susan felt growing anger at "the system." She began listening when the talk in Robby's circle turned to Marxism. Outwardly, however, she remained a conventional young wife, uninvolved in the counterculture. In 1966 she and Robby moved to Seattle to make a fresh start at the University of Washington. Susan enrolled in the graduate program in social work, Robby in law school. To the world, she was Mrs. Robert Stern, dutifully typing her husband's law school papers.

In March 1967 Robby brought home a quarter ounce of marijuana. Suspicious at first, Susan tried a little. She loved it and stayed stoned after that. But no drug could expel her demons. She clung to Robby, yet resented his strength and popularity. She spent hours rocking back and forth, torn between love and hate, fantasizing about beating him to a pulp—no way, she knew, to repay a knight. Marrying Robby was supposed to free her. Instead, she found herself trapped in the prison of a cultural type, the neurotic, high-maintenance princess.[19]

She tried to break out. She left Robby temporarily in the spring of 1967, to sample the hippie life in San Francisco, then permanently in June 1968. Her interests had taken a feminist turn when, earlier that year, she discovered *The Feminine Mystique*. Friedan's book struck her as a revelation: Millions of other women were as fed up as she was. She threw herself into feminist study and organizing. On April 19, 1968, she and five other members of Seattle Radical Women pulled paper bags over their heads and mounted the stage to protest the appearance of a Playboy bunny at the University of Washington homecoming. Angry jocks wrestled them off the platform.

Stern decided that liberation required a new style. She discarded her jeans for a miniskirt, pierced her ears, bought pink-tinted glasses, "and, honey, when I walked, I threw back my head, and moved with determination. People moved out of my way as I strode through them. When I entered a room, I did so with a flourish, and people looked at me, and God damn it, when I talked they listened, finally they listened." When Robby tried to interrupt her during a public, amphetamine-fueled tirade against their marriage, she erupted, screaming at him to "sit down and shut up, it's my turn now." When he complied, she felt "a surge of power in my body I had never felt before. And that was the very first moment of my life!"[20]

In June 1968 Stern moved to San Francisco and sang in Grant Street cafés, but found the hippie scene too Last Summer. Bored and broke, she applied for a job as a topless dancer at a North Beach bar. She teased her hair, penciled in her eyebrows, stripped to her mesh bikini panties, fed change into the jukebox, and auditioned before a grinning Italian bartender. She gave him a Mona Lisa smile; he said she could start that night. Three months after leading the protest against the UW Bunny, she found herself working at the Bunny Club, in the vortex of the commercialized sexual revolution. It was an odd way to begin her liberation, she admitted, though she would resort to sex work often. Organizing for SDS in New York later that year, Stern freelanced for a "flesh" agency. "When I needed money, I gave them a call. They would get me a body-painting job, or a topless job, or arrange for me to make a dirty movie." Her hourly pay was about ninety times better than "dehumanizing" secretarial work. Besides, the money was going to pay for SDS pamphlets.[21]

It was through SDS that Stern fell under the influence of a string of charismatic radical personalities. The first was Mike Klonsky, the kinetic national secretary, whom she met in August 1968. Stern had left San Francisco for Los Angeles, where she found herself doing grunt work in a sweltering SDS regional office. Klonsky took her aside, told her to get out of L.A. and join the big protest at the Democratic convention in Chicago. There she received her baptism of fire and her true membership in the national SDS family. "You could travel almost anywhere, and you would have an enclave of friends who would welcome you," she discovered. "You always had a place to crash, some food, some dope, and some sex." Sleeping with the leadership, the "tough, handsome, virile SDS men" like John Jacobs, proved the biggest attraction. "As embarrassed as I am to admit it," Stern wrote, "sex motivated most of my political ventures" in the peripatetic months after Chicago.[22]

But Stern wanted more than sex from SDS. She also wanted a new identity. She wanted, more precisely, to be Bernardine Dohrn. The fiery Dohrn's mix of toughness and glamour—she kept an eye-liner pencil in her breast pocket during riots—proved irresistible. She was the revolution's "high priestess." Stern longed to be a part of her court. When Dohrn led the Weatherman walkout at the chaotic June 1969 SDS convention, Stern unhesitatingly joined her, experiencing the moment as a conversion. Repressing all doubts, she died to her old, unhappy bourgeois self and was born again as a Weatherman, discovering the true purpose of her life. Not content to enter radical heaven, she aspired to the exalted place reserved for the vanguard. Her memoir notes, composed in white heat in prison, capture her state of mind when she talked her way into Weatherman:

> i was convinced that i had finally found my niche in life, and i was so full of sparkling enthusiasm that i was sure it would vibrate out and capture dozens, hundreds, thousands and eventually millions of other people. i was a weatherman cheerleader. i was a religious zealot. i was a crazy fool in love with the notion of rev without any idea of its concept. i was an old age teenager in love with life and living vibrantly for the first time. my lips were parted for the rev, my legs were spread for the rev, my arms were open wide for the rev, my heart was beating, my blood racing, and my tongue was pouring out endless homages for the rev, and i didnt understand a damn thing about the rev, and failed it miserably, but i couldnt have known it then, and even if i had, i would have ignored the truth.

The truth, that Weatherman had no positive program beyond its bring-the-war-home destruction, would dawn on Stern over the coming months. At the time, she was thrilled to have found the most not-daddy thing of all. No more pampered victim. No more dependent wife. "Weatherman had swung a pendulum in me. The vogue was to be tough and macho, and I was as overzealously aggressive and abandoned as a Weatherman as I had been timid and frightened prior to it."[23]

There was a rub. Stern joined Weatherman with the intention of having it both ways. She would give up her life for the revolution, but not her partying or go-go dancing. Discipline was jive. The Weather Bureau thought otherwise and purged Stern in January 1970. She half-heartedly tried to kill herself by swallowing sleeping pills. She survived and joined the Sundance Collective of the Seattle Liberation Front (SLF). This was a loosely knit antiwar organization founded by Michael Lerner, a young philosophy professor at the University of Washington. Though the SLF repudiated Weatherman's extreme tactics, its countercultural and social-ist agenda otherwise matched Stern's own. She moved into Sundance and mouthed the SLF line, but privately maintained her allegiance to Weath-erman. "The Bureau had kicked me out of Weatherman, but they couldn't kick Weatherman out of me."[24]

Neither could the authorities. In late 1970 Stern and seven other de-fendants faced charges of conspiracy and violation of the 1968 Federal Anti-Riot Act, better known as the Rap Brown Law. (One defendant re-mained underground, hence Seattle Seven instead of Eight.) Nobody backed off during the trial. Stern likened the judge, George Boldt, to Pon-tius Pilate and kept at him until the courtroom erupted in a wild shout-ing match, quelled by marshals with blackjacks and mace. She went to prison for contempt, serving five months on this and other charges. But the trial was her big break. The media played up her role as the lone fe-male defendant. She found herself starring in the judicial equivalent of a Broadway play, tended by an army of legal assistant stagehands. Queen Bee, at last. Transcripts at her elbow, Stern made sure that the trial, allit-eratively fresh in the public mind, featured in *With the Weathermen,* her tell-all memoir.[25]

The history of her book says as much about the youth revolution's complicated relation to capitalism as Stern's own troubled life. Con-ceived in prison as a moneymaking quickie, the book evolved into a therapeutic autobiography. In 1973 David Obst, the counterculture's unofficial literary agent, negotiated a contract with Doubleday, securing

Figure 8 and Figure 9 Radical makeover: Susan Tanenbaum at her father David Tanenbaum's fiftieth birthday party. He threw the party for himself, hired a band, and had Susan perform. In the 1960s Susan, under her married name of Stern, rebelled against her father and everything else. Seeking identity and emotional security in progressively more radical causes, she wound up in Weatherman and the 1970 Seattle Seven conspiracy trial. Photographer Pete Liddell caught her leaving the courthouse in her micro mini, next to co-defendant Charles "Chip" Marshall.

Figure 8 and Figure 9   *(continued)*

a hefty advance and a talented editor in Thomas Congdon, who would soon shepherd *Jaws* onto the best-seller list. The publicity campaign that accompanied the release of Stern's book, in June 1975, drafted off the Patty Hearst sensation. Like the kidnapped heiress, Stern had gone over to the wild side.[26]

The book caused a small stir. Radicals and feminists dismissed it as an embarrassing sell-out, provincial reviewers as a sordid memoir by a pathetic little rich girl. Only the in-house reviewer for the FBI, which bought three copies, was unstinting in his praise. Yet Stern also landed a Susan Brownmiller essay in the *New York Times,* a long review in *Newsweek,* and a two-column feature in *People,* complete with the news that she planned to give most, but not quite all, of her royalties to the poor. "I would really like a color TV," she explained. She was on television herself now and pulling no punches. The talk-show switchboards lit up with calls from viewers who said, in as many words, that she belonged in jail rather than the studio.[27]

Stern's feisty celebrity was short-lived. By late 1975 memory of the war was fading, the national mood changing. Her other writing projects stalled. The bookers quit calling. She was unsure about having children. She had already had three abortions and a miscarriage. She wasn't, as she put it, go-go material any more. Depressed, using cocaine heavily, she broke up with her lover, Raymond Potts. Puffy-faced and bug-eyed, binging on alcohol and Quaaludes and cocaine, she collapsed in the basement sauna of her Seattle collective early in the morning of July 25, 1976. She suffered irreversible brain damage, the same fate met by two later Culture War celebrities, Nancy Cruzan and Terri Schiavo. The doctors put Stern on a respirator. Her family took her off. The *New York Times* and *Washington Post* ran obituaries. Universal City Studios optioned the rights to her book.[28]

As it happened, the Seattle Seven did enter cinematic history, though not through Stern's memoirs. Joel and Ethan Coen's 1998 movie, *The Big Lebowski,* featured a pot-smoking radical-turned-slacker modeled on Jeff "The Dude" Dowd, the mop-haired son of Cornell radical economist Douglas Dowd. The Dude had stood trial with Stern, chanting "Kill the kids" when the proceedings erupted in a melee. He had been with Stern the night she overdosed—had, in fact, taken her to the hospital. When *The Big Lebowski* turned into a cult classic, he became a celebrity. Dowd parlayed it into a career as an independent film publicist and fixture at the Lebowski Fest, a Star Trek convention of the counterculture, plus bowling. Stoners, too, could be famous for being famous.[29]

Bandits

The point is not that radical opposition to the war was farcical, or that radical leaders were all head cases. It wasn't, and they weren't. The point is that people whose lives were deeply troubled, and whose behavior was by any standard aberrant, could still attract respectful media attention. *People* may not have been the first celebrity magazine, but it was the first to publish a grinning candid of an unrepentant Weatherman. This proliferation of subversive images was at the very heart of the moral revolution in postwar America and continued long after moral counterrevolutionaries futilely tried to put a stop to it.[30]

In the heyday of Time-Life and the three national networks and the code-conscious studios, media culture was homogeneous and relatively tame. There was, of course, a standing temptation to spice up the product with erotic, violent, and lurid details. As John Bartlow Martin said, the trick was to find the edge of the obscene and stop. Then the Warren Court turned stop to go, undercutting obscenity-law enforcement while vigorously protecting commercial free speech. The last barriers to mainstreaming the bachelor vices of the Victorian underworld fell. Hugh Hefner cheekily offered discounted *Playboy* subscriptions to ministers. Madison Avenue pushed its own envelope. By 1975 J. Walter Thompson Company executives were thinking of emulating the "tastefully done" nude ads popular in Europe. Their research showed that over half of American adults had no objection.[31]

"Thinkers prepare the revolution," remarks one of novelist Mariano Azuela's characters, "bandits carry it out." In the moral revolution, thinkers and bandits were often hard to tell apart. Hefner the publisher was also Hefner the philosopher, kicking the corpse of Puritanism in his editorial columns. He hired big-name talent, offering Arthur Schlesinger Jr. $10,000 to become a contributor and consulting editor. (Schlesinger was willing to write for *Playboy,* but balked at having his name on the masthead.) Reuben Sturman, king of the peep shows, spread his mountain of quarters around Jewish charities, the Cleveland Symphony, and the Cleveland Ballet. Larry Flynt, Sturman's hard-core heir, went the political route. He entered the 1984 presidential primaries as a Republican, though not of the Reagan variety. "If elected," Flynt promised, "my primary goal will be to eliminate ignorance and venereal disease."[32]

Hollywood's primary goal was making money. Between *The Sound of Music's* last hurrah in 1965 and *Easy Rider's* lucrative debut in 1969, this objective fell more unmistakably into line with the industry's prevailing left-liberal temperament. Edgy work scored with media peers and boomer audiences. Studio executives, overwhelmingly of urban background and secular disposition, were sympathetic to personal freedoms and antipathetic to religious conservatives. Meta Rosenberg, producer of *The Rockford Files*, caught the mood when she said, in answer to a question about small towns, "Jesus Christ, they did vote for Nixon." The president may have trounced McGovern, but Rosenberg and other television producers were cleaning up in fly-over country. Average viewing jumped 50 percent between 1965 and 1975, an increase so startling that researchers assumed the result was a data-coding error. It was not. Ten hours a week had become fifteen.[33]

One of the most popular viewing times for adults—and for children careful to keep the volume down—was between 11:30 PM and 1:00 AM eastern time. That was the slot of *The Tonight Show,* a program that, in its heyday, produced 17 percent of NBC's total profit. Johnny Carson, who hosted the show from 1962 to 1992, is remembered as the classy king of late-night television: the modest, flappable everyman who reddened a little when a starlet overflowed her dress. The private Carson was another matter: a moody loner fond of cigarettes, booze, tennis, yachts, and poker, and who was on his fourth wife when he died, of emphysema, in 2005. During a commercial break Carson reportedly confided to Madalyn Murray O'Hair that he too was an atheist. Why not come out publicly, she asked. "Who wants to buy a suit from an atheist?" he said, referring to his line of men's clothing. He dared not push the envelope too far.[34]

But push it he did. His topical monologues, the culture's real nightly news, were a billboard for the sexual revolution. Carson stayed safe by staying in character, the Nebraska boy poking fun at big-city ways. The raised eyebrow, the puzzled innocence, the mock horror conferred the necessary distance when he riffed on material like X-rated movies. Beneath the cover of satire, though, provincial viewers glimpsed the cultural headline. Porn was hot in the metropolis. And it showed more than man, woman, and missionary position.[35]

Carson played sidekick Ed McMahon for booze jokes, the house musicians for pot gags. Bandleader Doc Severinsen winked back:

Johnny: Interesting item today in the paper . . . Jimmy Carter, the president, is backing the decriminalization of marijuana. A lot of controversy there, but he declared support for the removal of all federal criminal penalties for possession of "an ounce or less' of marijuana—which is bad news for our band, because they don't know what 'an ounce or less'' means.

Doc: It means you're about out.

After the monologue came the guests, sit-down and stand-up. "A lot of the stuff I was doing was pretty hip for the crowds," remembered comedian Robert Klein, "but he'd really laugh you up and encourage them to laugh, too." Other guest comics included the pony-tailed George Carlin, of seven-dirty-words fame, and Richard Pryor, the brothel-raised prodigy who pushed comedy's edge from the white underworld to the black. Producer Fred de Cordova had to be careful. If irreverence worked, vulgarity did not. When Hawaiian singer Don Ho groped a pretty young woman planted in the audience, heartland viewers penned shame-on-you letters. But he had few such messes to clean up. Most of the subversion was quieter: Truman Capote lisping in the guest seat, or Gore Vidal, patrician atheist, slicing up the benighted with his wit.[36]

De Cordova, the son of world-class con artists George and Margaret de Cordova, studied law at Harvard but decided that he liked show business better. After a movie career that included directing Elvis Presley and Ronald Reagan, he took the reins of *The Tonight Show* in 1970. He found guests by scouting the morning television news shows and combing through the *New York Times, Washington Post, Hollywood Reporter,* and *Daily Variety,* a reading list that guaranteed a left-liberal, bicoastal, and show business tilt. In May 1972, when the show moved from New York City to Burbank, California, the tilt became specifically West Coast. Broadway stars were out, movie stars were in. Carson made them all look good. He was unfailingly gracious, attentively curious, and politely tolerant. Carson exemplified an American ideal, wrote Steve Martin, one of many comedians who launched his career on the show. "You're nuts but you're welcome here."[37]

"Here" meant in millions of American homes, including the one at 1600 Pennsylvania Avenue. "Ronnie and I always enjoyed him on the 'The Tonight Show,'" Nancy Reagan said at the time of Carson's death. (She presumably had not enjoyed Carson calling her religion "Christian Dior," but spoke no ill of the dead.) The *Washington Times,* Ronald Reagan's

Figure 10   Gore Vidal and Johnny Carson, September 7, 1976. *The Tonight Show*'s producer, Fred de Cordova, repeatedly invited Vidal to be a guest host. "After all," de Cordova said, "when you're in that chair, you're the king." "No," Vidal replied. "I may be in the chair but everyone knows the king is elsewhere."

favorite newspaper, eulogized Carson as a class act, regretting his passing in degenerate times. In fact, Carson had midwived the times. A talented magician, he had performed the ultimate deception. In 1992 he pocketed his Presidential Medal of Freedom and entered the pantheon as America's perpetual little boy, retiring after thirty years running the night shift of the moral revolution's celebrity marshalling yard.[38]

The affably square Mike Douglas ran the day shift. In the 1960s and 1970s his popular afternoon talk show introduced housewives to John Lennon singing "Imagine" and *Kiss*'s platform-booted, Kabuki-masked Gene Simmons proclaiming himself the incarnation of evil. Shock the bourgeois was more like it. Kids dug his costume death's head and ran to the record stores. The hip-meets-square formula outlasted glam rock.

Roger Ailes, Douglas's first producer and later television adviser for Nixon, Reagan, and George H. W. Bush, would ultimately take it to *Fox News,* where the zany and the scantily clad appeared under the cover of combative conservative commentary. You're nuts but your body is welcome here.[39]

Provided you had the right body. Television narrowed the range of acceptable appearance even as it broadened the range of acceptable behavior. Profit explained the paradox. The attractive, the strange, the controversial, and the violent all drew an audience, hence Susan Stern's radical-cutie book advance. Mass media in the 1970s became a "colosseum of infinite tiers," full of shapely bodies and bizarre and bloody acts. *The Tonight Show* was the emperor's box. The celebrities invited to its couch were the only truly complete citizens in an artificial but vastly influential social world that was wider and shallower than anything Americans had known before, and that was getting more permissive all the time. "Do we really need young women in bra-less sweaters running and bouncing across a set because someone has said dinner is ready?" asked a disenchanted Norman Lear. He knew the sexual antics had nothing to do with plot or character. They were about moving up in the ratings.[40]

Yet Lear himself had stretched the envelope in the 1970s. His most famous sitcom character, *All in the Family*'s Archie Bunker, was the dependable butt of the rights revolutions, the bigoted schlump who called blacks "spades" and Michelangelo "that dago artist." His outspokenly liberal opposite, Maude Findlay, the heroine of Lear's sitcom *Maude,* decided to have an abortion when she found herself pregnant, by her fourth husband, at age forty-seven. "Maude's Dilemma" drew both stellar ratings and 24,000 protest letters. "The people who wrote to us were not cranks and crazies," remembered star Bea Arthur. "They were genuinely interested in and felt sincerely about the right to life." But neither she nor the writers shied away from other controversial issues, alcoholism and pot among them. By the time the series had finished its run, in 1978, Maude was seated in Congress and the only subject left untouched, Arthur joked, was hemorrhoids.[41]

Counter Bandits

If Arthur's correspondents were sincere, the same could not always be said of the entrepreneurs who organized their fears and resentments. Conservative religious reaction, like all emotive reform movements, had the potential to degenerate into a racket. It did so when money, fame, power, or sex lured its leaders onto the very paths they condemned.

Billy James Hargis yielded to all four temptations. An orphan and Ozark Bible College dropout, Hargis led the Christian Crusade, an interdenominational anticommunist organization that he founded in 1950. With the help of W. L. Foster, a Tulsa oil man, and L. E. "Pete" White Jr., a Tulsa ad man who specialized in preachers (and who charged 15 percent plus fees), the orotund Hargis rode the anticommunist wave until he had his own broadcasting and publishing empire. Five- and ten-dollar donations from his mostly rural audience of "lonely patriots" kept him living in style on a 700-acre ranch. "He just impressed me as being in it for what he could get out of it, and to glorify his own name," said Julian Williams, Hargis's research director. Williams, a clerkish, facts-first anticommunist, wearied of his boss's exaggerations. But he stuck with Hargis for the chance to pursue his calling. A job was a job, and the pay was fulltime.

By the late 1960s Hargis was syncopating his anticommunist beat with notes of moral subversion. The slicks glamorized deviance, he complained. The networks mocked the Bible. The Beatles pushed drugs. Communists and liberals, who shared "interlocking directorates" and "harmony of purpose and organization," conspired to destroy the national character. The red flag never failed to rouse the bull. He sold, or so he claimed, 250,000 copies of a book called *Is the School House the Proper Place to Teach Raw Sex?*

In 1974 Hargis ran afoul of schoolhouse sex himself. Two students from his American Christian College discovered, during their honeymoon, that they had both lost their virginity to Hargis, who had presided over their wedding ceremony. The ensuing uproar over this *droit de seigneur* and revelations that Hargis had seduced male members of his All-American Kids choir, whose souvenir albums he peddled, ended his sojourn in the big time.[42]

Hargis was more than a Tartuffe in a fat-man suit. The real lesson of his career is how he managed, with paid professional help, to exploit the fears and resentments of his beleaguered audience, who felt less lonely and less powerless when they tuned in to Billy James. He climbed to the peak from which he fell by preaching solidarity against the common foe. He needed, and used, his enemies in the same way that Rush Limbaugh later vilified the Clintons, or the National Rifle Association (NRA) leadership, culture warriors to a man, demonized the gun-grabbers. Their enemies made sure to return the favor after every assassination and school massacre. The watchdog business was symbiotic. No Klan, no Klanwatch. All activists kept "oppo files," photocopying choice clippings so often that they seemed sprayed with a mist of birdshot.

If Azuela had lived through the Culture War instead of the Mexican Revolution, he might have written that it was hard to tell the bandits from the counterrevolutionaries. Fear kept the war chests full, and war chests kept the conflicts roiling. The process could be unexceptionable, as when the *National Review*'s circulation and advertising revenues rose on the conservative tide of the late 1970s and 1980s. But it could also be grotesque, as when Reverend Bob Harrington, "the Chaplain of Bourbon Street," staged Bible-Belt debates with Madalyn Murray O'Hair. She played the atheist virago for 45 percent of the gate. He would recite the Pledge of Allegiance until the words "under God," when she would grab the microphone and the crowd would go wild. Their act wound up on *The Phil Donahue Show* and *Good Morning America*.[43]

The ogre-media symbiosis helps explain a small mystery, why so many Culture War celebrities exhibited signs of narcissistic, histrionic, borderline, or antisocial behavior. O'Hair, Stern, and Hargis fit the pattern, as did Betty Friedan, Roy Cohn, Katherine Harris, and many others who became regulars (and sometimes hosts) on the talk-show circuit. Not since the "blundering generation" of Civil War infamy did so many impetuous and erratic people gain such visibility and influence in American public life, to say nothing of the four presidents, Johnson, Nixon, Clinton, and George W. Bush, chained to the same wobbly oar of self-preoccupation. Profit and competition, the same forces that eroticized popular culture, degraded political culture, as broadcasters and publishers sought out ideological gladiators. Culture warriors, Bill O'Reilly remarked, did not abide by the Geneva Convention. That was especially true when they performed in the colosseum of infinite tiers. Television producers loved no-holds-barred combat. They even recycled their meretriciousness, having celebrity-commentators deplore the media's coarsening effects. Thus no money was left on the table.[44]

Momentum

Thomas Hughes, the historian of technology, has shown how the relationship of key inventions to society reverses over time. In the beginning, society controls the invention. As the invention becomes intermeshed with daily life, it begins to control society. We drove cars, then cars drove us. This "technological momentum" is just as evident in the history of mass communications. The censors once held the studios and networks in tenuous check. Somewhere between *Gunsmoke* and *Charlie's Angels* the balance shifted. Broadcasters drew larger and larger audiences toward their natural profit centers of consumerist fantasy, novelty, controversy, celebrity, voyeurism, sex, and violence. Hefner had already perfected the formula in *Playboy*, save that his corpses appeared in Gahan Wilson's cartoons. If individuals developed their sense of self by modeling figures in their social environment, and if mass media became a dominant part of that environment, displacing other forms of civil society weakened by the movement of women into the workforce, men out of marriages, and the population to the suburbs, then the shift in media content mattered tremendously. "There is only one truth," observes a character in Don DeLillo's *Underworld*. "Whoever controls your eyeballs runs the world."[45]

Catching the eye became easier as two new consumer technologies, cable television and VCRs, spread during the 1970s and 1980s. Kids begged their parents for cable so they could watch Music Television (MTV). Pay cable services like Home Box Office, free of FCC censorship and fear of boycott, showed unedited movies; pay-per-view services, like the Playboy Channel, showed outright pornography. Video technology was a boon for the hard-core industry, which cut its costs, expanded production, exploited home privacy, and squeezed new profits out of its film libraries. The one apparent change of fortune, the closure of roughly two-thirds of adult movie theaters between 1981 and 1987, only meant that X-rated fare had migrated to homes, half of which were by then equipped with VCRs.[46]

"One paradox of the last decades of the century," wrote historian Kenneth Cmiel, "is that while conservatives have been winning an increasing number of elections, they have not been able to change the visual culture." Or change the culture, period. Expanding media and new forms of contraception and a flood of heavily promoted consumer goods reshaped social life and expectations in worldly ways. Technological momentum was reinforced by demographic and corporate momentum, in the form of an unusually large, affluent, educated, and self-centered boomer generation on which advertising and business elites depended and to which they were temperamentally attuned. The boomers would, as they grew older and wealthier, give economic conservatism a hearing. Like other Americans, they would become preoccupied with crime. But they remained disinclined to regulate private sexual behavior or reimpose censorship. In 1984 only 30 percent of Americans in their thirties thought pornography should always be illegal, compared to 64 percent of those in their sixties.[47]

Religious conservatives remained determined to attack obscenity and vice, and were in a stronger position to do so as they organized during the 1970s. The Saturday night ruckus had awakened them, and they were angry. Their growing power created a historic opportunity for Republicans, but also a governance dilemma, resolved by the tactic of bait and switch. Whatever they said in the primaries, Republicans in office generally followed Nixon's example, limiting their counterrevolutionary efforts to strategic laws and appointments aimed at base-pleasing headlines. Crime and welfare reform were safer than media violence and sex: It was awkward for Republicans to inquire too deeply into what Rupert Murdoch was beaming through his satellites or the Mormon-run Marriott chain was showing in its hotel rooms. New Right activists knew what was going on, but on the whole the tactic worked. And it worked in no small part because their Democratic opponents, President Carter among them, managed to so thoroughly alienate morally conservative voters.

6

BABE IN CHRIST

The Siena Research Institute's Presidential Survey asks historians and political scientists to rate every occupant of the Oval Office in twenty areas, ranging from personal integrity to foreign policy. One question, though, is particularly intriguing. It asks about each president's "luck." On that measure, Jimmy Carter surely had a low score. Elected in 1976, in the false spring of the bicentennial, he had to confront resurgent inflation, the collapse of the steel industry, rising global competition, a renewed energy crisis, Islamic revolution, Soviet aggression, and a drumbeat of bad news about American families, unions, courts, and cities. New York's siren-filled summer of 1977, with its blackout looting, torched buildings, coke-fueled discos, and .44-caliber killer, provided a tabloid script of urban breakdown. Any Democratic politician would have had trouble confronting so many crises, which were compounded by the growing power of political reaction.

Carter's Politics

Having served just two terms in the Georgia Senate and one term as governor, Carter had no experience of national politics. He did, however, possess a Moderate Protestant temperament, a likely asset for anyone who aspired to lead a divided nation. Carter had acquired his character from his father, a prosperous Baptist farmer and businessman who kept one eye on the world and one on salvation. Mr. Earl, as he was known, was prompt to take a peach-tree switch to misbehaving children. Jimmy was whipped six times, and he remembered every one of them. Yet Earl Carter also liked his cards and bourbon, and liked taking his son hunting, telling him stories, and helping with his homework. Jimmy loved and resented his father, whose standards he struggled to meet. He took after him in all important ways save one. Growing up with black playmates in rural Southwest Georgia, he acquired few hang-ups about race and had no use for segregation. In this he shared the outlook of his mother, an independent-minded nurse everyone called Miss Lillian.

Carter's second potential asset was his moderate liberalism. He was a fiscal conservative interested in social-welfare projects but mindful that governments had to live within their means. Carter had taken to heart his father's mantra, "always a reckoning." He had risen by watching his money and filling his hours with work. He read *War and Peace* in the eighth grade, ranked high in his 1946 Naval Academy class, and was chosen to help develop America's first nuclear submarines. The man who picked him, Admiral Hyman Rickover, was a taskmaster who became for Carter a second strict father. The traits Rickover modeled—unshakable belief in his own ideas, perfectionism, and obsession with details—combined with Carter's own aloofness, stubbornness, and penny-pinching to give his character a rigid, Scrooge-like aspect. Carter wasn't just a Baptist, journalist Bill Moyers decided. He was a Calvinist and all business. As president, he made time in his eighty-hour weeks to digest the IRS Code and check the cost of White House magazine subscriptions.[1]

Carter drew his energy from fear of failure. Missing a Rhodes Scholarship in 1948 had plunged him into depression, from which he rebounded by gaining admission to the prestigious Submarine Officer Course. When he left the Navy in 1953 to take over his late father's farmland and peanut-warehouse business, drought threatened to ruin the enterprise. He and his wife, Rosalynn, scrimped and toiled. When the rains returned, they prospered. Defeated in a rigged 1962 legislative election, the sort where voters cast their ballots in alphabetical order, Carter pursued every recourse until he was awarded the Georgia senate seat he had rightly won. Then he enrolled in a speed-reading course, so he could honor his pledge to read every bill before voting on it. In 1966, finishing third in the Democratic primary for the Georgia governorship, he experienced another bout of depression. He found solace in a deepened faith—Carter was born again after the election—and renewed hope that he could win the governorship in 1970. Systematic canvassing and a bit of deception turned the trick. Carter posed as an anti-forced-busing, pro-death-penalty son of the soil challenging a city slicker he dubbed "Cufflinks Carl."

In office, Carter showed his true colors as an efficiency-minded reformer and racial moderate, happily unveiling a portrait of Martin Luther King Jr. in the state capitol and joining in when the audience sang "We Shall Overcome." As he would in the White House, he preferred important but morally uncontroversial projects like government reorganization or better health care. Though he fell back on populist language in his campaigns, the reform tradition to which he really belonged was that of turn-of-the-century Progressivism. When people asked Carter what he did, he replied that he was "basically a planner"—the perfect middle-class Progressive answer.[2]

The realization that they had elected an engineer instead of a redneck came as a disappointment to the segregationists who had voted for Carter in 1970. It is unlikely that he would have won a second term as governor. But Carter's Georgia record proved to be an asset in the shifting national politics of 1972 to 1976. The Democratic Party's reforms had moved the action to the primaries. In September 1974 the early favorite, Senator Edward Kennedy, announced that he would neither seek nor accept the nomination. He cited family problems; pundits recalled Chappaquiddick. When several pretenders to Camelot's throne split the Democratic left, Carter won a majority of delegates as a respectable southern alternative to Wallace, still haunting the party in his wheelchair. Carter ran as a nonliberal liberal, the populist enemy of special interests who would restore competent, honest government with a reformed welfare system and lower but fairer taxes. It was a shrewd strategy, focusing the Democratic base's attention on the issues of class and unfair privilege that had traditionally united the party, rather than those of race and morals that had lately divided it.

McGovern, as it happened, had been thinking along similar lines. One long summer evening in 1975 he visited Hubert Humphrey and floated the possibility of a Humphrey–McGovern ticket. Let's heal the 1972 split, McGovern said. Let's reunite the labor and progressive wings of the party. You announce for the presidency, and then say you want me as your running mate. Humphrey said he would think about it. But McGovern could see, in the light of the dying sun, the tears welling up in Humphrey's eyes. "I think he had already had some warning about the cancer that took his life a couple of years later," McGovern remembered. A month passed, and then Humphrey turned him down.[3]

Throughout the 1976 campaign Carter spoke with unfeigned sincerity about his faith and how it shaped his commitment to public service.

Left-liberals winced, but stuck with Carter in the general election. A few purists held out; Arthur Schlesinger Jr. could not bring himself to vote for anyone who believed in Adam and Eve. The voters who mattered, white Southerners, had no problem with a favorite son who knew his Bible. They paused in their exodus from the party. Carter got 58 percent of the vote in the nation's most heavily Baptist counties. In some Wallace strongholds, where Humphrey and McGovern had collected a paltry 4 to 32 percent of the votes, Carter romped home with 59 to 80 percent. Enough white Evangelicals joined with black voters to tip every former Confederate state except Virginia into the Democratic column. The Solid South's last hurrah gave Carter a 297 to 240 electoral vote victory over Gerald Ford, who had closed late by charging his opponent with fuzziness. Then Ford himself seemed fuzzy when he asserted, in the second presidential debate, that the Soviets didn't dominate Eastern Europe. That was just the thing to keep workers whose names ended in vowels from voting Republican again.[4]

Carter was fuzzy in 1976, though not insincere. He meant what he said about turning politics to Christian purposes. But that meant improving people's lives by improving their government, not launching crusades or holding prayer services in the White House. Carter, who disliked mixing church and state, was content to read the Bible and show moral leadership by showing moral character—*his* moral character. He was an individual moralist, not a culture warrior. The Navy and Georgia politics had taught him to steer clear of mine fields. Unfortunately, there was no avoiding the one into which he was headed when, on January 20, 1977, the newly inaugurated president stepped from his black limousine and, in the company of his cloth-coated wife and skipping nine-year-old daughter, walked, grinning and waving to the astonished crowd, a mile and a half down Pennsylvania Avenue toward the White House.[5]

Sexual Politics

Two of the biggest political mines in Carter's path were the ERA and abortion rights, intertwined issues of great concern to the rising feminist wing of his own party and to their fast-mobilizing enemies. Modern feminism's roots, like those of civil rights, extended deep into the nineteenth century. They reached back to the movement from farm to city, to the spread of female education and activism, to the growing importance of women's paid labor, and to the changing expectations of marriage and family life, whose emotional limitations Betty Friedan named and against which Susan Stern rebelled. The rush of liberation Stern felt in 1968 was experienced, if less dramatically, by the rising generation of activist women who developed a feminist consciousness over the next few years. "One of the bizarre features of 1969, 1970, and 1971 was this deep divide in experience," Todd Gitlin remembered. "The time was agonizing for movement men, exhilarating for tens of thousands of women."[6]

In 1972 Nixon signed two landmark women's rights bills, the Equal Employment Opportunity Act and Title IX of the Education Amendments Act. For good measure, Congress finally passed and submitted for ratification the ERA, a constitutional amendment declaring "equality of rights under the law shall not be denied or abridged by the United States or by any State on account of sex." By March 1973, a year after submission, thirty of the required thirty-eight state legislatures had voted approval, many adding ERAs to their own constitutions. That same winter feminists secured another victory when seven justices, including all but one Nixon appointee, ruled broadly against the constitutionality of state laws criminalizing abortion.

What happened next, and in no small measure because of *Roe,* was that the ERA lost its apparent innocence. Moral rightists saw a Trojan horse looming outside the battered walls of the traditional family. The role of Laocoön fell to Phyllis Schlafly, who founded STOP ERA in 1972. The amendment, Schlafly warned, was part of the "anti-family, anti-children, and pro-abortion" agenda of "women libbers" who viewed "the home as a prison, and the wife and mother as a slave." What they failed to appreciate was that "most women want to be a wife, mother and homemaker—and are happy in that role." Ratification would enable liberals in the courts, Congress, and the bureaucracy to draft women, simplify wife-dumping, legalize homosexuality, and finance abortions with tax dollars. The last fear was reinforced when abortion-rights activists filed briefs demanding just such financing under state ERA measures.[7]

Schlafly's blunt words concealed a subtle mind. Equipped for life with a rosary and a Phi Beta Kappa key, she consulted God for guidance and books for ideas, packing an extra suitcase full of them when she departed on her honeymoon. A tireless organizer and a prolific writer, she divided her energy between her growing family and the Goldwater wing of the GOP. Combining the new spirit of moral counterrevolution with the old economic faith, she became, during the ERA fight, the bridge between

Don't Let "ERA" Give the Feds More Power

Figure 11 In the mid-1970s ERA opponents attacked the proposed constitutional amendment as a power grab by left-liberals determined to impose their agenda. The pamphlet in which this cartoon appeared predicted changes in marriage, divorce, alimony, child custody, abortion, and homosexual rights. The identification of a common federal enemy strengthened the alliance of moral and economic conservatives that ultimately put Ronald Reagan in the White House.

conservatism's past and its New Right future. Schlafly despised Carter, not just for supporting the ERA, but for supporting all things federal save the Pentagon. She made sure the wrecking ball she swung through the ERA kept right on going through the Carter administration and into the tottering edifice of Democratic liberalism.

Schlafly had three advantages: good timing, grassroots support, and superior tactics. By 1973 moral rightists were thoroughly alarmed at the progress their opponents had made in the federal courts and were wary of ceding more ground. Young mothers and housewives who had never before participated in politics signed on because they saw the ERA as a runaway constitutional chariot threatening their identities, beliefs, marriages, and families. They came from conservative religious traditions: Church of Christ, Southern Baptist, independent Evangelical, Mormon, Orthodox Judaism, and confession-box Catholicism. Insofar as the Protestants had political weight in Oklahoma and several southeastern states yet to ratify (ditto Mormons in the Mountain West and Catholics and Jews in battle-ground Illinois), this unusual coalition was well placed to lobby against ratification.

Schlafly taught volunteers how to debate and testify, including what makeup to wear and which colors worked best on television. Better than her feminist opponents, who instinctively fell back on the civil rights tactics of demonstration and boycott, she knew that honey worked better than vinegar in the statehouse. "Get Maud Rogers and that pretty young girl who had the baby and the nice looking redhead to commit themselves to talk personally with ten [Arkansas] legislators," ran a typical Schlafly instruction. "That would be thirty. Pick the ones who are wavering and go for it."[8]

Schlafly's smiling, thank-you-note-writing volunteers slowed, and then stopped, the ERA's ratification. Three states approved the ERA in 1974, one in 1975 and one more in 1977, leaving the amendment three states short. A frustrated Gloria Steinem threatened "every form of civil disobedience possible in every state of the country." Schlafly told her troops to remain poised when attacked. She had followed her own advice when, during a 1973 debate at Illinois State University, Betty Friedan blurted out that she would like to burn Schlafly at the stake. "I'm glad you said that because it just shows the intemperate nature of the proponents of ERA," she replied, the pro showing the amateur how to win.[9]

Venting rage against an anti-ERA opponent was one thing; venting it against a pro-ERA Democratic president was another. Yet the feminist leadership, particularly in the National Organization for Women (NOW), relentlessly criticized Carter. They said he should do more to secure ratification of the ERA, that his austerity measures had cut programs for women and children, and that his views on abortion were unacceptable. Only the last charge had real weight. State legislators answered to their constituents, not the president. Carter's budget cuts, dictated by economic circumstance, affected many programs, not just feminist favorites. The disagreement over abortion, though, was raw and principled.[10]

Carter the Baptist saw abortion as a sin. Carter the engineer saw it as a failure of contraception. He thought better family planning services would help make abortion rare. But, rare or not, he would uphold *Roe*. He could not change the Court's decision, though he had no objection to governments regulating abortion within its framework. "If a woman's major purpose in life is to have unrestricted abortions," he said during the campaign, "then she ought *not* to vote for me." In office, he supported the Hyde Amendment, which Congress passed in 1976 and which took effect in 1977. It eliminated federal funding for the 300,000 or so annual abortions for which Medicaid was then paying. Pregnancies that endangered a woman's life or that arose from rape or incest were exempted, though Carter said he wanted the rules strictly interpreted to weed out bogus cases. Asked if it was fair to deny abortions to those who could not afford them, Carter replied that life wasn't always fair, and that it wasn't always the business of the federal government to make it so, "particularly when there is a moral factor involved." If these words accurately expressed Carter's ambivalence about abortion (and the welfare state), they deeply affronted the feminist leadership, committed to an agenda of social equality and reproductive freedom.[11]

Carter had yet one claim on their patience. He had honored his pledge to appoint women to his administration. As of December 1979, 22 percent of his appointees were female, more than any previous president, or any subsequent president until Bill Clinton. He had named several feminists to high-profile positions dealing with women's issues. Among them were Margaret "Midge" Constanza, Bella Abzug, and Sarah Weddington. The winning attorney in *Roe*, Weddington raised hackles in the pro-life camp, but otherwise proved herself a diplomatic and loyal Carter aide. Constanza and Abzug were another matter.[12]

Midge Constanza was a fast-talking, high-energy, sexually ambiguous Democratic activist of Sicilian immigrant parentage: Marin Scorsese in a pantsuit. She told *People* that she hadn't married because she hadn't met anyone more interesting than her work. Initially the only woman on Carter's senior staff, with an office a few feet from the president's, she saw herself as strategically placed to press the feminist (and, more delicately, the gay) agenda on the administration. Done privately, and with tact, this approach might have succeeded. But Constanza's motor ran in two gears, public and brash. She ridiculed Carter's abortion policy and rallied feminists inside and outside the government to oppose it. Hamilton Jordan, Carter's chief adviser and enforcer, reduced Constanza's duties and reassigned her to a basement office. She took the hint and resigned in August 1978. Commenting on her departure, the *Washington Star* noted that Carter's greatest political problem was to hold on to voters who "thought he represented a chance to have the welfare state side of what the Democratic Party has historically stood for without giving up Middle American cultural values the way its McGoverns seem to want them to."[13]

Carter's appointment of Abzug to two high-profile positions compounded the problem. Abzug was a progressive's progressive. In 1951 she had, as a thirty-year-old attorney, traveled to Mississippi to handle the final appeals of Willie McGee, a black man convicted of raping a white woman. He died in a portable electric chair in the courtroom in which he had been condemned. Abzug battled McCarthyism, helped found the Women Strike for Peace, and called for defense dollars to be transferred to health care, day care, and New Yorkers, whom she represented in Congress from 1971 to 1977. But irenic causes belied her true character. "I spend all day figuring out how to beat the machine and knock the crap out of the political power structure," Abzug wrote in her congressional journal. She was a brawler, and she made enemies on both sides of the aisle. Ralph Nader, the consumer activist, judged that any measure she sponsored started twenty to thirty votes in the hole.[14]

Abzug's congressional career ended when she tried for the Senate and lost the 1976 Democratic primary to Pat Moynihan, who nosed ahead with the help of a flowery *New York Times* endorsement. Carter put her back in the game when, in March 1977, he picked her to head the National Commission on the Observance of International Women's Year. Then, in June 1978, he appointed her co-chair of the National Advisory Committee for Women. Even ERA supporters, including Rosalynn Carter, warned him to name someone else. Abzug was soon demanding a feminist replacement for Constanza and openly attacking Carter's budget priorities. She challenged his commitment to women's issues, confronting the president himself during a meeting. When Hamilton Jordan sacked her, in January 1979, more than half the women on the committee resigned. Steinem called the affair "the Friday night massacre." Carter's relationship with the feminist leadership hit a new low.[15]

Unrequited Politics

Those relations then proceeded to worsen, as did much else during 1979 and 1980. Faced with renewed inflation and the Soviet push into Afghanistan, Carter retrenched domestically, increased military spending, declared a boycott of the 1980 Moscow Olympics, and proposed to restore draft registration, this time for women and men. Right-conservatives heard "women." Left-liberals heard "draft." Both camps wanted Carter gone.[16]

The right-conservative champion was Ronald Reagan, who bested Republican establishment candidate George H. W. Bush in the primaries and then fatefully offered him the vice presidential nomination. The left-liberal champion was Ted Kennedy, who had come to despise Carter long before he announced his nomination challenge on November 7, 1979. He found Carter's folksiness to be studied, his willingness to listen only pretended. He was really a humorless know-it-all, the sort who invited senators to the White House, hustled them through a boozeless buffet, and then lectured them for three hours on African politics. Worse, he had betrayed the hopeful spirit of his party with timidity on universal health care and self-defeating talk of national decline. He had to go. Kennedy thought he could oust Carter and then handily beat Reagan in the general election.[17]

At first Kennedy led Carter in the polls. But the Iranian hostage crisis, unfolding even as Kennedy threw his hat in the ring, rallied Americans to the president. By December Carter had retaken the lead. He trounced Kennedy in the early caucuses and primaries, then faltered in the spring when the economy and the hostage-rescue mission both crashed. Newscasters numbered the hostages' days of captivity. So did pickup drivers, in masking-tape numbers under their gun racks. The late-night gags, liver-lipped caricatures, and populist doggerel ("Jimmy Carter's politics are so perplexed / that Russia may take Alaska next") were blood in the water. The candidate of competence, reassurance, and community seemed impotent, besieged, and isolated. Nixon had higher approval ratings in the depths of Watergate. Kennedy began winning big industrial states, though his votes were more anti-Carter than pro-Camelot. The president still managed to secure enough delegates for a first-ballot nomination, but Kennedy arrived at the Madison Square Garden convention that August in a mood for a fight.[18]

So did Carter's feminist enemies. As early as December 1979 the NOW executive board voted to oppose his renomination and reelection regardless of who was running against him. "He must be held accountable," explained board member Sue Errington. The defiance continued at the convention when the delegates (49 percent of whom were women, up from 33 percent in 1976) approved two minority planks opposed by the president. They were federal funding for poor women's abortions and the denial of party support for *any* Democratic candidate who opposed the ERA. Speakers who rose to point out that it was a bad idea to help Republicans win elections were treated to boos and catcalls. NOW continued to withhold its endorsement, the Carter people not being "exactly where they should be" on its issues. Presidential press secretary Jody Powell told the anti-Carter feminists that, if they got Reagan, they deserved him. Considering that a Reagan win would kill any lingering hope for the ERA, threaten Democrats down the ticket, and possibly change the balance of the Supreme Court, he had a point. The stakes were high—higher, in fact, than in any other presidential election between 1968 and 2000. Why, then, did feminists cut off their party's nose to spite its nominee's face?[19]

The simplest answer is that, in 1979 and 1980, they had alternatives to Carter. Kennedy was available in the primaries, John Anderson in the general election. Anderson was an owlish Republican social liberal who ran as an independent candidate. He was for the ERA, Medicaid-financed abortions, gun control, and taxing gasoline to encourage conservation. Even Jacqueline Kennedy Onassis, widow of a Democratic president, picked Anderson over Carter. Anderson wound up with 6.6 percent of the vote, costing the Democrats Massachusetts, New York, and possibly Connecticut. To these Reagan added forty-one other states. Weddington, who considered the landslide a disaster, thought some feminist leaders were so convinced of their own importance that they believed they would have a policy say regardless of who won. Twelve years of exile disabused them of the notion and put them in a more accommodating frame of mind when another Southern Baptist who did not always stick to the feminist script became president.[20]

A more subtle answer involves fund-raising. You don't mail out an appeal, as Weddington put it, proclaiming the president "has just been wonderful on the ERA." As if to prove her point, NOW contributions shot up after Reagan's election. Life really was unfair, said Jody Powell—though he got a revenge of sorts when NOW's membership fell back 40 percent between 1982 and 1986. Crisis-mongering also worked in internal feminist politics, with hard-liners moving up the organization. In 1975 Karen DeCrow ran for NOW's presidency with the slogan, "Out of the Mainstream: Into the Revolution," and won. Granted, the same tendency was on display at New Right meetings, where choir-faced orators vied for leadership spots by sounding as alarmist as possible. But the feminist equivalent was aggravated by a preference, New Left in origin, for cathartic speech. Friedan was not the only one who wished Schlafly dead, or who said so in public. However liberating the uninhibited expression of anger may have been, it looked intolerant to outsiders and divisive to anyone watching the convention.[21]

Finally, there is a psychological answer, that the emotional stakes overwhelmed the political ones. The battles over the ERA and abortion rights sprang from differences of religious temperament. These differences were aggravated by class divisions, which themselves grew out of value-based choices, such as starting a family rather than starting college. But the basic disagreements over gender roles and fetal status ultimately stemmed from irreconcilable worldviews. Activist opponents of the ERA, virtually all of whom belonged to churches, believed that sex differences were biological and scriptural givens that justified special status for women. STOP ERA meant *Stop Taking Our Privileges*. "I want the right to stay in my home and raise my little children," wrote an Illinois woman. "I do not intend to sacrifice my *superior* rights as a woman to become 'equal' with men." Because the sexual division was natural, stable, and divinely ordained, it followed that the ERA was unnatural, destabilizing, and sinful. So were abortion, pornography, homosexuality, godless schools, and other targets of what came to be called the pro-family movement. The ERA, said Illinois State Senator Betty Hoxsey, marked something bigger. Its supporters also favored "free choice for abortion, the mandatory hiring of homosexuals in school systems, and many things of that sort. And that goes against my moral feelings."[22]

Pro-ERA activists derided the pro-family movement, disputing its claim to speak for the family, a social unit in no way limited to Mom and Dad and Buddy and Sis. Overwhelmingly feminist and secular—only 15 percent declared religion to be very important in their lives, compared to 92 to 100 percent of their opponents—they believed that social institutions and roles could be reshaped to maximize freedom and happiness. A vote against the ERA was a vote against the Enlightenment. Flak from hick zealots was bad enough, but when educated women like Schlafly joined the attack, it was treason.[23]

No politics are more personal than sexual politics. To condemn sex outside marriage, abortion, childlessness, lesbianism, or even day care was to condemn things hardly unknown in feminist circles, or in the educated class generally. Forty percent of the women in the Harvard/Radcliffe class of 1970 anonymously admitted to having had one or more abortions. On a gut level, the fight over women's issues was a fight over who was a bad person. For feminists, this was go-to-the-wall territory. When their party nominated an ERA showboater who refused to stand up to the Christers for a woman's right to choose, the issue on the table was hardly endorsement. It was how fast they could wipe the grin off the bastard's face.[24]

In 1991 journalist E. J. Dionne Jr. published *Why Americans Hate Politics*, a book that elevated Democratic bloodletting to the level of tragedy. Carter had run afoul of the impatient liberals, by which Dionne meant the party's economic as well as moral left, united in the Kennedy insurgency. Yet it was the unloved Carter, not the glamorous Kennedy, who had the last real chance to preserve the New Deal coalition of intellectuals, middle-class liberals, northern and southern blue-collar workers, and racial minorities. Carter had begun brilliantly in his 1976 campaign. What happened next was a "bad case of unrequited politics," and it led to the collapse of the party and the era of finger-pointing, moral posturing, and Washington wheel-spinning that inspired Dionne's title.

In essence, the liberals failed to appreciate how important Carter was to their coalition, and Carter failed to appreciate how important the liberals were. Many of his campaign pledges, such as comprehensive health insurance, fairer taxes, and full employment, offered attractive common ground. But Carter was no Johnson. His high-minded disdain for politics and legislative ineptitude, together with growing corporate influence over campaign finance, a weakening economy, and a skeptical press, blooded by Watergate and still keen on the chase, made it hard to enact his liberal agenda. Democrats in Congress grew increasingly restive and fragmented. They did pass legislation to deregulate the airline and trucking industries, consumer-friendly policies backed by Carter and Kennedy as well as many Republicans. But they had to watch as the administration, increasingly concerned about inflation, sacrificed full employment on the altar of fiscal and monetary restraint. The result was the sharp "Carter recession" that began in the second quarter of 1980 and continued through the election. A sense of economic crisis not felt since the early 1930s gripped the country. "Working-class voters weighed Carter's policies of retrenchment against Reagan's buoyant optimism," Dionne concluded, "and decided that Reagan really did sound more like Franklin Roosevelt than the Democratic nominee."[25]

Feminists did not think that Reagan sounded like Roosevelt. But Carter did not either, and they meant both Franklin and Eleanor. Feminists denied that the 1980 election represented a repudiation of liberalism because, for them, Carter was no liberal. And yet, for Carter's enemies on the religious right, that was exactly what he was, or at best a lapdog of the secular humanists who had plunged the country into moral crisis. Dionne's diagnosis of unrequited politics is correct but requires the addition of a co-morbid condition. Even as Carter was falling out with the liberals and the feminists, he was getting into deep trouble with their temperamental opposites on the same issues. "Time and again," wrote historian Philip Jenkins, "Carter demonstrated his unique gift for alienating both sides at once."[26]

Engineered Politics

White Evangelicals felt more than alienated; they felt betrayed. Having gone for Nixon four-to-one in 1972, they had cast at least half their votes for Carter in 1976, giving him the South and the presidency. In office, he repaid them with appointees and policies they thought soft on abortion, drugs, communists, and homosexuals. His IRS commissioner, Jerome Kurtz, proposed guidelines that threatened the tax-exempt status of newly established Christian schools. Though overwhelmingly white, these schools also served the purpose of conservative religious instruction. Why didn't the president stop the IRS meddling and let Evangelicals do what Catholics had long done? "I voted for Carter because he was a Christian," ran a typical letter. "All I can say is that he must still be a babe in Christ because he hasn't taken stands that a truly born again Christian would take." Writer after writer begged Carter "to stand firm on traditional moral values." His bewildering failure to do so led a Lubbock, Texas, woman to doubt whether she could support him again. "You might convey to Mr. Carter that the majority of my Christian friends are going to vote for Reagan," she added.[27]

The man who did the conveying was the Reverend Robert Lee Maddox Jr. Like the president he served, Maddox was a Southern Baptist, Georgian by birth and Moderate by temperament, who had come to share King's vision of racial brotherhood. Belatedly appointed special assistant for religious liaison in 1979, he was to the Carter administration and the religious right what the Opana Point radar station was to Pearl Harbor and the Japanese Navy. What he saw in the last year and a half of the doomed administration bears retelling.

Beyond the clutter of unhappy souls digging out their writing tablets, Maddox detected a steady, growing blip of organized reaction. At its center was a group of televangelists, the most important of whom was Jerry Falwell. Born in Lynchburg, Virginia, in 1933, Falwell acquired his entrepreneurial skills from his bootlegger father and his faith from his long-suffering mother. At twelve he was hustling minnows to early-rising fishermen for 50 cents a dozen. At fourteen he was picking his drunken father up off the ground, slinging his arm over his shoulder, and walking him home. At eighteen, drink having put his father under the ground, grace quietly entered Falwell's life. As he sat at his widowed mother's table, eating hoecakes and bacon, he listened to radio preacher Charles Fuller broadcasting from Long Beach, a continent away. "I felt like crying," he remembered, "but I wasn't sad." He dwelled on the lesson. Conversion was possible electronically, across great distances, in the privacy of people's homes.[28]

Falwell decided in Bible college that he would apply these principles to his own ministry. In 1956 he launched Lynchburg's Thomas Road Baptist Church with thirty-five adult members. He used shoe leather and primitive broadcasts to acquire congregants and money. The cost of local television time, $90 per half hour, was a bargain for its attention-getting value. Falwell built up a thriving Christian empire, adding missions, recovery houses, camps, a school and college, and, as funds permitted, more television outlets. By 1971 more than 300 stations were broadcasting his *Old-Time Gospel Hour.*[29]

As a young preacher Falwell had endorsed the wisdom of separating whites from blacks and religion from politics. Accounts differ as to when and why he rethought these views: Falwell had a habit of backdating sensitive events. But by the early 1970s he was talking cultural politics rather than race. *Roe* hit him hard. Christians, he decided, needed to stand up the way the clergy-led civil rights people had. "This idea of 'religion and politics don't mix' was invented by the devil to keep Christians from running their own country," he said in 1976.[30]

Those sentiments were music to the ears of New Right organizers such as Howard Phillips, Paul Weyrich, and Richard Viguerie. Though raised in other faiths, they all understood the importance of mobilizing conservative Protestants. Their goal was to transform American conservatism from a narrow-based and high-toned movement of principled losers, personified by Bill Buckley, to a broad-based and openly populist movement of hardball winners. The trick was to marry Wallace to Goldwater, adding issues like busing and abortion to traditional worries about communism and federal economic interference.

Coalition-building on this scale did not just happen. It required copying opponents' organizational tactics, or what Weyrich called "reverse engineering the left." If left-liberals had prospered by means of political action committees, foundations, and think tanks, then right-conservatives needed to follow suit—and they did so in the 1970s with the help of financial backing from regulation-averse corporations and individual donors like beer baron Joseph Coors and industrialist John Olin. If left-liberals monopolized the broadcast media, right-conservatives needed to acquire their own. They should follow Pat Robertson's lead in setting up the Christian Broadcasting Network and making it available through cable and satellite. That, or they needed to develop alternative media, such as computerized direct mail. Viguerie had reputedly acquired 30 million names and a machine that could apply stamps askew, as if affixed by hand. One piece was still missing, however. If left-liberals had media-savvy coalition-builders like Ralph Nader, right-conservatives needed the equivalent. A popular southern televangelist like Falwell was perfect for the role.[31]

Falwell at first declined to head a national organization. But after participating in ad hoc campaigns against gay rights in Florida, the ERA in Virginia, and the upcoming White House Conference on the Family (allegedly stacked in favor of homosexual and feminist interests), he relented. Weyrich summed up the situation in a May 1979 planning meeting at the Lynchburg Holiday Inn. "Out there," he began, "is what one might call a moral majority—people who agree on principles based on the Decalogue, for example—but they have been separated by geographical and denominational differences and that has caused them to vote differently. The key to any kind of political impact is to get these people united in some way, so they can see that they are battling the same thing and need to be united."

"Go back to what you said earlier . . . ," Falwell interrupted. "You started out by saying there is something out there . . . what did you call that?"

"Oh, I said there is a moral majority."

"That's it!" Falwell said. "That's the name of the organization."

In fact, it became the name of two organizations established that June: the Moral Majority, Inc., a political lobby, and the Moral Majority Foundation, its media arm. Falwell provided the public face. Although he made no bones about his own Protestant fundamentalism, he welcomed nonfundamentalists, Catholics, "conservative Jews," Mormons, and non-believers. All that was required were "pro-life, pro-traditional family, pro-moral, and pro-American" values.[32]

The last meant both strong national defense and strong support for Israel. Like many fundamentalists, Falwell believed that the restoration of the Jewish nation was foretold in the Bible as a necessary prelude to the Second Coming. More subtly, the pro-Israel stand deflected charges of anti-Semitism and created common ground with the Jewish-led neoconservative reaction. Irving Kristol, Norman Podhoretz, Nathan Glazer, and other neoconservatives ("neo" because they were new to conservatism, most of them having come from socialist backgrounds) had become alarmed by left-liberalism's unintended consequences. Using a small but influential network of magazines and think tanks, they had spelled out how its policies, formulated by bureaucrats and defended by entrenched interest groups, had disrupted markets, ruined cities, demoralized the poor, bred fatherless criminals, and exposed America and Israel to Soviet and Arab aggression. Whatever they privately thought of Bible prophecy, the neoconservatives' Zionist and Straussian outlook inclined them toward alliances that were good for Israel and bad for moral decay.

Rank-and-file Jews also worried about Israel. As early as May 1975, Schlafly had predicted that they might yet join the conservative cause once they realized that the *détentistes* were "selling out" Israel the way they had sold out Southeast Asia. The 1978 recognition of the People's Republic of China, which seemed to leave Taiwan in the lurch, raised similar fears. So did the sale of advanced military aircraft to Israel's Arab neighbors. Then, in March 1980, the United States supported a UN resolution condemning Israel's failure to dismantle settlements in territories it occupied after the 1967 war. Furious Jewish voters helped to deliver the New York primary to Kennedy by an eighteen-point margin. Those same votes might, under the right circumstances, swing to Reagan or another favorite of the religious conservatives.[33]

Maddox thought that would be a tragedy. When sure of his company, he described Falwell's far-right followers as "neo-fascist." Jews were crazy if they thought these people were their friends. Maddox had to admit, though, that Evangelical disenchantment was real. Right-conservatives, he wrote in August 1979, had built a powerful coalition around emotive issues of morality, family, and national defense. Evangelicals were upset about the Panama Canal "giveaway" and strategic arms limitation as well as abortion, the ERA, the IRS, and school prayer. Implacable enemies threatened America at home and abroad. Carter seemed unwilling to confront them. If, as Maddox judged, there were 40 million conservative Protestants in the country, and if the Moral Majority and its allies were doing everything in their power to get them registered, the political consequences of that failure were enormous.[34]

Maddox saw two bright spots. Carter's main rival within the party was Ted Kennedy. No matter how upset religious conservatives were

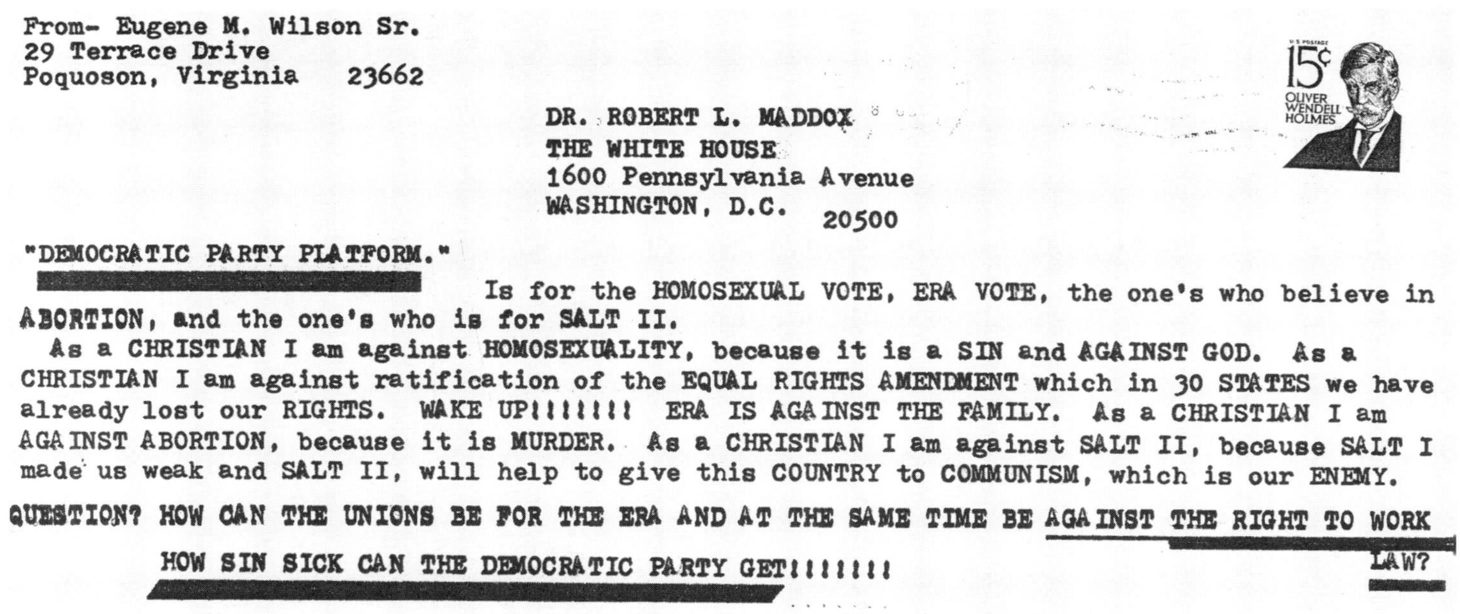

From— Eugene M. Wilson Sr.
29 Terrace Drive
Poquoson, Virginia   23662

DR. ROBERT L. MADDOX
THE WHITE HOUSE
1600 Pennsylvania Avenue
WASHINGTON, D.C.   20500

15¢
OLIVER
WENDELL
HOLMES

"DEMOCRATIC PARTY PLATFORM."

        Is for the HOMOSEXUAL VOTE, ERA VOTE, the one's who believe in
ABORTION, and the one's who is for SALT II.
    As a CHRISTIAN I am against HOMOSEXUALITY, because it is a SIN and AGAINST GOD. As a
CHRISTIAN I am against ratification of the EQUAL RIGHTS AMENDMENT which in 30 STATES we have
already lost our RIGHTS. WAKE UP!!!!!!! ERA IS AGAINST THE FAMILY. As a CHRISTIAN I am
AGAINST ABORTION, because it is MURDER. As a CHRISTIAN I am against SALT II, because SALT I
made us weak and SALT II, will help to give this COUNTRY to COMMUNISM, which is our ENEMY.

QUESTION? HOW CAN THE UNIONS BE FOR THE ERA AND AT THE SAME TIME BE AGAINST THE RIGHT TO WORK
LAW?

HOW SIN SICK CAN THE DEMOCRATIC PARTY GET!!!!!!!

Figure 12   Robert Maddox served President Carter as a religious affairs adviser, liaison, and flak catcher. One man who wrote Maddox in 1980 was so upset that he opened fire on the envelope.

with the president, they would sooner support the Antichrist than the senior senator from Massachusetts. The other hope was that Carter could yet retain a substantial portion—some aides thought half—of the conservative Protestant vote. No one doubted the president's personal faith. Judging from the agonized mail, people wanted to save him from backsliding as much as they wanted to save the country. Maddox urged Carter to use his Baptist belief in church–state separation to explain why, as much as he deplored abortion and valued prayer, he could not outlaw the one or require the other. What he could not explain, Maddox hinted, he should soft-pedal. Keep the ERA "low profile" to staunch further losses among conservative Christians and Mormons—the opposite of the advice coming from the feminist desk. Above all, make nice with the Evangelical leadership. Carter should speak before the National Association of Religious Broadcasters and then meet personally with a select group of prominent televangelists and ministers. Each of these men influenced large blocs of voters. Some, like Jim Bakker, were friendly. They might be kept in Carter's camp.[35]

On January 22, 1980, Maddox finally got his private meeting. It came too late and ended badly. Jerry Falwell, Tim LaHaye, Robert Dugan, and other Evangelical leaders gathered in the White House dining room to question Carter on such matters as abortion, family policy, and school prayer. Carter gave scripted answers they considered vague, evasive, or just plain wrong. D. James Kennedy accused the president of lying about vulnerability to Soviet missile attack. LaHaye was appalled when, in response to a question about the lack of Christians in senior positions, Carter said that he had named *religious* people, among them Vice President Walter Mondale and Anne Wexler, a top political aide. LaHaye, who counted Mondale as an unabashed humanist and Wexler as a Jewish feminist, found the examples telling. "We had a man in the White House who professed to be a Christian, but didn't understand how un-Christian his administration was," he recalled. While waiting to leave that cold, gray morning, "I stood there and I prayed this prayer: 'God, we have got to get this man out of the White House and get someone in here who will be aggressive about bringing back traditional moral values.'" Unbeknownst to LaHaye, several of the other ministers present silently offered the same prayer. They resolved to work more actively for candidates committed to their values.[36]

Ten months later Ronald Reagan won 61 percent of the votes of "born-again white Protestants," compared to Carter's 34 percent. Admittedly, even if Carter had maintained his 1976 level of support among Evangelicals, his poor showing among Catholics and Jews, must-win Democratic constituencies who gave Carter fewer than half their votes, would have killed his chances. Carter got the blame for the long-brewing economic crisis of the 1970s, a decade in which median real family income fell by 16 percent while inflation-driven "bracket creep" raised everyone's taxes. The neoconservative critique lent respectability to elemental political resentments. If welfare programs encouraged self-defeating lifestyles, then the ends of taxation were as doubtful as the means. Compounding the mood of anger and anxiety were the twin disasters of election-year stagflation and the endless hostage crisis. Carter seemed hapless, and not just on moral issues.[37]

In other ways, though, the 1980 Evangelical revolt marked a watershed in American politics. In 1980 the Democrats lost control of the Senate as well as the White House, with Frank Church, Gaylord Nelson, and other liberal stalwarts going down to defeat. Targeted by the National Conservative Political Action Committee, McGovern lost his seat in a contest that resembled the 1974 Dole–Roy slugfest, right down to the baby-killer fliers under the wiper blades. Catholics, who made up 20 percent of South Dakota's voters, as well as Evangelicals turned against the three-term incumbent. "Abortion was the key to it," McGovern said later. In heavily Protestant Oklahoma and Alabama, Baptist voters propelled Don Nickles and Jeremiah Denton, two pro-life Catholic Republicans who courted the religious right, to upset Senate wins. The old politics of denomination and region were giving way to the new, engineered politics of temperament.[38]

Nor was 1980 a one-time victory. The voters Falwell and his allies had organized remained active in politics—Republican politics, the Democratic Party's progressive atmospherics and platform having made it anathema. Candidate Carter had interrupted their movement out of the party; President Carter had resumed it. That movement, concentrated in the fast-growing and vote-rich Sunbelt, became the decisive electoral fact of American politics during Reagan's two terms. It also ensured that future Republican candidates, whatever their actual views and policies, would curry favor with the energized religious conservative base. Evangelical empire-builders like Falwell were happy to assist them, having tied their own prestige, fund-raising strategies, and dreams of moral reaction to the party of Reagan. Thus was cultural warfare institutionalized in American politics.[39]

Reagan's Politics

What bothered Maddox in 1980, and what has intrigued commentators since, was why religious conservatives should have embraced Reagan. Though the former actor was not, by Hollywood standards, a libertine, he had married twice, slept around between marriages, and wed his second wife, Nancy Davis, when she was pregnant with their daughter, Patricia. While governor of California, he had signed laws making it easier to obtain abortions and divorces. He was a remote parent, unconcerned with modeling piety (or much else) for his four children. Charity absorbed little of his income, church less of his time. "I do not think that Ronald Reagan wants to establish a state church," Moynihan quipped, "it would require him to attend services more often than he is disposed to do." Though Reagan had, partly as a reaction to his father's alcoholism, developed traits of determination, discipline, and self-concealment, he was known to blow his stack, cursing and sending objects flying around the room. And he did not mind a drink himself, or a ribald joke. Put the two men before St. Peter, and Carter seemed a better bet.[40]

Reagan's temperament was so Genteel as to barely qualify as Christian. He was never drawn to Calvary. He belonged to the Enlightenment, not to the Reformation. At eleven he had been baptized in the Disciples of Christ, a liberal offshoot of nineteenth-century Presbyterianism. His mother Nelle, an enthusiastic Disciples convert, had schooled him in a practical, hopeful faith that dealt with evil by finessing it. Everything was part of God's plan. "If something went wrong," Reagan remembered Nelle saying, "you didn't let it get you down: You stepped away from it, stepped over it, and moved on. Later on, she added, something good will happen. . . ."[41]

Reagan recalled those words when he lost jobs, lost the 1976 Republican nomination, and nearly lost his life in 1981 to another bullet-spraying assassin. In normal times, though, God's plan was for people to get ahead. Reagan had done so himself, before a growing audience, as high school president, heroic lifeguard, letter-winning athlete, radio broadcaster, movie star, Screen Actors Guild president, General Electric spokesman, California governor, and presidential candidate. An economics major turned political monomaniac ("You bore me! Get out!" was how actress Jane Wyman commenced their divorce), Reagan finally found his future in the past, in classical liberalism. He arrived at this view during his General Electric years (1954–1962), helped along by a dynamic labor relations executive named Lemuel Boulware and long hours of reading while traveling by train as company ambassador. (Reagan was afraid to fly.) He discovered the virtues of markets and the means of bypassing union leaders by pitching a free-enterprise message directly to workers and their families. Having voted for Roosevelt four times and Truman once, Reagan quit the Democrats because he thought left-liberals had taken the party too far left on taxes, regulation, and minority rights. He wanted a government that would lift its heavy hand from business and put it where it belonged, on foreign and domestic malefactors.[42]

Reagan's was a sunny individualism, one that had much in common with Emerson's optimistic spirit of self-reliance. He often quoted Emerson and Thomas Paine. Reagan even used Paine's "we have it within our power to begin the world over again" in a 1983 speech to the National Association of Evangelicals, an audience hardly well disposed toward Enlightenment bromides. The theological gap was at least as large as the temperamental one. Reagan did not believe in original sin or think that there was any evil, including the "evil empire," that was beyond human power to eradicate. Tellingly, he disliked funerals, nature's way of rebutting cosmic optimism. He was a self-directed improver who, as one biographer put it, kept God but got rid of the guilt. Which returns us to Maddox's question: How did Reagan wow conservative Christians who clung to both?[43]

For a start, he channeled their anger toward common enemies. In 1980 that meant Kremlin communists and the Washington establishment, the liberal judges, legislators, and bureaucrats who, Reagan charged, were silently imposing socialism, destroying the family, and undermining the Judeo-Christian tradition. "I'm told that throughout history, man has adopted about four billion laws," he informed a national Evangelical audience gathered in Dallas in August 1980. "But . . . in all that time we haven't improved by one iota on the Ten Commandments." Carter had improved on nothing. He had failed to stop the erosion of values, security, and incomes, eaten up by inflation and rising taxes. When, in a presidential debate televised from Cleveland—a once-prosperous industrial city that had, in 1978, become the first in America since the Depression to default on its bonds—Reagan asked voters if they were better off than they were four years ago, he landed the campaign's most telling blow.[44]

Reagan offered a solution that was at once moral and practical. High marginal tax rates (he had hit 94 percent in his Warner Brothers days) cheated productive citizens and ultimately robbed the Treasury. Who wanted to work or invest for pennies on the dollar? Cutting taxes, he said, would unleash enterprise and raise more money at a fairer rate. The additional revenue, combined with judicious cuts in social spending, would reduce the nation's debt and interest rates with money to spare for shoring up its defense.[45]

The cuts would include undeserved aid for the undeserving poor. It was wrong to treat people, Reagan reminded his Dallas audience, as if they were wards of the government. He drew white religious conservatives and libertarians together on social policy by stressing their common belief in individual responsibility. It was not that Reagan denied prejudice. Growing up, he had seen how it affected his Irish Catholic father and the blacks relegated to the balcony of his small-town Illinois theater. But the best redress was private. "My parents constantly drummed into me the importance of judging people as *individuals*," he wrote. "There was no more grievous sin at our household than a racial slur or other evidence of religious or racial intolerance."[46]

Refusal to judge by creed and color did not mean refusal to judge by accomplishment and character. Like Nixon, Reagan removed the language of race from conservative politics without removing its disdain for underclass behavior. Weakness was for Reagan a want of will, a failing of the sovereign self. He was an antisociologist, though more adept than Nixon at concealing his lack of empathy beneath a genial, self-deprecating façade. Adviser Martin Anderson called Reagan "the most warmly ruthless man I've ever seen." That note of ruthlessness was precisely what backlash voters wanted to hear on social issues at the end of two disorderly decades.[47]

Voters concerned with sexual morality liked Reagan's stated opposition to the ERA and abortion. In 1967 he had reluctantly affixed his governor's signature to a therapeutic-abortion bill drafted by a Beverly Hills Democrat. "Therapeutic" meant cases where pregnancy jeopardized physical or mental health. Too late Reagan realized that California psychiatrists construed the latter in liberal terms. There were 82,000 legal abortions during his first term as governor. Reagan thereafter swore himself an opponent of permissive abortion laws. "Interrupting a pregnancy means the taking of a human life," he explained in 1979. That could be justified only when the mother's own life was in danger.[48]

Republican feminists did not care for this stance. But Reagan's promise to enforce antidiscrimination laws and to consider appointing women to high positions, including the Supreme Court, kept them in line after the 1980 convention. Meanwhile pro-life Democrats were crossing the line. Randall Terry, a senior in Bible college, at first thought he would vote for Carter. A dope-smoking rock 'n' roller who left home after his father blackened both his eyes, Terry had been born again in September 1976. He was thrilled by Carter's election that same fall. But then he zeroed in on abortion. "For me, it was *the* single issue," he remembered. "I'm a young man, it's my first vote, and I'm a devout Christian, and abortion is murder, and Jimmy Carter has caved in and has betrayed his faith. Ronald Reagan, I'm not sure where he stands with his Christianity, but he says that he wants to fight to make abortion illegal again. I'm votin' for him." Terry quoted Jesus: Judge a tree by its fruit.[49]

The same maxim should be applied to Reagan's presidential record. He did little for moral conservatives worried about immorality, and set them back for years when he named a pro-choice, pro-ERA woman to the Supreme Court. "Good-bye, we don't need you," was how activist Connie Marshner interpreted Sandra Day O'Connor's nomination. Though sincere in his opposition to abortion, Reagan gave the issue low priority. He knew, as Bob Dole put it, that he could keep his base "without diving into the crowd." He need not even bother to appear before the crowd. Michael Deaver, Reagan's stage manager, made sure he spoke to pro-life rallies through a telephone hookup. Though Reagan named abortion opponents to head the Department of Health and Human Services and the Office of the Surgeon General, his pro-life gestures, such as removing abortion coverage from federal employees' health insurance, felt closer to 2 percent than to 20. What Reagan gave the religious right, wrote historian Sean Wilentz, was speeches.[50]

None of this is surprising. Reagan knew that religious conservatives were not going back to the Democrats, and he had long made it clear where his priorities lay. "Government is not the solution to our problem," he said in the signature line of his inaugural address, "government is the problem." What was surprising, given his libertarian credentials, was that big government was even bigger when he left office in 1989 than when he assumed it in 1981.

143

7

ACT RIGHT

Reagan's budget director, David Stockman, had always wanted to go into politics. At first, though, he did not know what his politics were. A farm boy raised on Republicanism, hard work, and occasional trips to the woodshed, he became a coffeehouse Marxist and antiwar organizer at Michigan State University in the mid-1960s. Disenchanted by violent protest and having second thoughts about socialism, he was inching back to the economic right when he sought shelter from the draft at the Harvard Divinity School in 1968.

Stockman spent little time pondering the Divine. He did acquire knowledge of political economy, a high draft number, and useful mentors. Pat and Elizabeth Moynihan hired him as their live-in babysitter. Pat Moynihan spent his weekdays in Washington, advising Nixon. But when he returned to Cambridge on the weekend and settled in by the fireplace with a brandy, he regaled young David with stories of how Washington worked. Stockman hung on every word. He began peeking at the White House memos Moynihan stored in his office. "The more I read, the faster my heart pumped," Stockman wrote in his memoirs. "I *had* to get down there."[1]

Sam Giancana, the mobster, said that anything that makes a man's heart race is a weakness. So it proved with Stockman. For the next fifteen years he pursued his Washington dreams, only to have them turn to disillusionment and defeat, albeit with a Wall Street parachute. At first, though, he knew only success. With the help of journalist David Broder and the Moynihans, who put the right words in the right ears, Stockman landed a job on Republican Congressman John Anderson's staff. He rose swiftly from mail drudge to Capitol Hill policy jock, becoming executive director of the Republican Conference in December 1971.

Stockman focused on economic issues. "I had too much of the East Lansing coffee house still in me to start screaming about abortion and school prayer," he admitted. "I believed in the first and not in the latter." Having rejected both economic and moral regulation, he was, by the mid-1970s, squarely in the libertarian camp. What mattered to him now was the production of wealth. What interfered with it was redistribution by the state. That was the message he preached to rural Michigan voters when he ran, successfully, for his own congressional seat in 1976.[2]

The Headsman Who Missed

Reagan preached the same message four years later. Whether the voters were supporting Reagan's doctrine or opposing Carter's performance was another matter, but the election gave Stockman a shot at real power. He and Representative Jack Kemp, a fellow supply-sider, persuaded the transition team to appoint Stockman director of the Office of Management and Budget. At thirty-four, he was the youngest cabinet-level official in a century and the one facing the most urgent crisis. The prime interest rate stood at 21.5 percent, the national debt at nearly a trillion dollars, and the economy on the brink of another recession. Stockman's busy calculator revealed that the only way to bring down taxes and inflation (itself a disguised form of taxation that pushed workers into higher brackets) without incurring huge deficits was by making deep budget cuts. Congress would go along or risk fiscal ruin. The revolution was at hand. "My attitude was that revolutionaries don't cut deals, they cut heads."[3]

Stockman's ax claimed fingers and toes, but no heads. On February 18, 1981, Reagan outlined his priorities before a joint session of Congress. He asked for a phased 30 percent reduction in individual taxes, regulatory relief, monetary restraint from the Federal Reserve, more military spending, and $41.4 billion to be cut from eighty-three programs, from arts to welfare. The Great Society needed to be pruned, not uprooted. Government should be "active, but limited; engaged, but not overbearing." That meant, Reagan said, excellent schools and health care as well as secure retirement and defense.[4]

Reagan's priorities were popular, expensive, and likely to become more so over time. The same applied to his tax bill, which Congress passed that summer. It lowered the top rate on earned and unearned income from 70 to 50 percent. His budget boosted defense appropriations but made no significant reductions in the entitlement programs that accounted for most federal domestic spending, setting the pattern for the next several years. Edwin Meese, James Baker, and Michael Deaver, who respectively headed the administration's right-conservative, pragmatic-centrist, and public relations factions, all thought deep cuts in programs like Social Security to be suicidal. "We didn't get any help from the White House," complained Dole, who chaired the Senate Finance Committee. "We got rolled." The president himself declared defense off-budget, reasoning that "you spend what you need."[5]

Stockman, who retained a healthy measure of skepticism for the Pentagon from his antiwar days, was the one person in the Executive Office Building who thought nothing sacred. He wanted to cut practically everything, from farm subsidies to unearned Social Security benefits. But Washington did not reward ideological consistency. Washington rewarded those who pleased influential constituencies, a truth Stockman ruefully acknowledged when he titled his memoirs *The Triumph of Politics*.

The chief consequence of the failure to rein in spending was a record deficit, exacerbated by a recession that finally wrung the inflation out of the economy in 1981–1983. Standing at $79 billion in 1981, the annual deficit surged to $208 billion in 1983 and averaged $212 billion over the next ten years. "Thanks to a half-revolution adopted in July 1981, more than a trillion dollars has already been needlessly added to our national debt—a burden that will plague us indefinitely," Stockman wrote in 1986. Flush times offered scant consolation. What looked like consumer heaven, warned fellow fiscal conservative Peter G. Peterson, was simply the result of wild deficit spending. The "tax and spend" regime of the 1970s had been replaced by a more insidious one of "borrow and spend."[6]

The deficit would have been even worse had Reagan not agreed, in 1982, to scale back some corporate and individual tax cuts. The following year Congress increased payroll taxes for Social Security and Medicare. Another round of reform in 1986 lowered tax rates across all incomes; dropped the top individual and corporate rates; and increased personal exemptions, standard deductions, and the earned income credit. These breaks were offset by increasing capital gains rates and eliminating many tax shelters. When the dust finally settled, the overall level of federal taxation remained about the same. The poorest half of the population paid a slightly higher share of their income to taxes in 1988 than in 1977, the richest half slightly less. The top 5 percent did the best, both in lower taxes and higher income. Their average family incomes rose from $120,000 in 1979 to $148,000 in 1989. The gain equaled the price of a new luxury car and a resort vacation. Family income for the poorest fifth meanwhile fell by $559—the cost of a clunker and a week's groceries.[7]

There was more to the rising inequality than tax policy. Manufacturing job losses from global competition fell most heavily on families with less education, while income losses from divorce and abandonment fell most heavily on women and children. Couples with degrees and two jobs prospered. "Dink" (double income, no kids) joined "yuppie" in the lexicon of wealth. Yet Reagan's borrowing did create a special opportunity for the affluent. They could afford to purchase the low-risk, high-real-interest bonds flooding from the Treasury and salt away the proceeds thanks to lower personal taxes. Bond traders screaming orders into the phones did even better than their clients.[8]

If the results of Reaganomics are clear, its intentions remain in dispute. Some thought Reagan was "an amiable dunce" incapable of seeing that his supply-side premises were wildly optimistic. Well rehearsed in attacking liberalism, he lacked the rigor to question his own assumptions. He left details to his staff and cabinet, saying "you fellas work it out." Nearly seventy when he took office, his mental energy declined further with age, injury, and illness. He sought refuge in the routine and the familiar, which meant stories and factoids rather than hard thinking about hard data. It was Stockman, not Reagan, who poured over the budget books.[9]

Stockman was of several minds about what caused the deficit explosion. At various times he said that Reagan was too soft, that his advisers forbade touching popular programs, that interest groups had too much influence in Congress, and that the 1981 tax-reduction bill was less an act of supply-side revolution than a "Trojan horse" to bring down the top rate. The last remark, featured in an *Atlantic Monthly* article and then, gleefully, on the network news, landed Stockman in the doghouse. Reagan let him out, saying "Dave, I want you to stay on. I need your help."[10]

Moynihan later claimed that the deficit itself was the sneaky object of the 1981 tax cuts. The idea, dubbed "starve the beast," was to crowd out social-welfare spending with debt. When he advised Nixon on the Family Assistance Plan, Moynihan complained, "the subject of cost scarcely arose. It was simply a given that if the idea was defensible on its merits, the money would be found." Reagan ended that quaint notion. Growing entitlements for the elderly, growing military spending, and growing debt service left less and less for the poor and minorities. By 1990, one year's federal interest payments cost more than four years of Medicaid appropriations. Though Moynihan's strategic-deficit idea caught on among Democrats, Stockman disavowed any intention to use the tax cut to create a huge deficit. "Not six of the six hundred players in the game of fiscal governance in the spring and summer of 1981 would have willed this outcome," he wrote. Murphy's Law, not Machiavelli, explained the fiscal disaster.[11]

Intention is not everything. What began as a blunder could have evolved into a strategy, the silver lining of the deficit occurring to anti–welfare-state conservatives after the fact. There is also a simpler explanation than conspiracy. It is that politicians in both parties had discovered that they could shift costs for present consumption to the future. The temptation was always there, but the inbred fiscal conservatism of voters and the limits of credit markets had restrained it. Even FDR had come to office pledged to stop the flow of red ink—which was why, Reagan said, he'd liked the man in the first place. But FDR's emergency program had become a welfare state, and Johnson had expanded it in a way that entitlement spending kept increasing over time. Even Reagan's defenders admitted that he had largely failed to stop this growth, the single most important reason for the 1980s deficit surge. Instead of *laissez faire,* Americans got *laissez les bon temps rouler.* Keeping the good times rolling required unprecedented overseas borrowing, widening current-account deficits, and an increasingly "financialized" economy short on manufacturing and long on IOUs. When Reagan assumed office the nation had net foreign assets of $141 billion. By 1985 it had net foreign liabilities of $111 billion, a quarter-trillion-dollar swing. Critics charged that, for all Reagan's talk of freedom and optimism for the future, he had jovially presided over a great barbecue that necessarily left coming generations less free and less hopeful.[12]

Cheerleader for the Counterrev

Having delivered little to the religious conservatives at the heart of the New Right and small-government conservatives at the heart of the Old Right, Reagan may seem, at first glance, to have failed twice as a conservative. Only cold warriors rejoiced in his first term, and they became nervous when Reagan began striking arms deals with Mikhail Gorbachev in his second. For all the conservative adulation of Reagan, Robert Bork remarked, he had just "one and a half good ideas. One was to re-arm, and one was to cut taxes."[13]

The missing half of the tax-cutting idea was spending restraint. Instead of building a modest welfare state on the foundation of a regulated capitalist economy, as Franklin Roosevelt had done, Reagan restored a partially deregulated capitalism on the foundation of an enlarged defense and welfare state. In fact, Reagan made defense the welfare state's most privileged branch. Privately, Republicans warned him of fraud and featherbedding. Nixon told him he could safely cut 10 percent of the civilian employees in the Defense Department. Reagan ignored him. He compartmentalized military spending, locking it away, as biographer Lou Cannon put it, "from his bedrock belief that government was inevitably inefficient."[14]

It was not the first time Reagan said one thing and did another. As governor of California, he had promised to "squeeze, cut, and trim." Voters remembered his gestures, like selling off toll collectors' revolvers. Yet Reagan's last budget was twice that of his Democratic predecessor. State spending rose twice as fast as inflation between 1967 and 1974. Then Reagan took his magic act to Washington. When he left office a second time, in 1989, the federal government had more of everything—employees, guns, butter, debt, and corruption—than when he entered it. Even the Department of Education, which Reagan had pledged to eliminate, had a much larger budget at the end of his presidency. Adjusting for inflation, the federal government was also spending more on welfare services, despite a dip during Reagan's first term. Business boomed anyway. Going by the numbers, Reagan looks like a stealth Keynesian, a false market prophet whose chief domestic legacy was big-government conservatism.[15]

Reagan's policies toward the communist world were, by contrast, more conservative and more consistent. His determination to confront Soviet misbehavior, modernize the nuclear arsenal, develop a high-tech missile defense, and support anticommunist movements sprang from a conviction that America had to regain its Cold War initiative. True, Reagan's assertiveness and moral tone played well with his patriotic and religiously conservative base. But that was a side benefit, not a primary motive. When Reagan challenged Gorbachev to tear down the Berlin Wall, he meant it—and wowed even right-conservatives who thought he dithered on domestic reform. Historians have also generally given Reagan higher marks on foreign policy, where he had room to maneuver, than on domestic policy, where he faced more entrenched opposition—the general pattern for Republican presidents in the second half of the twentieth century.

But there is more to a president's domestic legacy than budgets and bills. Bork's aphorism slights Reagan's historic role as a spokesman for free enterprise and an apologist for corporate wealth. CEOs, who averaged twenty-nine times the pay of a typical manufacturing worker in 1979, made ninety-three times as much by 1988. Meanwhile, Fortune 500 companies shed 3 million employees, including nearly a third of their middle managers. The social norms that had constrained inequality and shielded employees collapsed during the 1980s, a sea change not unlike the sexual revolution of the 1960s. The root causes of the new inequality admittedly lay elsewhere, in overseas competition, the decline of manufacturing, the retreat of unions, the increase of single-parent families, and the influx of immigrants from poorer countries. The gap between rich and poor began widening in the 1970s, before Reagan won the presidency. Yet his homilies provided ideal cover for the new concentration of wealth. Reagan was to money what Hefner was to sex: an iconic cheerleader for a profound moral change in an age when celebrities created as well as reflected values. Going over the heads of his opponents, he persuaded millions of ordinary citizens that great wealth was good, growth was preferable to redistribution, unregulated markets to regulated, unorganized labor to organized, and the private sector to the public. "When I was in college I thought that only dummies went to business school. Smart people went to work for the government," remembered Robert DuPont, a psychiatrist and future drug czar who arrived at the National Institutes of Health in 1966. Reagan reversed that prejudice.[16]

But he did not reverse the mores of the 1960s, which permeated the leisure of boomers and their children. The paradox of the 1980s was that the culture continued to drift to the left while the political conversation drifted to the right. Activists in both parties grew increasingly frustrated and shriller as the decade wore on. Reagan, though, seemed to regard the situation with equanimity. His individualist faith reassured Americans that they could have it both ways, that they could reconcile the self-liberating impulses of the 1960s with the free-market opportunities of the 1980s. Hippies and Republicans, as Charles Reich put it, made "more freedom" the national mantra. Reich thought expanding corporate power made the quest chimerical, but less sensitive sorts grabbed for whatever they could get. Reaganism's anesthetizing mix of patriotism, consumerism, and nostalgia gave them political cover and distracted religious loyalists from the creeping solipsism, materialism, and debt. Traditionalists versed in Edmund Burke and Russell Kirk knew the dangers of capitalism operating in a spiritual vacuum, rationalized by a conservatism of greed. But Reaganism marked for them an end, not a beginning. Fashionable neoconservative and libertarian thinkers dismissed them as "paleoconservatives" and mocked their fusty irrelevance.[17]

As he recedes into history, Reagan resembles one of those era-defining figures, like Thomas Jefferson or Andrew Jackson, whose influence on the political culture was as important as what they did in office. Speaker Thomas P. "Tip" O'Neill and the Democratic leadership won their share of the budget fights. But Reagan managed to challenge, as never before, the assumptions behind their Great Society liberalism. To an unusual degree, Reagan's political career was about ideas. His biggest idea, that less was more, reignited the seemingly settled debate over the role of a democratic government in a just society. Reagan changed the national subject. Compassion and safety nets were fine, but no excuse to drain the nation's Treasury or pauperize its citizens. "God damn it, Tip, we care about those people," Reagan exploded when O'Neill chided him for neglecting the unemployed. Then he calmed down, turned the meeting over to his aides, walked over to the jowly, white-haired speaker, and said, "Dave tells me we're really not that far apart." Details were negotiable. The principle was not. Reagan thought patience the wisest course when history was on his side.[18]

So did Lee Atwater. Self-styled Machiavelli to Reagan's prince, Atwater was a political operative of humble origins and a haunted past. He learned his hardball in South Carolina congressional races, worked for Strom Thurmond, climbed through Reagan's Office of Political Affairs, picked the right horse in Vice President Bush, masterminded Bush's 1988 campaign, took over the Republican National Committee, and then succumbed to a brain tumor in 1991. In the midst of all this he managed to assemble a rhythm and blues band, seduce countless women, and wolf down mountains of fried food seasoned with Tabasco. He atoned by running daily and smoking only on Fridays, his two futile concessions to health. He died a legend, the spinmeister who rubbed the Democrats' noses in Willie Horton while blasting power chords on his Stratocaster.

Atwater knew that boomers had dominated American culture for a generation. By 1988, he told a Cato Institute symposium, they would also dominate the electorate. Education, women's employment, television, new technologies, and the moral revolution had made them tolerant on social issues, especially those involving sexual and reproductive freedom. Having suffered through the Carter years, they had responded to Reagan's appeals for tax reform and strong defense. But theirs was no authoritarian conservatism. The implication, though unstated, was obvious: Watch out for religious conservatives. Just as the administration risked defeat by cutting too much too quickly from the budget, it should not become preoccupied with policing sexual morality or criminalizing abortion, which Atwater thought a terrible idea. Like Baker and Deaver and other administration pragmatists, he feared getting stuck in the right-conservative corner. Just look at what had happened to the left-liberal Democrats.[19]

The price for Reagan's compromises, aside from a rising deficit, was activist discontent. Reagan noted the howls arising from the Viguerie camp, but neither he nor his advisers felt threatened during the first term. Rearmament gave Reagan what peace-with-honor had initially given Nixon—credibility among right-conservatives. His telling the Joint Chiefs to spend whatever it took to make America unassailable and "our men and women proud to wear their uniforms again" was music to their ears. Flags came out in the early 1980s—more flags and bigger ones. Their stately flapping semaphored a nationalist revival unencumbered by social solidarity. Economic conservatives also gave Reagan big points for 1981, when he had backed his free-enterprise message with cuts in taxes and welfare. He had named cabinet secretaries, such as Secretary of the Interior James Watts, who were opposed to the core missions of their agencies. He had fired air-traffic controllers who struck against federal law, sending shock waves through the public-employee unions, organized labor's last great hope. And he had honored his deregulation pledge, pleasing free traders and consumer advocates while exposing union workers to more competition. The number of pages of proposed new regulations published annually in the *Federal Register* fell by nearly half during Reagan's first term, before creeping upward again in his less successful second.[20]

Economic conservatives took comfort in Reagan's friends, as well as his enemies. He got help from British Prime Minister Margaret Thatcher, from Nobel laureates who extolled the market, and from think tanks and political action committees (PACs) flush with corporate money. Manufacturers averse to regulation, taxes, and lawsuits, including tobacco and alcohol companies, ponied up. So did wealthy conservatives who saw nothing wrong with strategic subsidies in the marketplace of ideas. Charles Murray, author of the 1984 anti-welfare best-seller *Losing Ground*, had his salary, travel, and publicity costs covered, including hundreds of

Figure 13 Reagan's staff meticulously scripted and stage-managed his presidential performances. Here Elizabeth Board, director of the White House Television Office, prepares Reagan for a national address on the drug crisis, September 14, 1986.

free copies for opinion leaders at home and abroad. Money talked, or at least talked back, in Reagan's America. But what the think-tank angels could not buy, and what Reagan provided, was a charismatic focus. Reagan was to Reaganism what Marx was to Marxism, the indefatigable and incorruptible spokesman for a revolutionary movement that ultimately attracted millions with its message of hope, prosperity, and freedom. With his radio voice and actor's looks, Reagan played the part for forty years, first at General Electric, then in Sacramento, and finally on the world stage. Deaver's settings displayed his gifts to full advantage. In a culture geared toward spectacle, a pomaded ex-cavalry officer standing erect before D-Day veterans at Pointe du Hoc was tough to beat.[21]

Crime and Punishment

Though Reagan's deepest beliefs were libertarian, he salted his freedom talk with populist appeals. In 1966 he swept into the governor's office vowing to keep the death penalty for murderers and to deal with the student troublemakers at Berkeley. "I'd like to harness their youthful energy," he said, "with a strap." Reagan excoriated violent protesters, arrogant bureaucrats, tax-happy legislators, welfare queens, and bleeding-heart judges. He made it clear that, if society had fewer rules, the penalties for breaking them would be strictly enforced. Criminals belonged behind bars. "Sociology majors" who sympathized with them belonged someplace other than the federal bench.[22]

Americans overwhelmingly agreed with him. Between 1960 and 1980 the national rates of murder, rape, and robbery increased by two, four, and five times, respectively. Fear of crime—a fear that cut across all social and temperamental lines—grew as fast as crime itself. In 1965 a third of Americans said that there were neighborhoods within a mile of their homes in which they would be afraid to walk alone at night. By 1982 half said they were afraid, despite rapid suburbanization. Throughout the 1970s crime control ranked as the number-one issue on which people thought the government should spend more money.[23]

Spending alone would not have solved the crime problem. The underlying causes were too deeply rooted: more teenagers, intoxicants, cars, portable goods, anonymity, self-indulgence, and vice; fewer blue-collar jobs for the poor; fewer family restraints on poorly socialized young men without fathers or wives. Between 1974 and 1986 the number of men in their early twenties living with spouses dropped from four to about two in ten. But few voters thought in those terms. They wanted more and swifter punishment. Stories of judges approving cheap plea bargains to clear their calendars, or of murderers being released after serving only a few years, appalled them. Leniency would stop neither criminals nor juvenile sociopaths who treated the system as a joke.[24]

The popular view that punishment should be swift, severe, and certain was soon adopted by politicians in both parties and by criminologists who had begun rethinking the premises of their field. The received wisdom stressed flexibility and rehabilitation. By judiciously applying carrots and sticks, judges and corrections professionals could reform individual criminals and reintroduce them to civil society. Schools and jobs and families and communities would do the rest. Criminal justice played a part—the most coercive part—in an inclusive welfare state. When crime rates were low, this "penal welfarism" had attracted little notice, except when a Big House parolee went off the rails. But by the mid-1970s crime rates were no longer low. Attitudes toward indeterminate sentences (which might range from a few years to life, with parole boards determining the actual length) changed, and on all sides. Penal welfarism died in the middle of a circular firing squad, manned by radicals skeptical of expert control, neoconservatives skeptical of expert rehabilitation, moral conservatives skeptical of expert intentions, and fearful citizens skeptical of whether experts would actually put criminals behind bars and keep them there.[25]

Legislators had cracked down on crime before. They had increased penalties for trafficking in women and drugs and had passed "Lindbergh laws" that made aggravated kidnapping a capital offense (and sent Caryl Chessman to the San Quentin gas chamber). But these had been scatter-shot reactions in the context of a broader movement toward measured justice and rehabilitation. What was different about the crisis of the 1970s was that modernity finally lost its grip on the field. The whole criminal justice enterprise began shifting toward retribution, deterrence, and incapacitation. The capacity to incapacitate, to lock criminals away or to kill them, was precisely what angry voters wanted to restore. Over the next three decades politicians gave it to them. They abolished or restricted parole; funded more and harder prisons; added police and corrections officers; imposed longer sentences, particularly for violent, drug, and repeat offenders; increased the number and powers of prosecutors; and reduced judicial discretion. The point was for bad things to happen to bad people automatically, and damn the budget consequences. Fear turned out to be the shortest and surest path to big government. As Reagan had said of defense, you spend what you need.

California led the way. In 1977 the state adopted determinate sentencing and a new death-penalty statute. It then embarked on an imprisonment binge, culminating in the 1994 three-strikes initiative and statute. Enacted after a parolee with a long criminal history abducted Polly Klaas from a Petaluma slumber party and strangled her in his car, this law imposed twenty-five years to life in prison following a third felony conviction—*any* third felony conviction. Three strikes and you're out, or consigned to internal exile, which was what the policy amounted to. California built so many new prisons that private pilots began using them as a chain of navigational aides. "People have this image of California beach politics and the left coast," said one state senator. "The truth is California is a law-and-order state."[26]

America soon became a law-and-order nation. California-style hardening of penal codes drove the daily prison census upward. Stable at a rate of about 1 per 1,000 from 1925 to 1975, it rose every year thereafter, until it reached nearly 5 per 1,000 in 2000. Adding local jail inmates bumped the rate to 7 per 1,000. All told, 2 million Americans were locked up by 2002. Nothing remotely like it had occurred in the history of the country, or of any other advanced democracy.[27]

Nor was more prison time the end of it. States stripped away the protections accorded juvenile criminals. Confronted with the depredations of Willie Bosket, a fifteen-year-old psychopath who shot subway riders in the head before stealing their rings and wallets, New York's Governor Hugh Carey convened a special session of the legislature to enact the Juvenile Offender Act of 1978. Henceforth defendants as young as thirteen could be tried for murder as adults. Over the next two decades most states made it easier to lock away violent teens. Between 1979 and 1999 the number of incarcerated juveniles rose by nearly 50 percent.[28]

Carey held the line on the death penalty. His experience liberating the Nordhausen concentration camp had left him doubtful of the wisdom of killing inmates. But elsewhere capital punishment, which had seemed on a path to extinction, came roaring back. In 1972 the Supreme Court had ruled that existing death-penalty laws were unconstitutional because they yielded arbitrary results. Being condemned was like being struck by lightning, as Justice Potter Stewart put it. Legislators in thirty-five states went back to their drafting boards, looking for lightning-proof sentencing procedures that would reasonably determine which killers should live and which should die. Voters fed up with a system that seemed to offer neither justice nor protection strongly supported their efforts. On July 2, 1976, the Supreme Court ruled that nothing in the Constitution forbade the death penalty per se and that some of the new state laws passed judicial muster.

Six months later Gary Gilmore was seated before a Utah firing squad with a white target pinned to his breast. His was the first of 598 executions carried out between 1977 and 1999. Most took place in the South, a region that history had endowed with a high murder rate and a conviction that life-for-life was the way to deal with it. Death-penalty abolitionists, left-liberal activists who saw their cause as an extension of the civil rights struggle, made themselves sand in the gears of the execution machine. They fought back with every appeal at their disposal. The grim marathon that ensued, in which a state like Oklahoma might require fifteen years and millions of dollars to put a man to death, and then limit the cost of his final meal to $15, satisfied no one. The issue, however, would not go away.[29]

The reason it would not go away was its usefulness in everything from local judicial and district attorney races to statewide executive contests. California's George Deukmejian and New York's George Pataki, both Republicans, captured governorships by campaigning for the restoration of capital punishment. Reubin Askew, a racially liberal Democratic who served as Florida's governor from 1971 to 1979, defied the state's Republican trend by calling a special legislative session to restore the death penalty. Firmness on sentencing and parole restriction paid similar dividends. "You go to prison for a long time," summed up one criminologist. "I stay in office for a long time."[30]

Or advance to a higher office. From Truman to Nixon, every president had been a prominent federal official. They had either served in the Senate or, in Eisenhower's case, as a five-star general. When the Cold War was at its most intense, foreign-policy experience carried great weight. But from Carter to George W. Bush, every president save one had served as a governor, an executive position that provided an opportunity to demonstrate resolve on crime, not to say taxes and spending. Bill Clinton made a point, during his 1992 New Hampshire primary campaign, of flying back to Arkansas to oversee the execution of Ricky Ray Rector. The condemned man had killed two people, one a police officer, in a botched convenience-store robbery. Inconveniently, Rector had rescrambled his own brains with a gunshot to the head. He was so far gone that he thought he could save the pecan pie from his last meal for after his lethal injection. Clinton let his executioners strap him to the gurney anyway. Politics now required parasitizing the parasites.

Massachusetts Governor Michael Dukakis was the exception who proved the rule. In the final 1988 presidential debate, CNN's Bernard Shaw asked Dukakis whether he would favor the death penalty for someone who had raped and murdered his own wife. The unexpected question trailed a political lifeline. During his first term, Dukakis had vetoed legislation to end weekend prison furloughs for first-degree murderers. Willie Horton, a black robber who had fatally stabbed a gas-station attendant, subsequently took off on a weekend pass. Horton made his way south, burglarized a home in Washington's Maryland suburbs, tortured its owner, raped his fiancée, and stole his red Camaro, easily spotted by the police who captured him after a high-speed chase and crash. Though Bush avoided mentioning Horton directly, his surrogates and media advisers exploited the issue. The only question for the Bush campaign, as Roger Ailes put it, was whether to show Horton "with a knife in his hand or without it."[31]

Then Shaw lobbed his dead-wife question over the plate. Dukakis could have clobbered it, saying that, yeah, as a matter of fact, he'd like to kill the guy himself. But that was not Michael Dukakis. A lifelong opponent of the death penalty, he had been asked similar questions on countless other occasions. "I think the problem was that I answered it as if I'd been asked a thousand times," he said later, "and I kind of forgot that 90 million people were watching." He replied, matter-of-factly, that he'd always opposed capital punishment and, besides, there were better policies to deal with violent crime and the flood of drugs.[32]

Dukakis's aides winced: Here it comes. Brutal killers deserved to die, Bush said. Cop killers too. Capital punishment deterred criminals. That included drug overlords targeted by the latest crime bill, which Congress was finally acting on. Thus Bush assumed, by means of death-penalty ju-jitsu, the strategic role of crime-fighting executive. There would be no more talk, as in his mushy reformer days, of the respect for law gained by legislating flexible sentences.[33]

All of this is to say that the outcry against crime arose independently of Reagan, outlasted his presidency, affected all branches of government, and would have brought changes regardless of who occupied the White House. Democrats understood the stakes. John and Robert Kennedy had made juvenile delinquency prevention and organized crime signature issues. The Johnson administration had initiated omnibus crime and drug-control bills. Ted Kennedy had come out for sentencing reform in 1975. Yet the issue ultimately proved of greatest benefit to Reagan Republicans. Crime-control dovetailed with and reinforced their priorities: rebuilding national strength, restoring personal responsibility, creating incentives. Reagan's contempt for relativism, insistence on hard power, and fondness for tough talk came through in both his crime and early foreign-policy speeches. He stayed, so to speak, in character. Anyone could succeed in his America, but God help them if they did not, or if they broke the law.

Moral rightists loved the attitude, as well as Reagan's promise to name strict judges. It was "red meat" for white ethnics and New Right populists, a sure way to energize the base and pull in the victims-rights groups. As a bonus, it gave the fire-eaters something useful to do. "They can play a key role in publicizing the issue at the grassroots level," a White House political adviser pointed out in a discreetly anonymous 1983 memo. "Right-wingers will get the attention they crave by advocating positions that attract conservative and moderate voters to our side. They get the involvement, the President gets the votes." Let Weyrich or Viguerie play the Agnew role. "By spearheading the anti-liberal-judge side of the campaign, they can draw fire away from the President, as they have on the abortion and school-prayer issues."[34]

This cynical advice rested on an honest premise. Reagan's White House staff had imposed order on the judicial nomination process, vetting candidates for their constitutional and social views. The preferred type was a younger, male, upper-middle-class, often Catholic judge hostile to judicial activism and Warren Court criminal justice precedents. Picking such nominees was less costly than backing controversial legislation or constitutional amendments. It was easier, too, when the Republicans held a majority in the Senate and Strom Thurmond chaired the Judiciary Committee. By mid-1986, more than one in every three sitting federal judges was a Reagan appointee.[35]

Reagan burnished his law-and-order reputation by signing election-year crime bills in 1984, 1986, and 1988. The 1984 law began an overhaul of federal sentencing and incorporated many of the restrictive state trends. The 1986 and 1988 legislation highlighted drug enforcement and punishment. As it turned out, these laws were moral conservatism's most significant federal victories. They were also its most revealing, for what they showed both about tensions within the conservative camp and about the enduring roles of race and class in American politics.

The Drug War

Because most illicit drugs originated outside the United States, or were shipped across state lines, Americans expected the federal government to take a leading role in their suppression. The problem was that, after Nixon's overhaul, the drug-control system still failed to prevent widespread trafficking and abuse. By 1979 roughly two-thirds of high school seniors had tried an illicit drug, most often marijuana. Alcohol remained the drug of choice for bingeing, but seniors who admitted daily use preferred pot. Reefer was an easy high. It was not necessarily the last. Alarmed pharmacists saw kids buying cigarette papers later coming back to score insulin syringes. Alarmed parents walked into head shops and saw cases full of space bongs and coke spoons.[36]

In the middle class, panic gives way to organization. Families in Action, founded in 1977, and a succession of similar parents' groups worked to end paraphernalia sales, clean out the schools, confront kids about the dangers of drugs, and stop the legalization movement in its tracks. Suburban and morally conservative, their leaders embraced traditional family and gender roles. Beyond getting them high, pot threatened to lure their kids into the youthful counterculture, where they might disappear in the quicksand of defiance, promiscuity, academic failure, hard drugs, and crime. "I am here to protect my children," Joyce Nalepka explained to the Senate Judiciary Committee in 1980. "I am also here to protect my neighbor's children and the children of this nation." Protection meant zero tolerance for illicit drugs and for Carter bureaucrats who spoke the language of decriminalization and harm reduction. By the end of 1980 the parents' groups had momentum, a national federation, and a president-elect more to their liking.[37]

The election's real prize, though, turned out to be the first lady. Nancy Reagan had spoken out against drug abuse during the campaign and gradually decided, during her first year in the White House, to make its prevention and treatment the centerpiece of her public activities. To her critics, the first lady's to-doing was an act. Even her astrologer had told her the best way to repair her Queen Nancy image was to find a cause. Whether kids on drugs was the right one her advisers at first doubted. Yet they could see the advantages: her personal interest, an aroused constituency, lack of organized opposition. It was like child pornography, pointed out one aide. "No supporters, only suppliers. It is a safe issue." It also turned out to be a popular one. By January 1985, Nancy Reagan's approval rating stood at 72 percent, 10 points above her husband's.[38]

The one issue more sensitive than young people on drugs was young people in uniform on drugs. When Reagan took office more than a third of all military personnel, and nearly half of the youngest ones, were using marijuana and other illicit drugs at least occasionally. The bodies of six of the fourteen men who died in a fiery May 1981 crash landing aboard the carrier *Nimitz* tested positive for cannabis. The discovery of a sizable marijuana stash aboard the *Midway* a few months later confirmed that the Navy was less than bone dry. The Pentagon got serious about screening. Meanwhile, Reagan's senior drug adviser, an expert on cannabis chemistry named Carlton Turner, made youthful marijuana smoking his top priority. Federal spending on marijuana interdiction, crop eradication, and propaganda increased. Spending on treatment for impoverished narcotic addicts declined. Methadone was worse than passé. For Turner and his allies in the parents' movement, maintenance epitomized the fatuity of the "New York" psychiatric crowd. Let kids get high, work their way up to heroin, and then put them on methadone? That was a sick joke.[39]

When Richard Nixon made his drug war a White House operation, he introduced a standing question into American politics, "How's the president doing on drugs?" At first Reagan seemed to be doing pretty well. In April 1983 the administration released survey data showing declining marijuana use. In 1978, on Carter's watch, one in nine high school seniors had lit up daily. Now it was one in sixteen. Marijuana use by enlisted military personnel had dropped 40 percent since 1980. The new approach was succeeding both practically and politically, progress on drug abuse (as on crime generally) having become the new gold standard of executive legitimacy.[40]

There matters might have stood had not the administration's drug policy ruptured at its weakest point. While Carlton Turner and Nancy Reagan concentrated on teens and marijuana, the cocaine revival that had begun in the 1970s gathered steam. By 1985 an estimated 25 million Americans had tried the drug. Nearly 6 million were still using it, half compulsively. Supply intersected with fashion. Andean peasants grew more coca. Colombian traffickers shipped more cocaine. Jordached boomers found a new lift. Celebrities freebased. Richard Pryor ignited. Crack caught on in poor black and Latino neighborhoods. Ten bucks, no spike, big high. "I'll do this drug until the day I die," a Harlem woman thought after her first hit.[41]

In the early 1980s, when crack smoking began spreading from Los Angeles, Houston, and Miami, it was just another drug fad. The field reports that landed on high-level desks in Washington in 1984 and 1985 prompted no action. Crack was formidable, yes, but only one type of cocaine abuse, and concentrated in the inner cities. Things were going well on the marijuana front, which was what mattered. Or what mattered until late 1985 and 1986, when major news organizations picked up the crack story. Though they sensationalized its worst aspects, cocaine smoking had plainly become a social problem. That summer impresario Bill Graham made a nostalgic trip back to the Bronx, only to find the building he had grown up in reduced to rubble and dealers touting their wares. "What are you looking for, man? What do you need? We got the best. You want any *snap?* Any *pop? Luudes?* You want *pussy?*" Everything was for sale in crack neighborhoods.[42]

Early in the morning of June 11, 1986, Len Bias, a twenty-two-year-old University of Maryland basketball star, collapsed in his dorm suite. Two hours later doctors pronounced him dead. When cocaine turned up in his body, he became, as one writer put it, the Archduke Ferdinand of the drug war. If cocaine could kill Bias, it could kill anybody. When Congress reassembled in July an aroused Tip O'Neill, to whose Boston Celtics Bias had been bound, set his committee chairmen to work on comprehensive legislation. He demanded fast action, with passage before the November elections. The hearings-free result was a stew of law enforcement, diplomatic pressure, and military interdiction. "Give me the Army, the Navy, the Air Force," shouted one Democratic congressman. Though it included funds for education, treatment, and research, the bill stressed supply reduction and punishment, with mandatory minimum sentences determined by drug weight. Congress put its finger on the scales. Deal 500 grams of cocaine powder, get at least five years without parole. Deal 5 grams of crack, get the same.[43]

The White House, anxious to avoid being outmaneuvered, put together its own crisis agenda. Point one was a drug-free federal workplace, with urine testing for those in high-level or sensitive jobs. Reagan himself submitted a sample, inspiring "jar wars" among lesser politicians. Point two was drug-free schools, a potent backlash issue. "Here in Chicago schools you can get gang jackets, dope and birth control devices but no education," Alderman Edward Vrdolyak, then running for mayor, told a crowd of Southeast Side supporters. "Go, Eddie, go," they chanted. Reagan called for federal leadership on drug-free schools and, rounding the policy bases, more treatment, prevention, public awareness, international control, and prison time for dealers. He addressed the nation twice that summer, in August and again in September with Nancy Reagan. The first couple stuck to a primal theme: Americans had to pull together to save the country and its children. It was like World War II, when

Figure 14   The bipartisan drug-war dog pile inspired Jim Morin's cartoon of September 14, 1986. "I'm afraid this bill is the legislative equivalent of crack," said Massachusetts Democratic Congressman Barney Frank. "It yields a short-term high but does long-term damage to the system. And it's expensive to boot."

Americans had mobilized to battle fascism. There could be no moral middle ground, no substitute for victory. Dick Wirthlin, the president's pollster, judged that the public's reaction had never been more favorable. The only complaint, voiced by 44 of the first 229 viewers who called the White House, was that the president had not gone *far enough* in proposing stricter penalties for users and dealers. Here indeed was a safe issue.[44]

Here also was the reason why America's drug policy diverged from that of the rest of the developed world in the 1980s and 1990s. The intensification of hard-drug use and the spread of HIV/AIDS prompted most European nations to move toward harm-reduction policies rather than simply arresting more users. Better to provide medical care, clean needles, injection rooms, or even a legal supply, the thinking went, than turn addicts into infectious outcasts. European officials, less constrained by federalism and more insulated from populist pressure, could work out such public health solutions. The death penalty stayed dead in Europe for much the same reason. National political and judicial elites, who thought execution barbaric, did not need it to retain office.[45]

Republican politicians did need something, or someone, to throw to baying populist voters. Those who sold or used illicit drugs were obvious candidates. The fact that the National Institute on Drug Abuse, the government's own research arm, had amassed evidence that addiction was a brain disease was off the political point. Drug boot camps were on it. As a bonus, the drug crusade bought time on more divisive issues. "Politically drugs is the only issue strong enough to occupy the attention of the nation and overwhelm the difficulties inherent in the abortion issue," James Burke, chairman of the Partnership for a Drug Free America, pointed out to President George H. W. Bush in a private memo. "Upscale, educated women" were pro-choice. They thought abortion restrictions "unfair to the poor." Few Americans saw the drug war in those terms, at least in 1989.[46]

Neither Reagan nor Bush pursued the drug war as a strategic distraction. They thought the crisis real, as did Nixon. But they also knew that the drug war would let off activist steam and keep Republicans marching in the same direction. "Tough criminal penalties and increased user accountability," Bush drug czar William Bennett pointed out in 1989, united the party and divided its enemies. Democrats who balked made themselves "vulnerable to charges of softness on crime." The one danger, Bennett thought, was that congressional Democrats would get their act together and begin outbidding the Republicans on drugs. As long as the administration was out front, however, the issue afforded the political opportunity of doing good while doing well.[47]

Republican Roosevelt

From 1966 on, Republicans faced a recurring dilemma. They could successfully *run* as reactionaries, deploring the excesses of liberalism. But vested corporate interests, boomer lifestyle preferences, middle-class and retiree entitlement expectations, and secular media influences meant that they could not *govern* as reactionaries. The best, or worst, that they could achieve was a program of selective reaction—Nixon's 20 percent.

This principle explains the confusion about the fate of conservatism in the Reagan era. At first glance, its crime and drug policies seem proof of reactionary triumph. Nobody in Lyndon Johnson's America dreamed of a future in which millions of mostly poor people would be sleeping on concrete beds next to stainless steel toilets. When considered as part of the larger Culture War, however, crime and drugs look like big but isolated victories. The Reagan administration remained wary of pushing other conservative social causes. Restrictions on immigration and affirmative action risked offending employers who hired low-cost, nonunion Latino and Asian workers under a diversity rationale. Restrictions on abortion threatened to turn the "gender gap"—56 percent of male voters had chosen Reagan in 1980, compared to 47 percent female—into a chasm. Gay bashing not only invited payback, it ran contrary to Reagan's inclinations. Hollywood had taught him not to ask, not to tell, and not to stew. True, he disliked gay militants and ignored the AIDS epidemic until his friend Rock Hudson died in 1985. But when he finally gave an AIDS speech in May 1987, it contained nary a hint of God's wrath or personal antipathy.[48]

If Reagan despised anyone, it was welfare cheats. He told and retold the story of a Chicago woman who reputedly milked the system with eighty aliases, thirty addresses, and four fictitious husbands, all conveniently deceased. Reagan had called for welfare reform since his California days, and he continued to do so as president. But on this issue congressional Democrats stalled and then outmaneuvered him. The 1988 Family Support Act, crafted by Moynihan, actually expanded welfare expenditures under the cover of work requirements and stricter child-support enforcement. More comprehensive reform would have to wait.[49]

Not so the crackdowns on crime and drugs, which enjoyed bipartisan support. "It's sort of, 'I don't know if this is going to work, but nobody is going to blame me for not being tough,'" admitted Michigan Democratic Representative John Conyers. Georgia Representative Bob Barr, a Republican drug warrior who later renounced the campaign, thought fear of being labeled "soft" discouraged debate. No one looked closely at the costs or could even tell him how many law-enforcement personnel the federal government already employed. Yet Reagan knew a winner when he saw one. He added crime and drug control to his economic and defense agenda and competed with Democrats for leadership on these issues.[50]

But Reagan showed no enthusiasm for more divisive causes. Or he faked enthusiasm, as when he backed a school-prayer amendment the administration knew was doomed. "Good," a White House aide told a vote-counting Republican Senate staffer, "we just wanted to make sure that it could not pass before we began the battle." "It was all a mirage," recalled Ralph Reed, who left for the more fertile pastures of grassroots organizing. Paul Weyrich agreed. "What I didn't understand in 1981," he said later, "was that conservatives, when it came to many of the cultural issues, would run screaming from the room. They had no real stomach for them." Those who did stuck with Reagan anyway. His positions on the Kremlin, judges, crime, and drugs kept them in line.[51]

If moral conservatives were reassured by crime and drug policy, fiscal conservatives were not. The 1986 drug bill carried an initial price tag of $4 billion over three years. The longer-term cost lay in the mandatory sentencing provisions. Imprisoned dealers who sold as little as $400 worth of crack wound up costing taxpayers over $100,000. The overlapping drug and crime wars deepened the deficit, squeezed state budgets, enlarged public-employee unions, and intruded federal and state governments into local and private affairs. The more politically untouchable the justice bureaucracy became, the more it grew. In California, the state correction officers union lobbied hard for the 1994 three-strike initiative and then spent freely to block efforts to reform its costly provisions. With the prisons packed and overtime at $37 an hour, the union's political kitty remained full. That was more than could be said for the state treasury. By 2004 California was spending six times as much on corrections as in 1985.[52]

National statistics were almost as startling. By 2006 four times as many Americans were in jail or prison as when Reagan took office, and American taxpayers were spending four times as much money on law enforcement and a corrections system that housed a quarter of the planet's prisoners. Small-government Republicans found themselves caught between the rock of populist politics and the hard place of constitutional principle. Reagan himself had backed off his inclination to veto, on states-rights grounds, a 1984 federal law imposing a uniform national drinking age of twenty-one. The measure was simply too popular with parents, activists, and legislators who wanted drunken teens off the roads.[53]

The conflict between freedom and coercion was central to modern conservative thought, whose principal division, papered over by anticommunism, lay between self-restraining traditionalists and self-assertive libertarians. The conflict became conspicuous in Republican politics in the early twentieth century. Republican Progressives, mostly middle-class Protestants, sought to regulate private behavior and public markets, achieving social justice through social control. They were antilibertarian, as were their drug-warring descendants, who recaptured the institutions of the welfare state the Progressives had inspired and put them to their own purposes. Skeptical free-marketers like Milton Friedman despised the statist do-gooders. So did yuppies who wanted them out of their bedrooms and away from their stashes. Reaganism was supposed to be about assuming risks, not obsessively preventing them by locking away threats or stamping out temptations. Yet libertarians mostly stuck with the president for the same reason moral conservatives did. Half a revolution was better than none. Reagan had the rare combination of self-assurance, flexibility, and two-faced charm necessary to hold together a temperamentally divided coalition. He truly was the Republican FDR.[54]

Reagan also won over many of FDR's supporters, white Southerners and blue-collar workers. These were lifelong Democrats who had become fed up with the party's solicitude for minorities and support for higher taxes, which Senator Walter Mondale dutifully pledged to raise when he accepted the 1984 nomination. The party he led had seven officially sanctioned caucuses: women, blacks, Hispanics, Asians, gays, liberals, and "business/professionals." Each pursued an agenda at best tangential to the party's crumbling working-class and southern base; each proved Reagan's charge that Democrats cared about groups, not individuals. The vice presidential nomination of Geraldine Ferraro, a pro-choice Catholic woman, confirmed the left-liberal tilt. So did the platform, which supported gay and abortion rights while opposing landing rights for South African aircraft.[55]

In 1984 disgruntled "Reagan Democrats" joined with a united Old and New Right to give the president a virtual reelection sweep. He lost only the District of Columbia and Mondale's home state of Minnesota, and that barely. In no southern or border state, except for Tennessee, did Reagan command less than 60 percent of the white vote. He won New York, a traditional Democratic stronghold, by eight points. He ran well among all the state's white ethnic groups, except for non-Orthodox Jews. Two out of three of New York's Irish Catholics voted for Reagan. Their issues, wrote a Moynihan staffer, were opposition to taxes, abortion, and blacks in their neighborhoods.[56]

The Democrats, caught in the shift from the New Deal politics of class and region to the fissiparous politics of identity, had blown apart again. This time the consequences were lasting. With no third-party alternative in 1984, Reagan had made voting Republican respectable for millions of Americans who considered themselves cradle Democrats. Trent Lott, future leader of the Senate Republicans, had "never met a live Republican" growing up in Mississippi in the 1940s and 1950s. Yet, by early 1985, a majority of white Southerners identified with the GOP. That was the final, and most significant, way that Reagan was like FDR. In realizing Nixon's dream, he turned his party into a national coalition capable of competing in elections at all levels, among all social classes, and on both sides of the Mason-Dixon Line. Wherever white folks and barbecue were found, so were Republicans. It would in fact be Republicans from southern states and suburbs—Lott, Newt Gingrich, Bob Livingston, Dick Armey, Tom DeLay, and George W. Bush—who would lead the next great offensive against liberalism, albeit with long-term results little better than those of the president who inspired them.[57]

White Man's Country

The Reagan era's winners and losers can be sorted by race, class, and gender as well as by residence, region, and party affiliation. Those who benefited most from Reagan's partial victories on taxes and deregulation were rich white men who built, owned, and ran corporations. Those who lost most from his more durable victories on crime and drug policy were poor black men who lived in inner cities. Mass imprisonment meant, for practical purposes, the institutional resegregation of surplus black laborers made idle by agricultural mechanization and industrial decline, unemployable by poor education and self-defeating attitudes, and dangerous by worsening ghetto conditions. As in other moments of intense domestic reaction—in the South during slave revolts and Reconstruction, or in the North during race riots—the primary object of fear, control, and punishment in Reagan's America was lower-class black men, hereditary holders of the nation's short stick.

There was no Wannsee on the Potomac, no conscious plan to use the justice system to eliminate the urban underclass. But there was tremendous pressure to do something about violent crime and drug dealing, of which young minority men did more than their share. One in six black males born in Washington, D.C., in 1969 would be arrested for selling drugs by his twentieth birthday. Dealers risked arrest, injury, and death for status, money, and excitement. Black teens in Detroit dismissed factory jobs as "lame-ass" and laughed out loud at Wendy's. What you wanted was a crew, some action, and big paper. Customers were fools anyway, don't be worrying about them. But rip-offs were on you, so you'd better start packing. "Whatever happens, happens," shrugged Terry Jackson, who sold in New Haven. "You don't have no feelings about whether you're facin' jail or you're gonna get killed." You just jumped into the game.[58]

Dealers like Jackson sold in their own neighborhoods or to outsiders who came in to score. Other crimes had less willing victims. The most important political fact about rising street crime in the 1970s and 1980s was that, while whites seldom preyed on blacks, blacks often targeted whites, 60 percent of the time in robberies. One Brooklyn crew cornered a truck driver, put a knife to his throat, and told him, as his bowels opened, "Listen you white motherfucker, you ain't calling the law." Subway muggers slashed another victim, an older Catholic woman, in her face. "It was a black girl and a Puerto Rican that done it," she said. "That finished me feeling sorry for them." Academics could talk about institutionalized racism all they wanted, but no sociological abstraction could overcome this sort of resentment. Muggers and junkies reinforced the hoariest of racial prejudices—that blacks could not govern themselves. Black crime divided the Democrats, stymied progressive politics, accelerated middle-class flight, and drove the sentencing revolution forward.[59]

The situation fed on itself. In 1974, 8.7 percent of adult black men had served time in prison. By 2001, 16.6 percent had, and statisticians projected that 32.2 percent of the black males born that year would eventually wind up behind bars. Employers shunned young black men. Single women could not find spouses. Children grew up without fathers, or never had one. Rates of out-of-wedlock births, as well as AIDS and other sexually transmitted diseases, ran higher in communities where scarce men could play the field without committing to marriage. Men reentering the marriage pool from prison were not good bets, either, given their poor education and employment prospects. The percentage of black men who had given up looking for work tracked the prison boom. The prison boom in turn concealed how bad black joblessness really was. Prisoners did not count in the unemployment statistics.[60]

Some found in the cloud of mass imprisonment a silver lining of progress for black women. Knowing that they would likely fend for themselves, they stayed in school. By 2000, more than a third of black women aged eighteen to twenty-four were in college, compared to a quarter of black men. Black women were also likelier to graduate, and a degree was the surest way out of the ghetto. "The affluent blacks have moved upward and outward and have left the ghettos with virtually no hope for the future . . . ," Nixon pointed out to Moynihan in 1987. For all "the sanctimonious hypocrisy about integration," those they left behind were as wretched as the poor in Disraeli's England.[61]

For once, sociologists agreed with Nixon. They described urban disaster zones where the middle class, employers, retailers, landlords, and lenders had all pulled out, worsening the unemployment–drugs–crime–prison tangle. Whites continued to flee to the suburbs, using their credit, cars, and mortgage subsidies to acquire their own schools, governments, police, and gated communities. Though white suburbanites paid less attention to denominational and ethnic distinctions than their parents—by 1990, over half of the Jewish population was marrying Gentiles—they remained highly sensitive to race and class. They knew that when Republicans spoke of lower taxes, fewer regulations, smaller government programs, and local control, they meant less help for idle blacks as well as more opportunities for industrious whites. Reagan married libertarian logic to racial and class resentment. His drug war cemented the bond, recasting the problem of the ghetto as one of criminality and personal irresponsibility rather than discrimination and unemployment.[62]

The media played the ghetto implosion story both ways and for maximum profit. CBS scored a ratings coup with a 1986 documentary, "48 Hours on Crack Street," while its future sister company, MTV, went about the business of mainstreaming rap. Corporate America took hip downtown, loaded it with chrome, and drove it back up Broadway. Ghetto kids became so engrossed in the hip-hop lifestyle—which was as much their contribution to American life as jazz had been their grandfathers'—that they spurned school and other conventional means of advancement. They imprisoned themselves in a subculture that combined the vanity, conformity, and materialism of Madison Avenue with the misogyny, myopia, and nihilism of the streets.[63]

The upshot of all this was that the black slums, no matter how heavily policed, kept right on producing criminals. By 2002, the year the prison population topped 2 million, over 45 percent of inmates were black, 34 percent white, and 18 percent Hispanic. More minority crime caused most of the difference, though criminologists judged police practices and statutory biases liable for perhaps a fifth of the higher black rate. In federal courts, judges spent two decades mechanically applying the strict crack sentencing guidelines to convicted defendants, the vast majority of whom were young black men. Crack offenders averaged ten years in prison, more time than those convicted of robbery, arson, manslaughter, or sexual abuse.[64]

However black convicts arrived behind bars, Republicans gained. Since 1964, blacks had been overwhelmingly loyal to the Democratic Party. Its goal, especially in the South, was to find enough white votes to add to the black bloc to win elections. But mass imprisonment and felon disfranchisement undercut the strategy. By 2004, eleven states, including battleground Florida, had disfranchised 15 percent or more of their voting-age black citizens. The GOP would not have commanded a narrow Senate majority during Clinton's last six years or won the 2000 presidential election if imprisonment rates had stayed at pre-1980 levels. For Republicans the rule became, you go to prison for a long time, I stay in office for a long time—even after you're released.[65]

None of this could be expressed publicly, nor need it be. Words like "crime" or "dealer" or "welfare" carried implicit racial modifiers. Republican politicians and speechwriters who forgot the coded language were quickly set right by their minders. Three advance readers jumped on the claim, in a 1987 Reagan speech draft, that the federal welfare system had "wreaked havoc on the black family, tearing it apart, eating away at the underpinnings of the black community, creating fatherless children and unprecedented despair." Why specify blacks? "The poor family," the euphemism Reagan actually used, would do nicely. So would his customary ending, "God bless you all."[66]

One cannot read those words without thinking of Nixon. He was the first Republican president to use coded speech to harness resentment of black criminals and welfare recipients, the first to launch a high-profile drug war, the first to toss bones to religious conservatives, the first to massively expand domestic spending while preaching self-reliance. For all its libertarian flourishes, Reaganism in practice was hypertrophied Nixonism, a conservatism compromised and corrupted by the very fear and greed that were supposed to yield market prosperity. That irony lay at the heart of Stockman's 1986 memoirs. Everybody wanted lower taxes and less red tape. But the rent seekers and the moralizers did not want less costly or less intrusive government, and neither did the glad-handing incumbents intent on keeping them happy. What Stockman could not have dreamed, in his worst libertarian nightmares, was how, fifteen years later, Islamic terrorists would make it possible for politicians to exploit fear and greed in unprecedented ways, creating the hypertrophied Reaganism of another supposedly conservative administration.

8

ROBERT BORK'S AMERICA

Reagan's fate resembled Richard Nixon's in another way. Scandal wrecked his second term, or at least the second half of his second term. Reagan cruised for two years after reelection. He broke the ice with Gorbachev at the 1985 Geneva Summit, consoled the nation after the January 1986 *Challenger* explosion, lit the refurbished Statue of Liberty, launched his drug crusade, and signed a second historic tax overhaul. In June 1986 Reagan announced that he was naming Associate Justice William Rehnquist to replace retiring Chief Justice Warren Burger, and Antonin Scalia to fill Rehnquist's vacant seat. Conservatives applauded both appointments.

Yet all was not well with the seventy-five-year-old president. When he signed the tax bill that October, he wrote "Reagan" before "Ronald" and wondered why he made the slip. He gamely campaigned for his party in the fall, donning his white cowboy hat and bolo tie. He blamed permissive judges for the plague of crime and drugs. Elect Republicans, he warned, or Teddy Kennedy and Joe Biden would call the judicial shots. But the Democrats, who had learned to trade blows on crime and drugs, had an issue of their own. Reagan's "Swiss-cheese economy" had let coastal elites fatten while heartland workers fell through the holes. Any recovery that left the unemployed on the streets and foreclosure signs on family farms was no recovery at all. That August Nixon privately warned Bob Dole that, if the economy didn't pick up fast, Republicans would suffer in November. It didn't, and they did. Enough lower-income and swing voters sided with the Democrats to cost the GOP control of the Senate.[1]

The day after the election, Wednesday, November 5, the Iran-Contra scandal began breaking in American newspapers. Reagan aides Oliver North and John Poindexter had secretly sent missiles to Iran in exchange for cash and Iranian influence to secure the release of Americans held hostage in Lebanon. That news was embarrassing enough for a president who publicly opposed deals with terrorists and nations that sponsored them. But diverting the proceeds from the Iranian arms sales to anticommunist guerillas battling Nicaragua's Sandinista government was more than unwise. It was illegal. As in Watergate, the question became what the president knew and when he knew it. Reagan grudgingly admitted that arms had been traded for hostages, but said he couldn't remember approving the deal or the diversion. That got him off the impeachment hook, but at a price. Reagan's self-chosen role, apostle for the rebirth of freedom, required that people trust him. Whether they thought he was lying or losing his marbles was beside the point. Reagan's approval rating plunged from 67 to 46 percent in November, the biggest one-month decline since pollsters began keeping track in 1936.[2]

Must Win

The conservatives' hopes revived the following summer. On June 26, 1987, just as the Supreme Court's spring term was ending, Associate Justice Lewis F. Powell Jr. announced his resignation. A Nixon appointee with conservative views on business and crime, Powell had otherwise cast a reliable fifth vote for liberals on affirmative-action, church–state, and abortion-rights cases. If the president named a right-conservative to replace him, the balance of the Court would shift on all three issues. Powell had loaded the bases and handed Reagan the bat. "Conservatives have waited for over 30 years for this day," Richard Viguerie said when the president promptly nominated Robert Bork. "This is the most exciting news for conservatives since President Reagan's reelection."[3]

More than a conservative, Bork was a conservative convert and apologist. The only child of nominally Protestant parents, his mother had instilled in him a love of reading and debate. Boxing and two stints in the Marine Corps equipped him for other sorts of combat, but he remained at heart a rationalist who trusted argument as the surest path to truth. In high school he embraced socialism, only to give it up for libertarianism at the University of Chicago Law School. He practiced antitrust law in Chicago, grew bored, and took a pay cut to teach at Yale Law School. There he felt socially welcome but intellectually isolated. The only untenured member of the faculty who admitted voting for Goldwater in 1964, Bork would sit around the faculty lounge, cigarette in one hand and cof-

Figure 15 Ronald Reagan, battling declining health and popularity, introduces Supreme Court nominee Robert Bork on July 1, 1987. Bored by ceremony, Bork loved the parry and thrust of argument—a trait his enemies soon turned against him.

fee cup in the other, taking on all comers. He and his best friend, constitutional law professor Alexander Bickel, did gleeful battle before enthralled students in a team-taught seminar. But when protests erupted at Yale in the late 1960s, the fun ended. Bork thought arguments should be won with reason and wit, not obscenity and arson.

Bork was also having second thoughts about libertarianism. Efficiency seduced people into thinking markets should allocate everything. That did not work for drugs and pornography. Worse, judges who struck down vice controls violated the Constitution, whose framers had never intended to forbid customary exercises of state police power. Unless amendments declared otherwise, judges should generally allow what the framers allowed. That included executions, which Bork successfully defended before the Supreme Court after state legislatures revamped their death-penalty laws. Nixon had appointed him solicitor general in 1973. Bork served in that post until 1977, when Carter took over the White House. Bork returned, without enthusiasm, to Yale. Bickel had died of cancer in 1974. Claire Davidson Bork, his ailing wife, met the same fate at the end of 1980.[4]

Reagan's election reversed Bork's fortunes. In 1982, the president named him to the D.C. Circuit, the second most important federal appellate court, marking Bork as Supreme Court timber. That same year he married Mary Ellen Pohl, a former Sacred Heart nun who looked like a younger version of Phyllis Schlafly and thought pretty much the same way. Fed up with her order's modernism, she had left in search of a husband and a chance to work for conservative causes. In Bork she found both. Bork himself became a Catholic later in life, entering the Church in 2003. He decided that the reality of the Resurrection was all that mattered, though he allowed that it was nice to have your slate wiped clean at seventy-six, when the big sins were behind you.[5]

Bork would have done well to convert sooner. Charges of agnosticism surfaced during his 1987 nomination fight, hurting him with his base. His appearance, a cross between a bearded professor and a dyspeptic bear, did not help either. Though Bork denied the agnostic charge, he had never been particularly religious. He valued faith in others as a bulwark of public morals, but that was hardly the same thing. He compounded the offense by going public, as he did with other controversial positions. "My weakness," he conceded, "was that I had written so much."[6]

Most embarrassing was a 1963 article attacking the public accommodations provisions of the pending civil rights bill. The one thing uglier than racial discrimination, Bork said, was the "unsurpassed ugliness" of outlawing it in a free society. Though he later backed off the position, the words did lasting damage. So did his 1971 attack on *Griswold* v. *Connecticut*, the 1965 decision overturning a state law against providing contraceptives to married couples. Bork thought Justice Douglas's discovery of "zones of privacy" in "penumbras" emanating from the Bill of Rights a mere smokescreen for the imposition of left-liberal values on local majorities. Yet the central value in the case—marital privacy, which the Court extended to unmarried couples in 1972—was hardly confined to judicial elites. Bork's argument looked sexually reactionary.[7]

Attorney General Edwin Meese, a longtime Bork champion, and President Reagan knew the nomination would be controversial. But they also knew that Bork offered something to everyone in the conservative coalition. An enemy of the regulatory redistributionist state with a foot in both the individualist and traditionalist camps, he would be the "archetypal judicial conservative," much as Reagan was the archetypal conservative president. Justice Department backgrounders predicted that Bork would use his vote and formidable intellect to reverse the tide of judicial activism. With his "healthy lack of respect for unprincipled precedent," he "would not hesitate to overturn constitutional aberrations such as *Roe* v. *Wade.*"[8]

Twenty years later, asked how the Supreme Court's rulings would have differed had he been confirmed, Bork immediately agreed that "*Roe* against *Wade* would have been overruled." Asked why his confirmation failed, Bork said the timing was bad. "If they had reversed the order of Scalia and me, we'd both be on the Court." Democrats controlled the Senate in 1987, but they weren't about to shoot down the first Italian-American nominee. Not one Democrat had voted against Scalia the year before. It was Rehnquist's elevation that drew their fire. When Bork, who was older than Scalia, finally got the nod, he appeared before the Senate Judiciary Committee without a decoy, without ethnic armor, and without much support from a weakened president and a scandal-distracted attorney general. He faced a Democratic chairman, Joseph Biden, who harbored presidential ambitions, and a determined enemy in Edward Kennedy.[9]

In a sense, Kennedy had himself to blame for the Bork nomination. The natural heir to his party's leadership, he had spoiled his own presidential chances by scandal and Carter's by his divisive challenge for the 1980 nomination. In 1985, however, Kennedy publicly renounced his presidential ambitions. He had decided to make his mark in the Senate, where he used his name, seniority, and legislative savvy to extend the New Deal legacy. He got help from talented staffers, who packed his briefcase with memos and call lists. He plowed through them at night and on weekends, provided the sailing off Hyannis Port was not too tempting. It was as if he was using his appetite for hard work to compensate for the less happy effects of his other appetites. But he got results. Over the next two decades he patiently rounded up votes from both parties to enact bills to protect workers, the mentally ill, AIDS patients, the disabled, medical consumers, and uninsured children. Even critics appreciated his Rooseveltian determination to make America a country in which no one was left out.

What they did not appreciate was his Rooseveltian demagoguery when he felt he had to win.

Knowing that Reagan would likely pick Bork, Kennedy had him squarely in his sights. Within an hour of Reagan's July 1 announcement, Kennedy delivered a stark philippic. Reagan, he said, "should not be able to reach out from the muck of Irangate, reach into the muck of Watergate, and impose his reactionary vision of the Constitution on the Supreme Court and on the next generation of Americans." Bork would tip the Court, and the nation, back into the constitutional Dark Ages:

> Robert Bork's America is a land in which women would be forced into back alley abortions, blacks would sit at segregated lunch counters, rogue police could break down citizens' doors in midnight raids, school children could not be taught about evolution, writers and artists could be censored at the whim of government, and the doors of the federal courts would be shut on the fingers of millions of citizens for whom the judiciary is—and is often the only—protector of the individual rights that are the heart of our democracy.

"Every line in it was a lie," Bork later said of the speech. But he knew why Kennedy had given it. Faced with a well-qualified nominee, Kennedy needed something with shock value to sow doubt and buy time. If he pushed the hearings past summer adjournment, he would have more than two extra months to organize the opposition. He and his allies could keep the story building through July and August, slow news months. And they could win. Kennedy had gotten thirty-three votes against Rehnquist's elevation the year before, when the Democrats had been in the minority. Eight more votes would give him enough to sustain a filibuster.[10]

As it happened, Kennedy did not need to talk the nomination to death. Bork lost 9–5 in the Judiciary Committee and 58–42 on the Senate floor. But Kennedy's campaign, and the tactics that inaugurated it, crossed a line in American politics. The Senate was, or had been, a place of pretense and courtesy. Few senators openly expressed the view that judges' politics colored their decisions. Kennedy said that Bork's would and that they were bad politics in the bargain. His candor might have been refreshing had he not, eight years before, warned his colleagues that no judge should be disqualified for "strong political views." The nominee on that occasion had been Abner Mikva, a liberal Democrat up for a seat on the D.C. Circuit. Kennedy's about-face on Bork did not sit well.[11]

Neither did his distortions. Bork had no use for bigots, creationists, renegade cops, or arbitrary censors. He bore no responsibility for Nixon's crimes. As solicitor general, he had drafted the government's brief against Spiro Agnew. He argued for a broad interpretation of the Voting Rights Act and against private schools that wanted to bar black students. Yet Kennedy had cried havoc and let slip the dogs of war. "Nothing personal, you understand," he told Bork when the nominee paid him a courtesy visit. He later offered the same consolation to Mary Ellen Bork, who, astonished, could not think of a reply.[12]

Kennedy's colleagues smelled trouble. Arizona Democrat Dennis De-Concini warned that, unless the Judiciary Committee conducted the hearings responsibly, the public would see the Democrats as fronting for "extreme left-of-center" interest groups. That was no way to win back the White House. The groups mobilizing against Bork, an armada of feminist, civil rights, labor, environmental, and nuclear-freeze organizations, also understood the risk. Bork had to be defeated, but without re-igniting the 1960s civil war. "DON'T create a 'circus-like atmosphere' through Rallies and Protest marches," warned NAACP lobbyist Althea Simmons. The stakes were too high. Write letters, work the phones, play it straight. Make Bork's views the issue, not their tactics.[13]

Biden and Kennedy took a similar approach in the hearings, which opened on September 15, 1987. Kennedy labeled Bork an extremist, one who appeared to believe in the inferior constitutional status of blacks and women. Biden played good cop to Kennedy's bad. He cast himself as a defender of the living Constitution and its legacy of human rights. The hearings, he informed Bork, weren't about his judicial qualifications. They were about his judicial philosophy. Biden said he worried about Bork's views on race relations, privacy, and free expression. Harvard Law School Professor Laurence Tribe and a parade of star witnesses that Kennedy had lined up over the recess repeated these concerns. "Privacy" proved an especially productive line of attack. It touched the sex and family nerves without mentioning abortion, the most divisive issue hovering over the hearings.[14]

Bork had his own big-name witnesses. But the one who mattered was Bork himself. During five days of grilling, he played the professor, rebutting criticisms, expanding views, poking the air to make a point. At other times he backed off his more controversial positions, giving rise to charges of "confirmation conversion." His biggest problem, though, was his failure to win over the national audience, the real prize in the televised drama over the country's direction. Oliver North had shown, in his Senate testimony two months before, that it was possible to parlay the weakest of hands—breaking laws and lying about it—into a telegenic win. North did it with six rows of decorations, a boyish mien, and earnest talk of helping freedom fighters. But Bork was the wrong kind of soldier, a sardonic wordsmith who relished intellectual combat. Alternately acerbic and technical, he seemed to care more about principles than people. Bork talked about constitutional neutrality, Biden about bedroom police. A week into the hearings, Bork's negatives had jumped from 12 to 26 percent.[15]

Bork still held some high cards. Five years earlier, the Senate had unanimously confirmed his appointment to the D.C. Circuit. The Supreme Court had never reversed an opinion he had written or joined. The Senate had not rejected such a well-qualified nominee since the 1968 Fortas affair. His critics misfired. Vermont's Patrick Leahy wanted to know why, from 1979 to 1981, Bork had earned such high consulting fees. It turned out that they were to pay for his dying wife's medical bills. Reporters snooping around video stores wanted to know what he had rented. He liked Alfred Hitchcock and Cary Grant—and where were his privacy rights? Biden got caught up in a plagiarism scandal during the hearings; cartoonists had a field day with Teddy Kennedy denouncing another man's sins. Combative testimony or no, how could a well-qualified, pro-death-penalty judge with easily caricatured liberal enemies lose a nomination fight in a country that was supposedly racing to the right?

The usual suspect is civil rights. To win, either in the committee or on the Senate floor, Bork needed the votes of sympathetic southern Democrats, such as Alabama's Howell Heflin. Indeed, Heflin's constitutional views were close enough to Bork's to earn him a spot on the administration's list of potential Supreme Court nominees. But Heflin and other southern Democrats faced a problem that Bork did not: reelection. With white Southerners tending Republican, they needed a heavy black turnout plus white moderate and liberal votes. With every rights organization in the country lined up against Bork, a yes vote threatened their base. "I've been talking to the folks on the floor, particularly southern Democrats," Bob Dole told an aide. "They see a no vote as a no-lose proposition. They can please blacks, women, liberals. And in the end they figure the administration will get another conservative on the Court." John Breaux, a freshman Democrat elected with 39 percent of Louisiana's white vote and 85 percent of its black, was more direct. "If you vote against Bork, those in favor of him will be mad at you for a week. But if you vote for him, those who don't like him will be mad at you for the rest of their lives."[16]

Bork had a possible way out. He or his surrogates could have made more of his lack of prejudice. He had married a Jew and then a Catholic. He had personally defended victims of religious, racial, and gender discrimination. (Witnesses to that side of his character testified late and but briefly.) Above all, Bork could have more forcefully disavowed his 1963 libertarian critique of the civil rights bill. Jeffrey Blattner, a Kennedy aide, passed a tense moment when it came up. He thought that if Bork turned to the camera and said, "Senator, that article was the biggest mistake of my life. I will go to my grave regretting it. I ask the nation's blacks to forgive me," then they were in big trouble. Howell Heflin could vote for that man.[17]

But there was no forgiving Bork's other sin, his denial of a privacy right. The threat that his vote would overturn *Roe* energized every abortion-rights organization in the country. NARAL, the National Abortion Rights Action League, added a thousand members a week during the confirmation fight. Kate Michelman, NARAL's executive director, blasted the nomination. Rita Radich, her opposite number at the National Pro-Life Democrats, urged support. Anticipating just this polarization, Reagan's speechwriters blue-penciled criticisms of *Roe* prior to the hearings. They wanted to avoid the impression that Reagan had picked Bork to reverse the ruling. They failed. The final Senate vote underlined the centrality of abortion: Every one of the six Republicans who voted against confirmation supported *Roe*. Oregon's Robert Packwood did not bother waiting for the hearings to end before announcing his opposition. "His problem is abortion," a Dole aide reported.[18]

Bork reached the same conclusion. "I was perceived as the swing vote on abortion," he later said. "I think *Roe v. Wade* was probably the litmus issue." More than that, *Roe* symbolized the power of an intelligentsia bent on revolutionizing society through its judicial institutions. "The battle was ultimately about whether intellectual class values, which are far more egalitarian and socially permissive, which is to say left-liberal, than those of the public at large and so cannot carry elections, were to continue to be enacted into law by the Supreme Court," Bork wrote. "That was why this nomination became the focal point of the war within our culture." Nor would piling up nomination victories necessarily end the war. Left-liberals got two bites at the apple. Conservative justices,

Bork observed, often moved left on moral issues. As members of the intelligentsia, they were sensitive to elite blandishments. They cared what the law reviews and the *New York Times* wrote about them. Resisting legal-cultural osmosis required a tough skin—the sort that belonged to a fellow who would stand up for Barry Goldwater in the faculty lounge.[19]

Yet Bork was an odd champion for moral conservatives, in that his religious temperament lay closer to their secular enemies than to their own. At one point a rumor circulated that Bork was Jewish. In a way, he was, having assimilated into a heavily Jewish intellectual world. At some dinner parties he found himself the only WASP in the room. When he pondered the origins of life, he thought more like Larry Tribe than Jerry Falwell. Even after his conversion, Bork disdained Falwell, shaking his head over someone who saw September 11 as God's wrath. ("Why didn't He destroy San Francisco, then?") But none of that mattered in 1987. Falwell and other Evangelical leaders saw in Bork's judicial philosophy a lever that, applied to the Archimedean fulcrum of a critical Supreme Court seat, might restore the America of their boyhoods, when local majorities had been able to say no to abortionists, no to homosexuals, and yes to praying schoolchildren. That was why they supported him. Bork's enemies saw exactly the same thing. That was why they opposed him. His confirmation had to be stopped, and at all costs.[20]

Lessons

On August 12, 1942, in the opening days of the battle for Guadalcanal, a Marine intelligence officer named Frank Goettge led a patrol to locate Japanese soldiers he believed were about to surrender. What he found instead was an ambush that cost his life and those of most of his men, whom the Japanese shot, bayoneted, and hacked with swords. The story became a legend among leathernecks, a grisly parable affirming that theirs was an all-out war against a treacherous foe.

The Bork affair was the Goettge patrol of the Culture War, the point at which a new strain of rage and an intense desire for payback entered conservative politics. Bork's champions viewed his treatment as nothing less than character assassination. One of them, Richard Mellon Scaife, replied spectacularly in kind by bankrolling much of the Clinton scandal-hunting in the ensuing decade. Bork himself made a cameo appearance in the great revenge drama when he helped prep Gilbert Davis, the attorney who in 1997 successfully argued the case of Clinton nemesis Paula Jones before the Supreme Court.[21]

In calmer moments, right-conservatives drew other lessons from the Bork defeat. The most obvious was that their opponents had won the public relations fight in the early rounds. The pro-Bork phone and mail campaigns launched from conservative think tanks and PACs had not been enough. Their enemies still held sway in the universities and the media establishment. Forty percent of the nation's law school faculty had written to oppose Bork. From Kennedy's opening shot, the networks had run with his out-of-the-mainstream story line. Bork's opponents had used paid and free media, relentlessly pitching top-drawer reporters. "Never before had I felt so much like raw meat," said the *New York Times'* Linda Greenhouse. If the still-outgunned conservatives were to have a chance in future nominations, they would have to move with more speed and discipline, imposing their frame on what was, for all practical purposes, a major political campaign.[22]

Plainly, the frame had to be something other than sexual morality. That point was so sensitive that protesters kept at Bork well after his defeat. In January 1988, while accompanying his wife to a midtown Manhattan church to hear a lecture by Joseph Cardinal Ratzinger, Bork ran into gay pickets. "One bigot going to hear another bigot," they shouted. Inside the building, protesters interrupted Ratzinger's reflections on biblical exegesis, rising on cue and chanting, "No more violence against AIDS," "Antichrist," and "Nazi!" Police dragged out the noisiest hecklers. When it was over, the police insisted on driving the Borks to the post-lecture dinner. They arrived at John Cardinal O'Connor's residence in the incongruous safety of a paddy wagon.[23]

Equally revealing was the change of heart over Surgeon General C. Everett Koop. A pediatric surgeon and outspoken Evangelical, Koop condemned abortion as an act of individual selfishness and cultural stigma of secular humanism. When Reagan named him surgeon general in 1981, "Dr. Kook" endured a confirmation battle more protracted than Bork's and almost as ugly. Thirteen major newspapers and most left-liberal organizations opposed confirmation. The director of the American Public Health Association said it were better that the office be abolished than Koop serve in it. Koop survived the storm by taking refuge in Carter's old position. The Supreme Court had spoken. He would not campaign against abortion while serving as a federal officer.[24]

As surgeon general, Koop so scrupulously observed that promise that pro-lifers boycotted a dinner in his honor. Opponents took a second look. Economic leftists and public health rationalists liked the way he bucked the administration's tobacco-friendly policies. Moral leftists liked his October 1986 AIDS report advocating early sex education, condom use, and sympathy for AIDS patients. Paul Weyrich and Phyllis Schlafly threw bricks. Planned Parenthood and Liz Taylor threw bouquets. By October 1987, at the very moment Bork's nomination was slipping beneath the waves, Koop, version 2.0, was deploring homophobia to progressive acclaim. By the time he left office, AIDS activists were leading chants of "Koop, Koop, Koop, Koop" when he spoke at their rallies. The lesson could not have been clearer. Moral leftists would fight to the last ditch over sexual morality. But they would embrace nominees who posed no threat to their agenda, or who supported it after confirmation.[25]

The obvious alternative to sex was crime. Even before the Senate formally rejected Bork, White House political advisers were thinking about how to repackage the next nominee as a law-and-order judge. To win the "outside game," as Jeffrey Lord called the public relations war, the administration needed a simple campaign theme. He thought "a tough judge" or "a Justice, not a Legislator" would do nicely.[26]

The simple could be adapted to the sophisticated. Judge Douglas Ginsburg, Reagan's next choice, had absorbed the wisdom of the free market at the University of Chicago, taught at an Ivy League law school, opposed judicial meddling, been unanimously confirmed to D.C. Circuit, and bore Meese's stamp of approval. He looked, in other words, a lot like Bork. But he was nineteen years younger and so would serve longer. He was Jewish, so he had ethnic cover. He had written on economic issues, so he would be hard to attack on civil and privacy rights. And he had prosecuted antitrust cases for the Justice Department, where he had called for harsher sentences for white-collar criminals. Reagan added the missing touch. Justice Ginsburg, he promised, would favor the victims of street crime, not "clever lawyers" looking to trip up the police.[27]

That would have been fine if Ginsburg himself had not broken the law. Reporters who set to work on the nominee discovered that he had smoked marijuana socially while teaching at Harvard in the late 1970s. They also learned that Ginsburg's second wife, obstetrician Hallee Morgan, had performed abortions during her medical training. She had kept her own surname and passed it on to her daughter—as had Ginsburg's first wife. "It is modern marriage taken to the ultimate," a friend unhelpfully explained. Faced with the prospect of a bearded Jewish libertarian boomer serving forty years on the Supreme Court, it was the moral right's turn to revolt. Secretary of Education William Bennett, an outspoken moral conservative, called Ginsburg and urged him to withdraw. Ginsburg hesitated, slept on it, phoned Reagan on November 7, and pulled out.[28]

Ginsburg's exit in no way changed the administration's public relations strategy. The White House talking points on Anthony Kennedy, the third and ultimately successful nominee, read like the profile of a polite hanging judge. Kennedy was a "courageous, tough, but fair jurist" who had ruled in favor of the death penalty, upheld life sentences for drug traffickers, and whittled away at restrictions on police. He was a clean-shaven Catholic family man with three children, one wife, no bong, and a firm belief in "judicial restraint." That ambiguous phrase implied that he would vote to limit criminal rights and *might* vote to limit abortion rights. Therein lay the rub. Because Kennedy had not ruled or written on abortion, no one knew how far his views would incline him against *Roe*. Pro-life groups divided over his nomination. "Our problem is we don't trust the White House in any way, shape or form," said Paul Brown, head of the American Life League. "We are not going to take good old boy assurances. I want to know where this guy stands on *Roe* vs. *Wade*."[29]

So did the coalition that had opposed Bork. But Judge Kennedy artfully dodged the issue during the hearings. Asked about the right of privacy, he replied that there seemed to be protection for a consensual *value* of privacy in the Fourteenth Amendment's liberty clause, but declined to go into detail about what it included or how it might be enforced. Asked about other sensitive issues, such as affirmative action, he proved equally evasive. He had not ruled on the matter as a circuit court judge and might yet face it on the Supreme Court, so it would be better not to comment publicly. Here was another lesson. The fewer positions a nominee had taken, the greater the wiggle room.

Judge Kennedy had one liability. The Supreme Court had lopsidedly reversed the restrictive positions he had taken in four civil rights cases. These embarrassments he finessed by blandly asserting that he had no trouble accepting the final dispositions, as if that somehow explained his original votes. That Democrats allowed him to skate on a civil rights record far worse than Bork's, who had never been reversed, makes it clear that *Roe* lay at the heart of Bork's defeat. With the new nominee politely unguessable on abortion and both sides weary of combat, Judge Kennedy looked like an acceptable half-loaf. He won easy confirmation.[30]

Meanwhile, Bork had decided to quit the bench. In February 1988 he became a resident scholar at the American Enterprise Institute and launched a career as a Culture War celebrity, author, and five-figure speaker. "Who wouldn't like George Armstrong Custer's version of events at the Little Bighorn?" he told appreciative crowds. Better than the money, though, was the chance to argue large ideas before a large audience. Bork's ordeal gave him what he had always wanted, a role as a public intellectual. He became America's shadow justice, an unrelenting critic of its unreformed Court. That was fine by his enemies, so long as he lacked the power of Lewis Powell's vote.[31]

Stealth

George H. W. Bush, who succeeded Reagan as president in 1989, learned another lesson from the 1987 showdowns. With the Democrats controlling the Senate and the abortion pot boiling, he had to weigh nominees' conservatism against their confirmability. When Justice William Brennan, the brains of the vanishing Warren bloc, announced his retirement on July 20, 1990, Bush conferred with White House Counsel C. Boyden Gray and Chief of Staff John Sununu. They narrowed the choice to Judge Edith Jones of Houston and Judge David Souter of New Hampshire. The dazed finalists were flown to Washington, stashed in separate houses, and snuck into the White House for private presidential meetings. Bush later insisted, against the collective incredulity of the press corps, that he never mentioned *Roe*. Satisfied that the generalities of a restrained judicial philosophy would resolve the particular grievances of his culture warriors, Bush scratched the unsafe questions from his list, interviewed the candidates, retired to his office, and jotted pros and cons on a legal pad. "Deemed to be right on key points 'interpret' vs legislating from Bench," he wrote of Souter. Though lacking southern ties, ethnic or gender cover, and "pizazz" [*sic*], Souter trailed "no political baggage" and "no abortion writing," making him "safer than Jones" and "more readily confirmable." So he got the nod.[32]

No pizzazz was putting it mildly. A bookish Yankee of reclusive manner and skinflint ways, Souter remained unmarried at fifty. Rumors flew. But Souter was straight, and Sununu swore by his character. It resembled the president's own, both men being Episcopalian Ivy Leaguers fond of manly exercise in the New England outdoors. Souter's youth and runner's trim promised long service. Yet, unlike Edith Jones, he had virtually no record on federal issues, having only recently been elevated from the New Hampshire Supreme Court to the U.S. Court of Appeals for the First Circuit. He lacked Jones's conservative profile, or much of a profile at all, having said little about his views. "UnBorkable" declared the *Wall Street Journal*. Cartoonists favored "stealth," after the new radar-evading planes. Team Bush had only to stay on message. Superqualified. Solidly conservative. No litmus tests. No further comment. Souter archeologists quizzed ex-girlfriends. He was a sweet guy. He liked Robert Frost.[33]

Nice date wasn't what the fire-eaters had in mind. Edith Jones would have been a home run, complained activist Patrick McGuigan. Souter was a "blooper single." He might not be that when "the bitch"—Nina Totenberg, the NPR reporter who broke the Ginsburg pot story—got done sniffing around. But Totenberg found nothing, and McGuigan and other battled-scarred Bork veterans reluctantly got on board. It helped that Souter had served as state attorney general and supported the death penalty. Get lots of police to testify for Souter, McGuigan advised Sununu. "Play up the cop angle. This is a winner."[34]

The administration hardly needed prompting. More interesting was the president's reaction to the right-conservative carping about Souter, which made him "*really* upset." Bush suspected that "the Vigueries and a handful of right-wingers" were raising money by crying betrayal and then rattling the cup. If so, they were not alone. NARAL dispatched its first appeal before Souter made the short list. Planned Parenthood sent an emergency plea, NOW an "express wire." Brennan's retirement was Christmas in July for direct-mail fund-raisers.[35]

While the armies massed, Souter watched hearings videotapes like a quarterback studying game film. He concentrated on Anthony Kennedy, who had avoided legalese and sidestepped confrontation. Asked in his own hearings that September if he'd ever crusaded for a cause, Souter said yes. What was it? Why, he'd opposed casino gambling. Asked about his views on *Roe*, he retreated into circumspection faster than a crab into its hole. When he popped out again, he was all inoffensive wit and humanizing charm. Biden called the performance a tour de force. Abortion-rights supporters called it grounds for rejection. The majority of Senate Democrats ignored them. Souter offered little to shoot at and nothing to gain. Bush was not going to offer anyone better. It was over before it was over. One woman who opposed the nomination wept outside the hearing room. Souter donned his Red Sox cap and headed for the Baltimore ball-park. He had won his game going away.[36]

Figure 16 The abortion issue turned confirmation hearings for Supreme Court nominees into a minefield. David Souter coolly walked through it, skirting the issue in a way that kept both sides guessing.

Whoop-dee damn-doo

So had the administration, whose handling of the nomination resembled the way it had wrapped up the Cold War. No one gloated, no one lost face. Yet when Justice Thurgood Marshall, last of the Warren-era liberal stalwarts, announced his resignation in June 1991, Bush abruptly changed course. He nominated Clarence Thomas, an outspoken right-conservative with a rags-to-riches story. Poor, black, abandoned by his parents, Thomas had been raised by his grandparents in a cinderblock house in Savannah. His grandfather, Myers Anderson, believed in hard work, frequent application of the belt, and regular attendance at St. Benedict the Moor School. The Franciscan Sisters did the rest. Thomas became an altar boy, tried the seminary, and wound up, in the late 1960s, at the College of the Holy Cross. There he flirted with black power and liberal politics, only to drift from both at Yale Law School. He had a maverick streak and stubborn ambition. He worked for the Missouri Attorney General's Office, discovered the black libertarian Thomas Sowell, and, in 1979, joined Republican Senator John Danforth's staff. Reagan's election opened doors. He became assistant secretary of education for the Office of Civil Rights and, in 1982, chairman of the Equal Opportunity Employment Commission. In October 1989 Bush named him to the D.C. Circuit. In March 1990 the Senate voted—Democrats warily—to confirm the appointment.[37]

When Brennan resigned that July, Bush considered naming Thomas to replace him. But he was still too green and Marshall was still serving. Two black justices was one too many. Marshall's resignation the following summer, in June 1991, flipped the racial possession arrow toward Thomas. The timing, just after the Gulf War triumph, was perfect. "When you have a 90 percent approval rating," Bush aide Leigh Ann Metzger remembered, "you can do anything you want." Conservative, confirmable, and forty-three, Thomas would give blacks a seat, New Right activists a victory, Democrats headaches, and the administration a chance for decades of influence.[38]

The catch was that Thomas, like Bork, had left tracks. He had criticized affirmative action, rebuked his sister for accepting welfare, and dropped hints, later denied, of opposing abortion. NARAL leaders thought it self-evident that he threatened *Roe*. The press thought it self-evident that Bush had not, as he insisted, nominated the best qualified candidate. Inexperience and unconventionality—Thomas championed natural law as well as a narrow constitutional interpretation—suggested another out-of-the-mainstream campaign. "We simply immediately 'Bork' him," Flo Kennedy—the black Bella Abzug—announced at a NOW press conference on July 5. "He doesn't deserve any opportunity for questions."[39]

Thomas and his coaches thought their feminist enemies didn't deserve any opportunity for answers, at least not about *Roe*. Thomas studied Souter's performance on videotape during the sleepless nights before his hearings that September. When sworn in and seated at the long, green-felt-covered witness table, he proved more brazen still. Thomas denied that he had ever debated *Roe* or held a position on its merits. Ted Kennedy thought him lying or stupid, the one being as much ground for disqualification as the other. No one else believed Thomas, either, though no one could impeach his testimony. Like Ali against Foreman, he met angry incredulity with tactical impassivity, covering up, lying on the ropes, letting the opponent punch himself out. "There is an inherent dishonesty in the system," Thomas later admitted, with a candor lacking in the hearings. "It says, don't be yourself. If you are yourself, like Bob Bork was, you're dead."[40]

Thomas lived. He escaped the Judiciary Committee with a seven-seven tie. Vote counters predicted Senate confirmation. Polls showed that a majority of blacks supported him, on the belief that it was better to have a black conservative on the court than no black at all. Civil rights organizations split, providing political cover. If the Southern Christian Leadership Conference could go along with Thomas, so could Democrats, or those among them standing for reelection in states with numerous black voters. It looked as if Bush's divide-and-conquer strategy had paid off. Democratic staffers grew desperate. Juan Williams, a reporter who had profiled Thomas, fielded calls asking if the nominee had taken money from the South African government, beaten his first wife, or fiddled his expenses. "Have you got anything on your tapes," an exasperated staffer finally asked, "we can use to stop Thomas?"[41]

On Sunday morning, October 6, Nina Totenberg awakened listeners of NPR's *Weekend Edition* with a startling report. The bitch was back, and she had news. Anita Hill, Thomas's personal assistant in the early 1980s, had accused him of sexual harassment. Hill had declined his requests to go out. He persisted, courting her with vividly recounted scenes of pornographic sex. Hill left the EEOC in 1983, taught law in her native Oklahoma, and then, urged on by confirmation opponents, faxed a statement to the Senate Judiciary Committee. The FBI investigated, interviewing Hill and Thomas. Thomas denied the allegations. The committee decided not to pursue the matter. But someone, likely Senator Howard Metzenbaum, arranged a leak to Totenberg. She parlayed it into an exclusive interview with Hill, who charged on air that the man responsible for protecting the rights of women in the workplace had violated them in his own. Humiliated, and with his credibility badly damaged, Thomas again denied Hill's story.[42]

The Judiciary Committee rehearings in October, viewed by a Super-Bowl-sized audience, featured lurid testimony by Hill and an angry rebuttal by Thomas, who likened the proceedings to a "high-tech lynching for uppity-blacks." The pornographic details and circus atmosphere prompted national outrage and a national conversation about sexual harassment, there being many Anita Hills with laundry to air. The object of Hill's accusations, though, was less to raise consciousness than to defeat Thomas. Worried about *Roe* and running out of time, his opponents had spread rumors, coaxed a reluctant Hill to come forward, and leaked her charges when the committee balked. The uproar prompted Senate leaders to delay the floor vote and send the matter back to the committee, where opponents had a second shot at the nomination.[43]

Like the Alger Hiss perjury trials of 1949–1950, the Thomas–Hill hearings revealed a tectonic clash of temperaments beneath the crust of party affiliation. Pro-choice Republican women called the White House to quit the GOP, angry Democrats to praise Thomas. One white man announced, "I'm a racist but Judge Thomas is totally qualified and would make one of our most dignified judges." Others—many others—doubted the moral character of those who sat in judgment. The sense of hypocrisy worked to Thomas's advantage, as did suspicions of manipulation, widespread among blacks. Thomas got help from female staff and colleagues who swore to irreproachable conduct. Sexual harassment often occurs as a pattern of behavior. Yet Hill was the only woman to publicly complain. Polls taken during and after the hearings showed that more Americans, including blacks, women, and union members, believed Thomas. The majority wanted him confirmed.[44]

Washington Post reporters who finally tracked down Thomas's videostore manager might have persuaded them otherwise. By the time they rushed into the newsroom, on October 23, it was too late. Thomas had already sworn his judicial oath, having squeaked through the Senate the week before. His wife, Virginia, took the call while he was in the tub. "You were confirmed," she said. "Fifty-two to forty-eight." "Whoop-dee damn-doo," he said, slipping deeper into the water. The problem now, he thought, was how to get his reputation back.[45]

Abortion and Democracy

Like Bork, Hill and Thomas received the consolation of celebrity. She went on to *60 Minutes* and six-figure earnings. He went on to the Supreme Court and a seven-figure advance for his memoirs. In them he told the story of a young woman who had worked against his nomination and then undergone a religious conversion. She came to Virginia Thomas in tears. She said, "We didn't think of your husband as human, and I'm sorry. We thought that anything was justified because our access to abortions and sex was at risk." When it was Thomas's turn to pitch his book on *60 Minutes*, he called abortion "the elephant in the room." Hill wasn't a victim. She was a weapon, wielded in defense of *Roe*.[46]

Though Hill could have been both, victim and tool, it would be wrong to dismiss Thomas's accusations as purely self-serving. "The harsh reality," Senate Majority Leader George Mitchell admitted during the final debate, "is that the politics of abortion now dominate the process of filling vacancies on the Supreme Court." That was true of every confirmation fight from Bork to Thomas. If *Roe* played a less disruptive role in the process after 1991, it was largely because the president's party—Democratic for Justices Ruth Ginsburg and Stephen Breyer, Republican for Justices John Roberts and Samuel Alito—controlled the Senate during confirmation. From 1987 to 1991, however, the party officially committed to keeping abortion legal controlled the Senate, the party officially committed to outlawing it controlled the Executive, and the Supreme Court stood closely divided. Thus were sulfur, charcoal, and saltpeter combined.[47]

But why did abortion become the most explosive moral issue? Why did Americans, as journalist Jeffrey Toobin put it, see the Supreme Court as deciding two kinds of cases, those involving abortion and those involving everything else? Part of the answer lay in the language of Justice Harry Blackmun's 1973 decision. *Roe* forced American abortion policy to the left of European democracies (and to the left of some communist nations) by prohibiting substantive restrictions on abortion until the point of fetal viability. A companion case, *Doe v. Bolton,* held that states could not make abortions unreasonably difficult to obtain by, for example, limiting them to accredited hospitals. That amounted to a charter for abortion clinics, whose fast growth and steady business produced, by 1980, a legal abortion rate well above that of European democracies. The scale of abortion, which ended nearly one pregnancy in three, and the inability to limit it troubled even those Americans—a majority—who thought abortion should remain legal in some circumstances. But the Supreme Court continued to strike down state attempts to limit abortion access until 1989. That year a divided Court ruled, in *Webster* v. *Reproductive Health Services,* that Missouri might impose some statutory restrictions. At the same time, and at Justice O'Connor's insistence, the constitutional status of abortion rights remained unchanged. Or unchanged for the time being, which vastly raised the stakes of the ensuing Souter and Thomas hearings.[48]

The underlying clash of temperaments aggravated abortion politics. The easiest way to see this is to compare the decade's two biggest pro-life movements, against nuclear weapons and against abortion. Opponents of the nuclear arms race, mostly moral leftists accustomed to locating evil in systems rather than persons, wanted the superpowers to control the menace through a feat of diplomatic engineering. Abortion opponents, overwhelmingly moral rightists, thought in terms of individual sin. The typical abortion compounded one grave offense, fornication, with two others, the shirking of responsibility and the taking of innocent life. Abortion was triply sinful, and of more pressing concern than nuclear winter. The clash of moral priorities explained why, outside some Catholic activist circles, the pro-life movements failed to converge. They proceeded from, and attracted people with, opposing religious temperaments. Eugene McCarthy caught the irony of the situation. "The liberals, being pro-choice and antiwar, don't want anybody to be born but they want everybody who's already alive to live forever," he observed in 1987. "Whereas the conservatives want everyone to be born that can be but they don't care how long they live or under what conditions—you can blow them up or starve them, just get them born. Those are the irreconcilable positions now."[49]

Juli Loesch lived the contradiction. A bookish, working-class Catholic boomer who drifted from the Church, she was an antiwar, antinuke feminist who found her way back to Rome during the 1970s. Drawn to sex but determined to resist it outside marriage, she struggled to remain chaste, meanwhile throwing herself into pacifist and social justice causes, pro-life feminism among them. As early as 1972, she had decided that pictures of aborted fetuses bore a strong resemblance to blasted Vietnamese babies. Killing was killing. Over the next two decades, though, she discovered that consistency counted for less than temperament. When she and a small band of allies handed out pro-life leaflets at antinuclear rallies, "some people just told us to fuck ourselves, you know, and to get out of there." Jeering feminists delivered a similar message to Daniel Berrigan, the antiwar priest, when he equated abortion with nuclear weapons in a 1978 speech at the University of Massachusetts. At MIT, feminists tore down pro-life posters bearing the names of Mahatma Gandhi and Lech Walesa. Pictures of aborted babies spray-stenciled on sidewalks outside the Pacific School of Religion in Berkeley vanished in a day. Similar memorials to the victims of Hiroshima went untouched.[50]

Loesch decided that pro-choice meant pro-self. Take away the utilitarian and hard-case rationales, and what remained was a touchy defense of "me and my lifestyle." This view was all but universal among pro-life religious intellectuals, who saw abortion as the symbol and backstop of radical sexual individualism. Why else did leather-clad homosexuals counter-demonstrate outside abortion clinics, chanting "Born-again bigots, go away / Racist, sexist, anti-gay?" The same applied to controversies, soon to intensify, over gay clergy, gay civil unions, and gay marriage. These things were at bottom plots, abetted by treasonous clergy and liberal judges, to overturn all sexual norms. Yet many abortion opponents, conservative Catholics included, remained suspicious of Loesch's seamless-garment position. They saw it as a potential cover for uncommitted secularists, weak and worldly hypocrites. They trusted only their own kind.[51]

Loesch witnessed a display of this temperamental affinity during Operation Rescue's spring 1988 protests in New York City. Led by Randall Terry, the most controversial leader of pro-life civil disobedience, Operation Rescue staged prayerful street actions aimed at blocking access to abortion clinics and persuading pregnant women not to resort to their services. The New York City campaign kicked off in Times Square Church, packed with Catholic and Protestant activists. Terry warmed up the crowd with a hymn and a jeremiad, and then turned the microphone over to Austin Vaughan, auxiliary bishop of New York City. Defying the law was something new to him, Vaughan said quietly. He'd grown up in a family of cops and priests. But none of the politicians talked about abortion anymore. Someone needed to confront the evil. A fellow bishop had given him a ring, a ring that had originally been a gift of Pope Paul VI. That ring symbolized his vocation. It bore the images of three men arrested—no, killed—by their governments. Those three men, Vaughan said, were St. Paul, St. Peter, and Jesus Christ.

The room erupted in wild cheering. Born-again Protestants leapt onto their seats and shouted "Halleluia!" Loesch had never seen anything like it. A generation before, even a decade before, it would have been unimaginable for Evangelicals and Catholics to rise in solidarity before a bishop sermonizing about a ring from the Pope. True, the solidarity was imperfect. Not everyone in that room accepted the Church's social teachings, and the Evangelicals had come to the pro-life cause later than the Catholics. Yet what John Courtney Murray had foreseen had come to pass. When battling on the Culture War's most desperate ground, it was natural for moral conservatives to close ranks with theistic allies. "Cobelligerency," Evangelical theologian Francis Schaeffer called it. Ecumenicism, originally a liberal movement, had become a sexually and religiously conservative one. Before the protest was over, Loesch counted one Catholic bishop, thirteen Catholic priests, eleven Evangelical pastors, four nuns in habits, two Orthodox rabbis, one Eastern Orthodox priest and deacon, and one New York Giants tight end (Mark Bavaro) among the hundreds of arrestees.[52]

The same solidarity that inspired Loesch alarmed her secular opponents, who understood as well as she that the struggle transcended abortion's legal status. "We're pro-sex and you're anti-sex," a male pro-choicer informed Christopher Lasch. Actually, Lasch was a brilliant but prickly contrarian who came close to being anti-everything: the American Diogenes. He disdained abortion as a manifestation of the creeping solipsism that topped his list of national cultural defects. Yet, emotionally, the charge rings true. Many advocates of choice, particularly women, feared that their opponents were closet theocrats bent on controlling their sexuality and suppressing dissent. And some protesters did hold extreme views, including fundamentalists who said they wanted to save babies but execute abortionists, lesbians, and blasphemers. Every temperamental spectrum ends at a cliff.[53]

Terry kept his distance from the precipice by evoking King's legacy. The son of teachers, Terry had grown up in a family of Democrats, the kind who watched the news every night and worked for civil rights. "I never had a problem with Dr. King," Terry said later. "A lot of the conservatives did." He adapted King's nonviolence pledge and had his followers sign it. But Terry also embraced strict biblical morality and gender-role assumptions. He surrounded himself with "preacher boys," Loesch observed, and "was quite deliberately subordinating women within the movement." Taunting his enemies with his bullhorn and provocative sound bites, he bore no resemblance to the nice Catholic ladies with too much makeup who had dominated the movement in the 1970s. Terry raised fears of misogyny and intolerance, as did sporadic attacks on abortion clinics and providers. Pro-choice fund-raisers made hay. Terry was a more natural villain than Bork, a misguided rationalist who had strayed too close to power. Nothing personal, as Ted Kennedy had said. Terry *was* personal, as personal as it got, as personal as the damnation to which he consigned his opponents. Kill your baby, burn in hell. That opened the checkbooks.[54]

Americans have often proposed constitutional amendments to resolve moral controversies. For practical purposes, however, the Senate's 1981 failure to pass an anti-abortion amendment took this option off the table. Without a filibuster-proof majority, and with Reagan and Bush confining themselves to pro-life speeches, appointments, executive orders, funding cuts, and vetoes, the real power defaulted to the Supreme Court and, by extension, the senators who confirmed its appointees. When Eleanor Smeal, president of the Fund for the Feminist Majority, testified against Souter, she reminded the members of the Judiciary Committee that their decision would likely affect women's rights more than all the laws they ever passed.[55]

Smeal was right about Souter's importance. She was wrong about his vote. He wound up coauthoring the lead opinion in *Planned Parenthood of Southeastern Pennsylvania* v. *Casey*. The 1992 ruling reaffirmed *Roe* while allowing regulations, such as mandatory counseling, that imposed no "undue burden" on a woman's right to choose an abortion before some unspecified point of fetal viability. Like a boxer after a tough round, wrote historian Donald Critchlow, *Roe* was bruised but still standing. Others went further, calling the decision a knockout of the pro-life movement, which by then was struggling with bad publicity, costly court battles, and repeated disappointment.[56]

One thing everyone agreed on was the surprising role played by Republican appointees. Bush himself had wondered, as he jotted his pluses and minuses, whether Souter might not turn out to be another Earl Warren. "No one thinks so," he reasoned. There went another damn-fool decision— *if* Bush was really that keen on outlawing abortion. Souter, O'Connor, and Kennedy all gravitated toward *Roe*'s defense and toward the center of the Court generally. Bork thought their centrism masked a radical usurpation of power, the triumvirate imposing its moderate policy preferences through the old trick of torturing the silent Constitution. Only Scalia and Thomas remained steadfast. Five trips to the plate, two hits. A good percentage in baseball was bad in Supreme Court appointments.[57]

Against this, Republican judicial appointments did have a measurable impact in other areas of constitutional law, and throughout the federal judiciary. In nonunanimously decided federal cases involving discrimination, organized labor, welfare, personal-injury claims, and other economic issues, Republican nominees voted on the conservative side roughly twice as often as Democratic nominees. The same was true of crime. Republican presidents wanted, and got, judges willing to limit the rights of criminal defendants. Right-conservatives appreciated the way their staff vetted federal judges, overwhelmingly prosperous white men determined to protect property and punish criminals. The ideologically disciplined use of the appointment power helped assure the continued loyalty of the base. Yet, like disappointed fans whose team piles up wins year after year, only to lose in postseason play, right-conservatives never achieved their ultimate goal, a Supreme Court that foreswore social tinkering and overturned *Roe*.[58]

By 1991 the right-conservatives' frustration had turned to outright anger, fanned by a sense that the other side would do anything to prevail. It comes down to this, former Reagan legal counselor Theodore Olson remarked after the Thomas fiasco: Openly conservative nominees faced not a process of confirmation, but a process of cynical inquisition that destroyed them and the public's faith in government. Charles Reich, for all his countercultural sympathies, agreed. He knew the Court's personnel, having clerked for Justice Black, befriended Justice Douglas, later befriended Bork at Yale, and supervised Clarence Thomas's thesis. Bork, he said later, was far superior to the nominees who followed him. They had learned to lie their way to confirmation, reciting their "all-purpose mantra" of no comment on matters on which they might have to rule. "Bork was not willing to do that. He told it like it was. . . . I say shame on the process, really. It's diminished the Court." Better to have an upstanding conservative than a mediocre, equivocating one.[59]

Or, from another point of view, better than one who might cast an unexpected vote. The confirmation dramas of 1987 to 1991 raised a fundamental question about American democracy. For those who cared about moral issues, abortion being chief among them, Robert Bork's America was less a right-conservative nation than a politically dishonest one. Democracy was reduced to supporting presidential candidates who, if elected, might name the right judicial nominees, who might survive confirmation if they kept their mouths shut and pasts hidden, and who might someday vote as hoped, depending on whether they surrendered to the blandishments of elites, the tradition of honoring precedent, or the temptations of swing-vote power. For the truest believers, pro-lifers in the front lines of the abortion wars, this approach was indefensible. They would act for themselves. And they would brook no opposition from that wimp in the White House, whose commitment to any cause larger than his own reelection they had come to doubt.

9

LIKE BATTLING THE DEVIL

Jimmy Carter and George Herbert Walker Bush would seem to have little in common, other than one-term presidencies. Carter was a country boy who made good. Bush was an Andover athlete, Navy pilot, Yale Bonesman, oil executive, congressman, U.N. ambassador, Republican National Committee chairman, China envoy, and CIA director before becoming vice president and president. Yet, setting aside the class differences, the two men shared important traits. Both were Protestant Moderates who took faith seriously and strove to please authoritarian fathers. Prescott Bush was six-foot-four, stern and dignified. "I never heard him fart," Jonathan Bush, the president's brother, remembered. Prescott led the family in prayer, shunned off-color jokes, required coats and ties at dinner, and put the fear of God in his boys. George "always placated his father," said a cousin who became a psychoanalyst. "Then, later on, he placated his bosses. This is how he relates—by never defining himself against authority." No one who knew Bush doubted his decency, friendliness, and sense of duty. What they questioned was his ability to think independently and act decisively. Bork called him "about as close to an empty suit as you could find."[1]

It was not that Bush ducked fights. He delivered more to moral conservatives than Reagan did. In private life he was what Reagan only pretended to be, a gifted athlete, war hero, and churchgoing family man. Yet right-conservative activists who worshipped the Gipper found Bush to be, at best, an erratic champion. For various reasons, most of which boiled down to differences in temperament, they never fully trusted him. Like Carter, Bush began his second presidential campaign in 1992 facing an untimely recession and a disenchanted base. That disenchantment stemmed from disappointment over the high hopes he had initially aroused among conservatives, moral and economic, during his victorious 1988 presidential campaign.

Reverse Plastic Surgery

In 1980, when he picked Bush to be his running mate, Reagan reached out to both the establishment wing of the party and to its rising oil interests, centered in Bush's adopted state of Texas. But Reagan imposed a condition on his pro-choice rival, that he support him on the abortion issue. Bush agreed. The vice presidency, as one biographer put it, was worth a Mass. (Or another Mass, Bush having first rolled over in 1964, when he attacked civil rights legislation in a failed bid for the Senate.) Nor was Bush alone in pro-life expediency. Barry Goldwater tacked right on abortion in a tough 1980 reelection battle, which he won by just 9,000 votes. But Goldwater, in the twilight of his career, did not have to worry about the future. Bush did. The switch made him seem unprincipled. Bush changed positions on abortion, a critic later jibed, the way Imelda Marcos changed her shoes.[2]

Bush faced three obstacles to victory in 1988: his history of flip-flopping, doubts about his role in Reagan administration scandals, and a crowded primary field. The two biggest rivals turned out to be Senate Minority Leader Bob Dole, a veteran campaigner with war-hero credentials, and newcomer Pat Robertson, a rakish son of a Democratic senator before his conversion and a popular televangelist after it. Robertson ran well in the kickoff Iowa caucus and in caucuses in several other states. Dole won Iowa outright and looked poised to seize the nomination from Bush.

Sometimes the pot calls the kettle black and gets away with it. Bush countered by attacking Dole at his weakest point, his conservative credentials. For the New Hampshire primary, which Bush had to win to stay alive, Lee Atwater and Roger Ailes crafted a television ad depicting Dole as a tax-happy fence-straddler. Dole failed to answer the charge promptly. In North Carolina, before the decisive round of Super Tuesday primaries, a Bush ad blamed Dole for the GOP losing control of the Senate in 1986 and then failing to provide the leadership to get Bork confirmed. Both defeats properly belonged at the White House door. But the charges served the purpose of casting Bush as Reagan's loyal heir, the good conservative son versus the bad pretender.[3]

Attracting religious conservatives required a different sort of makeover. Bush's Episcopal manners grated. But his religious liaison, Doug Wead, and his prodigal eldest son, George W. Bush, were Evangelicals. They identified influential Evangelical leaders, arranged for personal meetings with the vice president, and made sure Bush signed *Time* covers bearing C. S. Lewis's portrait. Wead worked on the candidate's language. If asked whether he was born-again, he should say that he had acquired a "definite trust in the Lord as my Savior." Grace often came as a gentle rain rather than a deluge. There was nothing offensive in that or untrue to Bush's character. Yet the choice of words would please Evangelicals who had embraced Jesus as their personal Savior.[4]

Abortion was trickier. In a mock debate, Wead challenged Bush to explain why he had switched his position. "Well, frankly, I just thought that, you know, fifteen million abortions were enough," Bush said. Wead, playing Pat Robertson, cut in. "It's curious to me. Ten million abortions didn't bother you? You didn't see that as a threshold? Or five million abortions? It hadn't yet reached critical mass for you? Or a million abortions? Or what about one? What is it that's an issue—whether it's life or not life—not how many?" Ailes called a halt to the slaughter, studied the video playback with the candidate and his advisers, and came to the obvious conclusion. Bush did not have a good rationale, other than the unspoken one of harvesting Evangelical votes. He should therefore just state his position, take the heat, and clam up.[5]

Bush took the advice. He also went on cultivating Evangelical leaders. He was more adept in private settings than in public, where malapropism lurked. The stroking paid off. So did the Evangelical code words sprinkled into a private campaign interview, shown only in the South. It helped that Robertson, a Southern Baptist minister who had veered off toward Pentecostalism, was given to prophesying and speaking in tongues. That made Southern Baptists nervous. Most of them stuck with Bush through the primaries, helping him rack up wins in border and southern states, including South Carolina, where Robertson had hoped for an upset. Robertson labored under another handicap: the money and sex scandals that engulfed Pentecostal icons Jim Bakker and Jimmy Swaggart in 1987 and early 1988. Guilt by association pushed Robertson's already high negatives to insurmountable levels. Most Americans dismissed him as just another television preacher.[6]

They should not have. Robertson had made Phi Beta Kappa his junior year and graduated from Yale Law School, alma mater of culture warriors. He had the smarts to analyze his failure and the discipline to do something about it. He realized that a high-profile religious conservative had little hope of wresting the presidential nomination from political professionals, or of winning the general election. Had he done so, the liberals in the media and Congress would have destroyed his presidency anyway. God knew when to withhold miracles. Yet His people had plainly become a political force, wasted on the likes of Reagan, whose tokenism fooled Robertson not at all. What he should have done, he realized, was to build from the bottom up. Conservative Christians, mobilized and trained through a right-ecumenical grassroots organization, could work to recapture the party and, eventually, the Congress, thirty-plus state legislatures, and who knew how many city councils and school boards. In the end, people were policy. Get the right people in the right offices and the right decisions would follow. So would control of the GOP.[7]

In 1989 Robertson hired Ralph Reed, an adult convert with an acolyte face and a hardball past, as director of what became the Christian Coalition. Over the next nine years, Reed built the organization into a feared political machine. The surest way to win, Reed thought, was to find common ground for religious and economic conservatives, whose antipathy toward the federal government united them on many issues. "An 80 percent friend," he once observed, "is not a 20 percent enemy." Reed proved so accommodating that critics said his organization resembled a business coalition more than a Christian one. Yet there was no denying his growing clout, or the growing influence of his Christian Coalition, which by 1992 was a quarter of a million strong.[8]

One thing that made the success of religion-based political organizations possible was that more elections were taking place in safe districts, thanks to population shifts and gerrymandering. When, as one congressman put it, politicians picked voters, rather than the other way around, campaigning and governing became a morality play. Liberals proved how liberal they were, conservatives how conservative, and minorities how attentive to minority issues. This dynamic not only contributed to the growing polarization of American politics in the 1990s and beyond, it created opportunities for partisan operatives like Reed to groom and run right-conservatives in districts with the requisite number of churches, gun shops, SUVs, and white people. Once in office, they had every incentive to keep up the attack on their enemies, echoing their denunciations through the "niche outlets" popping up in cable television's twenty-four-hour news cycle.[9]

Diverse electorates required a different strategy. Presidential politics remained unsafe. Candidates were subject to the votes of all Americans, or at least the tens of millions who resided in contested states. The winners were those who tacked toward the activist base during the primaries, then scrambled toward the center in the general-election campaign. In a Republican primary, Nixon advised Dole, 40 percent of the primary voters might be well to the right, compared to only 4 percent in a general election. Ergo, "run as fast as you can back to the middle." That meant soft-pedaling activist platform planks while doing everything possible to magnify the extreme positions of opponents. It also meant that, once in power, successful candidates risked alienating centrists and independents if they devoted themselves too wholeheartedly to the activists' agenda. Nixon's rules for national politics applied to governing as well as winning.[10]

Bush and his advisers had to do more than win; they had to win from behind. Gallup had Bush trailing Dukakis by seventeen points when the Democrats wrapped up their convention in July 1988. Dukakis thought the early numbers way too high, but acknowledged that he had a decent shot. With Iran-Contra still fresh and the Master lapsing into forgetful, henpecked irrelevance, a third Reagan term was not necessarily what the country wanted. In August Bush handicapped himself further by making Indiana Senator Dan Quayle his running mate. Quayle was supposed to play the role of Nixon in the 1952 Eisenhower campaign, the rising young senator who would help the older, experienced statesman reach across generations, regions, and party divisions. Unfortunately, Quayle had nothing like Nixon's gravitas. Reporters took to calling him "Ken doll." Bush would have done better to pick a heavyweight.[11]

The Bush campaign made up the lost ground, and then some, by performing what Bill Clinton called "reverse plastic surgery" on Dukakis. Genuflecting to the base in his acceptance speech, a Peggy Noonan concoction of vigilant defense, more jobs, live babies, dead murderers, praying students, and no drugs or new taxes—Reaganism leavened with the promise of "a kinder, gentler nation"—Bush and his surrogates proceeded to intensify the attack they had been preparing all summer. Like Carter before him, Dukakis ran as the candidate of honest competence, Governor Fix-It come to repair the leaky ship of state. The Bush campaign turned him into Governor Failure, a big-city liberal who could not keep criminals locked up, the Soviets at bay, taxes down, or his own Boston Harbor cleaned up. A "card-carrying member" of the American Civil Liberties Union, Dukakis had vetoed a bill requiring that Massachusetts school teachers lead children in saying the pledge of allegiance, whose God-affirming words Bush recited at every opportunity.[12]

Dukakis's religious temperament lent credibility to the imputation of godlessness. The son of successful immigrants who had drifted from the Greek Orthodox Church, Dukakis and his wife Kitty, a nonobservant Jewish divorcée, had not had their children baptized, though they did celebrate Christmas and Passover with them. Garry Wills, no Bush fan, thought Dukakis "the first truly secular candidate we had ever had for the presidency." Asked if this were true, Dukakis denied it, saying that his Christian upbringing had profoundly shaped his philosophy. People were born to help other people. That's how they earned their salvation. In 1954, in his hitchhiking days, Dukakis had listened incredulously to a born-again Southerner explain how "his kids would never go to school with nigger kids as long as he's on this earth." That was following Christ? But Dukakis could not see past his own temperament, could not understand how Evangelicals might pose the same question about his pro-choice liberalism. He simply looked irreligious to them. The Bush campaign was quick to remind them that socialism flourished in the soil of irreligion. "Card-carrying" added an ominous touch.[13]

Dukakis tried to talk tough on drugs. He deplored the deficit. He posed in an oversize helmet in the turret of an M1 tank, a clumsy piece of stage business that Atwater held up to devastating ridicule. But the mistake Dukakis most regretted was not responding aggressively to Atwater's attacks. He thought the country was fed up with Reagan-style polarization, and he had prevailed in the Democratic primaries with a positive campaign. But that was not how things worked in the general election. By September Dukakis was hemorrhaging votes in the South and the suburbs. New Jersey, a largely suburban state where Dukakis began with a comfortable lead, wound up going for Bush by 423,000 votes. Evangelicals rejoiced. "Michael Dukakis is almost the devil for us," said Jerry Provo, pastor of the Anchorage Baptist Temple and chairman of Alaska's GOP delegation. "For us, this is like battling the devil."[14]

Not One of Us

When the November results were in, Bush had won 53.4 percent of the popular vote, 72 percent of the most religious voters (all faiths), and, by some counts, over 80 percent of white Evangelicals. The last piece of news came as a mixed blessing. Bush's advisers wished the win had been more broadly based, that they had run better among Catholics (48 percent, all temperaments) and other religious groups. Too much of their support had come from one part of the religious spectrum. They were now beholden to white born-again Christians, who had great expectations. The Bush campaign had made Dukakis a symbol of godless modern liberalism and then had beaten him in forty states. Rout the devil, gain the Kingdom.[15]

The Kingdom was still to come. Bush had no coattails. Democrats added to their majorities in both the House and Senate. And it soon became clear that Bush would name few Evangelicals to prominent positions. His transition team seemed to be sweeping out the few religious conservatives inherited from Reagan, while tapping secularists indifferent to the pro-family agenda. If people were policy, the administration had gotten off to a disastrous start in sensitive agencies like the IRS, Health and Human Services, and the Federal Communications Commission.[16]

In a 1989 meeting with religious leaders, Chase Untermeyer, Bush's personnel director, was asked why Evangelicals held so few prominent posts—essentially the same question Tim LaHaye put to Carter in 1980. It wasn't constitutional, Untermeyer explained, to impose a religious test as a qualification for public office. "Isn't it interesting," Pat Robertson rose to say, "that you have no difficulty identifying evangelicals and their allies during the campaign, but you cannot find them after the election?" Laughter filled the room.[17]

In fact, finding qualified Evangelicals was not that easy. Historically, high-church Protestants, and then Jews and Catholics, had ridden the good-college escalator to government careers, acquiring a worldly perspective along the way. Few Evangelicals had the education, interest, experience, or insider knowledge that Untermeyer, who had been a Harvard government major, political reporter, Texas state legislator, Bush aide, and assistant secretary of the Navy, exemplified. Important jobs went to important people who knew their way around, not provincials who knew Jesus. It was hardly surprising that the administration's two most visible moral conservatives, Chief of Staff John Sununu and drug czar Bill Bennett, turned out to be, not Evangelicals, but Catholics from brand-name schools with multiple degrees and years of government experience.[18]

Whatever excuse scarcity may have provided for bureaucratic appointments, it offered none for judicial selections. One reason Souter rankled was that Reagan had been stocking the federal judiciary for eight years. There were plenty of right-conservative judges available, not least finalist Edith Jones. Yet Bush went with the Ivy League Moderate. Even before he added injury to insult by upholding *Roe*, Souter had aroused little enthusiasm among Evangelicals. Hence the Thomas pick, giving conservative Protestants a soul mate in the confirmable skin of a black Catholic Horatio Alger. Having zigged with Souter, Bush zagged with Thomas. That was fine, until Anita Hill came along and blew things way right. Warm phone calls from racists for Thomas were not what Bush had hoped for, any more than how-could-you letters from Republican women. Hill was a Carter-class piece of bad luck.

The 20 percent problem had solutions other than balancing appointments. Bush met periodically with Evangelical leaders and posed for photos with Mother Teresa, events Wead described internally as "schmooze sessions" and "lots of 'K & G' "—shorthand for "kinder and gentler." More tangibly, Bush's 1989 decision to invade Panama and overthrow its defiant, drug-trafficking dictator, Manuel Noriega, pleased both neo- and moral conservatives. At last, Midge Decter told the Committee for the Free World, the president had shown "that small twerps cannot push around great nations." In 1991, a big twerp faced the music, thrilling those Evangelicals who saw Saddam Hussein as the new Antichrist reigning in the new Babylon.[19]

Bush's other politically popular war was the one against drugs. He devoted his first prime-time television speech to the problem, deploring handicapped preemies, needle-strewn playgrounds, and cocaine-abusing kids. The emotion was genuine. Bush knew what it was to lose a child, in his case a daughter to leukemia. He was of a generation and class that equated drugs with death and degradation. What was not genuine was his prop, an evidence bag full of crack seized "just across the street from the White House." The accused dealer, a teenager who did not know where the White House was and thought Reagan still lived there, had to be lured to Layfayette Park so the speechwriters could have their *coup de théâtre*. But it made the intended point. Though casual use was ebbing, addiction still weighed on the nation. To finish the job, the president proposed the largest one-year drug-budget increase in history, $2.2 billion, with three-quarters of the new money going to supply reduction. "Not tough enough," said Joe Biden, who delivered the Democrats' televised response. He demanded more money for more police, prosecutors, judges, and cells to lock up drug thugs "for a long time."[20]

Bennett rode the issue even harder. A Jesuit-educated rebel who nearly joined the SDS and who once went on a blind date with Janis Joplin (they didn't click), Bennett acquired a Ph.D. in philosophy from the University of Texas and entered Harvard Law School in 1969. He did not

Figure 17 President Bush poses with confiscated crack before his drug-strategy speech, September 5, 1989. The photo op turned sour when, later that month, Michael Isikoff reported that the DEA had to lure the dealer near the White House so Bush could say the drugs had been seized nearby.

like the flagrant student drug use he saw at Harvard, or faculty tolerance of it. He came to view drugs as symptoms of the permissiveness foisted on a collapsing society by left-liberal meddlers—essentially Nixon's and Bork's position, arrived at through a similar combination of repugnance and reflection.

Bennett knew little about drug policy. He had served Reagan as head of the National Endowment for the Humanities, secretary of education, and lord high executioner of the pot-smoking Supreme Court nominee, Douglas Ginsburg. When Bush approached him about heading up the Office of National Drug Control Policy, Bennett said that that he considered drug abuse an exception to the conservative rule, a social problem that required vigorous federal action and leadership. He took the drug-czar job and turned it into a bully pulpit, traveling about the country lecturing on personal responsibility, accountability, and salvation. He was all for bringing drug abusers to God, Bennett told Southern Baptists in June 1990. At bottom, the drug problem was a moral and spiritual problem, a crisis where "one can speak of the Great Deceiver, the Great Deceiver everyone knows." Moynihan rolled his eyes. He thought Bennett a grandstanding ass, called him a "poor dumb slob," and accused him of rank opportunism. Bennett returned the favor.[21]

Moynihan was not alone in suspecting the purity of Bennett's motives. Some Bush advisers thought Bennett was campaigning for himself as well as against drugs, buttering up adulatory moral conservatives for a future presidential run. They expressed few regrets when, in November 1990, he left his post to pursue a career as a cultural samurai in the floating world of lectures, book signings, and talk shows. On the way out he accepted, then rejected, an offer to replace the ailing Atwater as RNC chairman, reportedly saying he could earn $700,000 a year flying solo. Robert Martinez, an ex-Florida governor in need of a job, had no such scruples when he took the vacant drug-czar post. By the time the Senate confirmed Martinez, in March 1991, the drug issue had gone off the front burner, largely due to a temporary decline in use among middle-class kids. But crack was still burning through the cities, where heavily armed drug gangs were driving homicide rates back into record territory.[22]

If the drug war was cheap grace, the same cannot be said of Bush's stance on abortion. The president vetoed several bills that liberalized policy, including a 1989 measure that would have provided federal funding of abortions for women victimized by rape or incest—a position two-thirds of Americans favored. The vetoes, and his defense of the "gag rule" forbidding abortion counseling at family-planning clinics receiving federal dollars, reassured mainstream pro-lifers and most Evangelicals. But, as James Burke had foreseen, pro-choice Republicans bridled. They pleaded with Bush to keep the tent big. This was the view of most senior- and mid-level aides, who groaned when abortion came up at meetings. Female staffers were particularly sensitive. Opposing choice went against their personal views.[23]

Did it also go against Bush's views? He plainly felt uncomfortable discussing the question. "You mention abortion to the President," Atwater said, "and he stares at the floor, fiddles with his glasses, paces around the room, trots out some old story to change the subject." In private letters Bush distinguished between family planning, which he supported, and abortion, which he said he had come to oppose in principle. That he made this distinction consistently, and to personal friends, suggests that Bush felt abortion crossed some moral line. But the line did not keep him from campaigning for pro-choice Republicans. Nor did it relieve him of the desire to be rid of the question. "Don't you love these issues that divide friends?" he complained in one letter. In another, "I hate this divisive issue."[24]

What pro-lifers wanted was someone who hated abortion, not the *issue* of abortion. The problem, wrote a Dominican priest, was that Bush seemed "arbitrary and insecure." To avoid the appearance of hypocrisy, he needed to make an unequivocal moral statement about why he regarded abortion as the destruction of innocent human life. What Reagan had done effortlessly, Bush could not seem to do at all. The main way he emulated Reagan's abortion rhetoric was to channel it through a one-way telephone hookup when addressing rallies in Washington. Once he delegated the task to Dan Quayle while he went fishing on the Potomac. That shows you Bush's priorities, wrote activist Tim Wildmon.[25]

Randall Terry felt the same way. Traveling to Maine, Terry tried to meet with the vacationing president. He was fobbed off with an excuse, "Golf days mean an awful lot to a fellow," and reminded to obey the law. "I think the president and Sununu and his advisers viewed us as a political liability," Terry said later. They exemplified "that lukewarm, mealy-mouthed, 'pro-life' Republican position that has no teeth and that is really of very little use to ending this slaughter." Bush was just a foreign-policy mandarin who wouldn't give you the time of day on the one issue that really imperiled the nation.[26]

Bush's foreign-policy successes aggravated, in a roundabout way, his problems with right-conservatives. The collapse of the Soviet empire ended the Cold War, though not the Culture War. The 1990s, like the 1960s, were a long decade. They began in September 1989 with East Germans chanting "We want out!" and they ended with the Islamist terror attacks of September 2001. In that interval the Culture War replaced the Cold War as the most explosive topic in American politics. In political terms, Bush found it harder to sweep his leftward zigs under the carpet of anticommunism, as Nixon and Reagan had done.

The Persian Gulf crisis and war of 1990–1991 briefly returned the spotlight to foreign policy. Bush got credit for erasing the Vietnam stigma, for letting Americans feel like winners again. When the parades ended, though, he had to confront a sliding economy. The percentage of Americans who told pollsters the country was going in the wrong direction jumped from 31 percent in January 1991 to 60 percent in October. Schlesinger, who judged presidents for a living, got Bush in a sentence: confident in foreign affairs, inept in domestic ones. Unless the recession ended or an overseas crisis erupted, he thought the White House ripe for Democratic picking in 1992. More sympathetic historians have likened the situation to 1945, when Winston Churchill faced inward-turning voters who admired his statesmanship but doubted whether he was up to the crisis at home.[27]

Right-conservatives entertained more than doubts. Bush had backed the 1990 Americans with Disabilities Act (ADA) and the 1990 Clean Air Act Amendments, two laws that pleased liberals, plaintiffs, and trial lawyers far more than GOP activists. It did not help that gays, who had turned up at the White House signing ceremony for the 1990 Hate Crime Statistics Act, were also present at the signing of the ADA. The same administration that made medical research on AIDS—God's firm no to immorality—a funding priority seemed not to care at all that the National Endowment for the Arts funded sacrilege, including a notorious photograph of a crucified Jesus immersed in piss. Evangelicals reacted to that one, Wead remembered, the way Jews reacted to swastikas on synagogues.[28]

Wead's kibitzing and insinuations about such contretemps led to his dismissal. His departure, in August 1990, reinforced Evangelical fears of a secular putsch behind a Carter-like front man. "President Bush might be a born again believer in Christ," a retired Baptist minister told Communications Director David Demarest, "but he, you, and his entire staff are turning into the biggest compromisers and traitors to the cause of our Lord I've ever encountered." Bobbie Greene Kilberg, who worked for Demarest, and who was herself a prime suspect, tried to reason with religious conservatives. What more could they want from the president, she asked, when he was with them on abortion, school prayer, and guns? "And they'd just say, 'He's not one of us.' "[29]

Declaration of War

Economic conservatives felt the same way. For them, Bush's worst apostasy was the 1990 budget deal. In exchange for entitlement reforms, discretionary spending caps, and a "pay as you go" budget process, the president agreed to tax increases ultimately equivalent to about one dollar for each two and a half dollars in reduced spending. Yet Bush had thrice denied any such concession in his 1988 acceptance speech, culminating with his famous "Read my lips: no new taxes." The pledge held until the spring of 1990, when Budget Director Richard Darman began looking for a bipartisan deal. Reagan's bills could no longer be put off. The combination of inherited deficits, inflation-linked entitlement increases, and an expensive bailout of failed savings and loan depositors, together with Bush's own selective promises of new spending without new taxes, was unsustainable. Something had to give. That June Bush publicly agreed to put taxes on the negotiating table.

Republican House Minority Whip Newt Gingrich rebelled. He thought the way to break the Democrats' hold on Congress was to keep hammering wedge issues after the elections. If it cost Bush his job, too bad. Come the true revolution, Gingrich planned to occupy the Oval Office himself. Playing for such stakes, Gingrich had no interest in compromise. Not in public, anyway. Though he had privately agreed to the budget deal, he refused to appear before the cameras at the September 30 Rose Garden announcement. He was soon denouncing the pact outright, as were Viguerie and other activists. Bush, who hated anything that divided Republicans and brought out the pot-bangers, could not believe Gingrich's behavior. "You are killing us," Bush told him, "you are just killing us."[30]

Right-conservatives thought the president was killing them. After the Berlin Wall came down, taxes were the single most important issue holding moral and economic conservatives together. In repudiating his pledge, Bush alienated every important conservative faction within the GOP and a good many independents outside it. He angered supply-siders, libertar-

ians, entrepreneurs, investors, starve-the-beasters, tax-wary suburbanites, and coalition-builders like Ralph Reed. He was called an American
Brezhnev, a status-quo hack indifferent to reform. In the end, so few Republican representatives voted for the deal that Democrats did a little
progressive reneging of their own, withholding their votes until they got
fewer restraints on entitlements and higher taxes on income instead of
gasoline. Conservatives watched the deal go from bad to worse, and then
watched again as voters punished Republicans in the fall elections, when
the GOP lost one seat in the Senate and eight in the House.[31]

Dissatisfaction with Bush spilled over into open rebellion, as it had
with Carter in the winter of 1979–1980. This time the role of challenger
fell to Pat Buchanan, who had served both Nixon and Reagan and prospered as a television commentator. A paleoconservative with a common
touch, Buchanan disliked Bush's tax policy, trade policy, foreign policy,
and the patrician cut of his jib. Having spent much of 1991 denouncing
"King George" from various talk-show perches, he entered the New
Hampshire primary and won 37 percent of the Republican vote. As with
McCarthy in 1968, many Buchanan voters simply wanted to take a poke
at an unpopular incumbent. Turnout was ominously high: 62 percent, up
11 points over 1980. The *Manchester Union-Leader* ran a three-inch
headline, "READ *OUR* LIPS."[32]

Though Buchanan reveled in the campaign, he suffered no illusions
that he was other than a protest candidate with shallow pockets. Bush's
other challenger, H. Ross Perot, was a Texas billionaire with bottomless
pockets and many illusions. Perot was clear on one thing: The deficit had
grown too large. He proposed to shrink it by cutting spending and raising
taxes. An eclectic populist rather than a right-conservative, Perot also favored tariffs, term limits, campaign-finance reforms, and personal choice
short of drugs and machine guns. His core message, Washington is broke
and I can fix it, resonated with secular Republicans, libertarians, and independents fed up with politicians, partisan gridlock, and the state of the
nation, no better in 1992 than in 1980. Perot was Bush's John Anderson,
the third-party spoiler who hurt the incumbent more than his major-party
challenger. He wound up with one vote in five, and might have done
better had he not run a peek-a-boo campaign. Perot unofficially entered
the race in February, drummed up support on talk shows, withdrew in
July, then, in early October, jumped back in and began spending heavily
on television. He appeared in the first presidential debate, performing
as well as Clinton and better than Bush. When Bush said his experience

distinguished him from his rivals, Perot conceded the point. "I don't have any experience," he said, "in running up a $4 trillion debt."[33]

Bush had another experience problem, the lack of it among his campaign directors. Atwater was dead and Ailes was on the sidelines. The one thing everyone agreed on was the need to rally the conservative base. After New Hampshire, Bush fired NEA Director John Frohnmayer, a Buchanan punching bag, and then, in March, called the tax increase "a mistake." (He decided not to confront another mistake, Quayle, who declined to quietly depart.) In August the campaign swung hard to the moral right, delivering the platform and the Houston convention to religious conservatives. Reed called it "four dozen roses" to a long-neglected spouse. Robertson and Buchanan got prime-time speeches. Robertson used his to attack Democrats who cared more about spotted owls than families. Buchanan used his to declare war.[34]

George Bush, Buchanan told the cheering crowd, was one of us when it mattered. He had, at age seventeen, heeded his country's call to arms. His opponent had heeded his by ducking the draft. Bill Clinton, his "lawyer-spouse" Hillary, and his nominal running mate, Al Gore, were liberals and sexual radicals "cross-dressing" as moderates and centrists. Their agenda—abortion on demand, gay unions, secular schools, women in combat, children suing parents—was intolerable in a godly nation, whose character would be assayed that November:

> Friends, this election is about much more than who gets what. It is about who we are. It is about what we believe, and what we stand for as Americans. There is a religious war going on in this country. It is a cultural war, as critical to the kind of nation we shall be as the Cold War itself, for this war is for the soul of America. And in that struggle for the soul of America, Clinton and Clinton are on one side, and George Bush is on our side.

Buchanan also made plain which side of the divide ghetto blacks were on. Praising the young soldiers who had faced down a cursing mob of rioters in Los Angeles that spring, using "the one thing that could stop it—force, rooted in justice, and backed by courage," Buchanan closed with a metaphor that inverted Norman Mailer's historical logic. On one side were the hip, the black, the poor, and the bad; on our side were the straight, the white, the prosperous, and the good. This time, Buchanan said, our side was on the offensive. "As those boys took back the streets of Los Angeles, block by block, my friends, we must take back our cities, and take back our culture, and take back our country. God bless you, and God bless America."[35]

Bill Clinton, the white Negro inside the piñata, coolly appraised Buchanan's speech. "His job was to stop the hemorrhaging on the right by telling conservatives who wanted change that they couldn't vote for me, and he did it well," he wrote later. Republican professionals disagreed. Wead thought Evangelical outreach should be done early, privately, and below the radar. Houston was late, public, and "waaaay over the top." Even Randall Terry winced. "If Pat had just smiled a couple of times, it would have been OK." He'd neglected the essential spoonful of Reagan sugar. (Years later Terry took his own advice, running for the Florida Senate as a "Ronald Reagan Republican," the sheer black humor of the appellation lost on him.) Ralph Reed worried less about the speeches than the delegates. He watched as hotheads interrupted reporter Nina Totenberg, stalked her across the floor, and called her a "whore," of Babylon or garden-variety not specified, but plainly payback for Anita Hill. This is nuts, Reed thought. Where was the muscle to show these clowns the door? Pro-choice delegate Tanya Melich, tired of being accosted, turned in her credentials and fled Houston. She went to work for the Clinton campaign.[36]

Leigh Ann Metzger, a twenty-eight-year-old Republican comer who inherited Wead's job, saw Houston as part of a larger pattern, Bush's tendency to cross-pressure his base. With the abortion vetoes, the Thomas nomination, and the 1992 platform, Bush had done his conservative bit. But he had lurched the other way on taxes, the ADA, and environmental and civil rights legislation. With nobody minding "the consistency meter," the atmosphere became schizophrenic. Nixon had the skill to manage domestic zig-zagging. Bush did not.[37]

Darman thought the problem went deeper, to the misfit between Bush's character and Reagan's legacy. A patrician of centrist instincts, Bush found it hard to hold together the moral conservatives, libertarians, entrepreneurs, populists, and blue-collar Democrats who had flocked to Reagan. He had done it in 1988 by uniting them in an antiliberal crusade against an unexpectedly weak opponent. In office, he confronted a dilemma. If he tried to give something to all of the factions, he would look like a waffler. If he consistently sided with one group, he would lose the others. It was not so much that Bush lacked a vision, Darman concluded. "It was that there was no vision that could satisfy all the competing factions in the unsettled Reagan coalition."[38]

A Totally Improbable Life

Bush's Democratic challenger, Bill Clinton, did have a vision, one reinforced by the election of 1988. That disaster, no less than those of 1968 and 1972, confirmed his belief that Democrats had lost control of the White House because they had allowed special interests, identity activists, and crafty Republicans to paint them into the left-liberal corner. His aspiration was to lead them out of it, making himself president in the process.

"I had a totally improbable life," Clinton once said. Losing his thrice-divorced traveling-salesman father to a car accident three months before his birth, he had grown up in Arkansas with a resilient mother who liked to flirt and gamble and an alcoholic stepfather whose rages young Billy learned to quell by brandishing a golf club. Clinton made the same discovery that Nixon had. Life had equipped him to fight back. He was Nixon's equal in intelligence and memory, his superior in rhetoric and music, and much his superior in physical and social graces. Clinton's garrulous, hunky magnetism—he reminded everyone of Elvis—was the opposite of the whining petulance that plagued Nixon, a man genuinely effusive only when talking to Coach George Allen after the Redskins upset the Cowboys. Clinton could be effusive with anybody.[39]

Born in 1946, Clinton came of age when good schools were opening up to middle-class talent. In 1964 he entered Georgetown, where he did so well one of his professors tried to recruit him into the Jesuits. Clinton laughed and said he was a Southern Baptist, and, anyway, he'd have trouble with the celibacy vow. What Clinton had in mind was a career in politics, like his hero John Kennedy. He had applied to Georgetown because of its proximity to the capital. In 1966 he got a part-time staff job with Arkansas Senator J. William Fulbright, then in the process of breaking with Lyndon Johnson over Vietnam. Clinton watched, fascinated, as the chairman of the Foreign Relations Committee presided over the great foreign-policy showdown of the 1960s. Clinton himself became an ardent opponent of the war.

After two years in Oxford on a Rhodes Scholarship, and prolonged machinations to avoid military service, Clinton enrolled in Yale Law School in the fall of 1970. There he showed himself less intent on law than politics. He threw himself into the McGovern campaign, but remained wary of the counterculture. Clinton never rejected the system. He wanted to run the system and do it with flare. Tellingly, he rated Bork his favorite first-term professor. He did not care for Bork's conservatism, but

Figure 18　Bill Clinton and George McGovern, Love Field, Dallas, September 1972. Clinton helped coordinate McGovern's Texas campaign, an enterprise so obviously doomed that Texas Democratic candidates steered clear of the nominee. Clinton took a lesson from the thrashing: avoid the left-liberal tag. Photograph by Dave Garland.

he admired his intellectual high-wire act and his willingness to let others try to knock him off.

Clinton also admired Hillary Rodham, a second-year law student with nerdy glasses and a palpable strength of character. Raised in suburban Chicago, she was the oldest child in a prosperous but emotionally turbulent family. Her father, Hugh Rodham, was a self-made businessman, a Taft Republican, and a martinet. If one of his three children left the cap off the toothpaste, he would throw it out the bathroom window and make them hunt for it in the bushes, snow or no snow. At first Hillary dutifully emulated her father's politics. She worked as a "Goldwater Girl" in 1964, knocking on the doors of Chicago's Robert Taylor Homes to check for fraudulently registered voters. But her heart was already with the suspects. The cue ball hit her hard in 1961, when she twice heard Dr. King speak in Chicago. King's eloquent call to conscience, abetted by a young Methodist minister named Don Jones, inspired her to become a lifelong champion of racial justice.[40]

As late as 1968, Hillary Rodham hoped the GOP would serve the cause of racial progress. Nixon's law-and-order acceptance speech killed that dream. Henceforth she would work through the Democratic Party. Bill Clinton, who shared her racial-justice vision and Social Gospel faith, looked to go far in Democratic politics. She wanted to go with him. She fell for the big charmer who talked his way past a guard into a closed Yale Art Gallery, there to court her before the Rothkos. As their relationship deepened, she sensed that her strengths complemented his. If he skated on talent, got lost in dreams, and failed to spot malevolence, she was hard-working, hard-headed, and hard-nosed: the couple's bouncer. She may have escaped her father's politics, but she never fully escaped his bossy and controlling character.

The tragedy of Hillary Rodham's life was that the person she loved most, the person on whom she pinned her hopes, was the one person she could not control. The man carried too much canvas in his sails. For all his talent and idealism, he was manipulative, impulsive, and prone to bouts of rage, self-pity, gluttony, and lechery. He craved, a mistress later reported, the sort of sex that involved blindfolds, high heels, and plastic honey bears. When asked to name his favorite actor, Bill picked Humphrey Bogart, "great as a good guy and a bad guy." He was really describing himself. Good Bill wanted a brilliant wife. Bad Bill wanted a string of hot girlfriends. Hillary filled the first requirement. He proposed in 1973. She saw trouble. She said no. He kept asking.[41]

Hillary had another worry: Arkansas. Bill planned to launch his political career back home. For an ambitious graduate of Wellesley and Yale Law School, life as provincial politician's wife held little attraction. Then again, Bill looked to be headed for the top. In 1975 Hillary said yes, though she kept her maiden name. His political career went according to plan: state attorney general in 1976, nation's youngest governor in 1978. He became the youngest ex-governor in 1980, losing reelection, but then came back to win the governorship five straight times. He built a record as a pro-growth reformer focused on jobs and schools. She did corporate legal work. They attended Renaissance Weekends, high-end Chautauquas whose mix of brainy panels and celebrity schmoozing expanded their network of ambitious people. Far from being the countercultural radicals of Buchanan's parody, the Clintons were classic bourgeois-bohemian social climbers who blended the progressive aspirations of the 1960s with the careerism of the 1980s.

Clinton studied Reagan. He admired the way he said things simply, negotiated amicably, and accepted a fair compromise. He thought Democrats should do likewise, moving toward the dynamic center on social issues. Above all, they had to confront economic reality. Globalization and the information revolution required leaner, more flexible models of business and government, not industrial-style bureaucracies. Better to marry market means to progressive ends through such innovations as tax credits for private day care. "The two things we learned in the eighties were entirely contradictory," said James Pinkerton, a Bush domestic-policy adviser. "Socialism doesn't work, and the most ideological President of the twentieth century, Ronald Reagan, couldn't put an end to the welfare state. He couldn't even put a dent in it." Clinton agreed. What was needed was "a third way" between socialism and libertarianism.[42]

Clinton joined and ultimately chaired the Democratic Leadership Council (DLC), a group of like-minded, mostly southern Democratic centrists founded after the 1984 Mondale disaster. In May 1990 he gave the DLC keynote address—a jeremiad, really—in which he said the middle class had quit voting Democratic in national elections because it had quit trusting the party on defense, traditional values, and spending. "Our burden is to give the people a new choice, rooted in old values, a new choice that is simple, that offers opportunity, demands responsibility, gives citizens more say, provides them responsive government—all because we recognize that we are a community. We are all in this together, and we are going up or down together."[43]

Many observers had expected Clinton to carry the DLC banner into battle against Bush in 1988. He might have, save that Colorado Senator Gary Hart, another presidential aspirant of inhibited liberalism and uninhibited sexuality, withdrew from the race in May 1987 after journalists exposed him as an adulterer. The rules had plainly changed. Clinton was clearly vulnerable. He opted out. He fell into a funk, then another affair, then screaming fights with Hillary. In the end, ambition proved more compelling than the charms of Marilyn Jo Jenkins. Clinton backed away from divorce, entered counseling, and promised, in the words of aide-minder Betsey Wright, to be a "puppy dog." Much in the coming decade would turn on his incomplete housebreaking.[44]

The mid-life crisis passed, Clinton ruminated on the next election. In his memoirs, he claimed that Bush adviser Roger Porter called in July 1991 to warn him off. A pro-growth, anticrime southern DLC governor, Clinton was the only Democrat who worried the White House. If he bided his time until 1996, he could win the presidency. If he ran in 1992, the Republicans would destroy him, spending whatever it took to take him out early. "Ever since I was a little boy," Clinton recalled, "I have hated to be threatened." This bully he could confront. Bush had neglected the economy, stuck in a mid-life crisis of its own. Clinton knew his character would be used against him. His enemies in Arkansas had been doing it for years. But if he responded quickly and kept the focus on middle-class worries, he might prevail. The Democratic field was thin in 1992. If he won the nomination and lost a close election, he would still be odds-on favorite for 1996. So, on October 3, 1991, he pushed his chips into the presidential pot.[45]

What happened next has entered political legend. Skipping Iowa, where favorite son Tom Harkin had a lock, Clinton concentrated on New Hampshire, a state whose retail politics were like those he had mastered in Arkansas. Then, in late January, scandal erupted. Gennifer Flowers, a big-haired singer, divulged, for tabloid cash, a twelve-year affair with Clinton. Bill and Hillary went on *60 Minutes*. He denied the specific charges, admitting only that he had caused "pain in his marriage." He loved Hillary, and they had stuck it out. If there was a character issue here, it was the frivolous character of the press, playing "gotcha" in a recession. He resorted to more ju-jitsu in early February, after damaging charges surfaced that he had lied to draft officials. In Dover, New Hampshire, he fought back, charging that moral politics had become a snare of false consciousness:

> I'll tell you what I think the character issue is: Who really cares about you? . . . Who is determined to change your life rather than to just get or keep power? . . .
>
> I'll tell you what I think the character issue in this election is: How can you have the power of the presidency and never use it to help people improve their lives? . . .
>
> I'll tell you something. I'm going to give you this election back, and if you'll give it to me, I won't be like George Bush. I'll never forget who gave me a second chance, and I'll be there for you 'til the last dog dies.

Clinton finished a strong second in New Hampshire, surprising journalists who had written him off. The "Comeback Kid" went on to win Georgia, sweep the southern primaries on Super Tuesday, then rack up big-state wins in Illinois, Michigan, New York, and California, where he bested the state's own former governor, Jerry Brown. That May Clinton walked the riot-scarred streets of South Central Los Angeles, preempting Bush, who belatedly toured the ruins in a bullet-proof limousine. Throughout the spring Bush seemed unconcerned, detached. He still led Clinton in the polls. He doubted that Americans would elect someone of his flawed character.[46]

He forgot that character can be made over. The Democratic convention that July offered a clinic in restorative plastic surgery. The convention film, *The Man from Hope*, showed young Bill in Boys State garb clasping President Kennedy's hand, taking the torch on behalf of his generation. Bill in casual duds, Hillary in a pageboy, Chelsea in a dance costume—the footage purred family. In 52 convention speeches, orators mentioned "family" or "families" 164 times, "welfare" 31 times, and "AFDC" just twice. Clinton's DLC positions and trade- and welfare-reform plans hardly appealed to the party's economic left. But he passed muster on the nonnegotiable issues of race and sexual morality. He was for affirmative action, though against quotas; for gay rights, though against gay marriage. Above all, he was for choice. He promised to make *Roe* a litmus test for judicial appointments. No stealth, no pussy-footing.[47]

This was the position of DNC Chairman Ron Brown and other party leaders, who denied Pennsylvania Governor Bob Casey's request to speak against the abortion plank. An Irish Catholic whose orphaned father had worked in the anthracite mines at eleven, and then worked his way through Fordham Law School, Casey had his own ideas about family. The historical point of the party, he thought, was to extend dignity and opportunity to the powerless. Why not include the unborn in the expanding circle of human rights? His appeal to progressive conscience had a practical kicker. Casey had spanked his pro-choice Republican opponent by a million votes in the last election. Pennsylvania was a crucial swing state.

The leadership ruled Casey's request out of order and exiled him to the cheap seats. There he watched as Kathy Taylor, a pro-choice Republican who had worked for Casey's defeated opponent, sat on the platform as an honored guest. A delegate peddling buttons of Casey in papal regalia did a brisk business. "I have never seen a more rigid, predictable, or doctrinaire group of people in my life," he wrote later. "Nor have I felt such deep, bitter hatred—the tyranny of the far left, up close and personal."[48]

Better to say the moral left. Surveys showed Democratic delegates to be overwhelmingly secular. The group they most despised, by a wide margin, was Christian fundamentalists. Over 22 percent of the Republican delegates, by contrast, *were* fundamentalists, and over half said they were members of or sympathetic to "the Christian right." Abortion had become the stake-out issue for activists in both parties. Casey lecturing Democrats about the bright sunshine of unborn human rights invited hissing disaster. That was why party officials sacrificed him in the name of unity—and why Republicans promptly invited him to give his speech at their convention. Casey declined on the ground that, in office, Republicans waffled on abortion anyway. The same could not be said of the Democrats. Their 1992 strategy, and Clinton's, was small tent on abortion, big tent on almost everything else.[49]

Clinton chose Al Gore as his running mate. The Tennessee senator's reputation for seriousness and probity cut the "Slick Willie" smell, while Gore's DLC credentials and Baptist faith reinforced the ticket in the Upper South. Black voters liked southern boys who had gotten past bigotry, though Clinton was careful to throw the occasional racial change-up. That June he blasted Sister Souljah, a rapper who suggested black folks should try killing white folks for a change. In July, surrounded by a rainbow squad of Houston cops, Clinton pledged "to be tough on crime and good for civil rights." Above all, he promised to be good for the middle class, whose anxieties he kept front and center throughout the campaign.[50]

On November 3, Bill Clinton won the election with 43 percent of the popular vote. Ross Perot got 19 percent and George Bush 37 percent, a smaller share than Hoover in 1932. The key factor, mentioned by 41 percent of voters in exit polls, was the sour economy. But Clinton had also made inroads on the Reagan coalition. He had won two-thirds of the independent votes, half the suburban votes, and half the self-described "moderates." He ran well among Catholics and mainline Protestants disenchanted with Bush's sexual politics. One Republican in four deserted Bush for Clinton. Religious conservatives, with no place else to go, remained the president's most reliable supporters. Bush's 168 electoral votes came from the most morally conservative regions, the South, the Midwest, and the Mountain West.[51]

That moral conservatives should favor an Episcopalian over a Southern Baptist captures the essential change in religion and politics since the

1960s. Voters had learned to look under the hood of denomination at the engine of temperament. Religious conservatives understood that Clinton was not a "real" Southern Baptist, or even a Carter Baptist. Say what you will, Jimmy had kept his own nose clean. Though a high-church Moderate, Bush stood nearest to them on moral issues, most crucially on abortion. Bush's problem in 1992 was not the religious right, save that he paid too much for the bouquet he tossed it. His problem was that he had to defend his economic record against two articulate opponents in the midst of a lingering recession. In 1992 Bush received 10 million fewer votes than in 1988, though 13 million more Americans had gone to the polls, thanks largely to Perot. Many thought Perot a stroke of luck for Clinton, that the hectoring little Texan had siphoned off fiscal conservatives, Anderson voters, and angry populists who might otherwise have gone Republican. Yet, in politics as in baseball, luck was the product of design. Clinton's DLC-plus-choice strategy left him perfectly positioned to win, if only with a minority of popular votes.

Then Bill Clinton made a mistake. He forgot that Nixon's rules also applied to the governing cycle of the permanent campaign. In the eyes of his implacable enemies, he had barely been elected when he, and the scheming feminist who had sneaked into the White House with him, let their true colors show.

10

The struggle over morality that plagued Clinton's presidency and led to the climactic battle of the Culture War, the Monica Lewinsky scandal and impeachment drama of 1998–1999, began one week after the 1992 election. Asked if he would honor his pledge to let gays serve openly in the armed forces, the president-elect said, "Yes, I want to." Those words shot like a current through Evangelical and senior military circles. A pro-homosexual draft-dodger was about to become commander in chief.[1]

Clinton's transition was troubled in other ways. He spent too much time devising a cabinet that "looked like America" and not enough assembling an experienced staff or ordering its priorities. Those priorities were thrown into further doubt when, on January 6, Clinton learned that the deficit would be a third larger than projected, thanks to the recession and entitlement spending increases. The 1990 budget deal had not been enough. Having pledged to cut middle-class taxes and the deficit, while investing in education, jobs, and health care, Clinton saw that he could not do everything, even with defense savings and higher taxes on the rich.[2]

Clinton spent much of his first year sorting out the implications of the unwelcome news. The real legacy of Reaganism, he saw, was not conservatism, but a structural deficit. Over twelve years, in good times and bad, its "anti-tax theology" and spend-as-usual politics had raised the debt from $1 to $4 trillion. Now the rate at which the government was borrowing, and hence driving up interest rates, had to be controlled, lest the economic growth that underwrote the progressive project collapse entirely.[3]

Clinton seemed to be boxed in. But he was the Captain Kirk of American politics, the doughty survivor at his wily best when trapped. In February 1993 Clinton proposed to raise taxes on higher-bracket incomes and energy consumption while delaying the middle-class tax cut and many of his social programs. For every dollar in new spending, Clinton compensated with two dollars in overall deficit reduction. He hung on to one key progressive feature, expanded tax credits for lower-income workers who might otherwise abandon the labor market for welfare.[4]

It took six months of hard bargaining and a series of cliff-hanger votes to get the budget through Congress. It took another concerted effort to get Congress to approve the North American Free Trade Agreement (NAFTA), a U.S.–Canada–Mexico tariff reduction negotiated on Bush's watch. Had Bush still been president, protection-minded Democrats would never have allowed passage. Clinton negotiated side agreements on labor and the environment and then induced 102 House Democrats to join 132 Republicans in voting yes. Nixon, then in the last year of his life, approved. Hanging tough on NAFTA, he advised Clinton, would gain him a reputation for independence from his party's interest groups. "He's got to continue to do that," DLC founder Al From told a reporter at the end of the first year.[5]

Stealth Liberals

Clinton's failure to do so goes a long way toward explaining the 1994 election disaster, which cost his party control of both houses of Congress. A series of ill-fated legislative initiatives on health care, crime, and welfare belied his New Democrat pretensions, making it easy for Republicans to portray the president and his influential first lady as stealth liberals.

For all the money lavished on health care, upwards of 40 million Americans still lacked basic health insurance when Clinton took office. Bill entrusted Hillary to lead the effort to provide them with affordable coverage. That was a political mistake because it put such a personal stamp on health-care reform. Had Clinton invited congressional leaders to frame legislation consistent with his broad goals, he might have succeeded. Republican John Chaffee had already introduced a managed-competition bill that phased in individual mandates. Everyone would be required to buy tax-deductible, government-defined coverage through purchasing alliances that would keep down costs and force insurance companies to accept all comers. Republican leaders, particularly Dole, initially supported the scheme. Clinton could have put them on the spot had he said, early on, "I endorse your plan. Now let's work out the details."

Instead, the first lady and 500 unnamed consultants retreated to the Executive Office Building and set to work on their own proposal. Nine

Figure 19   Hillary Clinton testifying on Capitol Hill, September 29, 1993. Though she displayed impressive knowledge, her high-profile advocacy of the complex health-care plan proved to be a mistake. It lent credence to the charge that she and her husband were really big-government liberals and gave Republicans added incentive to oppose the bill.

months passed before the president outlined the still-incomplete Health Security Act before a joint session of Congress. In November he finally submitted a bill, nearly as long as *War and Peace,* designed to achieve universal coverage through mandates on individuals *and* employers. The federal government would spell out the minimum benefits and require everyone to obtain coverage through large purchasing alliances, which states would oversee. While there was no single-payer system, the bill was sufficiently complex and intrusive to invite big-government caricature. The insurance lobby ran ads featuring Harry and Louise, a middle-class couple forced to choose among bureaucrat-designed policies that required everyone to pay the same rate, regardless of age or health habits. The bill's abortion coverage bothered religious conservatives. Tobacco-tax increases angered swing-state Southerners.

In late 1993 the ghosts of Arkansas past intruded themselves. White-water and Troopergate, controversies about the Clintons' land dealings and Bad Bill's use of state police to procure women, lit the fuse of the sex-and-perjury scandal that would explode during his second term. Initially, however, the gossipy news drew attention from health-care reform and changed its political calculus. As Republicans sensed the possibility of big gains in the 1994 election, they made defeat of the Clinton plan, or any plan, top priority. Bill Clinton made matters worse in his first State of the Union address, when he brandished his pen and promised to veto any bill that did not provide universal coverage. Left-liberals in his administration, not least Hillary, held him to that pledge, which made it impossible to cut an improved-coverage deal. By the summer health care was dead. The smell lingered. As presidential blunders went, adviser David Gergen confided to Moynihan, this one ranked with Vietnam.[6]

Clinton hoped to recoup his losses with his crime bill, which squeaked through Congress in late August 1994. News of drive-by shootings, the Los Angeles riots, Polly Klaas, O. J. Simpson, and the rape-murder of seven-year-old Megan Kanka filled the airways from the spring of 1992 through the summer of 1994. As never before, Americans feared that strangers would claim their lives. Polls ranked crime the worst problem facing the country and the one most neglected by Washington officials.[7]

When official Washington finally acted, it produced another gigantic crime bill. New Democrat advisers spun it as a "tough, smart, balanced" mix of "stuff that works." The bill was balanced, in the sense of a Christmas tree hung on every branch. To the usual populist stand-bys—more police and prisons, longer sentences for repeat offenders, drug boot camps, and a wholesale expansion of the federal death penalty—Democrats added $7 billion for nominally crime-preventing social programs, from midnight basketball leagues to public transportation. Republicans simply reframed the package as pork.[8]

Their NRA allies went further. Clinton had already signed the Brady Bill, a handgun-purchase background-check measure that had languished since 1987. He compounded this offense by insisting that his crime bill ban large-magazine automatic weapons. NRA leaders, who regarded any regulation as a slippery slope and the Clintons as mortal enemies, declared war. They could not defeat Clinton until 1996, but they could target congressmen who defied their wishes. Jody Powell, watching from the sidelines, tried to warn the White House. Voters believed the NRA's claim that gun control would inconvenience or disarm them, but not violent criminals. "You will be asking some good Democrats to cast a very tough vote for no good end—and in a year in which you are already going to be asking for more than a few tough votes."[9]

Democratic congressmen would have been less endangered if Clinton had meanwhile succeeded in reforming welfare. When Congress enacted Aid to Dependent Children in 1935, the money had gone to widows with children. Renamed Aid to Families with Dependent Children (AFDC) in 1962, the program grew steadily larger and more controversial. The number of families on welfare rose from less than 1 percent in 1936 to 15 percent in 1994. The typical recipient evolved from a widowed mother to a divorced mother to a mother who had never married, who did not work, and who received AFDC, food stamps, and Medicaid services, often for years. Temporary assistance for the deserving poor had become, in the eyes of most Americans, a promiscuous way of life. Welfare made possible generations of fatherless children prone to delinquency, dropout, unemployment, crime, and welfare dependency themselves. Then there were the frauds, like the Newark residents caught turnstile-jumping in Manhattan while carrying New York and New Jersey welfare cards. For conservatives, moral and economic, the welfare mess proved liberal good intentions no match for human nature.[10]

Clinton thought that welfare could work if done right. As governor, he had advocated work requirements for Arkansas welfare recipients. He had encouraged other governors to obtain federal waivers to launch their own reform experiments. As president, he called for both state experimentation and systemwide reform. AFDC was a joint program, with the federal government providing guidelines and the bulk of the funding while the states set benefit levels and handled administration. Clinton wanted to phase in national requirements for recipients to find work after two years, but with the training, child care, and, as a last resort, publicly funded jobs that would enable them to do so. The additional cost would be about $9 billion over five years.[11]

Gingrich wanted reform that would save money. He linked welfare dependency to criminality, saying its abolition was as basic to preventing future crime as locking up current criminals. The fewer bastards, he reasoned, the fewer sociopaths. If welfare mothers kept having children, then cut them off. If their children had children, then refuse AFDC for minors. The same logic would, of course, dictate legal abortion. Yet Gingrich and his neoconservative allies had to tread carefully on choice. It was far safer to target the sexual behavior of unwed, implicitly black, welfare mothers than the reproductive freedom well established in the broader culture.[12]

Clinton pushed health-care reform first and tried to link welfare reform back to it. If everyone had insurance, he argued, welfare recipients could take low-skill jobs without worrying about losing Medicaid coverage. Republicans and centrist Democrats scoffed. The welfare system was in crisis, not health care. Addressing health care first was about keeping the liberals happy. In January 1994 Moynihan, whose patience had worn thin, called Clinton's bluff. "Ending welfare as we know it" was just talk, "boob bait for the Bubbas." If the administration didn't get serious about a welfare bill, Moynihan hinted, he'd use his own position as Senate Finance Committee chair to hold up the health-care plan.[13]

When Clinton finally introduced his welfare bill in June, he could not get it past a coalition of Democrats who did not want to limit benefits and Republicans who did not want to lose a wedge issue right before an election. With things going their way, Republicans preferred to leave the welfare boil unlanced. They got help from an unexpected quarter, left-liberals in the administration who leaked damaging stories suggesting that welfare reform would not work or that Clinton was not really serious about it.[14]

Clinton was serious about reforming welfare and later admitted he should have tackled it first. Americans overwhelmingly supported making recipients work, though in a way that did not leave them or their kids destitute. Failure to capitalize on that sentiment left Clinton banging his head against the wall, and historians scratching theirs. If he had led off with welfare-to-work, his centrist credentials, bolstered by the budget deal and NAFTA, would have been unassailable. He could have leveraged them into better health care—another winner in the polls—and left Republicans banging their heads. The political future turned on the mistakes of 1993–1994. Granted, Clinton had little fiscal room for maneuver. Cost was an issue for any new program. He also had to contend with the lemmings in his own party and the spoiler tactics of Republicans, intent on killing his bills without leaving fingerprints. His best chance was to make a stand against both factions. Welfare reform offered the most favorable political ground.[15]

Clinton paid for his errors. "He managed to unite doctors, insurers, gun owners, religious conservatives, motorcyclists, smokers, country-club Republicans, and blue-collar workers," remembered Mark Souder, one of the Republican congressmen elected in 1994. At meetings tattooed long-hairs, cigarettes dangling from their lips, rose to support him. Gingrich saw that he could turn the midterm elections into a national referendum against big government and one-party control. He had Republican candidates sign "The Contract with America," a manifesto of lower taxes, longer sentences, tort and welfare reform, term limits and other issues popular with Reagan and Perot voters. Though the Contract was only a set of talking points, the resentment Gingrich meant to tap was real. By November 1994, 65 percent of Americans said the country was on the wrong track, a record that stood until the second Iraq War went sour. Clinton's fumbling enabled Gingrich to achieve what George H. W. Bush had not, the reunification of the Reagan coalition.[16]

Gingrich made sure the Contract avoided sexual issues. Otherwise, he told Ralph Reed, liberal columnists would spend two weeks writing about the religious right and the GOP. Besides, Clinton had whistled up his own religious opposition. Early in his administration, when news broke that he was preparing to lift the ban on gays in the military, Robertson had his viewers deluge Capitol Hill with phone calls. Dole wondered aloud whether the president's "top defense priority" wasn't repayment for all those gay activists and "Hollywood elites" who donated to his campaign. When Clinton realized his cause was futile, that Congress would pass veto-proof legislation authorizing dismissal, he acquiesced to a policy of "don't ask, don't tell." But the White House and Justice Department went ahead and added sexual orientation to their own nondiscrimination policies.[17]

Clinton's stance on abortion was, if anything, more provocative. With Hillary urging him on, he promptly reversed restrictions imposed by his Republican predecessors. He salted pro-life wounds by signing the orders on the twentieth anniversary of *Roe*. He tried, and failed, to get Congress to repeal the Hyde Amendment. He succeeded in placing two pro-choice justices on the Supreme Court. They saw to it that *Roe* marked other anniversaries.

By 1994 conservative religious opposition to Clinton had reached fever pitch. The man who did the most to mobilize it was Ralph Reed. His fast-growing Christian Coalition distributed 33 million "voter guides" that selectively distorted Democratic candidates' records. Reed also benefited from a wave of mostly Democratic retirements, which left open an unusually large number of seats, and from Pat Robertson's daily attacks on the president. Turnout soared. Religious conservatives, who had cast a quarter of all votes in 1992, cast a third in 1994. They gave 70 percent of their votes to Republicans, who drew 40 percent of their total support from

Evangelicals and morally conservative Catholics. Representative Dave Mc-Curdy, a popular Oklahoma congressman and Clinton DLC ally, summed up his defeat for an open Senate seat with "God, gays, and guns."[18]

That fall the GOP gained a net of eleven governorships, fifty-two House seats, and eight Senate seats—nine after Alabama's Richard Shelby switched parties. The Democrats lost the South, the Congress, and nearly half the state legislative chambers, where Republicans approached parity for the first time since FDR. Democratic heavyweights, including House Speaker Tom Foley, went down to defeat. Mario Cuomo, who had unwisely refused Clinton's offer of a Supreme Court appointment, lost the New York governorship. Ann Richards met the same fate in Texas, putting George W. Bush on the road to the presidency. The Dow rose 30 points before the polls closed on leaked exit-interview results. Republican conservatives had never ridden higher. "Let the show trials begin," Viguerie remembered thinking. "This finally," Robert Novak gloated, "was the realigning election I had awaited for a generation."[19]

Trench Warfare

Big-time Washington journalists like Novak generally attributed the Clintons' early failures to excessive ambition and amateur indiscipline. If they had refrained from shooting the moon on health care, exercised firmer control over their agenda and image, charmed the press and Georgetown establishment, and better managed a series of minor embarrassments, such as the requests for Whitewater papers, they would not have been repudiated in the 1994 elections.

There is, however, another way to interpret the events of 1994. Bill Clinton's first two years closely resembled John Kennedy's. As of November 1962, Kennedy had signed few laws save for the benefit of large corporations, confused everyone about his pro-business policies by delivering a tongue-lashing to price-hiking steel executives, failed to secure health insurance for the elderly, dithered on civil rights, and presided over a crisis-driven foreign policy. He took astonishing sexual risks, including affairs with a nineteen-year-old intern and his own wife's press secretary. Yet he also took a 61 percent approval rating into the midterm elections. The Democrats gained three Senate seats and lost only four seats in the House. First ladies aside, the difference was that Kennedy's failures occurred in a congenial institutional and media environment. Clinton's occurred in a competitive, polarized, and scandal-obsessed one.[20]

In 1970, when Moynihan told Nixon he was outgunned, he meant that left-liberals commanded the institutional strongholds. From them they could beat back attacks and sally forth to conquer new territory. By 1993, however, right-conservatives had built fortifications of their own. These included think tanks like the Heritage Foundation, litigation shops like the American Center for Law and Justice, Evangelical schools like Liberty University, and advocacy groups like the Federalist Society. Though their agendas varied, they all enjoyed the patronage of conservative donors, corporations, and foundations. They also benefited from the rise of direct mail, subsidized "opinion-leading" magazines, conservative publishing houses, and talk radio. The *Drudge Report,* an Internet news-and-rumor site, and the *Fox News Channel,* a cable and satellite network, came on line after Clinton took office, but in time to compound his woes.

The think tanks functioned as disciplined alternative universities, with a hierarchy that ran from summer interns to sinecured counterintelligentsia. Republican presidential dominance in the 1980s and congressional dominance after 1994 offered postgraduate training for ambitious young conservatives as staffers, lobbyists, and federal appointees. These jobs taught them that amending social policy required patience and preparation. Inertia and vested interests worked against change on Capitol Hill, where the default vote was no. But when dramatic events got the attention of the president and the congressional leadership, change became possible. Institutions with off-the-shelf plans, a well-framed message, and a Rolodex of talking heads had the advantage when the policy window opened. The conservative institutional renaissance created a shadow government.

New and alternative media gave its shadow ministers an unfiltered outlet for their views, broadening the policy debate and extending the spectrum of ideas rightward. They also provided outlets for shrewd polemicists like Ann Coulter. A latter-day Clare Luce—in fact, a fan of Luce—Coulter perfected the blonde-who-hates-liberals act. Her polemics sold briskly. But so did the books of more phlegmatic conservatives, who benefited when conservative foundations duplicated Nixon's trick of subsidized purchases. Best-sellerdom enabled them to book a string of talk-show interviews and get their ideas out to the real audience.[21]

The most influential host, Rush Limbaugh, usually dispensed with guests, relying on monologues and call-ins to sustain the attack. The odd duck in a family of Republican lawyers and judges—young Rusty liked radio and sports—Limbaugh created a solo act that combined the *National Review* with the *National Lampoon*. Economic conservatives loved his ideology, moral conservatives his jibes at political correctness. Though Limbaugh could be thoughtful, he knew his ratings depended on authoritarian rants and dismissive insults, the frat-house equivalents of Coulter's sorority-queen put-downs. Limbaugh was at least frank about his primary motive. He wanted "to attract the largest possible audience I can so I can charge confiscatory ad rates." The Clintons put him in a position to do just that.[22]

When critics accused Limbaugh and other conservative impresarios of bias, their invariable response was they were simply balancing liberal bias. Try finding pro-life women in New York newsrooms, Ailes said. Establishment journalists skewed to the moral and economic left, and voted overwhelmingly for Clinton. Yet, if that were true, why did organizations like the *New York Times* join the Clinton hunt begun by billionaire Richard Mellon Scaife and conservative organs like *The American Spectator?*[23]

The answer is that three independent events—the Watergate apotheosis of Woodward and Bernstein, the growing public fascination with celebrity scandal, and the intensified competition among proliferating media—had transformed political journalism from a high-toned profession into a klieg-lit roust. The filtered coverage of Kennedy's day collapsed in the face of constant pressure for stories that cut politically. Matt Drudge teared up when he hit "Enter" for his Lewinsky scoop. He knew that his life was about to change. Sure enough, Limbaugh read his reports on the air, the mainstream media took up the story, and he was a made man.[24]

Conservative muckrakers had an abundance of sources. Another post-Watergate development, the 1978 Ethics in Government Act, enabled the attorney general to appoint independent prosecutors to investigate criminal allegations against White House officials. Clinton, thinking actual innocence would protect him, asked Attorney General Janet Reno to clear the air by appointing an independent counsel. In August 1994 a three-judge panel with a conservative majority used perceived conflict of interest as a pretext to replace Robert Fiske, the original counsel. Fiske had fallen from Republican favor. His replacement, Kenneth Starr, was more to their liking, though not the president's. Making matters worse, the November election put Republicans in charge of the congressional banking committees, providing another base from which to investigate

Whitewater and leak damaging information. The "vast right-wing conspiracy," Bill Clinton later remarked, hardly seemed a conspiracy at all. It was wide open and operated with remarkable boldness.[25]

Clinton recalled a conversation he had with Wyoming Senator Alan Simpson in October 1995. Simpson was a Republican, but friendly. The fact that there was nothing to Whitewater, he told Clinton, wouldn't make it go away. The press may have voted for him, but they thought like his enemies. Clinton asked him what he meant. "Democrats like you . . . get into government to help people," Simpson said. "The right-wing extremists don't think government can do much to improve on human nature, but they do like power. So does the press. And since you're President, they both get power the same way, by hurting you."[26]

Clinton brooded on these words for months. When he finally decided that Simpson was right, he felt liberated, freed from his fatuous dream of collective progress. If his enemies hated him and envied his power, there was nothing to do but go on fighting, even after the bell had rung. Whitewater dragged on for fourteen months after he left the White House. Elections resolved nothing. Politics had become nonstop partisan warfare, driven by bilious resentment and endless polling. Nixon had set the ball rolling, mounting his permanent campaign because he imagined his enemies were always campaigning against him. But Clinton, facing implacable and sophisticated opposition, had no choice. What he regretted was that he and Hillary had made matters worse by hoisting the Old Democrat flag over their lines in 1993. Their enemies in the freshly dug trenches opposite had only to zero in, cry "Remember Bork!" and fire away.[27]

White Hats and Black

The man who led their charge over the top was Newt Gingrich. After the 1994 election, the incoming House speaker mocked the humiliated president and first lady as "McGovernicks." The 1960s-driven civil war was over, Gingrich said. The New Reconstruction would marry the entrepreneurial freedom of the digital age to the wisdom of the Victorians. Its revitalized work ethic would bring the ghetto-centered nightmare of pregnant teens, gang-bangers, AIDS, and illiteracy to an end.[28]

Gingrich was himself a fair specimen of the work ethic. The product of a doomed teenage marriage, he grew up with his mother and artillery-officer stepfather in a peripatetic army family. He could not finish, he told a reporter, *The Great Santini,* Pat Conroy's autobiographical novel about a son's struggle to live up to the expectations of his overbearing Marine father. Mad for animals, lists, and books, near-sighted, bespectacled, and flat-footed, Gingrich was not the warrior type, though he did become fascinated with all things martial. A visit to Verdun, where he glimpsed bones piled in an ossuary, taught him that the fates of nations hang on the decisions of political leaders. He fantasized that he was the brainy hero who would save Western civilization, inflicting on one teacher a 200-page, single-spaced paper on the balance of naval power. "I think," Gingrich said, "I was pretty weird as a kid."[29]

Gingrich's dream of salvation was secular and revolutionary. Like the campus radicals, he wanted to defy corrupt authorities and smash their institutions. The difference lay in his ultimate target, the welfare state. Though he appreciated the wisdom of tongue-clucking over a crapulous culture, Gingrich was not religious. Like Clinton, he had earned degrees at prominent universities before teaching college and plunging into politics. He won his House seat in 1978, the same year Clinton became Arkansas governor. Gingrich shared his contemporary's enthusiasm for grand ideas, though he could be strident about them, the professor unwinding before a captive audience. "Newt Gingrich was the worst guy to have at the tip of the spear," lamented Randall Terry. "He was mean. He was angry. He was too pompous."[30]

Clinton thought Gingrich missed a chance for a historic debate. Did Clinton's third way represent the best response to the emerging global information economy? Or did Gingrich's libertarian vision? That was a fair fight. What drove Clinton crazy—but gave him an opening—was the way Gingrich insisted on moralizing it. "The core of his argument was not just that his ideas were better than ours," Clinton wrote, "he said his *values* were better than ours, because Democrats were weak on family, work, welfare, crime, and defense, and because, being crippled by the self-indulgent sixties, we couldn't draw distinctions between right and wrong." Instead of exchanging new ideas, Gingrich wanted to exploit old liberal stereotypes. The obvious counter was to depict him as a blowhard and extremist.[31]

The man who showed Clinton how to do this was Dick Morris, a cocksure political consultant with a take-it-from-me style. He was trolling for clients when he met Clinton in Little Rock in 1977. Clinton talked faster and thought more strategically than any Southerner Morris had ever met. They dished for hours, taking lunch at Clinton's desk.

Morris tutored Clinton on the polling and public relations aspects of the business, and advised Clinton during his 1978 gubernatorial campaign, which he won handily.[32]

In the statehouse, the wonder boy proceeded to take on too many issues, rile up too many constituents, and raise a too-conspicuous tax on license plates. He made another mistake in parting company with the abrasive Morris, who told him that he was going to lose the 1980 election. He did. A humbled Clinton asked Morris to craft his 1982 comeback, which featured Clinton apologizing for his mistakes. Hillary apologized in her own way, changing her married name from Rodham to Clinton. Morris stayed on as consultant, advising Clinton until 1990, when the two volatile men again parted in anger.[33]

After Clinton became president, Morris reprised his role of Machiavelli to the rescue. Using Hillary as a conduit, he remained in touch, warning of the 1994 congressional tsunami. The survivors turned to him after it struck. Though Morris remained in the shadows, meeting only with the Clintons and a small group of White House advisers, his influence over domestic policy and campaign strategy eventually rivaled Hillary's. He dominated meetings, rattling off numbers from his pocket computer and telling everyone what they had to do to win. He reminded George Stephanopoulos of Dustin Hoffman's autistic savant in *Rain Man,* except that Morris looked like a pompadoured sausage. Stephanopoulos hated him. So did most of the inner circle, who watched with glee as the *consigliere* had to resign during the August 1996 convention. Morris's obsessions, a tabloid revealed, included the toes of his favorite call girl.[34]

The Morris who advised the president in the mid-1990s was in other respects a different man from the one Clinton met in 1977. Though he had worked for McGovern, Morris had come to disdain Democratic weakness on social spending, crime, welfare, defense, and the economy. Voters wanted hard-headed policies to deal with hard problems, not posturing or bickering. He told Clinton to embrace the parts of the Gingrich agenda the public embraced and to oppose the parts the public thought extreme or mean-spirited. He should apologize again, but in a measured way. Reactionary politics were like the doses of digitalis or other poisons doctors prescribed. Titrate to the right amount, and the patient improved; overshoot the mark, and the patient died. Instead of vital signs, Dr. Morris had polls on every imaginable subject, from tobacco marketing to public school uniforms—both of which made surprise appearances in the 1996 State of the Union address.

Clinton also got help from his enemies, none more so than Timothy McVeigh. The embittered Gulf War veteran wanted to teach the federal government a lesson for taking away guns and suppressing dissent. McVeigh designed a truck bomb with fellow conspirator Terry Nichols, then drove it to Oklahoma City on the morning of April 19, 1995. The date marked the second anniversary of the fiery federal raid on an armed compound near Waco, Texas, in which David Koresh and scores of his Branch Davidian followers had died. McVeigh parked in front of the Murrah Federal Building, lit two fuses, the second to be sure, and walked away. He killed 168 people, including 3 pregnant women and 19 children, most of them in the employee day-care center. Federal bureaucrats did not look so faceless any more.[35]

McVeigh presented Clinton with the most golden of presidential opportunities, the chance to denounce terrorists as "evil cowards," console the shocked nation, and lead the effort to bring mass killers to justice. "A. Temporary gain: boost in ratings," Morris wrote to Clinton. "B. More permanent gain: Improvements in character/personality attributes—remedies weakness, incompetence, ineffectiveness found in recent poll. C. Permanent possible gain: sets up Extremist Issue vs. Republicans." It did not hurt that the bombing occurred against a backdrop of rising violence against abortion clinics and providers. Arsons, bombings, and shootings spiked in 1993 and 1994, after the 1992 *Casey* decision and presidential election frustrated more conventional means of combating abortion.[36]

Then Republicans lit a fuse of their own. The main domestic fight in 1995, as in 1993, was over the budget. Gingrich demanded big cuts in taxes and spending, including occupational safety and environmental protection. Clinton proposed modest trims, confining tax cuts to the middle class and sparing health and education. Many congressional Democrats disliked his compromise proposal, but the public found it reasonable. Morris loved the idea of the president brokering a deal between bickering parties. The trick was to avoid giving away too much.

In November Congress passed budget resolutions that, among other provocations, cut education funding and canceled a scheduled decrease in Medicare premiums. If Clinton vetoed them, the government would run out of operating funds. Confronting the leadership just before the shutdown, he said, "If you want to pass your budget, you're going to have to put somebody else in this chair. I don't care what happens." Gingrich looked stunned. He'd underestimated his enemy. The irresistible force of his revolution had just met the as-yet-immovable object of a presidential veto.[37]

When the government began suspending nonemergency operations the next day, Clinton had agency heads prepare lists of their most popular services. Nobody liked closed national parks or shuttered Social Security and passport offices. Absence provoked, if not fondness, then recognition of the large role government played in daily life. A quarter of Americans blamed the president for the crisis, half the Republican leadership. It was a clear win for Clinton.[38]

The two sides agreed to temporarily restore funding. But then the government shut down again, this time for three weeks, when Clinton vetoed another take-it-or-leave-it Republican budget. "Most people don't commit suicide twice," Morris wrote, "but Gingrich did." He alienated pensioners, independents, white Southerners, and Reagan Democrats. Reagan, in fact, had refused to provoke a similar shutdown to force Democrats to cut budgets. "I wear the white hat," Reagan told a conservative activist, "and the man in the white hat doesn't force that kind of crisis." Clinton had absorbed the Master's lessons and improved on them. He had twice vetoed cuts, switched hats in the process, and let Gingrich take the blame. "Clinton's essential insight and his political salvation," wrote biographer John Harris, was that "people might not like government in the abstract, but they like it in the particulars that touch their own lives."[39]

No better epitaph could be written for the failure of small-government conservatism after Nixon. Gingrich's cry for revolution had again fallen on deaf ears, except among libertarian intellectuals and New Right activists, who were furious when the Republican leadership caved in January and settled on the president's terms. But the number of true small-government conservatives was small, no more than one voter in ten. Another 22 percent claimed to be conservative, yet, when questioned, favored more public spending for preferred causes. They shunned the liberal label because they also favored things like the death penalty and school discipline. Clinton wanted to shun the label too. If, with Gingrich's clumsy help, he could add these pro-spending "conflicted conservatives" to the Democratic base, he would be unbeatable.[40]

Footwork

Clinton had to be careful, though. He had gotten his symbolic wires crossed more than once. He knew conservatives still had momentum on issues of personal responsibility. That momentum kept him from doing things he wanted to do, like refining drug policy. It also pushed him toward doing things he did not want to do, like signing a Republican welfare bill.

By the mid-1990s the excesses of the drug war were obvious, as was its failure to curtail the black market. But the libertarian solution, taxed sales to adults, remained politically radioactive. One reason Clinton fired Surgeon General Joceyln Elders, in December 1994, was that her controversial remarks about teaching masturbation in school followed earlier and equally controversial remarks about studying drug legalization. Yet proponents of a broader harm-reduction agenda—more treatment, more equitable penalties, more needle-exchange programs—had a plausible case. Their nimbler, thriftier, evidence-based policies fit the third-way model.

Only their timing was off. Adolescent cannabis use began ticking up in 1992. Heroin made a comeback in bohemian and fashion circles. Amphetamine, seemingly vanquished in the 1970s, returned via meth labs, prescription diversion, and club drugs. With editorialists warning against drug-war retreat, Clinton was in no position to embrace harm reduction. Nor could he embrace a recommendation to reduce penalties for crack distribution and money laundering. There was no way, he said in October 1995, that he would "let anyone who peddles drugs get the idea that the cost of doing business is going down."[41]

Three months later Clinton nominated General Barry McCaffrey as his new drug czar. A decorated Vietnam and Desert Storm veteran whose only pertinent experience was interdicting drug trafficking while head of the Southern Command, McCaffrey had reluctantly taken the job after his father told him to "shut up and do what the president tells you to do." Clinton introduced McCaffrey during his January 1996 State of the Union address, the same speech in which he declared "the era of big government is over." It was not, of course, and neither was the drug war. Having cut the drug czar's staff in 1993, Clinton pledged to restore a full complement of personnel. The promised beef-up and McCaffrey's appointment provoked cries of cynical maneuver. They did not bother Morris, who wanted the rightward tacking to be as blatant as possible.[42]

McCaffrey disliked the war metaphor. He thought fighting drugs was like fighting cancer, something sustained, holistic, and guided by medical advice. He recommended reducing the crack-sentencing disparity. He backed drug courts to get users into treatment. But he drew the line at federal funding of needle-exchange programs. Clinton's health advisers wanted to distribute sterile needles to prevent infections. McCaffrey thought that was like handing car keys to a drunk. It undercut the message that drugs were wrong and deadly. He forwarded letters to the White House from conservative allies who saw the plan as welfare for junkies, a subsidy for immorality, and a sop to the AIDS crowd. Fifty-seven percent of the public strongly opposed the scheme. "There's just no way we could have done it," Clinton said later. Needles for addicts had gays in the military written all over it. The price of this political realism was a rate of new HIV infections twice what it would have been had the government backed needle exchange. If the wages of sin were death, so were those of expediency.[43]

Moynihan and many other Democrats feared that political expediency would also endanger poor children. Though he favored AFDC reform, Moynihan fretted that Clinton would let Republicans gut the system. He suspected that they planned to use the savings to offset another tax cut for the rich without providing the means to move poor, single mothers from welfare to work. The administration that had just proposed history's most gargantuan entitlement program, Moynihan reflected bitterly, now appeared ready to abandon kids whose sole offense was having been born to the wrong parents. "Thus ends the progressive era."[44]

Far shrewder was the assessment of an anonymous administration official who said that AFDC was the bone the White House could toss to the hounds baying at the welfare state's door. Clinton and ascendant centrist advisers like Bruce Reed and Rahm Emanuel just wanted to leave as little meat on the bone as possible. In late 1995 and early 1996, Clinton vetoed the first two Republican welfare-reform bills. Too weak on work, he said, too tough on kids. But each time they revised the legislation it became harder to say no. Dole, who had nailed down the GOP nomination by mid-March, was playing a titration game of his own. The perfect Republican bill had just enough poison to make it hard for Clinton to swallow, but not enough to make it easy for him to explain a veto. Democrats who wanted to save AFDC winked at the strategy. Once again, it looked like Clinton had been backed into a corner.[45]

He broke out on July 31, 1996. He had no objection to replacing AFDC with temporary welfare assistance and work requirements. But he hated the blatantly political provisions like food stamp restrictions or the denial of benefits to legal immigrants. The whole thing, he decided, was "a decent welfare bill wrapped in a sack of shit." Old civil rights allies saw only the sack. They wanted another veto. So did most of the cabinet. Morris dissented. Kill the bill, and you'll be three points behind Dole. Sign it and you'll be fifteen points up. Early television advertising in key states had pitched Clinton as a sensible centrist. Signing would confirm it and assure victory. Reed reminded him that a veto could also cost congressional seats. This was his best, and maybe his last, chance to deliver on welfare reform. Clinton agreed. He broke the news himself, telling reporters he would sign the third version of the bill. He would try to amend its flaws later, but he wanted to help people escape the trap of welfare dependency.[46]

When other presidents signed legislation that party activists considered wrapped in shit, they paid a steep price. Every sitting president from Ford on who lost a general election did so at a time of rebellion in the base. Clinton himself worried that a dissident faction would make noise at the August convention. Maybe, he joked, he should sneak "welfare reform" into a string of applause lines and whisper the words so that nobody heard them. He need not have worried. DNC staff simply flipped the welfare plank, which sailed through the platform committee. Given what had happened to other presidents, particularly Carter, why were activists so willing to accommodate Clinton?[47]

There were, for starters, the lessons of the recent past. Having witnessed the disasters of 1980–1994, left-liberals decided they could live with welfare reform, along with school uniforms and benefit caps. Just as importantly, Clinton was temperamentally *simpático*. Though fond of market incentives, he remained progressive in his ends. Even his womanizing confirmed, in a backhanded way, his moral-left leanings. To those who thought Clinton had sacrificed too much of the soul of the Democratic Party, Representative Barney Frank tellingly replied, "What was our soul? He stuck with us on affirmative action, on choice, on gay rights, on immigration. What was our soul?" Clinton had the right moral enemies.[48]

He also had the right political ones. Early in the primaries, it looked as if the flamboyant Buchanan might actually win the GOP nomination if he managed to throttle back a little. Buchanan eked out a win in New Hampshire, but then showed up for the pivotal Arizona primary with a black cowboy hat and a shotgun. He slipped to third. Dole rallied his party and corporate backers, bought lots of television, won South Carolina and then a string of March primaries. His chief virtue was safety. If he lost, he would not drag the GOP down with him. Clinton fantasized about a showdown with Black Pat. But he knew, as Morris put it, that Republicans "don't nominate nuts for president."[49]

Clinton studied Dole during the 1995 budget negotiations. He watched how he would nod when Gore or Chief of Staff Leon Panetta suggested a likely compromise. "But then Gingrich or Armey speaks up," Clinton told Morris, "and he pulls his head in like a turtle and says nothing. He really let those guys run him." Dole shared Bush's predicament. The logical nominee by dint of long service—at seventy-three, he was the oldest major-party candidate in American history—Dole's cautious pragmatism held little appeal for libertarians. They saw him as a deal-maker, a Nixon-style pro. Religious conservatives were just as wary. They knew Dole had voted against abortion, but suspected him of big-tent tendencies.[50]

Dole stuck to the conservative script. He attacked Jocelyn Elders, the United Nations, bureaucrats, drug dealers, liberal judges, and Hollywood's "nightmares of depravity." Activists also gave Dole points for his vice presidential pick, Jack Kemp, who was popular in free-market and Christian Coalition circles. Even so, Evangelical turnout was under 50 percent in November. It was as if religious conservatives had become the blacks of the Republican Party. The danger was less that they would vote for the other party than that they would not vote at all.[51]

Clinton made it hard for Dole to whip up enthusiasm on traditional Republican issues. Welfare had been reformed. The deficit was coming down. So was crime, which a quarter of Republicans actually thought Clinton better able to handle. "Clinton had good footwork," Dole admitted. He knew how to skim centrist and conservative votes, adding them to his Democratic blocs. His one big foreign-policy crisis, Bosnia, had subsided. He did not mention foreign affairs until fifty minutes into his convention speech. Most crucially, the hard fiscal decisions he had made in 1993 had fostered recovery. The election, Dole thought, was less a referendum on Clinton than on the economy, which was in good shape. One dead-on cartoon had a housewife in hair curlers telling a pollster, "I'm for the scumbag." Clinton won nearly half the popular votes. Dole got 41 percent. The rest went to Perot and other third-party candidates.[52]

Republicans fared better in Congress, losing eight seats in the House and gaining two in the Senate. Robert Novak breathed a sigh of relief. Realignment was intact. Other Republicans were not so sure. Clinton had come back from the dead. He had trounced Dole 379 electoral votes to 159. Ralph Reed and his Christian Coalition, masters of the political universe two years before, had been powerless to stop their nemesis. "He was so against their interests," Weyrich said, "yet he won so clearly."[53]

J'accuzi

Weyrich was about to witness a resurrection still more astonishing. Sure of his footing now, and facing a more compliant Gingrich, Clinton spent the first six months of his second term working out a new budget deal. It balanced the federal budget and provided a tax cut, but increased spending on children's health care and education and restored the welfare benefits to legal immigrants sacrificed in 1996. What made these miracles possible was fast growth and ample revenue. Anticipating a government surplus and fearing that Republicans would attempt to divert it into a tax cut, Clinton planted a rhetorical question in his January 1998 State of the Union Address. "What should we do with this projected surplus?" he asked. "I have a simple four-word answer: Save Social Security first." Democrats jumped to their feet and roared. Gingrich and the stunned Republicans followed with reluctant applause. "In that instant," thought speechwriter Michael Waldman, "a trillion dollars silently shifted on the budget ledger from the column marked 'tax cut' to the column marked 'Social Security.' "[54]

More remarkably, Clinton gave that address in the shadow of a sex scandal so spectacular that his survival prompted a flabbergasted Weyrich and other religious conservatives to despair of victory in the Culture War. It began on November 15, 1995, during the first government shutdown, when Monica Lewinsky, an unpaid, twenty-two-year-old White House intern, flirted with a very interested president. Lewinsky was a *zaftig* Susan Stern, a lost-puppy rich girl whose fantasy object happened to be Bill Clinton rather than Bernardine Dohrn. They carried on a hugger-mugger, eighteen-month affair whose erotic details were evoked by Lewinsky's gifts: knee pads with the presidential seal, edible gummy boobs, a phone-sex novel, and an antique cigar holder.

Lewinsky blabbed about the affair to a confidante, Linda Tripp, who taped and betrayed her. Attorneys for Paula Jones, a former Arkansas state employee whose sexual harassment suit against Clinton the Supreme Court had allowed to go forward, added Lewinsky to their witness list. Jones's attorneys, backed by conservative activists, wanted corroborative sexual evidence and dirt on the president. On December 17, 1997, a worried Clinton called Lewinsky in the small hours. He suggested that she

Figure 20 The State of the Union, January 27, 1998. Sidestepping the Lewinsky affair, Clinton delivered a confident, policy-packed speech interrupted for applause 104 times. Any budget surplus, he declared, should first go toward stabilizing Social Security—a welfare winner that caught the Republicans off guard. Newt Gingrich looks on: outmaneuvered again.

could avoid deposition by signing an affidavit. This she did on January 7, 1998. She denied any sexual involvement. Clinton friend Vernon Jordan helped her find a job in New York City. When the president was deposed in the Jones case, on January 17, he denied sexual relations with the intern, a friendly gal who delivered pizza and documents.

He had just walked into another trap. Starr asked for and got permission to expand his Whitewater probe to include perjury and obstruction of justice in the Jones case. On January 16 his operatives confronted Lewinsky with evidence that she had lied in her deposition. They pressed her to testify. On January 21, six days before the State of the Union address, the story broke in the national press. Clinton denied it, saying he had not had "sexual relations with that woman." What he meant was that he had not had vaginal intercourse. Over the next six months Starr used grand jury testimony and an immunity deal with Lewinsky to assemble evidence, including a semen spill on Lewinsky's blue dress, that proved he had done just about everything else.

That August Clinton reluctantly came clean. He confessed to a furious, sobbing Hillary. He lied, he said, to protect her and Chelsea. On August 17 he admitted sexual intimacy to the grand jury, but clung to his definitional defense. On television he admitted misleading others about the relationship but rebuked Starr for prying into his private life. Starr returned fire on September 9, presenting his referral to the House Judiciary Committee. On September 11 the committee presented it to the world. Full of prim pornographic detail, *The Starr Report* read like a prosecutorial novel, complete with an omniscient narrator, devoted to a single theme. We nailed you. Leave now. Stay and face impeachment.

Clinton later claimed that the impeachment crusade was retaliation for luring his fellow white Southerners away from the politics of division that enabled the wealthy few to maintain power by demonizing minorities. So they had demonized him and tried to drive him from office. At its deepest level, though, the scandal had less to do with calculated exploitation than with sex, morality, and temperament, the basic emotive divisions of the Culture War. Opposing letter-writers called Clinton a degenerate creep and a lying weasel and Starr a fanatical reincarnation of Joe McCarthy. World War II veterans were particularly hard on Clinton, seeing his immorality and his draft-dodging as two sides of the same selfish coin. Left-liberal Jews were particularly vituperative toward Starr, about whom they detected a distinct whiff of pogrom. Clinton consistently got his highest approval ratings from Jews and blacks, his lowest from the group notionally his own, white Evangelicals. With Starr, it was just the reverse. There was also a decadal divide. Starr symbolized the 1950s, Clinton the 1960s. Supporting or denouncing Clinton after Starr's revelations became a way of voting on the 1960s.[55]

Both sides understood this at the time. "I hate Clinton . . . ," said Harvey Golden, a Houston salesman. "He's a product of the '60s, and he has no sense of morality." "Thank God for the '60s!" countered New Yorker Alisa Mitchell. "The '60s got us more personal freedom and the right to abortion. That may be in danger now, if the right wins this war." "You want to know why the left swallows hard and defends Clinton?" asked Sidney Zion, a New York City writer. "It's because they don't want to give a victory to the racist scum, the anti-abortionists and the Christian right. That's who's trying to bring him down, and that's what's at stake here."[56]

Zion's point applied with special force to feminists. Clinton had done things with young subordinates that Clarence Thomas had only dreamed of doing and had betrayed the First Feminist in the process. The logic of Monica plus "the personal is political" was his nuts in a sack. But feminists saw Starr's supporters as implacable enemies of their own liberation. Betty Friedan, Gloria Steinem, Kate Michelman, Geraldine Ferraro—the big feminist and pro-choice names lined up behind Clinton. "They had to dance with who brung 'em," said Randall Terry. Journalist Nina Burleigh said she would be happy to perform for the president the same sexual favor he was accused of receiving from Lewinsky "just to thank him for keeping abortion legal." Weyrich thought abortion the core of the Bork, Thomas, and Clinton fights. "If abortion hadn't been the issue, we would have had an entirely different result with Bork," he said. "Thomas almost didn't survive because of the abortion issue and, again, I think people supported Clinton *because* of the abortion issue."[57]

Hillary Clinton faced a tougher choice. "A lot of people thought I just should have thrown his clothes off the Truman Balcony and kicked him out of the house," she confided to her friend Diane Blair, "but you know, it's just not that easy." It wasn't that easy because of her daughter, her faith, her ambition, and her love for Bill. Then there was her hatred for the man who rubbed her nose in his infidelities. Starr was worth ten marriage counselors. Hillary stayed in Bill's corner, if no longer in his bed. She threw herself into the fall congressional races, campaigning for Democratic candidates in twenty states. "She was on fire," said an awed observer. Polls showed that every Democratic candidate she supported got a lift.[58]

Polls showed something else, record levels of personal popularity for Hillary Clinton and strong support for her husband's record, if not his character. Starr's apparent prurience offset Clinton's personal failings. So did the surging Dow, up more than 6,000 points on his watch. Republican determination to make his conduct an issue in the fall elections backfired. Gingrich, whistling in the graveyard, predicted a pickup of twenty-two House seats. The Republicans lost five. Exit polls showed that six in ten voters ignored the scandal in picking candidates. Two in ten used their votes to register support *for* Clinton; two in ten their opposition. Overall, 60 percent said they opposed impeachment. Over half approved Clinton's job performance.[59]

The biggest loser was Gingrich. He had been moving toward wary collaboration with the president in late 1997, but had to scurry away after the scandal broke. He sat in the speaker's chair on October 8, when the House debated and approved a Republican motion for the Judiciary Committee to conduct an impeachment investigation. Gingrich thought the moral crusade a poor substitute for his fiscal one, and feared his own sexual skeletons would tumble out of the closet, as they soon did. But he had made himself a symbol of reckless partisanship in other ways, and so he took the heat for the November losses. With one whipping boy in Starr, Clinton did not need another in Gingrich. Louisiana Representative Robert Livingston and other members of the Republican caucus asked Gingrich to resign. On November 6, he stepped down as speaker and said he would leave Congress when his term expired.[60]

Livingston, Gingrich's short-lived successor, met a similar fate. Outed as an extramarital frequent flier, the speaker-designate attempted a kamikaze resignation on December 19, in the midst of the House impeachment debate. The Judiciary Committee, chaired by Henry Hyde, the venerable anti-abortion leader, had approved four articles of impeachment on party-line votes. The gist was that Clinton had tried to fix the Paula Jones case. The Democrats said that Republicans were trying to fix the election, using the scandal to unseat the president. And here was Bob Livingston, accused of kinky adulterous sex, telling Clinton to resign. "*You* resign," shouted angry Democrats. Livingston told them he would do just that and urged the president to do likewise. Clinton would not. That afternoon the House voted two articles of impeachment against him, for perjury and obstruction of justice.

Privately, many Republicans and Democrats favored a weaker censure measure. But Majority Whip Tom DeLay, the real power now among House Republicans, had worked behind the scenes to block their compromise efforts. DeLay so hated Bill Clinton that his face flushed and his neck veins bulged at the mere mention of his name. DeLay got his rage from his father, an alcoholic Texas wildcatter who freely applied his belt. Pugnacious, hard-drinking, and neglectful of his own family, DeLay had found God during his freshman year in Congress, in 1985. He wept over a James Dobson video that seemed a catalog of his own sins. He saw, as did all converts, the futility of a self-centered life. He studied the Bible. He cut out the boozing and womanizing. But sobriety did not soften his anger, which Clinton summoned as reliably as Pavlov's bell. That man had slimed his wife and daughter, the nation's honor, and truth itself. Why, he even lied about golf. Ten handicap, my ass.[61]

DeLay knew that the best way to keep Republican congressmen lined up for impeachment was to keep firing up the base with blast-faxes and radio interviews. Bob Barr and his allies on the House Judiciary Committee had been using similar tactics for months, trying to get the attention of fellow Republicans busy schmoozing with lobbyists. Rather than twisting arms himself, DeLay used fund-raisers and local party officials and talk-show hosts as surrogates. Most Republican representatives came from safe districts. The real threat to their incumbency lay in a primary challenge from the right. They were less concerned with national polls, which showed two-thirds against impeachment, than with their own activists. They voted faithfully, gave generously, and wanted Clinton out. Right-wingers, said Barney Frank, were like people who had gone to sleep in a Norman Rockwell painting and awakened in one by Hieronymus Bosch. Clinton had led Americans astray. He had lowered their moral standards, Falwell claimed, more than Hollywood, television, and drugs combined. Impeachment offered exorcism and moral renewal. Battling the devil, round II, was not optional. DeLay tapped this reservoir of righteous anger and used it to vent his own.[62]

In the end, House Republicans tied the tin can of impeachment to Clinton's tail because DeLay succeeded in making a yes vote a safe vote. Ever since the early 1960s, when the John Birch Society had begun financing the campaign to remove Earl Warren, impeachment and its threat had become increasingly important partisan weapons. That was no accident. Close national division had made the usual constitutional repair process, amendment, practically impossible during the Culture War. Feminists who wanted the ERA, or pro-lifers the Human Life Amendment, stood little chance of securing two-thirds votes in the House and Senate and then approval by three-quarters of state legislatures. The bitter standoff made the unusual constitutional repair method, impeachment, more attractive. Frustrated partisans in both camps expected their generals to point this "rusted blunderbuss" at their most perfidious enemies. The thing could always go off, or prompt the white flag of resignation. Neither was likely with Clinton, given the nature of his misconduct and the necessity of a two-thirds vote for Senate conviction. But whatever happened in the trial, House Republicans knew that they could salute and report mission accomplished. Politically, impeachment was a base-pleasing gesture, the ultimate 20 percent.[63]

If impeachment was an expedient vote, it was not an entirely free one. Impeachment unified the Democrats and made Clinton seem what he claimed to be, the victim of unrelenting partisanship. His approval rating took a four-point bounce the day after the vote and stayed in the 60 percent range for the rest of his term. "Great president from the neck up," said Morris. During his impeachment trial, a record 81 percent approved his handling of the economy. Starr's *j'accuse* left the Jacuzzi buyers unmoved. "We've got money in our pockets. Who cares?" said a Massachusetts taxi driver. Most Americans thought the scandal boiled down to private sexual conduct, not crime. "I don't want people asking questions about the President's sex life," said one married woman, "because I don't want anyone asking about mine." "From a public-relations standpoint, he's won," Pat Robertson conceded. "They might as well dismiss this impeachment hearing and get on with something else."[64]

"Although I would always regret what I had done wrong," Clinton wrote in his memoirs, "I will go to my grave being proud of what I had fought for in the impeachment battle, my last great showdown with the forces I had opposed all of my life." He had not intended to enter history as a culture warrior. He had intended to lead the country *out* of the cultural warfare that had sustained the New Right and its Reagan-cloaked successors Yes, Democrats bore their share of responsibility for the disasters of the 1960s. But liberalism's mistakes were reparable, its vital center within reach. He admitted that he had begun his mission of reclamation badly. The Republicans had made him pay in the 1994 elections. But he had come back in the 1995 budget battle, and in the 1996 and 1998 elections. That made the score three to one. With the nation basking in peace and prosperity, that should have settled things. But DeLay and his allies were seething. They used their lame-duck Congress to force one last, bitter fight. "There was nothing to do," Clinton sighed, "but suit up and take the field."[65]

On February 12, 1999, the Senate acquitted him of all charges. The final score was four to one.

11

THE ILLUSION OF CONSERVATISM

Journalists voted the Lewinsky scandal the fifty-third most significant story of the twentieth century, a piece of news that prompted Clinton to ask, "What's a man got to do to get into the top 50?" The real significance of the story, though, had less to do with his travails than with the permanence of the moral revolution. Clinton's survival shocked religious conservatives. They lamented "the death of outrage" that Bill Bennett evoked in his best-seller of the same title. "If there really were a moral majority out there," Paul Weyrich wrote in February 1999, "Bill Clinton would have been driven out of office months ago."[1]

Culture warriors like Bennett and Weyrich were not the only ones who recognized Clinton's survival as a landmark, or who used the occasion to make millennial pronouncements. Alan Wolfe, a sociologist who studied the beliefs of ordinary Americans, and who was impressed by their growing toleration of moral differences, remarked in 1999 that "the right won the economic war, the left won the cultural war and the center won the political war." Substitute "rich people" for "the right"—a distinction often blurred—and Wolfe's words can, with a few other qualifications, be applied generally to post-1960s politics.[2]

First, the political collapse of liberalism and the old Roosevelt coalition (or, for that matter, of communism and the Soviet Union) did not mean the triumph of conservatism, moral or economic. The dreams of Bill Buckley, Adrian Rogers, and Ronald Reagan—to overturn the New Deal, to overturn the 1960s, to overturn people's reliance on government—remained unfulfilled. "America's right turn," the organizing cliché of late-twentieth-century history is, at best, a misleading half-truth.

The true part of the cliché is that moral politics and Republican power, both of marginal significance when Johnson swept into office in 1964, were enlarged and transmogrified by the populist reaction that became conspicuous after mid-1965. In exploiting this opportunity, Richard Nixon devised the durable Republican strategy of conservative symbolism and brokered policy zig-zags. The rightward zags of Nixon and his successors fell into a familiar race–class pattern, with ghetto men bearing the brunt of reaction. Race was postwar liberalism's single weakest point, before, during, and after the crisis of the late 1960s. It was also libertarianism's weakest point, in that reactionary crime and drug laws increased government's size, intrusiveness, and cost.

In contrast to race, the old hierarchy of European national origins and religious affiliation declined in political significance, as moral conservatives and liberals of different faiths formed new alliances along temperamental lines. Ethnic pluralism yielded (imperfectly) to moral pluralism, old-country neighborhoods to lifestyle neighborhoods, conflicts over creed and nationality to conflicts over personal identity and conduct. Temperamental warfare became entrenched as conservatives created their own institutions to challenge liberalism and secular humanism. Entrepreneurs built careers on the ensuing stalemate, demonstrating modern capitalism's ability to make secondary profits from problems generated by its primary activities.

In the dog's dinner of Republican policy, corporate conservatives fared better than moral ones. Paul Blanshard's offhand 1973 remark, "I am more definitely sanguine about the future of sex than about the future of socialism," was on the money. Yet, even though Republicans trimmed taxes and regulations, and attacked prevailing assumptions about government, they reined in neither popular entitlements nor overall spending. The broadest measure of their failure was national debt as a percentage of the gross domestic product. Every Democratic president from Truman through Clinton left office with that figure lower than when he entered. So did Eisenhower and Nixon. But every Republican president from Ford on left office with the debt percentage higher. Ford had to cope with recession for much of his brief presidency. Reagan and George W. Bush had no such excuse. They enjoyed partial or complete GOP congressional control for six of their eight years. The problem went beyond entrenched Democrats.[3]

Conservatism's intellectual decline was just as apparent. Buckley, James Burnham, and other *National Review* stalwarts had engaged in real debates, both with left-liberals and one another. True, Buckley was a showman and liked to lob the occasional bomb. But no one ever mistook him for a rodeo clown. People did so mistake his talk-show epigones.

They drowned out reasonable voices and reduced conservative argument to niche entertainment, pro wrestling with liberals in sheik costumes. The calculated zaniness and apocalyptic rhetoric resembled Yippie street theater, with money and war substituted for beads and love. Like the counterculture before it, conservatism degenerated into a faintly ridiculous but still lucrative national brand.[4]

Most people persist in calling that brand "conservatism." "Reaganism" would be a more accurate label for the mélange of big government, assertive foreign policy, lower taxes, higher deficits, mass imprisonment, acquisitive individualism, and moral and patriotic symbolism that became the Republican norm after 1980. The GOP's favorite intramural sport, arguing over who was or wasn't a "Reagan conservative," obscured the point that Reagan wasn't one either—not consistently. He was instead a master of optimistic illusion, the greatest in American politics since FDR.

The likeliest alternative to Reaganism was the third-way progressivism that Carter anticipated and Clinton partly achieved. Left-liberal antagonism and sabotage frustrated its development, handicapped both presidents, and intensified the disasters of 1980 and 1994. So did the Democratic identity politics that gave Republicans such a durable foil. Two, four, six, eight, here's my head, on a plate. Militancy made it simple to tap the fears of traditionalists, who understood—correctly—that progressive Democrats wanted to keep pushing the moral envelope.

Republican exploitation of Democratic cultural vulnerabilities nevertheless failed to bring about the end of legal abortion, moral conservatives' flagship issue after 1973. Ineptly handled by the Supreme Court, inherently hard to compromise, and involving existential questions of sexual responsibility, spiritual purpose, and human life, abortion was to the Culture War what slavery was to the Middle Period, the great, often unspoken matter lurking beneath, and linking, seemingly unrelated controversies. The failure to decisively restrict legal abortion was the single greatest defeat moral conservatives suffered during their apparent political ascendancy.

The failure to restrict abortion was part of a larger failure to restrict behavior once deemed criminal or deviant. The vices of the Victorian underworld had entered the mainstream and, with the exception of certain drugs, had become increasingly commercialized. The 1960s, a decade associated with civil rights, antiwar protest, and boomer *rumspringa*, had also marked a more subtle and permanent shift in American morality and marketing. What the headlines didn't show, Charles Reich remarked in

2008, the Internet did. The country had moved, and was still moving, toward less repression.[5]

The Lasting Revolution

In his memoirs, Ralph Reed itemized the moral conservatives' biggest worries. These were the decline of the traditional family, evidenced by widespread divorce, illegitimacy, teen pregnancy, and abortion; the neglect and abuse of children by absent dads, preoccupied moms, indifferent teachers, criminal predators, and drug dealers; explicit sex and violence in the media; commercialized vice; feminist and homosexual militancy; and the toleration of deviance in a revolutionized culture of anything goes. (Hence the logic of Clinton's impeachment: Anything does *not* go.) In the main, the statistical evidence bears out the reality of these trends and shows that the moral revolution that emerged full blown in the 1960s persisted through the end of the century and beyond.[6]

Nowhere was this clearer than in marriage and family life. The ratio of marriages to divorces, steady at four to one during the 1950s, fell to two to one during the 1970s and stayed there for the rest of the century. Men and women married later, or not at all. The number of cohabiting couples rose from less than half a million in 1960 to more than 5 million in 2005. In 1960 three quarters of households consisted of married couples, two-thirds of women over fourteen were married, and one infant in twenty was born out of wedlock. In 2005 fewer than half of households consisted of married couples, fewer than half of women were married, and more than one infant in three was born out of wedlock.[7]

Contraception, women's employment, divorce, and cohabitation brought about similar marital declines in Europe. What set Americans apart was their collective inability to stay put in one bed. They believed in the ideal of marriage, wrote sociologist Andrew Cherlin, but also the notion that individual unhappiness justified ending a relationship. Consequently they had more marriages and more divorces than any other Western people, and also more short-term cohabiting relationships that either ended in marriage or breakup. Sexual partnership became a carousel. Those who did not like their ponies stepped off and waited for others to come around. That included Evangelicals, whose circumspect ministers less frequently evoked biblical strictures against divorce and remarriage than those against homosexuality and abortion.[8]

In the general population, young women's approval of premarital sex rose from just 12 percent in the late 1950s to 73 percent in the late 1980s, while their average age of first intercourse fell from around nineteen to sixteen years. If boomers first did it in college, said psychologist Jean Twenge, their children first did it in high school—and a good deal more casually. Sex, explained a young woman she interviewed, had gone from marriage to love to recreation. Steady dating was for dweebs.[9]

Teen pregnancy rates rose alarmingly in the late 1980s, then declined during the 1990s. Researchers attributed the drop to more conscientious contraception and condom use. AIDS changed behavior. Teenage sexual activity also diminished, though self-reports often omitted, à la Clinton, the oral varieties. "The new third base" was more socially acceptable than intercourse and took care of the pregnancy problem. But moral conservatives could take no comfort in the trend, nor satisfaction in the news that self-reported extramarital sex was less than half of what it had been in Kinsey's day. That was simply an artifact of unhappy married couples breaking up, or happy unmarried ones shacking up.[10]

Women's participation in the labor force, both cause and consequence of changing sexual and marital behavior, rose from 37 percent in 1960 to 60 percent by century's end. In the Great Depression, when extra cash would have come in handy, more than four in five Americans disapproved of a married woman earning money if her husband could support her. During the Clinton boom, more than four in five approved. Once typecast as hubby-hunting dropouts, female students had become college all-stars. By 2001 thirteen women collected bachelor's degrees—the name itself a revealing anachronism—for every ten men. More striking was the growing presence of women in the service academies and armed forces. Women in combat, a bugbear in the ERA debate, vanished as an issue, despite the deaths of forty-eight female soldiers between 2003 and 2005. One pretty PFC, Jessica Lynch, did a turn as Helen of Troy after she was injured, captured by Iraqis, and rescued by special forces. Blondes in harm's way were fine by Fox News.[11]

As to Reed's complaints of relativism and vice, Americans had indeed become measurably more tolerant, foul-mouthed, obese, and slovenly. When Kennedy lay in state in 1963, mourners passed uniformly in somber suits, dresses, polished shoes, and skinny black ties. When Reagan lay in state in 2004, many bade their respects in casual shirts, jeans, sneakers, and even shorts. Compared to 1963, Americans in 2004 penciled in more wrong SAT answers, viewed more pornography, participated more often in the underground economy, owed more money, and filed more often for bankruptcy. They professed themselves less troubled by homosexuality, and had more openly gay and lesbian acquaintances. They smoked less, though that was because cigarettes had become a loser's vice linked to cancer and other deadly diseases.[12]

Casino revenue surged, rising from $9.6 billion in 1992 to $26.5 billion a decade later. Reed found it telling that, by century's end, 95 percent of Americans lived less than a four hours' drive from a casino, and that practically every state had some form of legal gambling. Reed's enemies found it telling that his friend, super-lobbyist Jack Abramoff, was caught working both sides of the tribal gaming street and funneling millions of Indian casino dollars to the campaigns of Republicans who nominally opposed gambling. The 2003 revelation that Bill Bennett had gambled away millions of his own dollars showed how ubiquitous the vice had become and how seductive. If the king of virtue could not resist video poker, who could? Arizona Republican Senator John McCain was almost as fond of the dice table. "Craps is addictive," he said.[13]

So was television, at least in the eyes of its critics. Program content, particularly on cable, became increasingly explicit. Edgy shows drew high ratings and advertisers stayed on board. Broadcasters quietly trimmed their internal standards departments. Gay characters and story lines proliferated. Overworked and sick of arguing, parents reached the point where they quit policing their children's viewing. Two-thirds of their bedrooms had televisions anyway. Shows aimed at teens ranked especially high in sexual content and innuendo. Movies served up sex with a double scoop of violence. MPAA ratings were supposed to give parents a measure of control while preempting unfriendly locals from establishing their own censorship boards. In practice, kids bought multiplex tickets and snuck into R-movies. "Ratings creep" insured that they got more mayhem, flesh, and profanity for their trouble.[14]

The most welcome statistical news for moral conservatives was that, during the 1990s, the number of property crimes fell by one-quarter, while the number of violent crimes and abortions declined by roughly one-fifth. The abortion drop, though, had mainly to do with an aging population, a greater willingness to bear children out of wedlock, contraceptive use, and the decline in teenage vaginal intercourse. No one in either camp thought anti-abortion protest responsible for the trend, though it did discourage medical students from considering abortion as a specialty practice. Young women continued to take choice for granted. A survey in Washington State revealed that most patients at the clinics did not know abortion had ever been illegal. Such restrictions as the Supreme Court allowed had minor effect. One, parental notification, may have increased the pressure on teenaged women to abort, mom and dad insisting that they go right ahead.[15]

In 2001 economists John Donohue III and Steven Levitt published another embarrassing piece of news. The surge of legal abortions in the 1970s and 1980s accounted for as much as half of the drop in crime in the 1990s, insofar as it had eliminated millions of unwanted (and disproportionately poor and minority) children at highest risk of becoming offenders. States that had legalized abortion first experienced the earliest drops in crime, while states with the highest abortion rates had the steepest drops. Right-conservatives faced a dilemma, which Bennett confronted in a controversial thought experiment. "You could abort every black baby in this country, and your crime rate would go down," he told a caller to his talk show. "That would be an impossible, ridiculous, and morally reprehensible thing to do, but your crime rate would go down."[16]

For all his disclaimers, Bennett had made explicit the trade-off between abortion, which many conservatives saw as a troubling but cost-effective form of race, class, and crime control, and mass incarceration, a more morally acceptable but cost-ineffective form of social termination. No wonder Republican politicians prayed that their judicial appointees would keep most abortions legal, or that they shifted the fight away from *Roe* to the safer issue of late-term, partial-birth abortions. "From the beginning, this was a Republican concept," said pro-life activist Judie Brown. "It was the least they could possibly get away with in order to receive the pro-life vote." "These guys are all fakers," Dukakis complained. "They tell their Evangelical friends they're pro-life, and they do nothing about it." Asked why Democrats didn't highlight Republican duplicity on abortion, he said, "We probably should. . . . We don't. Don't ask me why."[17]

George McGovern did have an answer. "Republicans," he said, "are better at negativism than Democrats are." The typical Democratic candidate wanted more government support for education, housing, and health care. The typical Republican had learned to say what was wrong with wanting more government assistance and with the lax morality associated with liberal policies. Reagan, Atwater, and Rove had taken Nixon's tactics to a new level, so tarring the liberals with the brush of excess and immorality that voters overlooked the Republicans' own failures to free the nation from big government and permissiveness. Only the rich had been freed from progressive taxes, at the price of record deficits—a species of fiscal hypocrisy McGovern found "maddening." Pro-life was an essential part of the deception. He did not doubt that the South Dakotans who turned him out of office in 1980 sincerely opposed abortion. But "the powers that be in the Republican Party don't really give a hang about abortion as such. They see it as a political device that works for them."[18]

Soft Religion

Thinning or otherwise, family life remained connected to religious practice. Those who avoided or delayed marriage were the least likely to be avid churchgoers. In 2001 only one in five who claimed no faith was married, compared to three in four members of the conservative Assemblies of God. Higher rates of marriage and fertility gave Evangelical churches a growth advantage. So did their richer emotional rewards, which made it easier to retain members and attract the disaffected. Outnumbered more than two to one by mainline Protestants in 1960, Evangelicals held a three-to-two edge by 2000. Yet, surprisingly, Evangelical growth did not translate into a fundamentalist makeover of American religious culture. Many observers detected the opposite—a liberalization of faith and practice even in churches that were still growing.[19]

The same was true of Catholicism. In 1963, 71 percent of the nation's 45 million Catholics attended Mass at least weekly. The number of vocations, the canary in the Church's *Gemeinschaft,* was still healthy: 10 seminarians for every 10,000 Catholics. By 1990, though, there was just 1 for every 10,000. Thanks in part to immigration, the number of Catholics kept growing, reaching 62 million by century's end. But only about a quarter of these attended weekly Mass, presided over by silver-haired priests whose average age had reached fifty-nine. If participation in the Mass and sacraments had not declined so precipitously, the bishops would have been still harder pressed to staff their parishes.[20]

Despite its official opposition to contraception and abortion, the Church no longer served as a bulwark of Victorian morality. On the contrary, it had gone on the defensive. In 2002 a long-simmering clergy sex-abuse scandal erupted in Boston and other dioceses. Moral leftists within and without the Church found a new stick with which to beat the hierarchy. Conservative Protestant clergy, who in other times would have gleefully piled on, said revealingly little. Long before the crisis, though, moral crusading had departed the parish pulpit. Richard Viguerie could remember his monsignor threatening hellfire to anyone who dared to watch Jane Russell in *The Outlaw* (1943). Now he could see more cleavage in the office on casual Fridays.[21]

Selective Catholicism became the norm. In 2005 three-quarters of Catholics told pollsters that they could still be "good Catholics" if they skipped Sunday Mass and practiced contraception. The younger the respondents, the more likely they were to hold such views. Catholicism had become another mainline denomination, a religion to which the majority remained sentimentally attached, but to which they paid less attention and obeisance, especially on matters of sexual morality. Judaism moved in the same direction. By the early twenty-first century, Reform congregations, welcoming gays and Gentile spouses and the selectively observant, had overtaken their conservative rivals to become the largest branch of North American Judaism.[22]

Some commentators, citing a run of poll data showing that more than four-fifths of Americans professed to believe in an afterlife and that overall church attendance remained stable at around 40 percent, insisted that America remained uniquely religious among Western nations. Those who looked at the evidence more closely thought otherwise. Churchgoing Americans had a knack for leading secular lives. Except for groups like the Amish, barricaded on the far right of the temperamental spectrum, they believed it possible to be both religious and modern. Things were quite otherwise in Europe, where few self-consciously modern citizens patronized institutions historically linked to establishment privilege, sectarian strife, and clerical meddling. This much was evident in the speed with which churches emptied out in modernizing countries like Ireland or Spain. Yet Americans, who regarded affiliation as a matter of personal choice in a benign religious marketplace, could attend services and remain responsible citizens. Indeed, friendly neighbors often asked newcomers which local church they intended to join. "None" was not a socially adept answer. In the South it came close to farting.[23]

That may explain why so many Americans lied to pollsters about churchgoing. Actual national weekly attendance in the 1990s stood closer to 20 percent than the reported 40 percent. One group of Catholics polled by phone claimed 51 percent; 24 percent showed up when researchers checked the parishes. People lied about skipping church at the same rate they lied about abortion, which they underreported by half. Clergy did their own fibbing, particularly about membership. Historian Andrew Walsh suspected that regular churchgoing, far from being stable, had weakened beneath misleading data. Political scientist Robert Putnam agreed. He found that postwar gains in religious activity began to erode during the 1960s, as did participation in community-based organizations generally.[24]

Theoretically, people can be religious without benefit of clergy. In 1988 four in ten unchurched Americans said that they had made a commitment to Jesus; six in ten that there was life after death; and eight in ten that they sometimes prayed. But to what did such avowals amount? Apparently to an updated form of Pelagianism, the heresy that denied original sin. Three-quarters of Americans polled in 2000 agreed with the statement "all people are inherently good when they are born." Though no one mentioned it during his feel-good 2004 funeral, Reagan's epitaph, which began "I know in my heart that man is good," repudiated Pauline Christianity—no surprise, perhaps, from a man who whistled up a cheerful conservatism similarly at odds with the classical strain.[25]

Doctrinal ignorance, theological indifference, and biblical illiteracy were other signs of the shift toward soft, privatized religion. By the early 1980s a sizable majority of American adults, 58 percent, could not identify who delivered the Sermon on the Mount or name even five of the Ten Commandments. These were nominal Christians who had a dusty Bible somewhere in the house, a disinclination to spend too many Sunday mornings in church, and a bland optimism in a benevolent but infrequently consulted God. They had their counterparts among the Jews, 42 percent of whom reported themselves strongly committed to Judaism but only 13 percent of whom regularly attended religious services. While participation in Jewish community life went beyond the synagogue, Reform Jews were nevertheless involved in explicitly religious activities far less often than the Orthodox. As far as the Orthodox were concerned, Reform Jews were unbelievers.[26]

"American religiosity," summed up Alan Wolfe, "is as shallow as it is broad." Christianity, agreed historian Thomas Reeves, had accommodated consumerism. It had become a consumer object itself, purchased only in such amounts that the cost remained low and customer satisfaction high. The children of the religiously liberal were the hardest sell. Half of all Presbyterian youth became unchurched adults. It was much the same in other mainline churches. "I think I was baptized Episcopalian, but I'm not quite sure," said a thirty-year-old Portland environmentalist. "I try to put those things out of my mind."[27]

The Structures of Self

Whether they welcomed it or not, most intellectuals conceded the robustness of the moral revolution, the dilution of faith, and the triumph of the self. Some, like Bork and Lasch, made second careers out of deploring the trends. They did not, however, agree on its underlying causes. To varying degrees, they set it down to the influence of capitalism, technological innovation, elite formation and ideology, family change, and political structure.

The cultural critics of capitalism composed variations on a theme by the German sociologist Max Weber. Religious discipline, Weber argued, had fostered the growth of capitalism, only to be undermined by the wealth that capitalism produced. "The higher the Dow," as Norman Mailer put it, "the lower the standards. Money destroys all other values." Like many theologians, Pope John Paul II drew a distinction between a regulated market economy, which harnessed individual creativity to the yoke of social progress, and unchecked consumer capitalism, which lured people toward an idolatrous life of "having" rather than "being." The heart of the problem, wrote political theorist Benjamin Barber, was that producer capitalism and its hard-nosed virtues had given way to a lax, infantile, narcissistic consumerism that was as bad for democracy as it was for faith.[28]

Thomas Frank sharpened the paradox, arguing that the moral abrasiveness of unfettered capitalism was also bad for Democrats. American business had learned to love the moral revolution. Profit drove cultural change, particularly in the youth market. Professors weren't the ones encouraging little girls to dress like whores, as Garrison Keillor put it. But liberal smarty-pants still got the blame. Duped blue-collar voters elected Republicans who let corporations do what they wanted. All they got in return, Frank wrote in *What's the Matter with Kansas?*, was "a crap culture" in moral free fall no thanks to "the grandstanding Christers whom they send triumphantly back to Washington every couple of years." Republicans won politically because they kept losing culturally. The commercialized moral revolution turned out to be an endless vein of Nixonian gold.[29]

Critics accused Frank of overstating working-class defections from the Democrats, confusing principled conservatism with crony plutocracy, reducing everything to anti-intellectualism and class resentment, and dismissing real moral differences aggravated by elite activism. Madison Avenue hadn't decided *Roe*. And why shouldn't blue-collar workers vote their consciences on issues like abortion if the educated classes voted theirs on issues like the environment? For all that, Frank had a crucial insight, that corporate profit promoted abrasive cultural change and therefore cultural conflict. The conflict, to extend his point, created new opportunities for profit. If the media bothered conservatives, then start *Fox News,* or a Christian entertainment division at William Morris. Corporations finessed temperamental differences by treating them as manifestations of a segmented market. Gays were big travelers, so schedule gay days at Disney World. If they wanted a wedding package too, let them have it. All this made pluralism and relativism more visible and legitimate, undercutting religious conservatives in the process.

As the old communities of birth lost their grip, Americans chose communities based on lifestyle. Gays congregated, not just in particular cities, but in particular zip codes. Self-sorting simplified redistricting and made local voting more lopsided. In the 1960 election, fewer than one voter in three lived in a county decided by 20 or more percentage points. In the 2004 election, nearly one voter in two lived in such a place. Bumper stickers served as ideological no-trespassing signs. Developers planned and named communities ("Covenant Hills") for particular religious temperaments. Marketers turned franchises and products into beacons of identity. Americans on the move—4 to 5 percent a year—looked for neighborhoods with the right kind of merchandise as well as the right kind of people. By their shops you shall know them.[30]

During the 1960s and 1970s, critics on both the economic left and moral right had attacked consumerism—though separately, their temperamental differences inhibiting anything like a Tory socialist coalition. During the 1980s and 1990s, however, consumerism triumphed absolutely. It erased the last vestiges of Victorian restraint from two decades that, historian Gary Cross realized, "were really not so conservative after all." He laid much of the blame at the doorstep of Reagan, whose FCC had thrown open the door to fully commercialized broadcasting. Between 1986 and 1994—years in which the number of television commercials exploded and programming itself became a marketing operation—the amount of income Americans said they needed to fulfill their dreams jumped from $50,000 to over $100,000.[31]

Consumption came at the expense of religion. Serious faith required prayer, contemplation, study of scripture, service to others, and communal worship. Quite apart from the self-assertion of its core message, consumer capitalism distracted Americans from these spiritual tasks by flooding the world with goods to be located, priced, purchased, assembled, operated, serviced, repaired, guarded, and amortized by unremitting toil. Americans worked more than the Germans, more even than the Japanese. By 2005 a third of them labored more than fifty hours a week. Ten million required more than an hour to drive to work, insofar as work remained a definable place. Securities trader Jim Cramer found himself discussing stock positions while arranging his mother's funeral and fielding a call about Fed moves during his daughter's birth. Alarm clocks—a Puritan invention—lashed everyone on. Thirty percent of adults got by on six hours of sleep or less. Some college students made do with four or five, prompting Duke University to cancel its 8:00 A.M. classes. Wired teenagers preferred electronic diversions to sleep, which was a "waste of time" and "boring."[32]

Sundays became a day for sleeping in—or for paying bills, watching television, and shopping. Americans who admitted to pollsters that they did not go to church cited, as the single most important reason, that they were just too busy. "We went church shopping," explained a mother in Alpharetta, a prosperous Atlanta suburb. "We found one, but it's a half-hour drive away. We don't have that kind of time." Studies of time diaries, detailed accounts of how many hours Americans spent on various activities, confirmed that religious worship and related social activities dropped by a third from 1965 to 1995. Children recorded even sharper declines.[33]

Computers and video games accounted for much of the shift. One college rewired its dorm rooms with ten outlets to accommodate students who averaged eighteen electrical gadgets apiece. Student reading of newspapers, literary fiction, and poetry went the way of chapel attendance. The Internet, a cloistered academic e-mail service that, during the 1990s, morphed into a global libertarian commons of untaxed commerce, switchblade opinion, raw gossip, and gaudy vice, became a primary source of temptation and distraction. So did cell phones, useful for hooking up and downloading as well as tweeting and calling mom.[34]

If merchandise was the opiate of the masses, and television the needle, then cable was the intravenous drip and wireless the dermal patch. Digital technology enabled consumerism and advertising to create a hologram of desire whose shimmering images captivated the limbic brain, mocked faith's invisible metaphysics, and kept everyone tuned to the shopping channel. Short of Luddism—Russell Kirk threw his television off his roof—there was no escape. Mennonites knew who Madonna

Figure 21   Digital etiquette: Florida Gators basketball star Joakim Noah with girlfriend Erin Kelly on the steps of a Gainesville restaurant, April 2006. In a time-pressured society, multitasking became the norm, particularly among the young. Photograph by Bob Self.

was. Screens in waiting rooms became as common as guard towers in prisons, the backup control system for the poor, the violent, and the illicitly narcotized.[35]

Shifts in education and elite formation contributed to the moral revolution's staying power. The old WASP establishment, those whom David Brooks called "dumb good-looking people with great parents," had yielded to a miscible educated class of bourgeois bohemians. These "bobos" had risen through a combination of merit and luck, the marital revolution being also a natal lottery. Children raised by married biological parents were, on average, happier, healthier, wealthier, and better behaved than those who were not. If their parents also happened to be professionals, they were more likely to have the cultural capital, vocabularies, and test scores necessary to enter prestigious universities. The stakes were huge. The average college graduate earned two-thirds more than the average high school graduate, while those from selective schools had the inside track for top careers. Everyone knew how the system worked. Phyllis Schlafly and Betty Friedan may have hated one another, but their sons ended up in the same doctoral program at Berkeley and with the same adviser, the prize-winning mathematician Isadore Singer.[36]

"You realize what you're talking about is the Jews taking over America," a Jewish woman told a startled Brooks. There was something in that, he reflected. Brooks himself was a Jew and had arrived at the pinnacle of punditry by way of the University of Chicago. He was hardly unusual in this: Jewish students and faculty at elite universities had grown rapidly after the admissions reforms of the 1950s. But his real point had been larger. The Cold War had opened universities to all talented students. In grinding their way to success, they had absorbed the ethos of the institutions they attended. Conservatives (Brooks included, when he felt like grousing) highlighted the academy's moral-left biases, manifest in everything from the GLBT center to the communal bass line blasting from the dorms. The more prestigious the school, the more liberal its academic culture, though, as nineteen-year-old Barack Obama discovered, even a small college like Occidental was well endowed with radicals and feminists and punk rockers. Universities, wrote one critic, had become "miniature liberal states themselves—prescribing nothing and allowing virtually everything." Morality, Brooks noticed, was the one subject on which students were reliably inarticulate.[37]

Moral certainty and the ethic of self-sacrifice survived in strict religious colleges and at the service academies. Most students, however, enrolled in secular institutions, and in growing numbers. In 2006 colleges and universities trained nearly three times as many students as they had in 1966. Republicans and Democrats alike funded the surge, increasing higher-education assistance from $4 billion to $106 billion annually over the same period. Taxes, endowments, loans, and grants subsidized a vast secularization machine in which the worldly lessons of the classroom were reinforced by the fleshly ones of the dorm. Tom Wolfe, who spent four years researching a campus novel, admitted that he would be "shocked out of my pants if I was at college now." He assigned the same fate to his heroine Charlotte Simmons, a rural innocent deflowered at a fictional Pennsylvania university whose bibulous, rutting students bore a fair resemblance to Duke undergraduates. In the 1960s, Wolfe said, people spoke of a sexual revolution. Now it was "a sexual carnival."[38]

So, to get anywhere young people went to college, and in college they relived the 1960s, the fun part, digitally enhanced, minus the burning buildings. The moral left's key institutions still dominated culturally, still shaped the outlook of the nation's ambitious young. The paradox was that the young had to work their way to hedonism. Admission and academic success required discipline and initiative, at least at selective universities. They sport long hair but work like Puritans, historian C. Vann Woodward said of his Yale students. That was exactly what Brooks had in mind. His bobos had embraced the self-liberation of the counterculture, but also the self-enriching possibilities of a liberated economy. After graduation they merged the two into a lifestyle of hard work, refined consumption, energetic but safe sex, New Age experimentation, and lots of Starbucks coffee. Having forged a post-Christian version of the Genteel temperament, they leavened self-assertion with sensitivity and good taste. As far as they were concerned, the Culture War was over. Historian Mark Lilla thought this true of the whole society by century's end. The cultural revolution of the 1960s and Reaganism turned out to be fundamentally harmonious, being grounded in the individualism that was America's most enduring legacy.[39]

Neo- and religious conservatives doubted whether any morally lax society could remain prosperous indefinitely. They put another item, the family, at the top of their list of defective character-forming institutions. So did Moynihan. As out-of-wedlock births had steadily risen, he pointed out in 1993, so had the number of poor kids, dropouts, delinquents, and sociopaths. The volume of their depredations had forced disciplinary triage. Gone were the days when a student might be suspended for saying "thanks a lot" sarcastically to a teacher. (As actually happened to Bork, who never learned to keep his mouth shut.) When assistant principals worried about having enough metal detectors, smart alecks got a pass. Institutions could afford to recognize only so much deviant behavior before they had to redefine as normal what they had once stigmatized. The enthusiasm for prison building and executions suggested that Americans were less willing to normalize violent or felonious behavior. But in other respects—dress, speech, sex—the rule held. That which does not kill me I learn to tolerate.[40]

Almost as an afterthought, Moynihan had a powerful insight: This downward redefinition of deviancy lay at the heart of cultural warfare. The constant lowering of standards was what drove moral conservatives crazy and what had prompted their chest-thumping display at the 1992

Republican convention. Moynihan thought there was nothing wrong with condemning self-defeating behaviors and felt that the social sciences, his field of sociology included, were the poorer for refusing to do so. But he did not hold out much hope for a swift upward revision of standards against the inexorable downward pressure of family disintegration, which had so far defied the government's best policy efforts. Good luck taking back the culture block by block.[41]

Evangelical psychologist James Dobson shared Moynihan's premises, though not his pessimism. Dobson thought it possible to take the culture back, if not block by block, then child by child. Through his popular radio and television programs and nonprofit organization, Focus on the Family, Dobson dispensed advice to worried parents, most often mothers. He told them that they needed to provide firm discipline as well as love, that moderate spanking was appropriate, and that they should be at home with their young, not at work. Time pressure was family enemy number one.

In 1983 Dobson co-founded the Family Research Council, an advocacy group that would become the religious right's most powerful lobby after the Christian Coalition unraveled in the late 1990s. Dobson wanted governments to do everything in their power to uphold traditional families and moral values. But neither Reed's coalition-building nor Gingrich's agenda impressed him, other than as proof that the GOP was to the cause of the religious right what Lucy was to Charley Brown's football. If you think you're going to get our votes every two years and then disregard God's moral law, he warned Republicans in a 1998 speech, "I'm gone, and if I go . . . I will do everything I can to take as many people with me as possible."[42]

But take them where, exactly? Not to the Democrats, or to the pro-choice Perot, or to the even more pro-choice Libertarian Party. Dobson's sensible distrust of bait-and-switch tactics could not resolve two problems: the futility of third parties and the necessity of sixty votes to break a filibuster in the Senate. Democrats and a handful of moderate GOP defectors could block any bill that threatened the status quo, especially on choice. Though Dobson did his best to hold Republican feet to the fire, he fared little better than his predecessors. His legislative 20 percent on life issues took the form of a 2002 law conferring legal rights on infants born alive during an attempted abortion; a 2003 partial-birth abortion ban, eventually upheld by the Supreme Court; a 2004 law recognizing fetuses as legal victims if injured or killed during violent crimes; and a 2005 private-relief bill granting Terri Schiavo's parents another appeal to stop the Florida-court-ordered removal of their vegetating daughter's feeding tube. Nothing changed. The abortion clinics went about their business. Federal courts refused to intervene in the Schiavo case, which turned into a public relations fiasco with Randall Terry as media-circus ringmaster.[43]

The Culture War thus taught conservatives what Vietnam had taught Cold War liberals, that it was possible to win tactically and lose strategically. The culture was the prize that mattered, Weyrich said, and conservatives had lost it to leftists who had understood to concentrate there rather than on politics. Whether his opponents had actually made a conscious strategic choice seems open to question, given that the most basic economic and social structures of postwar society favored a cultural shift in their direction. Capital thought for the moral left. Self-assertion was good for business.[44]

Few trends continue indefinitely. American consumerism ultimately depended on cheap energy and easy credit, making rising prices for both potential game-changers. Demography can also rearrange culture. As Kinsey noted, the irreligious had fewer hang-ups about sex than the religious. Yet frequent, guilt-free sex conferred no reproductive advantage when offset by contraception. In 2001 a third of high-achieving career women over forty remained childless, compared to a fifth of women in the general population. What churchgoing prudes lacked in ardor they made up for in confidence. Mutual disapproval of divorce meant that wives could count on support in raising their broods. Mutual disapproval of adultery reassured husbands that they were supporting their own children.[45]

Contraception and feminism were like homeostatic mechanisms that kept moral leftists from turning their economic and institutional advantages into a complete cultural rout. All Christians had to do to beat the antimarriage crowd, declared one homeschool advocate, was raise six kids in godly fashion. The hitch was that, by 2001, the cost (including foregone income) for a single middle-class child raised to age eighteen by a stay-at-home mom exceeded a million dollars. Even so, lower fertility put secularists—and Democrats—at a disadvantage. Republicans ran strongest in states and districts with the most marriages and the most children. In 2006 Republicans in Congress represented 7 million more children than Democrats. Theoretically, that meant more Republicans in the pipeline than Democrats, given that voters who identify with a party most often choose the one their parents supported. But the "fertility gap" was at least partly offset by immigration, which yielded more Democratic voters, particularly among Hispanics, who also had relatively high fertility. Party shifts like the one in Houston—just 39 percent Republican in 2009, down from 50 percent in 1989—explained why immigration re-emerged as a key issue in George W. Bush's second term and why Barack Obama could move formerly Republican states like Colorado into the Democratic column in the 2008 presidential election.[46]

In Europe, where immigration compounded rather than alleviated the secular parties' problems, fertility differentials posed a more serious challenge. From a fourth of the world's people in 1900, Europe had shrunk to an aging tenth in 2005. Its worldly young were unenthusiastic about having children, which put them at a demographic disadvantage against religious and patriarchal rivals. Commentators worried that Islam would inevitably expand into the demographic vacuum. If that happens, the global Culture War may have different outcomes in different regional theaters. A future in which Europeans are more religious than Americans is not impossible to imagine.[47]

Predation

Greater fertility aside, America's conservative culture warriors had little to show for their efforts as the new millennium began. They had shoved back the enemy's lines at the weak points of race and class, but had themselves been shoved further back on vice and sex. They had mounted one last big offensive, in the Lewinsky sector, and failed. Weyrich was right. If Clinton was winning, they were losing. Cultural critics made a bolder claim. As long as malls, Hollywood, Apple, bobos, and bottom-line Republicans were winning, moral conservatives were losing. The deck of daily life was stacked against them. Culture is what you know. What Americans knew in the year 2000 was commercialized desire.

Yet structure is not everything. Actors and contingencies also shape history. Like fluke plays at the end of a losing game, the disputed 2000 election and the 2001 terror attacks gave conservatives another chance. In the eyes of influential pundits like Paul Krugman, they gave conservatism an undeserved victory. Blessed with prosperity and an opponent with a 566 verbal SAT score, Gore should have cruised to victory. But, overreacting to the Lewinsky scandal, he distanced himself from Clinton and ran a clumsy campaign. Bush ran an adroit one under the banner of "compassionate conservatism." Following strategist Karl Rove's script, he deplored partisanship and wooed independents, adding them to his base of southern and rural white men, NRA members, small-business owners, executives, and religious conservatives. Strength in urban and industrial states gave Gore a half-million popular-vote advantage, yet he lost by four electoral votes. Nader's third-party candidacy tipped Florida to Bush. Gore would have won Florida anyway had not so many confused voters—27,000 in Duval County alone, concentrated in black precincts—spoiled their ballots. The debacle gave Bush, with a five-to-four assist from the United States Supreme Court, the state's crucial electoral votes.[48]

In office Bush moved quickly on the traditional Republican agenda of tax cuts, military upgrades, and selective environmental deregulation. He marked time on abortion and struck an awkward compromise on embryonic stem cells, permitting federal funding of research using existing cell lines. Bush's real priorities were the finance, insurance, real estate, and energy industries and taxpayers prosperous enough to worry about income, capital gains, and estate taxes. A third of the benefits of his tax cuts went to the wealthiest 1 percent of households. His was a strongly pro-business administration, though not a particularly popular one. By late summer it was headed into the rough waters of an economic slowdown.[49]

Then America awoke to a storm of planes. The rally-round effect of September 11 gave Bush the mandate he had failed to win in the election. His inner circle, dominated by Vice President Dick Cheney and a coterie of neoconservatives, seized the day. They expanded executive power, launched an ambitious war in Iraq, and attacked the Democrats, suddenly vulnerable on security. Republicans gained seats in the House and Senate in 2002 and again in 2004. They retained the White House when Rove, this time concentrating on the base, ran his man as the steely champion of security and faith. Surrogates deployed two new wedge issues, fear of terrorism and gay marriage. Democratic nominee John Kerry's Hamlet-like indecisiveness made him vulnerable to the one, while his Selective Catholicism made him vulnerable to the other. Temperament had so trumped denomination that Kerry found himself with the opposite of John Kennedy's problem. Kerry was not Catholic enough for Evangelicals or for the traditionalists of his own faith. "The true Catholic," said one Florida parishioner, "would have voted for Bush just on moral reasons alone."[50]

The true American, said Bush's critics, would have voted for Kerry on democratic reasons alone. The administration, they charged, had used its newfound power to suppress constitutional freedoms, torture detainees,

Figure 22 President George W. Bush addresses rescue workers in the ruins of the World Trade Center, September 14, 2001. As the new millennium began, Republican prospects looked bleak. Two extraordinary events, Bush's judicial victory in the disputed 2000 election and the September 11, 2001, terrorist attacks, temporarily reversed the party's fortunes and indirectly prolonged the Culture War. Photograph by Eric Draper.

spy on citizens, despoil the environment, and hinder science. The only hard data that interested Bush and his advisers were Rove's numbers. In pursuit of their authoritarian, imperialist, and corporate agenda, they had ignored the plight of minimum-wage workers, the uninsured, and the victims of predatory lenders, unleashed by usurious deregulation. Wall Street returned the favor, pumping money into the Bush reelection campaign. Investment bankers repackaged the record debt in opaque financial instruments, laying the ground for the financial crisis of 2008. Meanwhile, libertarians and Christian conservatives resumed their shaky alliance. In January 2005 Bush promised to try again for a federal constitutional amendment prohibiting gay marriage in exchange for their support for his plan to privatize Social Security.[51]

Neither scheme went anywhere. Therein lies the lesson of Bush's domestic record, or at least a good working hypothesis until more internal documents become available. Bush achieved neither a reactionary break with the New Deal nor a belated triumph of conservatism. On the contrary, he and his congressional allies increased federal discretionary spending at a faster rate than Lyndon Johnson. The No Child Left Behind Act, signed in early 2002, added nearly $7 billion to the federal education budget. Bush extended Clinton's drive for lower-income and minority home ownership with the 2003 American Dream Downpayment Act, which provided grants for qualified first-time homeowners. That, and business for grateful realtors and investment bankers who securitized their subprime mortgages. The 2003 Medicare prescription drug benefits, initially projected at $40 billion annually, were a windfall for pharmaceutical companies, whom the Republicans protected from price negotiation. Seniors also gained. By 2007 their total federal benefits averaged $524 a week, or nearly twice what minimum-wage workers earned. "You take anything," admitted Arizona Republican Representative Jeff Flake, "and we've grown it big."[52]

Tactically, even less had changed. Bush's advisers fine-tuned Nixon's permanent campaign and adapted it to new media opportunities. The political affairs staff rolled their eyes and "handled" the "nuts," the "ridiculous," the "goofy," and the "out of control" as if Colson was still managing the asylum. Rove, the chief strategist, had no apparent religious faith. Bush did, but lacked enthusiasm for "kicking gays," or for generously funding faith-based programs, or for making war on sin. He had spent too many nights in bars to imagine the culture plastic to his presidential touch. "It seems like the president, on our issues, just sort of laid down and died," admitted one Catholic right-to-life activist. Evangelicals were twice stuck, with the GOP and with a president hard to publicly criticize because of his war against terrorism and proud rebirth in Christ. Deference to authority and group loyalty, two ingrained traits of the religiously conservative, inclined them to stick with Bush. The two-party system gave them little choice.[53]

Only in one important respect did Bush fully live up to Evangelical expectations. His two Supreme Court picks were solidly pro-life. Roberts and Alito were both conservative Catholics, but conservative Protestants were fine with that. In fact, most preferred Alito to Harriet Miers, the president's personal lawyer and first choice to succeed O'Connor. Miers was an Evangelical convert and, as a woman, a good political fit. But she was also an ideological unknown, lacking in judicial experience. Conservatives smelled a swing vote. On October 26, 2005, Miers withdrew in the face of the mounting opposition. Her replacement, Federalist Society veteran Samuel Alito, enjoyed the support of both economic and moral conservatives. But even his reliable vote was not enough to offset Anthony Kennedy's. Though Kennedy voted to uphold the partial-birth abortion ban, his unwillingness to abandon *Roe*'s core principles left abortion opponents one tantalizing vote short.[54]

In other ways Bush closely followed Reagan. His telephone hookups to pro-life rallies, yearly spending increases for the drug war, missile-defense and space projects, record farm bills, merger-friendly Justice Department, delegation of fiscal details, and rhetorical opposition to racial quotas (conveniently leaving actual resolution of the issue to the courts and state legislatures) seemed a replay of the 1980s. Bush applied market ideology to taxes and trade but not to the welfare or the defense state, using spending to placate powerful constituencies and enrich key contributors. At times he dropped all pretense of free competition, as when he signed a prescription benefits bill that excluded identical but cheaper imported drugs, thereby enriching the domestic pharmaceutical industry. Economists who counted tax exemptions for private insurance and other off-the-books subsidies came to a surprising conclusion: Per capita public spending on health services in the United States matched that of Canada, the supposed bastion of socialized medicine. The difference was the way that interest groups had distorted American policy, making coverage patchy and spending wildly inefficient.[55]

It would be unfair to lay all of this at Bush's door. He simply added one more storey to the canted edifice Democrats and Republicans had been hammering together since 1935. It is easy to forget how much important health legislation—the 1954 health-insurance tax exclusion, the expansion of Medicaid eligibility in the 1980s, the 2003 Medicare prescription benefits—was enacted under Republican presidents. Indeed, government health spending neatly illustrates the theme of this book—the ragged continuity of left-liberal trends in an age of rising Republican fortunes. Both government expenditures and social permissiveness kept growing under the cover of selective reaction. Granted, the conservative emperor was not entirely naked. But he had gained weight, and it showed when he paraded in his NASCAR cap, gold cross, nightstick, and camo skivvies.

When Bush reprised Reagan's tactics, he got Reagan's fiscal results: a rapidly mounting debt sustained by steady overseas sales of bonds, denominated in dollars that commanded, if ever more tenuously, privileged status as the world's primary reserve currency. The federal ledger went from a surplus of $128 billion in fiscal 2001 to a reported deficit of $455 billion in 2008. The true deficit was over a trillion dollars, counting the "intragovernmental transfer" from the Social Security trust fund. Not coincidentally, the number of registered lobbyists and the amount paid to federal contractors almost doubled between 2000 and 2006. "It turns out, in the real world of Republican governance," neoconservative William Kristol wrote in 2008, "that there aren't a whole lot of small-government Republicans." Change the names and dates, and *The Triumph of Politics* could have been written during Bush's last years—though not by Stockman, who was by then busy fighting charges he had manipulated financial reports to deceive investors. That was legal only when done to taxpayers.[56]

Many have called Bush a radical version of Reagan. It would be as apt to call him a clumsy one. Reagan knew when to back off, amiably consolidating his gains. Bush was cocksure, stubborn, polarizing. Left-liberals hated him like nobody since Nixon, differing only as to whether he was the puppet or ringleader of the Gilded Age gang. Krugman set the tone, accusing the administration of restoring plutocracy under the cover of racial, patriotic, and moral reaction. He saw the New Deal receding in history's rearview mirror. He feared conservatives were winning because Bush's rich allies had grown fatter than ever. The essential irony, and the interesting complication, to Krugman's story was that economic conservatives simultaneously thought *they* were losing because government—state and federal—had grown fatter than ever.[57]

Almost to a person, they turned on Bush during his second term. "Not a conservative," decided Limbaugh. Buckley used the same words. "No conservative in the classic sense," wrote DeLay, as if he were Cicero. Less polite critics settled on impostor, traitor, spendthrift, socialist, and "bizarro." Bush was the Republican LBJ, right down to his reckless, mismanaged war. Buchanan thought Bush made Bill Clinton look like Goldwater. I'd vote for Clinton against Bush, said former Reagan aide Bruce Bartlett. Bob Barr, a champion of impeaching Clinton who later quit the GOP for the Libertarian Party, judged the Bush administration infinitely worse on civil liberties than its predecessor. "What does conservatism today stand for?" demanded fellow libertarian Lew Rockwell. "It stands for war. It stands for power. "It stands for spying, jailing without trial, torture, counterfeiting without limit, and lying from morning to night." Mike Huckabee, former Arkansas governor and 2008 GOP presidential hopeful, conceded that the problem went beyond the White House. The whole party had "advertised conservatism and delivered another product."[58]

Economist James Galbraith, son of John Kenneth, gave that product a name. He called it "the predator state," meaning "the systematic abuse of public institutions for private profit or, equivalently, the systematic undermining of public protections for the benefit of private clients." Free-market ideology, Galbraith wryly observed, had come to occupy the place of Marxism in the Soviet Union: the official myth taught to schoolchildren but ignored in setting policy. Market talk had become a bigger racket for Republicans than God talk. What Bush's actual policies demonstrated was not principled conservatism, but the diversion of public resources to a favored few. That included cronies dumped in the Federal Emergency Management Agency, whose botched 2005 response to Hurricane Katrina served as the American Chernobyl. Big government was one thing. Corrupt and incompetent government was another.[59]

Caught in an ideological crossfire, and with Bush's approval ratings sinking to Watergate levels, the Republicans lost control of the House and Senate in the 2006 elections. Evangelicals remained loyal to the GOP, but moral and economic moderates shifted decisively toward the Democrats. Two years later, Barack Obama, an Illinois senator with a Kenyan father and a left-liberal voting record, captured the White House with the biggest Democratic margin since 1964. He celebrated his victory in Chicago's Grant Park, flash point for the 1968 convention protests. That night, at least, the Culture War seemed to slip into history.

During the campaign, Republican nominee John McCain had tried to keep it alive by naming Alaska Governor Sarah Palin as his running mate. Palin was 20 percent in a designer jacket and peep-toe pumps. But even the media novelty of a sexy Evangelical politico-mom could not save McCain and the GOP from the twin disasters of an unpopular war and collapsing credit markets. As in 1980 and 1992, the swing voters of 2008 cared more about pocketbook issues than moral ones.

Worry over the economy provoked another unprecedented event in late 2008, the federal bailout of the financial industry. The government took over the nation's two largest mortgage companies and pledged $700 billion to help restore liquidity to credit markets. Bush insisted the government had acted solely to rescue the economy. Whatever his intention, the result was hardly free-market orthodoxy. In a pinch, government turned out to be the solution, not the problem.

Obama reaffirmed government's primacy in his 2009 inaugural address. The question, he said, was not government's size "but whether it works." Republicans denied his premise, yet freely admitted that they had overspent to buy support when they controlled the purse strings. It was they who had failed, not conservatism, which had never really been tried. But the voters had taken them to the woodshed and taught them a lesson. They knew better now. Besides, the Obama crowd was worse than they were. The rationalization, however clever, only highlighted the deceptions of the previous eight years.[60]

"All battles," Milton Friedman said, "are perpetual." Given the high stakes, lingering resentments, and cyclical character of partisan politics, it would hardly be surprising if Republicans return to power under the conservative banner. They may yet execute their right turn, at least in fiscal policy. Mounting deficits provide impetus and cover for spending cuts—though also tax hikes, which bitter medicine Stockman himself predicted that the GOP would finally have to swallow. ("Sorry, game over.") A moral turning seems less likely. Cash-strapped state governments may even legalize more vices and reduce prison time, trends already evident in bellwether California. But historians are denied the luxury of speculation. Like referees, they mark periods, make judgments, and keep score. I am content to assign the forty years from 1968 to 2008 a name, the Culture War. I find in them a unifying theme, the counterrevolution against left-liberalism. And I discern a surprising outcome. It was the messy failure of reaction, obscured by the illusion of conservatism.[61]

AI   Author interview

BL   George Bush Presidential Library, College Station, Texas

CBLP   Clare Boothe Luce Papers, Library of Congress Manuscript Division, Washington, D.C.

CL   Jimmy Carter Presidential Library, Atlanta, Georgia

DI   Robert J. Dole Institute of Politics Archive, University of Kansas, Lawrence, Kansas

DPC   Domestic Policy Council

DPMP   Daniel Patrick Moynihan Papers, Library of Congress Manuscript Division, Washington, D.C.

FTU   *Florida Times-Union*

GPO   Government Printing Office

JAH   *Journal of American History*

JBMP   John Bartlow Martin Papers, Library of Congress Manuscript Division, Washington, D.C.

LCMD   Library of Congress Manuscript Division, Washington, D.C.

NA II   National Archives II, College Park, Maryland

NPMS   Nixon Presidential Materials Staff, National Archives II, College Park, Maryland

NYRB   *New York Review of Books*

NYT   *New York Times*

PP   *Public Papers of the Presidents of the United States* (Washington, D.C.: GPO, various dates)

RL   Ronald Reagan Presidential Library, Simi Valley, California

RLMP   Robert L. Maddox Papers, Carter Library, Atlanta, Georgia

RRP   Richard Rovere Papers, Wisconsin Historical Society, Madison, Wisconsin

SSP   Susan Stern Papers, Special Collections Division, University of Washington, Seattle, Washington

WARP   William Allen Rusher Papers, Library of Congress Manuscript Division, Washington, D.C.

WCCPM   Wilcox Collection of Contemporary Political Movements, Spencer Research Library, University of Kansas, Lawrence, Kansas

STAP   Spiro T. Agnew Papers, University of Maryland, College Park, Maryland

WHS   Wisconsin Historical Society, Madison, Wisconsin

WJCL   William J. Clinton Presidential Library, Little Rock, Arkansas

WP   *Washington Post*

WSJ   *Wall Street Journal*

WT   *Washington Times*

I. HOW TO THINK ABOUT THE CULTURE WAR

1. Tape 31–128, October 18, 1972, Nixon Presidential Materials Staff, hereafter NPMS, National Archives II, College Park, Maryland, hereafter NA II.

2. Buchanan to John Ehrlichman, H. R. Haldeman, and Charles Colson, September 23, 1971, box 1, Pat Buchanan to Larry Higby, June 23, 1972, box 2, and Buchanan to Nixon, November 10, 1972, box 2, Buchanan chronological files, Staff Member and Office Files, White House Special Files, Contested Documents File, NPMS; Buchanan memoranda to Nixon, April 3, 1972, November 29, 1972, and November 30, 1972, box 7 of the uncontested Buchanan staff files, NPMS; Robert Mason, *Richard Nixon and the Quest for a New Majority* (Chapel Hill: University of North Carolina Press, 2004).

3. Moynihan to Nixon, November 13, 1970, box I:245, Daniel Patrick Moynihan Papers, hereafter DPMP, Library of Congress Manuscript Division, hereafter LCMD, Washington, D.C.

4. My notion of two revolutions follows Mark Lilla, "A Tale of Two Reactions," *New York Review of Books,* hereafter *NYRB,* 45 (May 14, 1998): 4–7.

5. Earl Black, "The 2004 Presidential Election," lecture at the University of North Florida, September 28, 2004.

6. Buchanan to John Ehrlichman, H. R. Haldeman, and Charles Colson, September 23, 1971, box 1, Buchanan chronological files, Staff Member and Office Files, White House Special Files, Contested Documents File, NPMS.

7. Philip Greven, *The Protestant Temperament: Patterns of Child-Rearing, Religious Experience, and the Self in Early America* (New York: Knopf, 1977).

8. Donald J. Bogue et al., *The Population of the United States: Historical Trends and Future Projections,* rev. ed. (New York: Free Press, 1985), ch. 18; "Religion in America," *The Gallup Report,* nos. 201–202 (June-July 1982): 20, 41, 44, 45; and Egon Mayer and Barry Kosmin, *American Religious Identification Survey 2008,* http://www.americanreligionsurvey-aris.org/, August 4, 2009.

9. Anaïs Nin, *Seduction of the Minotaur* (Chicago: Swallow Press, 1961), 124.

10. Jonathan Haidt and Matthew A. Hersh, "Sexual Morality: The Cultures and Emotions of Conservatives and Liberals," *Journal of Applied Social Psychology* 31 (2001): 191–221, concisely explores the roles of temperament and affect in moral judgment.

11. Patrick J. Buchanan, *Right from the Beginning* (Boston: Little, Brown, 1988), 340.

12. Greven, *Protestant Temperament,* and *Spare the Child: The Religious Roots of Punishment and the Psychological Impact of Physical Abuse* (New York: Knopf, 1991).

13. George Lakoff, *Moral Politics: How Liberals and Conservatives Think,* 2nd ed. (Chicago: University of Chicago Press, 2002), xv, 392.

14. Michael Mott, *The Seven Mountains of Thomas Merton* (Boston: Houghton Mifflin, 1984); Peter Occhiogrosso, *Once a Catholic: Prominent Catholics and Ex-Catholics Reveal the Influence of the Church on Their Lives and Work* (Boston: Houghton Mifflin, 1987), 65–78.

15. Julie Ingersoll, *Evangelical Christian Women: War Stories in the Gender Battles* (New York: New York University Press, 2003).

16. Jonathan Haidt, "What Makes People Vote Republican?" *Edge,* September 9, 2009, http://www.edge.org/3rd_culture/haidt08/haidt08_index.html; Hoffman quoted in *It Was 20 Years Ago Today* (Granada Television documentary, 1987); Constance Sommer, "'60s Drug Guru Timothy Leary Dies at 75," AP wire, May 31, 1996; *Takin' It to the Streets: A Sixties Reader,* ed. Alexander Bloom and Wini Breines (New York: Oxford University Press, 1995), 65, italics deleted *(Statement).*

17. Unpublished journal (TS, 1948), 22–23, box 3, Richard Rovere Papers, hereafter RRP, Wisconsin Historical Society, Madison, Wisconsin, hereafter WHS; Roth 2001 interview in *Fresh Air: Writers Speak with Terry Gross* (Minneapolis: High Bridge Audio Books, 2004).

18. The phrase is from Thomas L. Haskell, "The Curious Persistence of Rights Talk in the 'Age of Interpretation,' " *Journal of American History,* hereafter *JAH,* 74 (1987): 984–1012.

19. Joseph Cardinal Ratzinger and Vittorio Messori, *The Ratzinger Report: An Exclusive Interview on the State of the Church* (San Francisco: Ignatius Press, 1985 [based on 1984 interview]), 51, 146, 149, 173, quotation at p. 190; Buchanan, *Right from the Beginning,* 285; Michael O. Emerson and Christian Smith, *Divided by Faith: Evangelical Religion and the Problem of Race in America* (New York: Oxford University Press, 2000), ch. 4.

20. William Martin, *With God on Our Side: The Rise of the Religious Right in America,* rev. ed. (New York: Broadway Books, 2005), 100; Taylor Branch, *Pillar of Fire: America in the King Years, 1963–65* (New York: Simon and Schuster, 1998), 207 (quotations); Mark Felt and John O'Connor, *A G-Man's Life* (New York: Public Affairs, 2006), 112 (marathon); Ralph David Abernathy, *And the Walls Came Tumbling Down: An Autobiography* (New York: Harper and Row, 1989), 434–436; Megan Tench, "A Nightmare Recalled," *Boston Globe,* January 26, 2002; King autopsy report, http://foia.fbi.gov/king/mlk1b.pdf, October 25, 2005.

21. David J. Garrow, *Bearing the Cross: Martin Luther King, Jr., and the Southern Christian Leadership Conference* (New York: William Morrow, 1986), 375.

22. Garrett Epps, "The Discreet Charms of a Demagogue," *NYRB* 34 (May 7, 1987): 30–35; William A. Link, *Righteous Warrior: Jesse Helms and the Rise of Modern Conservatism* (New York: St. Martin's Press, 2008), 261–269; "Helms Pleads to Keep Clinton Out of U.N.," *New York Times,* hereafter *NYT,* February

1, 2005; Samuel Francis, "The King Holiday and Its Meaning," http://www.martinlutherking.org/articles.html, October 25, 2005 ("filth"); James Davison Hunter, *Culture Wars: The Struggle to Define America* (New York: Basic Books, 1991).

23. Howard Moody, "Pleasure, Too, Is a Gift from God," *Christianity and Crisis* 45 (June 10, 1985): 231; Clark Morphew, "Issue of Ordination of Gays Isn't Going to Go Away Soon," *Florida Times-Union*, hereafter *FTU*, February 10, 1990. Williams died of AIDS in 1992.

24. Karen Armstrong, *The Battle for God* (New York: Knopf, 2000).

25. Ralph E. Pyle, "Faith and Commitment to the Poor: Theological Orientation and Support for Government Assistance Measures," *Sociology of Religion* 54 (1993): 385–401.

26. Stephen Prothero, *Religious Literacy: What Every American Needs to Know—and Doesn't* (San Francisco: HarperCollins, 2007), 9.

27. Arthur M. Schlesinger Jr., *A Life in the Twentieth Century: Innocent Beginnings, 1917–1950* (Boston: Houghton Mifflin, 2000), 161–166; James H. Jones, *Alfred C. Kinsey: A Public / Private Live* (New York: Norton, 1997), 195, 609–610; Steve Miller, "Johnny Ramone: Rebel in a Rebel's World," *Washington Times*, hereafter *WT*, March 12, 2004; Michael Janofsky, "When Cleaner Air Is a Biblical Obligation," *NYT*, November 7, 2005.

28. Lakoff, *Moral Politics;* unpaginated journal, ca. 1949, box 315, Clare Boothe Luce Papers, hereafter CBLP, in LCMD; Bill O'Reilly, *Culture Warrior* (New York: Broadway Books, 2006), 186.

2. LIKE IT WAS WHEN I WAS A BOY

1. John B. Judis, *William F. Buckley, Jr.: Patron Saint of the Conservatives* (New York: Simon and Schuster, 1988), 162; James Dunn to Jimmy Carter, August 23, 1980 (Rogers), box 4, Robert L. Maddox Papers, hereafter RLMP, Jimmy Carter Presidential Library, hereafter CL, Atlanta, Georgia.

2. Reagan's words have been variously reported; my version is from the videotaped speech in *With God on Our Side*, part IV (Alexandria, Va.: PBS Video, 1996).

3. James Hitchcock, *Years of Crisis: Collected Essays, 1970–1983* (San Francisco: Ignatius Press, 1985), 57; Garrison Keillor, *Homegrown Democrat: A Few Plain Thoughts from the Heart of America* (New York: Viking, 2004), 4.

4. Hemingway to Perkins, July 26, 1929, reprinted in "Three Words," *New Yorker* special issue (June 24/ July 1, 1996): 75.

5. Daniel Yankelovich, "How Changes in the Economy Are Reshaping American Values," in *Values and Public Policy*, ed. Henry J. Aaron et al. (Washington, D.C.: Brookings Institution, 1994): 47 (poll); Sally Belfrage, *Un-American Activities: A Memoir of the Fifties* (New York: HarperCollins, 1994), 89, 199, 219–220.

6. Donald J. Bogue et al., *The Population of the United States: Historical Trends and Future Projections* (New York: Free Press, 1985), 275; John Bartlow Martin, *Butcher's Dozen and Other Murders* (New York: Harper & Brothers, 1950), ch. 6, and *It Seems Like Only Yesterday: Memoirs of Writing, Presidential Politics, and the Diplomatic Life* (New York: William Morrow, 1986), 80; "Youth Must Face Murder Trial," *NYT*, May 28, 1949; "Babich Found Guilty, Gets Life

Sentence," *NYT,* June 21, 1949. "A Century of News," *JS Online,* February 14, 2006, reports that Babich served nine years of the sentence.

7. "Richard Chamberlain Opens Up about Being Gay," AP wire, May 31, 2003; Howard Moody, "Pleasure, Too, Is a Gift from God," *Christianity and Crisis* 45 (June 10, 1985): 230.

8. Helen Vendler, *A Life of Learning* (New York: American Council of Learned Societies, 2001), 12.

9. Daniel Horowitz, *Betty Friedan and the Making of* The Feminine Mystique: *The American Left, the Cold War, and Modern Feminism* (Amherst: University of Massachusetts Press, 1998); David T. Courtwright, *Violent Land: Single Men and Social Disorder from the Frontier to the Inner City* (Cambridge, Mass.: Harvard University Press, 1996), ch. 10.

10. Benjamin C. Bradlee, *Conversations with Kennedy* (New York: Norton, 1975), 43–49; John H. Summers, "What Happened to Sex Scandals? Politics and Peccadilloes, Jefferson to Kennedy," *JAH* 87 (2000): 825–854; Bruce Allen Murphy, *Wild Bill: The Legend and Life of William O. Douglas* (New York: Random House, 2003), 291.

11. Belfrage, *Un-American Activities,* 33; Patrick Henry, "'And I Don't Care What It Is': The Tradition-History of a Civil Religion Proof-Text," *Journal of the American Academy of Religion* 49 (1981): 41, 46.

12. Andrea Tone, *Devices and Desires: A History of Contraceptives in America* (New York: Hill and Wang, 2001), ch. 1; Charles Bamberger memoirs (TS, 1943), p. 30, box 14, Ralph Ginzburg Papers, WHS.

13. "Targets . . . Montgomery Ward, 1944," box 17, Ginzburg Papers, WHS; Martin, *It Seems Like Only Yesterday,* 28.

14. January 5 entry, Truman's 1947 diary, http://www.trumanlibrary.org/diary/transcript.htm, February 21, 2006.

15. Mailer, "The White Negro: Superficial Reflections on the Hipster," in *Advertisements for Myself* (New York: G. P. Putnam's Sons, 1959), 337–358; William Plummer, *The Holy Goof: A Biography of Neal Cassady* (Englewood Cliffs, N.J.: Prentice-Hall, 1981), 55.

16. Mailer, "White Negro," 356.

17. Dwight Eisenhower to Edgar Eisenhower, November 8, 1954, *The Presidential Papers of Dwight David Eisenhower,* http://www.eisenhowermemorial.org/presidential-papers/first-term/documents/1147.cfm, February 21, 2006; George H. Nash, *The Conservative Intellectual Movement in America since 1945* (New York: Basic Books, 1976), especially ch. 6.

18. William C. Berman, *America's Right Turn: From Nixon to Clinton,* 2nd ed. (Baltimore: Johns Hopkins University Press, 2001), 13; F. Richard Ciccone, *Royko: A Life in Print* (New York: Public Affairs, 2001), 30, quoting Royko.

19. Mike Royko, *Boss: Richard J. Daley of Chicago* (New York: Plume, 1988), 31.

20. Gary Gerstle, *American Crucible: Race and Nation in the Twentieth Century* (Princeton, N.J.: Princeton University Press, 2001), ch. 5.

21. Milton Gordon, *Assimilation in American Life: The Role of Race, Religion, and National Origins* (New York: Oxford University Press, 1964), 165–166, 181, 205–206; Belfrage, *Un-American Activities,* 92; John Bartlow Martin, "Abortion,"

Saturday Evening Post 234 (May 20, 1961): 21 (Italian boy); Herbert S. Parmet, *George Bush: The Life of a Lone Star Yankee* (New York: Scribner, 1997), 18.

22. Mark Silk, *Spiritual Politics: Religion and America since World War II* (New York: Simon and Schuster, 1988), 70–83, 188 n. 12; Mark S. Massa, *Catholics and American Culture: Fulton Sheen, Dorothy Day, and the Notre Dame Football Team* (New York: Crossroad, 1999), ch. 1.

23. Peter Wallenstein, *Tell the Court I Love My Wife: Race, Marriage, and Law—An American History* (New York: Palgrave Macmillan, 2002), 253–254; David J. Garrow, *Bearing the Cross: Martin Luther King, Jr., and the Southern Christian Leadership Conference* (New York: William Morrow, 1986), 40–41; David A. Hollinger, "Amalgamation and Hypodescent: The Question of Ethnoracial Mixture in the History of the United States," *American Historical Review* 108 (2003): 1364.

24. Joseph W. Alsop with Adam Platt, "The Wasp Ascendancy," *NYRB* 36 (November 9, 1989): 56; Dan A. Oren, *Joining the Club: A History of Jews and Yale* (New Haven, Conn.: Yale University Press, 1985), 326; Patrick Allitt, "Perry Miller and American Religion," New England Historical Association paper, Deerfield, Mass., April 24, 1987, pp. 16–17; John Steele Gordon, "The Country Club," *American Heritage* 41 (September/October 1990): 82, 84.

25. Mark Rudd, "Why Were There So Many Jews in SDS?" http://www.markrudd .com/?about-mark-rudd/why-were-there-so-many-jews-in-sds-or-the-ordeal-of-civility.html, March 15, 2010; Francis Wilkinson, "Nixon's Real Enforcer," *NYT*, December 25, 2005; Marilyn Stasio, "Evan Hunter . . . Dies at 78," *NYT*, July 7, 2005.

26. Paul Blanshard, *American Freedom and Catholic Power*, 2nd ed. (Boston: Beacon Press, 1958), opposite title page; Jack Star, "The Vanishing Nun," *Look* 27 (October 22, 1963): 44; Tim Russert, *Big Russ and Me: Father and Son: Lessons of Life* (New York: Miramax Books, 2004), 180–181.

27. Patrick J. Buchanan, *Right from the Beginning* (Boston: Little, Brown, 1988), 72, 104–105; Joseph A. Califano Jr., *Inside: A Public and Private Life* (New York: Public Affairs, 2004), 35; Evan Thomas and Suzanne Smalley, "Growing Up Giuliani," *Newsweek* 150 (December 3, 2007): 32; Peter Occhiogrosso, *Once a Catholic: Prominent Catholics and Ex-Catholics Reveal the Influence of the Church on Their Lives and Work* (Boston: Houghton Mifflin, 1987), 46 (Stone).

28. Stuart Rose to John Bartlow Martin, August 11, 1960, box 173, John Bartlow Martin Papers, hereafter JBMP, in LCMD.

29. Francis Cardinal Spellman, *Communism Is* Un-American (New York: Constitutional Educational League pamphlet, n.d.).

30. John Courtney Murray, "Paul Blanshard and the New Nativism," *The Month* n. s. 5 (April 1951): 214–225, and "The Crisis in Church-State Relationships in the USA" (TS, October 29, 1950), p. 2 (quote), box 703, CBLP; *John Courtney Murray and the Growth of Tradition*, ed. J. Leon Hooper and Todd David Whitmore (Kansas City: Sheed and Ward, 1996), v-xv; and Paul Blanshard, *Personal and Controversial: An Autobiography* (Boston: Beacon Press, 1973), 114–115, 279–283.

31. Undated 1972 letter draft, Clare Boothe Luce to William F. Buckley Jr. ("square"), box 340, CBLP; Sylvia Jukes Morris, *Rage for Fame: The Ascent of Clare Boothe Luce* (New York: Random House, 1997), 285 ("yellow-haired").

32. "By Love Possessed" (TS, 1959) and "Last Résumé for HRL" (MS, July 17, 1960), both box 793, and Clare's undated profile (MS, 1961?) of Harry, box 794, CBLP; Wilfrid Sheed, *Clare Boothe Luce* (New York: E. P. Dutton, 1982), 92.

33. The borderline characterization rests on the foundations of two psychiatrically explicit autobiographical documents, "The Double Bind" (TS, 1962), box 322, and Clare Luce to Gerald Heard, November 20, 1959, box 796, CBLP. Morris's *Rage for Fame* paints a compatible picture of a narcissistic, insecure, depressive, needful, and preemptively cruel woman haunted by a miserable childhood and fear of rejection.

34. Accident report, box 731, CBLP; Clare Boothe Luce, "The 'Real' Reason," *McCall's* 74 (February 1947): 16–17, 116–135, "sleeping" at p. 130; (March 1947): 16–17, 153–176; (April 1947): 26–27, 76–90, with readers' replies (May 1947): 30, 112–116.

35. "The 'Real' Reason," 78; Morris, *Rage for Fame*, 95–96, 290, 525 n. 33; diary entries of April 10–12, 1925, January 5–6, 1926, and February 10–14, 1926, box 793, CBLP. "By Love Possessed," above, claims that Clare underwent three operations in a futile attempt to restore her fertility. Some caution is in order. Luce the playwright embellished her writings, and Luce the borderline made them self-aggrandizing. But the conversion story checks out, in that Wiatrak's long correspondence antedates her spiritual crisis and meetings with Sheen.

36. Stephen Shadegg, *Clare Boothe Luce: A Biography* (New York: Simon and Schuster, 1970), 209–211.

37. Arthur E. Payne to Luce, February 21, 1946, box 124, CBLP.

38. "The 'Real' Reason," 121, "attended church."

39. Luce, undated MS notes, "Notes and Fragments: Politics, 1970s" folder, box 341, CBLP.

40. Helen Lawrenson, "The Woman," *Esquire* 82 (August 1977): 152; Luce to John Courtney Murray, January 27, 1962, box 315; Luce to Murray, undated (1961 or 1962), box 795; LSD MS notes, January 8, 1961, box 793; Luce to Gerald Heard, November 20, 1959, box 796, CBLP.

41. Unpaginated journal, ca. 1949, box 315, CBLP; "Confessions," undated MS fragment, box 4 of separately filed additions to RRP.

42. "The 'Real' Reason," 122; Luce to Sidney Cohen, December 2, 1965, box 795, CBLP; Kevin White, *The First Sexual Revolution: The Emergence of Male Heterosexuality in Modern America* (New York: New York University Press, 1993); John Burnham, *Bad Habits: Drinking, Smoking, Taking Drugs, Gambling, Sexual Misbehavior, and Swearing in American History* (New York: New York University Press, 1993).

43. Beth Bailey, *Sex in the Heartland* (Cambridge, Mass.: Harvard University Press, 1999), 22; "Evansville briefing sheet" (TS, 1960), box 77, JBMP; Stephanie Coontz, *The Way We Never Were: American Families and the Nostalgia Trap* (New York: Basic Books, 1992).

44. Alan Petigny, *The Permissive Society: America, 1941–1965* (Cambridge: Cambridge University Press, 2009); Burnham, *Bad Habits,* 1–22; Hitchcock, *Years of Crisis,* 44–56; Bogue et al., *Population,* 166 (using crude rate).

45. Bernardine Dohrn, "Sixties Lessons and Lore," *Monthly Review* 53 (December 2001): 44; W. J. Rorabaugh, *Kennedy and the Promise of the Sixties* (Cambridge: Cambridge University Press, 2002), 212 (Huxley).

46. Tone, *Devices and Desires*, xv, 233, 239; Rovere, unpublished journal (TS, 1948–1949), 58–60, 301, RRP; Blanshard, *Personal and Controversial*, 114–115.

47. Robert Nisbet, "Individual Ethics," *Public Opinion* 9 (November/December 1986): 8.

48. George A. Akerlof and Janet L. Yellen, "An Analysis of Out-of-Wedlock Births in the United States," Brookings Institution policy brief no. 5 (August 1996), http://www.brookings.edu/papers/1996/08childrenfamilies_akerlof.aspx, including quotation.

49. Luce to Murray, January 27, 1962, box 315, CBLP; Clare Boothe Luce, "Birth Control and the Catholic Church," *McCall's* 94 (February 1967): 48, 198.

50. Leslie Woodcock Tentler, *Catholics and Contraception: An American History* (Ithaca, N.Y.: Cornell University Press, 2004), statistic at p. 134; Joseph Cardinal Ratzinger and Vittorio Messori, *The Ratzinger Report: An Exclusive Interview on the State of the Church* (San Francisco: Ignatius Press, 1985), 84.

51. Tone, *Devices and Desires*, 237 ("don't confess"); Tentler, *Catholics and Contraception*, 153, 235; Andrew M. Greeley, "Children of the Council," *America* 190 (June 7–14, 2004): 8–11; Peter Steinfels, *A People Adrift: The Crisis of the Roman Catholic Church in America* (New York: Simon and Schuster, 2003), 275 ("don't ask"); Ratzinger and Messori, *The Ratzinger Report*, ch. 3.

52. Thomas J. Carty, *A Catholic in the White House? Religion, Politics, and John F. Kennedy's Presidential Campaign* (New York: Palgrave Macmillan, 2004); Luce to Wilfrid Sheed, undated MS letter, probably 1972 or 1973, box 315, CBLP (quoting Kennedy).

53. Martin, 1960 campaign journal, n.p., box 76, JBMP.

54. Rorabaugh, *Kennedy and the Promise of the Sixties*, ch. 1, and *The Real Making of the President: Kennedy, Nixon, and the 1960 Election* (Lawrence: University Press of Kansas, 2009); Robert Dallek, *An Unfinished Life: John F. Kennedy, 1917–1963* (Boston: Little, Brown, 2003), 296.

55. Mark A. Noll, "The Eclipse of Old Hostilities *between* and the Potential for New Strife *among* Catholics and Protestants since World War II," in *Uncivil Religion: Interreligious Hostility in America*, ed. Robert N. Bellah and Frederick E. Greenspahn (New York: Crossroad, 1987), 86–109, Graham at p. 88; Luce to Wilfrid Sheed, undated MS letter, box 315, CBLP; Bradlee, *Conversations with Kennedy*, 166.

56. William Martin, *A Prophet with Honor: The Billy Graham Story* (New York: William Morrow, 1991), 310 (Cushing), 460, 491; Bruce Bryant-Friedland, "Graham Rally Courts Catholics," *FTU*, December 15, 1999.

3. OVERCOME

1. "The Ideas of Henry Luce" (TS, 1966), pp. 100–101, box 83, Henry Robinson Luce Papers, LCMD; W. J. Rorabaugh, *The Real Making of the President: Kennedy, Nixon, and the 1960 Election* (Lawrence: University Press of Kansas, 2009), 50.

2. Rovere, unpublished TS notes on March 17, 1962, interview with JFK, p. 4, box 12, RRP.

3. Joel Williamson, *The Crucible of Race: Black-White Relations in the American South since Emancipation* (New York: Oxford University Press, 1984), 57–59.

4. John Steinbeck, *Travels with Charley: In Search of America* (New York: Viking, 1962), 226–227.

5. Taylor Branch, *Parting the Waters: America in the King Years, 1954–63* (New York: Simon and Schuster, 1988), ch. 9; Arthur M. Schlesinger Jr., *A Thousand Days: John F. Kennedy in the White House* (New York: Houghton Mifflin, 1965), 74 (quotation).

6. Allen J. Matusow, *The Unraveling of America: A History of Liberalism in the 1960s* (New York: Harper and Row, 1984), part I; Branch, *Parting the Waters*, chs. 9–21, "little black girl" at p. 759; and W.J. Rorabaugh, *Kennedy and the Promise of the Sixties* (Cambridge: Cambridge University Press, 2002), ch. 3.

7. Jane Dailey, "Sex, Segregation, and the Sacred after *Brown*," *JAH* 91 (2004): 119–144, "Gospel" at p. 133; Taylor Branch, *At Canaan's Edge: America in the King Years, 1965–68* (New York: Simon and Schuster, 2006), chs. 13, 30, and Branch, *Pillar of Fire: America in the King Years, 1963–65* (New York: Simon and Schuster, 1998), "mad" at p. 579.

8. Anglican Orthodox Church Ephemeral Materials, folders 4–12, Wilcox Collection of Contemporary Political Movements, hereafter WCCPM, Spencer Research Library, Lawrence, Kansas. Quotations from "The Anglican Orthodox Church" (pamphlet, 1964?), folder 4, and "National 'Gay' Group Active in Ft. Valley," *Macon Herald*, March 20, 1975.

9. U.S. Senate, *"Equal Rights" Amendment: Hearings before the Subcommittee on Constitutional Amendments*, 91st Cong., 2nd sess. (1970), 337; Thomas F. Burke, *Lawyers, Lawsuits, and Legal Rights: The Battle over Litigation in American Society* (Berkeley: University of California Press, 2002), ch. 2.

10. G. Edward White, *Earl Warren: A Public Life* (New York: Oxford University Press, 1982); Ed Cray, *Chief Justice: A Biography of Earl Warren* (New York: Simon and Schuster, 1997), quotations at pp. 387, 337.

11. Cray, *Chief Justice*, 327–339; Robert A. Caro, *The Years of Lyndon Johnson: Master of the Senate* (New York: Knopf, 2002), 1030–1033.

12. Burke, *Lawyers, Lawsuits, and Legal Rights*, 8–13.

13. Lucas A. Powe Jr., *The Warren Court and American Politics* (Cambridge, Mass.: Harvard University Press, 2000), precedent statistics at pp. 405, 482.

14. Powe, *Warren Court*, quotations at pp. 188, 391, 410, 411; Escobedo cover, *Time* 87 (April 29, 1966); "People," *Time* 91 (February 16, 1968): 46; David Margolick, "Living Landmark Cites Harassment," *NYT*, September 17, 1984; "Man in Landmark Court Case Arrested in Tavern Shooting," *NYT*, September 27, 1985.

15. Alfred H. Kelly and Winfred A. Harbison, *The American Constitution* 4th ed. (New York: Norton, 1970), 1016; Powe, *Warren Court*, 493, 494.

16. Branch, *Parting the Waters*, 922.

17. Max Holland, "The Assassination Tapes," *Atlantic* 293 (June 2004): 82 ("Murder Inc."); Doris Kearns Goodwin, *Lyndon Johnson and the American Dream* (New York: Harper and Row, 1976), 178.

18. "President Lyndon B. Johnson's Remarks at the University of Michigan, May 22, 1964," http://www.lbjlib.utexas.edu/johnson/archives.hom/speeches.hom/640522

.asp, May 27, 2006; Robert Dallek, *Flawed Giant: Lyndon Johnson and His Times, 1961–1973* (New York: Oxford University Press, 1998), 82.

19. Lee Edwards, *Goldwater: The Man Who Made a Revolution* (Washington, D.C.: Regnery, 1995), and Rick Perlstein, *Before the Storm: Barry Goldwater and the Unmaking of the American Consensus* (New York: Hill and Wang, 2001).

20. Henry Luce, "The Significance of the Goldwater Nomination" (TS, 1964), box 83, Henry Robinson Luce Papers, LCMD; Perlstein, *Before the Storm*, 197 (Khrushchev).

21. Barry Goldwater, *With No Apologies* (New York: William Morrow, 1979), 11 ("dime-store"); Lisa McGirr, *Suburban Warriors: The Origins of the New American Right* (Princeton, N.J.: Princeton University Press, 2001); Richard H. Rovere with Bill Mauldin, *The Goldwater Caper* (New York: Harcourt, Brace and World, 1965), 45.

22. Paul K. Conkin, *Big Daddy from the Pedernales: Lyndon Baines Johnson* (Boston: Twayne, 1986), 25–29, and Monroe Billington, "Lyndon B. Johnson: The Religion of a Politician," *Presidential Studies Quarterly* 17 (Summer 1987): 519–530.

23. *The Public Records of Barry M. Goldwater and William E. Miller,* part 1, *Congressional Quarterly Special Report* (July 31, 1964), 1603; "Goldwater Had a Way with Words," *Arizona Republic,* May 29, 1998.

24. William Martin, *With God on Our Side: The Rise of the Religious Right in America,* rev. ed. (New York: Broadway Books, 2005), 80, 86.

25. "Is LBJ Slipping?" *National Review* 16 (October 20, 1964): 902.

26. Martin, unpaginated journal notes, September 15, 1964, box 78, JBMP.

27. Richard Rovere, White House notes (TS, October 1, 1964), p. 4, box 17, RRP; Martin memo to Bill Moyers re Pennsylvania (undated, early September 1964) and Martin to Moyers re Illinois, October 1, 1964, both box 78, JBMP; John Updike, *Self-Consciousness: Memoirs* (New York: Knopf, 1989), 135.

28. John B. Judis, "The Alrightnik of Arizona," *New Republic* 199 (November 28, 1988): 41–44; Stuart Spencer interview, November 15–16, 2001, p. 8, Ronald Reagan Oral History Project, http://webstorage1.mcpa.virginia.edu/library/mc/poh/rwr/transcripts/spencer_stuart.pdf.

29. "Right Wing Lost Popularity in Election, but Gave Up Nothing Else," *Group Research Report* 3 (November 14, 1964): 83; Branch, *Pillar of Fire,* 522.

30. Johnson's voting rights address, March 15, 1965, http://www.hpol.org/lbj/voting/.

31. William A. Schambra, "Progressive Liberalism and American 'Community,'" *Public Interest* no. 80 (Summer 1985): 32–37.

32. Author interview (AI) with Richard Viguerie, June 22, 2006; Johnson–McCone telephone conversation, August 18, 1965, http://whitehousetapes.org/clips/1965_0818_lbj_mccone.html.

33. H. W. Brands, *The Strange Death of American Liberalism* (New Haven, Conn.: Yale University Press, 2001), ch. 4.

34. Rorabaugh, *Real Making of the President,* 135 (Dallas); Goodwin, *Lyndon Johnson,* 251–252; Larry L. King, "Lyndon B. Johnson and Vietnam," *Historical Viewpoints,* 5th ed., ed. John A. Garraty (New York: Harper and Row, 1987), 411.

35. Kevin Phillips, *The Politics of Rich and Poor: Wealth and the American Electorate in the Reagan Aftermath* (New York: Random House, 1990), 203–207; Matusow, *Unraveling,* 213; Theda Skocpol, "Targeting within Universalism: Politically Viable Policies to Combat Poverty in the United States," in *The Urban Underclass,* ed. Christopher Jencks and Paul E. Peterson (Washington, D.C.: Brookings Institution, 1991), 418–419.

36. Matthew D. Lassiter, *The Silent Majority: Suburban Politics in the Sunbelt South* (Princeton, N.J.: Princeton University Press, 2006); Kevin M. Kruse, *White Flight: Atlanta and the Making of Modern Conservatism* (Princeton, N.J.: Princeton University Press, 2005), quotation (originally from Robert Reich) at p. 246.

37. Matusow, *Unraveling,* 175–176; Dale Russakoff, "In Motor City, Anger Yields to Pragmatism," *Washington Post,* hereafter *WP,* March 26, 2006.

38. Skocpol, "Targeting within Universalism," 411–436; Nicholas J. G. Winter, "Beyond Welfare: Framing and the Racialization of White Opinion on Social Security," *American Journal of Political Science* 50 (2006): 400–420.

39. Powe, *Warren Court,* 275; Ann Marlowe, *How to Stop Time: Heroin from A to Z* (London: Virago, 2002), 170 ("schvartzes").

40. Matusow, *Unraveling,* 365 ("burn"); H. Rap Brown, *Die Nigger Die!* (New York: Dial, 1969), 124 ("separate"); Goodwin, *Lyndon Johnson,* 305.

41. Dominic Sandbrook, *Eugene McCarthy: The Rise and Fall of Postwar American Liberalism* (New York: Knopf, 2004), 142–143.

42. George McGovern, *Grassroots: The Autobiography of George McGovern* (New York: Random House, 1977), 104 ("leg"); John Cooney, *The American Pope: The Life and Times of Francis Cardinal Spellman* (New York: Times Books, 1984), 325–327.

43. Harry McPherson oral history, part IV, March 24, 1969, LBJ Library transcription, p. 9, http://www.lbjlib.utexas.edu/johnson/archives.hom/oralhistory.hom/mcpherson/mcpher04.pdf; Sandbrook, *Eugene McCarthy,* 184.

44. *The Autobiography of Martin Luther King, Jr.,* ed. Clayborne Carson (New York: Warner Books, 1998), ch. 30.

45. "Elections" (1968 pamphlet), folder 2, SDS Ephemeral Materials, WCCPM.

46. Bill Ayers, *Fugitive Days: A Memoir* (Harmondsworth, Middlesex: Penguin, 2003), 64; Louis Menand, "College: The End of the Golden Age," *NYRB* 48 (October 18, 2001), 44; Kitty Kelley, *The Family: The Real Story of the Bush Dynasty* (New York: Doubleday, 2004), 297; Jerald G. Bachman and M. Kent Jennings, "The Impact of Vietnam on Trust in Government," *Journal of Social Issues* 31 (1975): 146.

47. Norman C. Miller, "The Wallace Boom," *Wall Street Journal,* hereafter *WSJ,* September 17, 1968.

48. Dan T. Carter, *The Politics of Rage: George Wallace, the Origins of the New Conservatism, and the Transformation of American Politics* (New York: Simon and Schuster, 1995), 346; Theodore H. White, *The Making of the President, 1968* (New York: Atheneum, 1969), 349; James Moore and Wayne Slater, *Bush's Brain: How Karl Rove Made George W. Bush Presidential* (Hoboken, N.J.: John Wiley and Sons, 2003), 125.

49. Pete Hamill, "The Revolt of the White Lower Middle Class," *New York* 2 (April 14, 1969), "strangle" at p. 24; "The Public Record of George C. Wallace," *CQ Weekly Report* 26 (September 27, 1968): 2563.

50. John Bartlow Martin, *It Seems Like Only Yesterday: Memoirs of Writing, Presidential Politics, and the Diplomatic Life* (New York: William Morrow, 1986), 297.

51. Ibid., 288–289; Brian Dooley, *Robert Kennedy: The Final Years* (New York: St. Martin's Press, 1996), 97–99, 124.

52. Martin to RFK, April 21, 1968, and June 3, 1968; "RFK Notes" (TS, June 28, 1968), 61, 70–71, 78, all box 82, JBMP.

53. Arthur M. Schlesinger Jr., *Journals, 1952–2000,* ed. Andrew Schlesinger and Stephen Schlesinger (New York: Penguin, 2007), 295; Bill Clinton, *My Life* (New York: Knopf, 2004), 122.

54. Dooley, *Robert Kennedy,* 16–17, 126–127, 130; Richard M. Scammon and Ben J. Wattenberg, *The Real Majority* (New York: Coward-McCann, 1970), ch. 9; George McGovern, AI, March 20, 2009; Arthur M. Schlesinger Jr., *Robert Kennedy and His Times* (Boston: Houghton Mifflin, 1978), 910 (Stevenson); C. David Heymann, *RFK: A Candid Biography of Robert Kennedy* (New York: Dutton, 1998), ch. 25; Evan Thomas, *Robert Kennedy: His Life* (New York: Simon and Schuster, 2000), 388 (suburbs).

55. Heymann, *RFK,* "straight-line" at p. 494; Donald T. Critchlow, *The Conservative Ascendancy: How the GOP Right Made Political History* (Cambridge, Mass.: Harvard University Press, 2007), 89; White, *Making of the President, 1968,* 298, 303.

56. Dallek, *Flawed Giant,* 556–564; John W. Dean, *The Rehnquist Choice: The Untold Story of the Nixon Appointment that Redefined the Supreme Court* (New York: Free Press, 2001), 3–4; Bruce Allen Murphy, *Fortas: The Rise and Ruin of a Supreme Court Justice* (New York: William Morrow, 1988), "Mallory" at p. 426; "Yale Law School Holds 'Fortas Film Festival,'" *NYT,* November 5, 1968.

57. Matusow, *Unraveling,* 438; Donald J. Bogue et al., *The Population of the United States: Historical Trends and Future Projections* (New York: Free Press, 1985), 665.

58. Scammon and Wattenberg, *Real Majority,* 174–175; Martin, 1968 Humphrey campaign journal, quotation at p. 122, box 85, JBMP.

4. TWENTY PERCENT OF WHAT THE NUTS WANT

1. Christopher Lasch, "The Baby Boomers: Here Today, Gone Tomorrow," *New Oxford Review* 60 (September 1993): 7; Maurice Isserman and Michael Kazin, *America Divided: The Civil War of the 1960s,* 2nd ed. (New York: Oxford University Press, 2004); Frank Kusch, *Battleground Chicago: The Police and the 1968 Democratic Convention* (Westport, Conn.: Praeger, 2004), 161.

2. Bill Clinton, *My Life* (New York: Knopf, 2004), 133.

3. "Half-Million Commemorate a Police Raid on a Gay Bar," *NYT,* June 26, 1989; David Obst, *Too Good to Be Forgotten: Changing America in the '60s and '70s* (New York: John Wiley and Sons, 1998), 101; Kusch, *Battleground Chicago,* 84.

4. Charles A. Reich, *The Greening of America* (New York: Random House, 1970), and *The Sorcerer of Bolinas Reef* (New York: Random House, 1976), quotation at p. 104.

5. Nixon to Pat Buchanan, February 10, 1971, box 4, memoranda name file, Staff Member and Office Files, White House Special Files, Uncontested Documents File, NPMS.

6. Clare Luce to William F. Buckley Jr., undated 1972 draft, box 340, CBLP; Mark Feeney, *Nixon at the Movies: A Book about Belief* (Chicago: University of Chicago Press, 2004), 14, 231.

7. Ken W. Clawson, "A Loyalist's Memoir," *WP*, August 9, 1979; John Osborne, "White House Watch: Gabbing with Harlow," *New Republic* 178 (May 13, 1978): 14.

8. My sketch draws on Fawn M. Brodie, *Richard Nixon: The Shaping of His Character* (New York: Norton, 1981); Stephen E. Ambrose, *Nixon,* 3 vols. (New York: Simon and Schuster, 1987–1991); Herbert S. Parmet, *Richard Nixon and His America* (Boston: Little, Brown, 1990); Richard Reeves, *President Nixon: Alone in the White House* (New York: Simon and Schuster, 2001); and David Greenberg, *Nixon's Shadow: The History of an Image* (New York: Norton, 2003).

9. Paraphrasing tape nos. 498–5, May 13, 1971; 505–4, May 26, 1971; 536–4, 536–10, and 536–16, July 3, 1971; 524–27, June 17, 1971; 559–23, August 10, 1971; 10–116, October 7, 1971; and 685–5, January 27, 1972, NPMS. Nixon's prejudices are also documented in H. R. Haldeman, *The Haldeman Diaries: Inside the Nixon White House* (New York: G. P. Putnam's Sons, 1994), and John W. Dean, *The Rehnquist Choice: The Untold Story of the Nixon Appointment that Redefined the Supreme Court* (New York: Free Press, 2001), Jewish seat remark at p. 73.

10. Tape 498–5, May 13, 1971, NPMS.

11. Tape 662–4, February 1, 1972, and Ehrlichman's MS notes of February 10, 1971, meeting, box 4, Staff Member and Office Files, White House Special Files, Ehrlichman Contested Documents File, both NPMS.

12. Allen J. Matusow, *Nixon's Economy: Booms, Busts, Dollars, and Votes* (Lawrence: University Press of Kansas, 1998); Deborah Hart Strober and Gerald S. Strober, *The Nixon Presidency: An Oral History of the Era,* rev. ed. (Washington, D.C.: Brassey's, 2003), 46 (Haldeman).

13. James Rosen, *The Strong Man: John Mitchell and the Secrets of Watergate* (New York: Doubleday, 2008), 71; address of March 16, 1972, *Public Papers of the Presidents of the United States,* (hereafter *PP*): *Richard Nixon, 1972* (Washington, D.C.: GPO, 1974), 425–429; address of November 3, 1969, *PP: Richard Nixon, 1969,* 909.

14. Strober and Strober, *Nixon Presidency,* 108 (Phillips). Nixon's domestic policy: Joan Hoff, *Nixon Reconsidered* (New York: Basic Books, 1994), part I; Melvin Small, *The Presidency of Richard Nixon* (Lawrence: University Press of Kansas, 1999), chs. 6 and 7 (60 percent at p. 154, hotel locks at p. 209); and Greenberg, *Nixon's Shadow,* ch. 8.

15. Tape 33–2, November 3, 1972, NPMS; Pat Buchanan to H. R. Haldeman, April 20, 1972 (abortion law), box 17964, Mariam Bell files, Ronald Reagan Presi-

dential Library, hereafter RL, Simi Valley, California; William Martin, *With God on Our Side: The Rise of the Religious Right in America,* rev. ed. (New York: Broadway Books, 2005), 98–99.

16. Charles Colson with Ellen Santilli Vaughn *Kingdoms in Conflict* (New York: William Morrow, 1987), 306–309.

17. Richard Scammon and Ben J. Wattenberg, *The Real Majority* (New York: Coward-McCann, 1970); *Haldeman Diaries,* 127 (Roth); Arthur M. Schlesinger Jr., *Journals, 1952–2000,* ed. Andrew Schlesinger and Stephen Schlesinger (New York: Penguin, 2007), 397 (Kissinger); Dean, *Rehnquist Choice,* 104, 113–116, 126, 145–146, 158.

18. Parmet, *Richard Nixon,* 509–514; Bruce Kehrli to H. R. Haldeman, December 29, 1970, President's Personal File, Alpha Name/Subject File, box 14 (most admired) and Buchanan to Nixon, June 23, 1970, box 23, Staff Member and Office Files, White House Special Files, Ehrlichman Contested Documents File, both NPMS. Quotes from speeches of September 25, 1970, series III, subseries 7, box 13, and March 25, 1972, series III, subseries 3.7, box 12, Spiro T. Agnew Papers, hereafter STAP, University of Maryland, College Park.

19. Moynihan to Nixon, November 13, 1970, box I:245, DPMP; Small, *Presidency of Richard Nixon,* 235; David Brock, *The Republican Noise Machine: Right-Wing Media and How It Corrupts Democracy* (New York: Crown, 2004), 19.

20. Max Frankel to Moynihan, n. d. (February 1970), box I:250, and Moynihan to Nixon, September 20, 1971, box I:245, DPMP.

21. Moynihan to Nixon, September 20, 1971, box I:245, and Moynihan to Nixon, January 16, 1970, box I:244, DPMP.

22. Robert D. Novak, *The Prince of Darkness: 50 Years Reporting in Washington* (New York: Crown Forum, 2007), 419. My sketch draws on Douglas Schoen, *Pat: A Biography of Daniel Patrick Moynihan* (New York: Harper and Row, 1979), and Godfrey Hodgson, *The Gentleman from New York: Daniel Patrick Moynihan: A Biography* (Boston: Houghton Mifflin, 2000).

23. Small, *Presidency of Richard Nixon,* 199–200, 221–222; Bruce J. Schulman, *The Seventies: The Great Shift in American Culture, Society, and Politics* (New York: Free Press, 2001), 27–29; Dean J. Kotlowski, *Nixon's Civil Rights: Politics, Principle, and Policy* (Cambridge, Mass.: Harvard University Press, 2001), chs. 4–5; David Hamilton Golland, "Only Nixon Could Go to Philadelphia," http://www.davidgolland.com/Golland/Publications/Only_Nixon.pdf, March 16, 2010.

24. Reeves, *President Nixon,* 294–295.

25. Small, *Presidency of Richard Nixon,* 209; John Ehrlichman, *Witness to Power: The Nixon Years* (New York: Simon and Schuster, 1982), 275; Brodie, *Richard Nixon,* 110.

26. Ehrlichman to Nixon, October 21, 1970, box 23, Staff Member and Office Files, White House Special Files, Ehrlichman Uncontested Documents File, and tape 498–5, May 13, 1971, both NPMS.

27. *Harvard/Radcliffe Class of 1970, 25th Reunion: Answers to the Anonymous Questionnaire* (1995), 57, furnished by the Harvard Alumni Office; *The*

Sixties: The Years that Shaped a Generation (2005), film by Stephen Talbot (Burdon).

28. Ronald H. Spector, *After Tet: The Bloodiest Year in Vietnam* (New York: Free Press, 1993), 276–277; Morton G. Miller to Daniel Patrick Moynihan, June 16, 1970, box I:270, DPMP.

29. *Congressional Record–House,* September 23, 1970, p. 33314.

30. Remarks of October 23, 1969, *PP: Richard Nixon, 1969,* 833 (quotations); David T. Courtwright, "The Controlled Substances Act: How a 'Big Tent' Reform Became a Punitive Drug Law," *Drug and Alcohol Dependence* 76 (2004): 9–15; David F. Musto and Pamela Korsmeyer, *The Quest for Drug Control: Politics and Federal Policy in a Period of Increasing Substance Abuse, 1963–1981* (New Haven, Conn.: Yale University Press, 2002), 56–62.

31. Paul Pietro, personal communication, March 28, 2007.

32. Tape 498–5, May 13, 1971, NPMS.

33. Ibid.

34. Ehrlichman's MS notes of September 8, 1972, meeting with Nixon and Krogh, box 6, Staff Member and Office Files, White House Special Files, Ehrlichman Contested Documents File, and tape 690–11 (quotation), March 21, 1972, both NPMS.

35. Michael Massing, *The Fix* (New York: Simon and Schuster, 1998), 84–131, Rockefeller quotation at p. 126; Musto and Korsmeyer, *Quest for Drug Control,* chs. 2–4.

36. Tape 393–11B, January 4, 1973, NPMS, and address of March 10, 1973, *PP: Richard Nixon, 1973,* 180–184.

37. Ralph Z. Hallow, "Buchanan Sees 'War' Within Conservatism," *WT,* May 17, 2005; Richard A. Viguerie, *Conservatives Betrayed: How George W. Bush and Other Big Government Republicans Hijacked the Conservative Cause* (Los Angeles: Bonus Books, 2006), 183.

38. Buchanan to Nixon, January 6, 1971, box 1, Buchanan chronological files, Staff Member and Office Files, White House Special Files, Contested Documents File, NPMS; F___ S___ (archival regulations prohibit the use of constituents' names) to Robert Dole, August 5, 1971, acquisition 329–74–160, box 10, Robert J. Dole Institute of Politics Archive, University of Kansas, hereafter DI; John B. Judis, *William F. Buckley, Jr.: Patron Saint of the Conservatives* (New York: Simon and Schuster, 1988), ch. 19, Rusher at p. 332.

39. Goldwater to Gilbert Wheeler, December 17, 1971, series III, subseries 7, folder 13, STAP.

40. Rusher to Ronald Reagan, January 5, 1973, box 75, and Rusher to Buckley, March 9, 1972, box 121, William Allen Rusher Papers, hereafter WARP, LCMD; William A. Rusher, *The Making of the New Majority Party* (New York: Sheed and Ward, 1975); Jack Anderson, "Viguerie: A Modern Wizard of Oz," *WP,* June 3, 1978 (tank).

41. Matusow, *Nixon's Economy,* chs. 7–10; *Haldeman Diaries,* 472.

42. Thomas Byrne Edsall and Mary D. Edsall, *Chain Reaction: The Impact of Race, Rights, and Taxes on American Politics* (New York: Norton, 1991), ch. 4;

Dominic Sandbrook, *Eugene McCarthy: The Rise and Fall of Postwar American Liberalism* (New York: Knopf, 2004), 219.

43. Haynes Johnson, "A Portrait of Democrats' New Delegate," *WP,* July 8, 1972; Rusher, *New Majority Party,* 85; Obst, *Too Good to Be Forgotten,* 207.

44. John Bartlow Martin, *It Seems Like Only Yesterday: Memoirs of Writing, Presidential Politics, and the Diplomatic Life* (New York: William Morrow, 1986), 323; Bruce Miroff, *The Liberals' Moment: The McGovern Insurgency and the Crisis of the Democratic Party* (Lawrence: University Press of Kansas, 2007), 89–97, 299–301; Michael Novak, "Errand into the Wilderness," *Political Passages: Journeys of Change through Two Decades, 1968–1988,* ed. John H. Bunzel (New York: Free Press, 1988), 257; tape 31–81, October 16, 1972, NPMS.

45. Buchanan memoranda of April 12, June 18, June 23, September 13, and October 23, 1972, box 2, Buchanan Contested Documents File, and Teeter survey, box 100, Charles W. Colson Uncontested Documents File, both in Staff Member and Office Files, White House Special Files, NPMS.

46. George McGovern, AI, March 20, 2009; Small, *Presidency of Richard Nixon,* 254.

47. . . . *For the People: The Platform of the Democratic Party* (1972 offprint), p. 4, box II:2947, DPMP; Kevin Phillips, *American Theocracy: The Peril and Politics of Radical Religion, Oil, and Borrowed Money in the 21st Century* (New York: Viking, 2006), 184; Buckley draft fund-raising letter of July 16, 1973, box 121, WARP.

48. Bob Woodward, *The Secret Man: The Story of Watergate's Deep Throat* (New York: Simon and Schuster, 2005); Charles Reich to William O. Douglas, May 1, 1973, box 366, William O. Douglas Papers, LCMD; Roy McHugh, "TV Reminder of Nixon Saga Haunts a 'Depressed' Bork," *Pittsburgh Press,* May 8, 1977.

49. Marshall Frady, *Billy Graham: A Parable of American Righteousness* (Boston: Little, Brown, 1979), 478; *With God on Our Side,* part II (Alexandria, Va.: PBS Video, 1996); Ambrose, *Nixon,* vol. 3, 420 ("real good").

50. H. W. Brands, *The Strange Death of American Liberalism* (New Haven, Conn.: Yale University Press, 2001), ch. 5.

51. James M. Naughton and Adam Clymer, "Gerald Ford, 38th President, Dies at 93," *NYT,* December 27, 2006; John Updike, *Memories of the Ford Administration: A Novel* (New York: Knopf, 1992).

52. Bill Roy, AI, August 19, 2006; Lou Cannon, "Roy-Dole Race Shatters Clean Campaign," *WP,* October 8, 1974.

53. Richard Ben Cramer, *Bob Dole* (New York: Random House, 1995), 80.

54. Quotations from AIs with Robert Dole, June 13, 2006, and Bill Roy, August 19, 2006. Private secretary: Roy personal communication, March 10, 2007. The 1974 race is described in Cramer, *Bob Dole,* 130–136, and Elizabeth Kolbert, "Abortion, Dole's Sword in '74, Returns to Confront Him in '96," *NYT,* July 8, 1996. Pertinent materials in DI include "Roy on Abortion," 329–91–031, box 2, "Election 1974 Abortion Ads," 329–91–273, box 25, and "Campaign Ads: 1974 Senate Election" (DVD), vol. II, no. 1, whence "eastern liberal."

55. "Dole Game Plan" (TS, n.d.), box VL 144, DI.

5. CHEERLEADERS FOR THE REV

1. Lawrence E. Harrison, *The Central Liberal Truth: How Politics Can Change a Culture and Save It from Itself* (New York: Oxford University Press, 2006), xvi.

2. Richard A. Easterlin, *Birth and Fortune: The Impact of Numbers on Personal Welfare* (New York: Basic Books, 1980); Diane J. Macunovich, *Birth Quake: The Baby Boom and Its Aftershocks* (Chicago: University of Chicago Press, 2002).

3. Cheryl Russell, *The Master Trend: How the Baby Boom Generation Is Remaking America* (New York: Plenum, 1993), 33, 136.

4. Wade Clark Roof, "The Baby Boomers' Search for God," *American Demographics* 14 (December 1992): 56, *A Generation of Seekers: The Spiritual Journeys of the Baby Boom Generation* (San Francisco: HarperSanFrancisco, 1993), and *Spiritual Marketplace: Baby Boomers and the Remaking of American Religion* (Princeton, N.J.: Princeton University Press, 1999). Roof's sample was taken from those born 1946 to 1962.

5. Charles S. Liebman, *The Ambivalent American Jew: Politics, Family, and Religion in American Jewish Life* (Philadelphia: Jewish Publication Society, 1973), 158. Education and religion: Donald J. Bogue et al., *The Population of the United States: Historical Trends and Future Projections,* rev. ed. (New York: Free Press, 1985), 411, 413, 656–657, and Charles Y. Glock and Rodney Stark, *Religion and Society in Tension* (Chicago: Rand McNally, 1965), ch. 14.

6. Steve Gillon, *Boomer Nation: The Largest and Richest Generation Ever and How It Changed America* (New York: Free Press, 2004), 35; Richard King, *The Party of Eros: Radical Social Thought and the Realm of Freedom* (Chapel Hill: University of North Carolina Press, 1972); Michael Harrington, "The Irony of Contemporary Life," *Washington Star,* September 6, 1970.

7. [Neil Postman,] "How Television Is Destroying Childhood," *San Francisco Chronicle,* March 1, 1981.

8. Thomas Frank, *The Conquest of Cool: Business Culture, Counterculture, and the Rise of Hip Consumerism* (Chicago: University of Chicago Press, 1987), 31.

9. "Address by Vice President, May 18, 1971" (TS, 1971), series III, subseries 3.7, box 13, STAP; Robert H. Bork, *Slouching towards Gomorrah: Modern Liberalism and American Decline* (New York: Regan Books, 1996), 37; *Vietnam: A Television History* transcript, http://www.pbs.org/wgbh/amex/vietnam/series/pt _10.html, February 24, 2007 (Chancellor, Rubin).

10. Paula S. Fass, "Bringing It Home: Children, Technology, and Family in the Postwar World," in *The Columbia History of Post-World War II America,* ed. Mark C. Carnes (New York: Columbia University Press, 2007), 82.

11. Lynn Z. Bloom, *Doctor Spock: Biography of a Conservative Radical* (New York: Bobbs-Merrill, 1972), ch. 6; Eric Pace, "Benjamin Spock, World's Pediatrician, Dies at 94," *NYT,* March 17, 1998 ("Bedtime"); David Obst, *Too Good to Be Forgotten: Changing America in the '60s and '70s* (New York: John Wiley and Sons, 1998), 107.

12. Thomas Maier, *Dr. Spock: An American Life* (New York: Harcourt Brace, 1998).

13. David T. Courtwright et al., *Addicts Who Survived: An Oral History of Narcotic Use in America, 1923–1965* (Knoxville: University of Tennessee Press, 1989), 314–315.

14. C. Vann Woodward, "What Became of the 1960s?" *New Republic* 171 (November 9, 1974): 18–19; Stephen E. Ambrose, *To America: Personal Reflections of an Historian* (New York: Simon and Schuster, 2002), 139–140, 228.

15. Mark Rudd, "Why Were There So Many Jews in SDS?" http://www.markrudd.com/?about-mark-rudd/why-were-there-so-many-jews-in-sds-or-the-ordeal-of-civility.html, March 15, 2010; Yuri Slezkine, *The Jewish Century* (Princeton, N.J.: Princeton University Press, 2004), 348–350; Allen J. Matusow, *The Unraveling of America: A History of Liberalism in the 1960s* (New York: Harper and Row, 1984), 308–309; Kenneth Keniston, *Young Radicals: Notes on Committed Youth* (New York: Harcourt, Brace & World, 1968).

16. AIs with David Obst and Cynthia Wills, June 15 and October 6, 2005; Mark Rudd, *Underground: My Life with SDS and the Weathermen* (New York: William Morrow, 2009), 122; Todd Gitlin, *The Sixties: Years of Hope, Days of Rage* (New York: Bantam, 1987), quotation at p. 107.

17. Susan Stern, *With the Weathermen* (New York: Doubleday, 1975), supplemented by manuscript drafts and letters. Susan's mother, Bunny Raymond, gave me permission to use the unpublished materials, which she subsequently donated to the University of Washington Special Collections Division, and which I hereafter cite as SSP. Many people who knew Stern generously shared information and leads: Mike Abeles, Thomas Congdon, Stephanie Coontz, Paul Dorpat, Todd Gitlin, Joe and Karen Kelly, Robert Kaplan, Mike Leavy, Michael Lerner, Roger Lippman, David Obst, Ray Potts, Arthur Raymond, Mark Rudd, Susan Schwartz, Judith Shapiro, Barbara Sikorski, Jeff Steinborn, Robby Stern, Roger Tanenbaum, Terry Tanenbaum, Michael Tigar, Cynthia Wills, and Barbara Winslow. Smell: "With the Weathermen," undated chapter outline, p. 3, SSP. "Princess": Bunny and Arthur Raymond, AI, July 13, 2005.

18. Robby Stern, AI, June 29 and December 3, 2005.

19. "With the Weathermen," draft outline, pp. 4–5, SSP; Stern, *With the Weathermen*, 3.

20. Stern, *With the Weathermen*, 11, 13, "With the Weathermen," draft outline, p. 5, SP.

21. "With the Weathermen," draft outline, p. 6, SSP; Stern, *With the Weathermen*, 13–14, 45–46.

22. "With the Weathermen," draft outline, p. 6, SSP; Stern, *With the Weathermen*, 31–32, 55.

23. TS prison notes [Congdon's designation], p. 4, SSP, minor typos corrected; Stern, *With the Weathermen*, 64, 72, 143–144; Gitlin, *The Sixties*, 385–86; Bill Ayers, *Fugitive Days: A Memoir* (Harmondsworth, Middlesex: Penguin, 2003), 168 (pencil).

24. Stern, *With the Weathermen*, 225.

25. Ibid., 260.

26. Susan Paynter, "Susan Stern: Personal Revolution," *Seattle Post-Intelligencer,* June 15, 1975 (moneymaking). The contract and publicity memos are in SSP.

27. Susan Brownmiller, "The Movers, the Moved, and the Movement," *NYT Book Review,* June 15, 1975, p. 6; Peter S. Prescott, "Stormy Weather," *Newsweek* 85 (June 30, 1975): 64–65; Jed Horne, "An Outcast Radical Rips the Weathermen," *People* 4 (July 7, 1975), 53. "Seattle Today Audience Reaction Recap" (TS, June 24, 1975) and newspaper reviews are in SSP. FBI: memoranda of July 1 and December 3, 1975, FOIPA file 1025198.

28. Stern, "Falling Flesh" (TS, 1976), and March 7, 1977, option agreement, SSP; AI with Ray Potts, October 1 and 2, 2005, Joe Kelly, August 1, 2005, Karen Kelly, August 2, 2005, and Martha Greer, August 11, 2005 (go-go). Stern's death: above interviews and Robby Stern, June 29, 2005, Mike Abeles, July 12, 2005, Bunny and Arthur Raymond, July 13, 2005, and Roger Tanenbaum, July 7 and 14, 2005; Dick Clever, "Author Susan Stern Ill, On Life Support Device," *Seattle Post-Intelligencer,* July 31, 1976; "Controversy over Death of Susan Stern," *Seattle Post-Intelligencer,* August 3, 1976; death certificate, July 31, 1976, and coroner's letter, August 17, 1976, SSP.

29. Stern, *With the Weathermen,* 323; "Controversy over Death;" "Lebowski Fest," http://www.lebowskifest.com/, March 16, 2007.

30. Kenneth Cmiel, "Drowning in Pictures," *The Columbia History of Post-World War II America,* ed. Mark C. Carnes (New York: Columbia University Press, 2007), 36–56.

31. Cathleen Falsani, "Hefner: 'I'm a Pretty Moral Guy,' " *Chicago Sun-Times,* September 26, 2004; Sys Morch, "Sociological Trends in the United States in 1973 and 1974" (TS, 1975), p. 25, J. Walter Thompson Company Archives, Writings and Speeches Collection, box 26, Special Collections Library, Duke University.

32. Mariano Azuela, *The Flies,* in *Two Novels of Mexico* (Berkeley: University of California Press, 1970), 13; Arthur Schlesinger Jr. to Richard Rovere, June 24, 1964, box 3, RRP; Eric Schlosser, *Reefer Madness: Sex, Drugs, and Cheap Labor in the American Black Market* (Boston: Houghton Mifflin, 2003), ch. 3; Rodney A. Smolla, *Jerry Falwell v. Larry Flynt: The First Amendment on Trial* (New York: St. Martin's Press, 1988), 42–43.

33. Benjamin Stein, "Whatever Happened to Small-Town America?" *Public Interest* no. 44 (Summer 1976): 17–26, with reply to Herbert Gans, 127–128 (Rosenberg); John P. Robinson and Geoffrey Godbey, *Time for Life: The Surprising Ways Americans Use Their Time* (University Park: Pennsylvania State University Press, 1997), 142–143.

34. Laurence Leamer, *King of the Night: The Life of Johnny Carson* (New York: William Morrow, 1989); Stephen Cox, *Here's Johnny! Thirty Years of America's Favorite Late-Night Entertainer,* rev. ed. (Nashville, Tenn.: Cumberland House, 2002), 182–183; Ted Dracos, *Ungodly: The Passions, Torments, and Murder of Atheist Madalyn Murray O'Hair* (New York: Free Press, 2003), 273–274.

35. *Tonight Show* program notes for October 16, 1970, box 1, Johnny Carson Papers, LCMD.

36. Cox, *Here's Johnny!,* 223 ("about out"); Jesse McKinley, "Comics Who Made It Big-Time Express Their Debt to Carson," *NYT,* January 25, 2005 (Klein); program notes and correspondence for December 4, 1972, box 15 (Ho), Carson Papers, LCMD.

37. Fred de Cordova, *Johnny Came Lately: An Autobiography* (New York: Simon and Schuster, 1988), 53; Richard Severo, "Johnny Carson . . . Dies at 79," *NYT,* January 23, 2005; Steve Martin, "The Man in Front of the Curtain," *NYT,* January 25, 2005.

38. "Famous Friends Remember Johnny Carson," http://abcnews.go.com/ Health/print?id=436228, January 25, 2005; "Good Night, Johnny," *WT,* January 25, 2005.

39. Tim Weiner, "Mike Douglas . . . Dies at 81," *NYT,* August 12, 2006.

40. George W. S. Trow, *Within the Context of No Context* (Boston: Little, Brown, 1981); Norman Corwin, *Trivializing America* (Secaucus, N.J.: Lyle Stuart, 1983), 115 (Lear), 139 ("colosseum").

41. Michael Novak, "Television Shapes the Soul," in *Inter/Media: Interpersonal Communication in a Media World,* 3rd ed., ed. Gary Gumpert and Robert Cathcart (New York: Oxford University Press, 1986), 583–596, Bunker at p. 589; Geoffrey Cowan, *See No Evil: The Backstage Battle over Sex and Violence on Television* (New York: Simon and Schuster, 1979), 31; Kirk Honeycutt, "'We Ran Out of Controversy,'" *NYT,* April 16, 1978.

42. John George and Laird Wilcox, *American Extremists: Militias, Supremacists, Klansmen, Communists, and Others* (Amherst, N.Y.: Prometheus, 1996), ch. 13; Laird Wilcox interview of Julian Williams, November 29, 1985, WCCPM; Harold H. Martin, "Doomsday Merchant on the Far, Far Right," *Saturday Evening Post* 235 (April 28, 1962): 19–25; "The Sins of Billy James," *Time* 107 (February 16, 1976): 52; Hargis newsletter, September 1968, folder 2101.3 ("interlocking . . . harmony"), Christian Crusade Ephemeral Materials, WCCPM.

43. "National Review Plan for 1989" (TS, November 14, 1988), pp. 3–4, box 122, WARP; Dracos, *Ungodly,* 122–125; Laird Wilcox, personal communication, August 23, 2005 (symbiosis).

44. Bill O'Reilly, *Culture Warrior* (New York: Broadway Books, 2006), 99.

45. Thomas P. Hughes, "Technological Momentum," in *Does Technology Drive History? The Dilemma of Technological Determinism,* ed. Merritt Roe Smith and Leo Marx (Cambridge, Mass.: MIT Press, 1994), 101–113; Don DeLillo, *Underworld* (New York: Scribner, 1997), 530.

46. Frederick S. Lane, *The Decency Wars: The Campaign to Cleanse American Culture* (Amherst, N.Y.: Prometheus, 2006) and *Obscene Profits: The Entrepreneurs of Pornography in the Cyber Age* (New York: Routledge, 2000); Timothy Egan, "Wall Street Meets Pornography," *NYT,* October 23, 2000; Frank Rizzo, "Hard-Core Change," *Hartford Courant,* January 5, 1987.

47. Cmiel, "Drowning in Pictures," 50; Thomas Exter and Frederick Barber, "The Age of Conservatism," *American Demographics* 8 (November 1986): 33.

6. BABE IN CHRIST

1. Jimmy Carter, *Why Not the Best* (Nashville, Tenn.: Broadman Press, 1975); Peter G. Bourne, *Jimmy Carter: A Comprehensive Biography from Plains to Postpresidency* (New York: Scribner, 1997), "reckoning" at p. 25; Arthur M. Schlesinger Jr., *Journals, 1952–2000,* ed. Andrew Schlesinger and Stephen Schlesinger (New

York: Penguin, 2007), 409 (Moyers); Burton I. Kaufman and Scott Kaufman, *The Presidency of James Earl Carter*, 2nd ed. (Lawrence: University Press of Kansas, 2006), chs. 1–2; Robert D. Novak, *The Prince of Darkness: 50 Years Reporting in Washington* (New York: Crown Forum, 2007), 302.

2. Bourne, *Jimmy Carter*, chs. 8–16, "planner" at p. 174; Betty Glad, *Jimmy Carter: In Search of the Great White House* (New York: Norton, 1980), 489–490.

3. George McGovern, AI, March 20, 2009. Carl Solberg, *Hubert Humphrey: A Biography* (New York: Norton, 1984), 451–452, confirms a unity meeting but attributes Humphrey's reluctance to distaste for fund-raising. However, as Humphrey had already received radiation and chemotherapy for bladder cancer, it seems likely that his health also played a role.

4. Schlesinger, *Journals*, 423; E. J. Dionne Jr., *Why Americans Hate Politics* (New York: Touchstone, 1992), 129, 224; Kaufman and Kaufman, *Presidency*, 18–19.

5. Kenneth E. Morris, *Jimmy Carter: American Moralist* (Athens: University of Georgia Press, 1996), chs. 6–7.

6. Todd Gitlin, *The Sixties: Years of Hope, Days of Rage* (New York: Bantam, 1987), 374.

7. Andrew Hacker, "Who Killed ERA? Women, Not Men," *WP*, September 14, 1980; Donald T. Critchlow, *Phyllis Schlafly and Grassroots Conservatism: A Woman's Crusade* (Princeton, N.J.: Princeton University Press, 2005), 218 (quote), 225.

8. Critchlow, *Phyllis Schlafly*, 224.

9. James Lardner and Neil Henry, "Over 40,000 ERA Backers March on Hill," *WP*, July 10, 1978; Critchlow, *Phyllis Schlafly*, 226–227.

10. Sarah Weddington, AI, July 13, 2007.

11. *Conversations with Carter*, ed. Don Richardson (Boulder, Colo.: Lynne Rienner, 1998), 53; Joseph A. Califano Jr., *Inside: A Public and Private Life* (New York: Public Affairs, 2004), 345–347; press conference of July 12, 1977, *PP: Jimmy Carter, 1977*, book II, 1237.

12. "Women Appointed to Top Government Posts by President Jimmy Carter" (TS, December 1979), box 34, Office of the Assistant to the President for Women's Affairs (Weddington), 1979–1981, CL; Susan M. Hartmann, "Feminism, Public Policy, and the Carter Administration," in *The Carter Presidency: Policy Choices in the Post-New Deal Era*, ed. Gary M. Fink and Hugh Davis Graham (Lawrence: University Press of Kansas, 1998), 230.

13. Constanza name file, CL; Garry [sic] Clifford, "As Midge Constanza Sees It, Her Cluttered Office Provides a Window to the President," *People* 7 (March 21, 1977), 34; "Why Midge Had to Go," *Washington Star*, August 3, 1978.

14. Abzug name file, CL; Laura Mansnerus, "Bella Abzug, 77, . . . Is Dead," *NYT*, April 1, 1998 (quote).

15. Max Frankel, *The Times of My Life and My Life with* The Times (New York: Random House, 1999), 377–379; Abzug name file, CL; John Dumbrell, *The Carter Presidency: A Re-evaluation*, 2nd ed. (Manchester: Manchester University Press, 1995), 66–71; Glad, *Jimmy Carter*, 438.

16. Philip Jenkins, *Decade of Nightmares: The End of the Sixties and the Making of Eighties America* (New York: Oxford University Press, 2006), 160.

17. Edward M. Kennedy, *True Compass: A Memoir* (New York: Twelve, 2009), chs. 17–18.

18. James E. Grice, undated poem, box 3, RLMP; Kaufman and Kaufman, *Presidency*, chs. 10–12.

19. Adam Clymer, "Board of NOW to Oppose Carter, Charging Lag on Women's Issues," *NYT*, December 11, 1979; Dumbrell, *Carter Presidency*, 67 (percentages); Leslie Bennetts, "Rights and Abortion Planks Are Achieved by Feminists," *NYT*, August 13, 1980, and "White House Reshapes Approach to Women's Issues to Aid Rights Plan," *NYT*, October 18, 1980 ("exactly"); Jody Powell, *The Other Side of the Story* (New York: William Morrow, 1984), 39–40.

20. Schlesinger, *Journals*, 506; Kaufman and Kaufman, *Presidency*, 245; Sarah Weddington, AI, July 13, 2007.

21. Sarah Weddington, AI, July 13, 2007; Powell, *Other Side of the Story*, 40; Mark D. Uehling, "Twenty Years from NOW," *Newsweek* 108 (December 15, 1986): 69; Critchlow, *Phyllis Schlafly*, 229; Jean Hardisty, *Mobilizing Resentment: Conservative Resurgence from the John Birch Society to the Promise Keepers* (Boston: Beacon, 1999), 3.

22. Donald G. Mathews and Jane Sherron De Hart, *Sex, Gender, and the Politics of ERA: A State and the Nation* (New York: Oxford University Press, 1990), xi, 158–159, 175–180; Dionne, *Why Americans Hate Politics*, 107–108; Mrs. Michael Mills to President Carter, February 16, 1978, Jesse Helms name file, CL; Critchlow, *Phyllis Schlafly*, 267; Steven V. Roberts, "Illinois Lawmaker Says No to E.R.A.," *NYT*, May 13, 1980.

23. Kent L. Tedin et al., "Social Background and Political Differences between Pro- and Anti-ERA Activists," *American Politics Quarterly* 5 (1977): 404; Carol Mueller and Thomas Dimieri, "The Structure of Belief Systems among Contending ERA Activists," *Social Forces* 60 (1982): 665.

24. *Harvard/Radcliffe Class of 1970, 25th Reunion: Answers to the Anonymous Questionnaire* (1995), 59, furnished by the Harvard Alumni Office.

25. Dionne, *Why Americans Hate Politics*, 141, 142.

26. Jenkins, *Decade of Nightmares*, 172.

27. Dionne, *Why Americans Hate Politics*, 227, 234; Novak, *Prince of Darkness*, 352; Joseph Crespino, "Civil Rights and the Religious Right," *Rightward Bound: Making America Conservative in the 1970s*, ed. Bruce J. Schulman and Julian E. Zelizer (Cambridge, Mass.: Harvard University Press, 2008), 90–105; Terry Miller to Maddox, August 21, 1980, box 4, Fletcher A. Brothers to Carter, August 7, 1980, box 8, and Faye Spoth to Maddox, July 14, 1980, box 3, RLMP.

28. Jerry Falwell, *Strength for the Journey: An Autobiography* (New York: Simon and Schuster, 1987), quotation at p. 103.

29. Falwell video interview, part 1, October 16, 2003, Archive of American Television, http://www.emmytvlegends.org/interviews/people/jerry-falwell, March 17, 2010; Falwell, *Strength for the Journey*, 313.

30. Susan Friend Harding, *The Book of Jerry Falwell: Fundamentalist Language and Politics* (Princeton, N.J.: Princeton University Press, 2000), 21–28, "mix" at 22.

31. Richard Viguerie, AI, June 22, 2006, and *America's Right Turn: How Conservatives Used New and Alternative Media to Take Power* (Chicago: Bonus Books,

2004), ch. 8; Nick Kotz, "King Midas of 'the New Right,'" *Atlantic* 242 (November 1978): 58. Kotz estimated that half of Viguerie's names were duplicates.

32. Harding, *Jerry Falwell*, 128–129; William Martin, *With God on Our Side: The Rise of the Religious Right in America*, rev. ed. (New York: Broadway, 2005), 200 ("moral majority"); Jerry Falwell, "The Maligned Moral Majority," *Newsweek* 98 (September 21, 1981): 17 ("conservative Jews"), and *Strength for the Journey*, 363 ("pro"), 364. Harding (285 n. 18) suggests that Falwell may already have had the name in mind.

33. Phyllis Schlafly to William Rusher, May 26, 1975, box 81, WARP; James B. Hunt Jr. to Robert Maddox, August 22, 1980, box 3, RLMP; Kaufman and Kaufman, *Presidency*, 209.

34. Maddox to Jody Powell, October 7, 1980, box 4, RLMP, and Maddox to Phil Wise and Anne Wexler, August 28, 1979, White House Central Files Subject File: Religious Matters, box RM-1, CL; Andrew R. Flint and Joy Porter, "Jimmy Carter: The Re-emergence of Faith-Based Politics and the Abortion Rights Issue," *Presidential Studies Quarterly* 35 (March 2005): 42–44.

35. Maddox to Fran Voorde, November 16, 1979, with Anne Wexler handwritten addendum, White House Central Files Subject File: Religious Matters, box RM-1, CL; Maddox to Jody Powell, undated memo, box 1, RLMP.

36. Robert L. Maddox, *Preacher at the White House* (Nashville, Tenn.: Broadman Press, 1984), 161–165; Maddox agenda memo, January 21, 1980, box 10, RLMP; Maddox, AI, June 23, 2005; Tim LaHaye, undated *Moral Majority Report* clipping, box 3, RLMP; Martin, *With God on Our Side*, 189. Falwell compounded the damage by publicly misrepresenting what Carter said about homosexuality during the meeting. Dudley Clendinen, "White House Minister Misquoted Carter Remarks," *NYT*, August 8, 1980.

37. Dionne, *Why Americans Hate Politics*, 227, 234; Theda Skocpol, "Targeting within Universalism: Politically Viable Policies to Combat Poverty in the United States," in *The Urban Underclass*, ed. Christopher Jencks and Paul E. Peterson (Washington, D.C.: Brookings Institution, 1991): 420. Among those who argue that deep-rooted economic problems limited Carter's options and ultimately destroyed his presidency are Edward Berkowitz, *Something Happened: A Political and Cultural Overview of the Seventies* (New York: Columbia University Press, 2006); William C. Berman, *America's Right Turn: From Nixon to Clinton*, 2nd ed. (Baltimore: Johns Hopkins University Press, 2001); and W. Carl Biven, *Jimmy Carter's Economy: Policy in an Age of Limits* (Chapel Hill: University of North Carolina Press, 2002).

38. George McGovern, AI, March 20, 2009.

39. Dionne, *Why Americans Hate Politics*, 142, 234–236; Dirk Smillie, *Falwell Inc.: Inside a Religious, Political, Educational, and Business Empire* (New York: St. Martin's Press, 2008), chs. 3–4.

40. Edmund Morris, *Dutch: A Memoir of Ronald Reagan* (New York: Random House, 1999), 281–282, 292; William Martin, "How Ronald Reagan Wowed Evangelicals," *Christianity Today* 48 (August 2004): 48; Moynihan on *This Week with David Brinkley*, September 9, 1984, box II:720, DPMP; Michael K. Deaver, *A Different Drummer: My Thirty Years with Ronald Reagan* (New York: HarperCollins,

2001), 3–4, 160–161, 186; John Patrick Diggins, *Ronald Reagan: Fate, Freedom, and the Making of History* (New York: Norton, 2007), 33–34.

41. Ronald Reagan, *An American Life* (New York: Simon and Schuster, 1990), 21.

42. Morris, *Dutch,* 387; Bob Colacello, *Ronnie and Nancy: Their Path to the White House, 1911 to 1980* (New York: Warner Books, 2004), 221 (quotation); Thomas W. Evans, *The Education of Ronald Reagan: The General Electric Years and the Untold Story of His Conversion to Conservatism* (New York: Columbia University Press, 2006).

43. Remarks of March 8, 1983, *PP: Ronald Reagan, 1983,* book I, 364; Lou Cannon, *President Reagan: The Role of a Lifetime* (New York: Simon and Schuster, 1991), 746 (funerals); Diggins, *Ronald Reagan,* 1–54, guilt at p. 27.

44. "Address . . . Dallas, Texas, August 22, 1980," Reagan 1980 campaign vertical file, RL; Jenkins, *Decade of Nightmares,* 66; Bourne, *Jimmy Carter,* 471.

45. Reagan, *An American Life,* 120, 231.

46. "Address . . . August 22, 1980;" Reagan, *An American Life,* 30.

47. Thomas Byrne Edsall and Mary D. Edsall, *Chain Reaction: The Impact of Race, Rights, and Taxes on American Politics* (New York: Norton, 1991), ch. 7; Adrian Wooldridge, "The Great Delegator," *NYT,* January 29, 2006; Richard Reeves, *President Reagan: The Triumph of Imagination* (New York: Simon and Schuster, 2005), 14 ("ruthless").

48. Morris, *Dutch,* 351–352; Reagan to Robert L. Mauro, October 11, 1979, in *Reagan: A Life in Letters,* ed. Kiron K. Skinner et al. (New York: Free Press, 2003), 197–198.

49. Catherine E. Rymph, *Republican Women: Feminism and Conservatism from Suffrage through the Rise of the New Right* (Chapel Hill: University of North Carolina Press, 2006), 228–230; Randall Terry, AI, August 12, 2005.

50. Martin, *With God on Our Side,* ch. 9, Marshner at p. 229; Robert Dole, AI, June 13, 2006; Sean Wilentz, *The Age of Reagan: A History, 1974–2008* (New York: HarperCollins, 2008), 274.

7. ACT RIGHT

1. David Stockman, *The Triumph of Politics: Why the Reagan Revolution Failed* (New York: Harper and Row, 1986), 28. Christopher Buckley ghostwrote the book, which doubtless accounts for its fluidity.

2. Ibid., 30.

3. Ibid., caption 10 following p. 118. I also draw on David S. Broder, "When the Woodshed Isn't Enough," *WP,* March 29, 2007, and Edmund Morris, *Dutch: A Memoir of Ronald Reagan* (New York: Random House, 1999), 422–423.

4. Address of February 18, 1981, with documents, *PP: Ronald Reagan, 1981,* 108–138.

5. Kevin Phillips, *The Politics of Rich and Poor: Wealth and the American Electorate in the Reagan Aftermath* (New York: Random House, 1990), ch. 4; John W. Sloan, *FDR and Reagan: Transformative Presidents with Clashing Visions* (Lawrence: University Press of Kansas, 2008), chs. 6, 8; Robert Dole, AI, June 13, 2006.

6. Congressional Budget Office, *Historical Budget Data,* table 1 (including net social insurance outlays), http://www.cbo.gov/budget/data/historical.pdf, July 17, 2007; Stockman, *Triumph of Politics,* 379; Peter G. Peterson, "The Morning After," *Atlantic Monthly* 260 (October 1987): 48.

7. Paul Krugman, "The Great Taxer," *NYT,* June 8, 2004; W. Elliot Brownlee and C. Eugene Steuerle, "Taxation," in *The Reagan Presidency: Pragmatic Conservatism and Its Legacies,* ed. W. Elliot Brownlee and Hugh Davis Graham (Lawrence: University Press of Kansas, 2003), 155–181; Phillips, *Politics of Rich and Poor,* 83; Robert Pear, "U.S. Reports Poverty is Down but Inequality is Up," *NYT,* September 27, 1990.

8. Lester C. Thurow, "A Surge in Inequality," *Scientific American* 256 (May 1987): 30–37.

9. Richard Reeves, *President Reagan: The Triumph of Imagination* (New York: Simon and Schuster, 2005), 15 ("fellas").

10. William Greider, *The Education of David Stockman and Other Americans* (New York: E. P. Dutton, 1986), 49; Stockman, *Triumph of Politics,* 3.

11. Stephen Engelberg, "Moynihan Asserts Stockman Said Reagan Doubted Tax-Cut Theory," *NYT,* July 11, 1985; Daniel Patrick Moynihan, "How the Great Society 'Destroyed the American Family,'" *Public Interest* no. 108 (Summer 1992): 60 (quote); Jackie Calmes, "The Voracious National Debt," *Congressional Quarterly* 48 (March 24, 1990): 896; Stockman, *Triumph of Politics,* 267–268.

12. Daniel Patrick Moynihan, "Reagan's Inflate-the-Deficit Game," *NYT,* July 21, 1985; Ronald Reagan, *An American Life* (New York: Simon and Schuster, 1990), 66–67; Andrew E. Busch, *Ronald Reagan and the Politics of Freedom* (Lanham, Md.: Rowman & Littlefield, 2001), ch. 5; John Patrick Diggins, *Ronald Reagan: Fate, Freedom, and the Making of History* (New York: Norton, 2007), 183; Kevin Phillips, *American Theocracy: The Peril and Politics of Radical Religion, Oil, and Borrowed Money in the 21st Century* (New York: Viking, 2006), part III; and Iwan Morgan, "Reaganomics and Its Legacy," in *Ronald Reagan and the 1980s: Perceptions, Policies, Legacies,* ed. Cheryl Hudson and Gareth Davies (New York: Palgrave Macmillan, 2008), 110 (swing).

13. Robert Bork and P. J. O'Rourke, "'Live' with TAE," *American Enterprise* 8 (May–June 1997): 24.

14. Lou Cannon, *President Reagan: The Role of a Lifetime* (New York: Simon and Schuster, 1991), 92.

15. Jackson K. Putnam, "Governor Reagan: A Reappraisal," *California History* 83 (March 2006): 33, 42; Martin Tolchin, "Paradox of Reagan Budgets Hints Contradiction in Legacy," *NYT,* February 16, 1988; John W. Sloan, *The Reagan Effect: Economics and Presidential Leadership* (Lawrence: University Press of Kansas, 1999), 19; Gareth Davies, "The Welfare State," *Reagan Presidency,* ed. Brownlee and Graham, 211–212; Larry M. Schwab, *The Illusion of a Conservative Reagan Revolution* (New Brunswick, N.J.: Transaction, 1991), 132–133.

16. Phillips, *Politics of Rich and Poor,* 180; Mark C. Carnes, "The Culture of Work," in *The Columbia History of Post-World War II America,* ed. idem (New York: Columbia University Press, 2007), 124; Paul Krugman, "For Richer," *NYT*

Magazine, October 20, 2002, pp. 65–66; Nolan McCarty et al., *Polarized America: The Dance of Ideology and Unequal Riches* (Cambridge, Mass.: MIT Press, 2006), ch. 1; Mark Lilla, "A Tale of Two Reactions," *NYRB* 45 (May 14, 1998): 6–7; "Conversation with Robert L. DuPont," *Addiction* 100 (2005): 1403.

17. Gil Troy, *Morning in America: How Ronald Reagan Invented the 1980s* (Princeton, N.J.: Princeton University Press, 2005); Robert M. Collins, *Transforming America: Politics and Culture in the Reagan Years* (New York: Columbia University Press, 2007), 5, 245–250; Charles A. Reich, *Opposing the System* (New York: Crown, 1995), 4; Ted V. McAllister, "Reagan and the Transformation of American Conservatism," *Reagan Presidency,* ed. Brownlee and Graham, 54–56.

18. Sean Wilentz, *The Age of Reagan: A History, 1974–2008* (New York: HarperCollins, 2008), 281–287; Hugh Heclo, "Ronald Reagan and American Public Philosophy," *Reagan Presidency,* ed. Brownlee and Graham, 18–19; John Aloysius Farrell, *Tip O'Neill and the Democratic Century* (Boston: Little, Brown, 2001), 599–600 (quotes), 603.

19. John Brady, *Bad Boy: The Life and Politics of Lee Atwater* (Reading, Mass.: Addison-Wesley, 1997); Lee Atwater, "The Politics of the Baby Boom," in *Left, Right and Babyboom,* ed. David Boaz (Washington, D.C.: Cato Institute, 1986), 31–36.

20. Ronald Reagan, *The Reagan Diaries,* ed. Douglas Brinkley (New York: HarperCollins, 2007), 72, 97 (Viguerie); Reagan, *An American Life,* 235; Busch, *Ronald Reagan,* 52–53; Joseph A. McCartin, "Turnabout Years: Public Sector Unionism and the Fiscal Crisis," *Rightward Bound: Making America Conservative in the 1970s,* ed. Bruce J. Schulman and Julian E. Zelizer (Cambridge, Mass.: Harvard University Press, 2008), 225; Benjamin Ginsberg and Martin Shefter, *Politics by Other Means: The Declining Importance of Elections in America* (New York: Basic Books, 1990), 106–107, 157.

21. Jean Stefancic and Richard Delgado, *No Mercy: How Conservative Think Tanks and Foundations Changed America's Social Agenda* (Philadelphia: Temple University Press, 1996), 58; William C. Berman, *America's Right Turn: From Nixon to Clinton,* 2nd ed. (Baltimore: Johns Hopkins University Press, 2001), 70–71.

22. Rick Perlstein, *Nixonland: The Rise of a President and the Fracturing of America* (New York: Scribner, 2008), 113; remarks of October 8, 1986, *PP: Ronald Reagan, 1986,* book II, 1348.

23. *Statistical Abstract of the United States,* 1962 and 1982 eds. (Washington, D.C.: GPO, 1962 / 1982), 149, 174, respectively; Stuart A. Scheingold, *The Politics of Law and Order: Street Crime and Public Policy* (New York: Longman, 1984), 39, 45.

24. David Garland, *The Culture of Control: Crime and Social Order in Contemporary Society* (Chicago: University of Chicago Press, 2001), 90–91; Phillips, *Politics of Rich and Poor,* 205.

25. Garland, *Culture of Control,* chs. 3–4.

26. Jonathan Simon, *Governing through Crime: How the War on Crime Transformed American Democracy and Created a Culture of Fear* (New York: Oxford

University Press, 2007), ch. 5; John Pomfret, "California's Crisis in Prison Systems a Threat to Public," *WP,* June 11, 2006.

27. Bruce Western, *Punishment and Inequality in America* (New York: Russell Sage Foundation, 2006), part I, rates at p. 13.

28. Fox Butterfield, *All God's Children: The Bosket Family and the American Tradition of Violence* (New York: Knopf, 1995), ch. 11; Western, *Punishment and Inequality,* 39.

29. Stuart Banner, *The Death Penalty: An American History* (Cambridge, Mass.: Harvard University Press, 2002), chs. 10–11; John Grisham, *The Innocent Man: Murder and Injustice in a Small Town* (New York: Doubleday, 2006), 214.

30. Andrew von Hirsch, "Retribution and the 'Desert' Model: Should Punishment Fit the Crime?" New School for Social Research Conference, "Punishment: The U.S. Record," New York City, November 30, 2006.

31. Simon, *Governing through Crime,* ch. 2; debate transcript, October 13, 1998, http://www.debates.org/index.php?page=october-13-1988-debate-transcript, March 17, 2010; Steve Takesian, *Willie Horton: True Crime and Its Influence on a Presidential Election* (author, 2002); Jack E. White, "Bush's Most Valuable Player," *Time* 132 (November 14, 1988): 21 (Ailes).

32. Michael Dukakis, AI, December 8, 2008.

33. Nancy Soderberg, AI, October 24, 2008 (winced).

34. "Crime and Judges: An Opportunity Issue for 1984" (TS, November 4, 1983), box 16024, White House Office of Public Affairs: Records, 1981–1988, RL, italics deleted from original. Putting sensitive material in blind, hand-delivered memos—a trick pioneered by Lee Atwater—discouraged leaks and ensured deniability. Brady, *Bad Boy,* 116.

35. David M. O'Brien, "Federal Judgeships in Retrospect," *Reagan Presidency,* ed. Brownlee and Graham, 327–353; "Myths and Realities—Reagan Administration Judicial Selection" (TS, July 1, 1986), p. 6, box 16024, White House Office of Public Affairs: Records, 1981–1988, RL.

36. Lana D. Harrison, "Trends in Illicit Drug Use in the United States: Conflicting Results from National Surveys," *International Journal of the Addictions* 27 (1992): 819; Stanley Urbine to President Carter, April 1, 1977, Peter Bourne name file, CL.

37. Michael Massing, *The Fix* (New York: Simon and Schuster, 1998), chs. 11–12, Nalepka at p. 153.

38. Kitty Kelley, *Nancy Reagan: The Unauthorized Biography* (New York: Simon and Schuster, 1991), chs. 18–19; Joan Quigley, *"What Does Joan Say?" My Seven Years as White House Astrologer to Nancy and Ronald Reagan* (New York: Birch Lane, 1990), ch. 2; James G. Benze Jr., *Nancy Reagan: On the White House Stage* (Lawrence: University Press of Kansas, 2005), ch. 2, "safe" at p. 58.

39. Benze, *Nancy Reagan,* 60; Massing, *The Fix,* 160.

40. "Update on Drug Abuse Prevention Campaign—Trends Improving," press release, April 28, 1983, box 9434, Carlton Turner files, RL.

41. Massing, *The Fix,* 36.

42. Bill Graham and Robert Greenfield, *Bill Graham Presents: My Life Inside Rock and Out* (New York: Doubleday, 1992), 487; Peter Kerr, "Anatomy of the Drug Issue," *NYT,* November 17, 1986.

43. Massing, *The Fix,* chs. 13–14; Dan Baum, *Smoke and Mirrors: The War on Drugs and the Politics of Failure* (Boston: Little, Brown, 1996), ch. 15, Ferdinand at p. 225; Edward Walsh, "House Votes Antidrug Legislation," *WP,* September 12, 1986.

44. Andrew H. Malcolm, "Chicago Expecting a 3-Way Campaign," *NYT,* December 7, 1986; Donald Regan to Ken Khachigian, September 16, 1986, and Joan De Cain to Anne Higgins, September 14, 1986, subject file SP 1091, RL.

45. David Garland, "Capital Punishment and American Culture," *Punishment and Society* 7 (2005): 347–376.

46. George Bush to John Sununu, August 12, 1989 (attaching Burke's memo), John Sununu Files, 01807, George Bush Presidential Library, hereafter BL, College Station, Texas.

47. William Bennett to John Sununu, July 26, 1989, John Sununu Files, 01807, BL.

48. Hugh Davis Graham, "Civil Rights Policy," *Reagan Presidency,* ed. Brownlee and Graham, 283–292. Biographers differ over Reagan's views on sexual morality, Morris taking the most conservative line. Cf. Morris, *Dutch,* 457–458; Troy, *Morning,* 201–202; Diggins, *Ronald Reagan,* 322–323; and Cannon, *President Reagan,* 812–819.

49. Cannon, *President Reagan,* 518; Davies, "Welfare State," *Reagan Presidency,* ed. Brownlee and Graham, 222–227.

50. Joseph B. Treaster, "Some Think the 'War on Drugs' Is Being Waged on the Wrong Front," *NYT,* nat. ed., July 28, 1992; Bob Barr, AI, March 17, 2009.

51. Richard Darman, *Who's in Control? Polar Politics and the Sensible Center* (New York: Simon and Schuster, 1996), 115; Ralph Reed, *Active Faith: How Christians Are Changing the Soul of American Politics* (New York: Free Press, 1996), 117; Paul Weyrich, AI, October 24, 2007.

52. Kent Markus to José Cerda, May 14, 1997, box 81, Domestic Policy Council (hereafter DPC): Bruce Reed: Crime, William J. Clinton Library (hereafter WJCL), Little Rock, Arkansas (cost data); Simon, *Governing through Crime,* 16–19, 45; Daniel Gardner, *The Science of Fear* (New York: Dutton, 2008), 208 (overtime).

53. Glenn C. Loury, *Race, Incarceration, and Human Values* (Cambridge, Mass.: MIT Press, 2008), 5; Adam Liptak, "Inmate Count in U.S. Dwarfs Other Nations'," *NYT,* April 23, 2008; "Reagan Said to Drop Opposition to a Bill to Set Drinking Age," *NYT,* June 13, 1984.

54. George H. Nash, *The Conservative Intellectual Movement in America since 1945* (New York: Basic Books, 1976), 184; James A. Morone, *Hellfire Nation: The Politics of Sin in American History* (New Haven, Conn.: Yale University Press, 2003), 452–453.

55. Jon F. Hale, "The Making of the New Democrats," *Political Science Quarterly* 110 (1995): 212–213.

56. Jonathan Rieder, *Canarsie: The Jews and Italians of Brooklyn Against Liberalism* (Cambridge, Mass.: Harvard University Press, 1985), 260; Tom Melia to Bob Peck, February 20, 1985, box II: 91, DPMP.

57. Earl Black and Merle Black, *The Rise of the Southern Republicans* (Cambridge, Mass.: Harvard University Press, 2002), Lott quote at p. 40; Hale, "Making of the New Democrats," 213.

58. Peter Reuter et al., *Money from Crime: A Study of the Economics of Drug Selling in Washington, D.C.* (Santa Monica, Calif.: Rand, 1990); Carl S. Taylor, *Dangerous Society* (East Lansing: Michigan State University Press, 1990), 45–46; Alan Burdick, "Looking for the High Life," *The Sciences* 31 (June 1991): 14–17; "Code of the Street," NPR *Talk of the Nation*, September 1, 1999, *http://www.npr.org/templates/story/story.php?storyId=1057946, March 17, 2010 (Jackson)*. .

59. Thomas Byrne Edsall and Mary D. Edsall, *Chain Reaction: The Impact of Race, Rights, and Taxes on American Politics* (New York: Norton, 1991), 113, 235–236; Rieder, *Canarsie*, 68, 77–78.

60. Thomas Bonczar, "Prevalence of Imprisonment in the U.S. Population, 1974–2001," http://www.ojp.usdoj.gov/bjs/pub/pdf/piusp01.pdf, December 1, 2007; Todd R. Clear, *Imprisoning Communities: How Mass Incarceration Makes Disadvantaged Neighborhoods Worse* (New York: Oxford University Press, 2007); Michael B. Katz et al., "The New African American Inequality," *JAH* 92 (2005): 81–83; Western, *Punishment and Inequality*, 94–97.

61. Stéphane Mechoulan, "The External Effects of Black-Male Incarceration on Black Females," SSRN: http://ssrn.com/abstract=997479, December 3, 2007; Karen Arenson, "Colleges Struggle to Help Black Men Stay Enrolled," *NYT*, December 30, 2003; Katz et al., "Inequality," 97–108; Nixon to Moynihan, August 10, 1987, box II:332, DPMP.

62. David C. Leege et al., *The Politics of Cultural Differences: Social Change and Voter Mobilization Strategies in the Post-New Deal Period* (Princeton, N.J.: Princeton University Press, 2002), ch. 9; Ginsberg and Shefter, *Politics by Other Means*, 105–106.

63. Orlando Patterson, "A Poverty of the Mind," *NYT*, March 26, 2006.

64. Paige M. Harrison and Allen J. Beck, "Prisoners in 2002," http://www.ojp.usdoj.gov/bjs/pub/pdf/p02.pdf, November 30, 2007; Western, *Punishment and Inequality*, 50; U.S. Sentencing Commission, *Sourcebook of Federal Sentencing Statistics*, http://www.ussc.gov/ANNRPT/2006/SBTOC06.htm, fig. J and table 61, district court cases.

65. Jeff Manza and Christopher Uggen, *Locked Out: Felon Disenfranchisement and American Democracy* (New York: Oxford University Press, 2006), ch. 8 and tables A3.4, A8.5.

66. Memos to Tony Dolan from Peter Germanis, William Henkel, and Ceci Cole McInturff, all February 18, 1987, box 318, White House Office of Speechwriting: Speech Drafts, 1981–1988, RL; remarks of February 20, 1987, *PP: Ronald Reagan, 1987*, book I, 167.

8. ROBERT BORK'S AMERICA

1. Edmund Morris, *Dutch: A Memoir of Ronald Reagan* (New York: Random House, 1999), 602; remarks of October 8, 1986, *PP: Ronald Reagan, 1986*, book II, 1348; Nixon to Robert Dole, August 26, 1986, "V.I.P. Letters: Nixon," DI; E. J. Dionne Jr., *Why Americans Hate Politics* (New York: Touchstone, 1992), 295–298.

2. Lou Cannon, *President Reagan: The Role of a Lifetime* (New York: Simon and Schuster, 1991), chs. 19–20, poll data at p. 704.

3. Ethan Bronner, *Battle for Justice: How the Bork Nomination Shook America* (New York: Norton, 1989), 17, 190 (Viguerie).

4. Robert Bork, AI, March 23, 2007; Charles Reich, AI, January 18, 2008; "Legends in the Law: A Conversation with Robert H. Bork," http://www.dcbar.org/for_lawyers/resources/legends_in_the_law/bork.cfm, March 17, 2010; Stuart Taylor Jr., "Bork at Yale," *NYT*, July 27, 1987.

5. Bronner, *Battle for Justice*, 91–92; Tim Drake, "Judge Bork Converts to the Catholic Faith," *National Catholic Register*, July 20–26, 2003.

6. Arthur B. Culvahouse Jr. to Howard Baker Jr., September 8, 1987, box 15149, Thomas Griscom Files, RL; Robert Bork, AI, March 23, 2007.

7. Bronner, *Battle for Justice*, 67–68, 74–75.

8. Bork candidate notebook (TS, n.d.), pp. 2, 10–11, box 15149, Arthur Culvahouse Files, RL.

9. Robert Bork, AI, March 23, 2007.

10. Bronner, *Battle for Justice*, chs. 5–6, speech at pp. 98–99; Robert Bork, AI, March 23, 2007.

11. "Notable and Quotable," *WSJ*, August 18, 1987.

12. Bronner, *Battle for Justice*, 103.

13. DeConcini to Moynihan, July 24, 1987, box II:1938, DPMP; Althea Simmons form memo, August 8, 1987, box 17718, Rebecca Range Files, RL.

14. U.S. Senate, *Nomination of Robert H. Bork . . . : Hearings before the Committee on the Judiciary*, 100th Cong., 1st sess. (printed 1989), part 1, 33, 95–96.

15. Bronner, *Battle for Justice*, chs. 7–9; Norma Vieira and Leonard Gross, *Supreme Court Appointments: Judge Bork and the Politicization of Senate Confirmations* (Carbondale: Southern Illinois University Press, 1998), ch. 14.

16. Candidate notebook, OA 15066, Culvahouse files, RL; Bronner, *Battle for Justice*, 325 (Dole); Vieira and Gross, *Supreme Court Appointments*, 87 (Breaux).

17. U.S. Senate, *Bork Hearings*, part 3, 2884–2886, 2980–2981; Bronner, *Battle for Justice*, 223 (Blattner).

18. Bronner, *Battle for Justice*, 215; Kate Michelman to Daniel Patrick Moynihan, August 6, 1987, box II:1938, and Rita Radich to Moynihan, October 3, 1987, box II:1939, both DPMP; Peter M. Robinson to Reagan, July 29, 1987, box 345, White House Office of Speechwriting: Speech Drafts, 1981–1988, RL; Tom McGough to Dole, September 21, 1987, acquisition 329–90–195, box 7.

19. "Legends in the Law;" Robert Bork, *The Tempting of America* (New York: Free Press, 1990), 337; "National Press Club Luncheon with Robert Bork," September 6, 2005, http://www.hudson.org/files/publications/natl_press_club_bork.pdf, February 18, 2008.

20. Robert Bork, AI, March 23, 2007.

21. Vieira and Gross, *Supreme Court Appointments*, 156; Ken Gormley, *The Death of American Virtue: Clinton vs. Starr* (New York: Crown, 2010), 220–223.

22. Bronner, *Battle for Justice*, 149 ("raw"); Patrick B. McGuigan and Dawn M. Weyrich, *Ninth Justice: The Fight for Bork* (Washington, D.C.: Free Congress Research and Education Foundation, 1990), espec. 207–226.

23. Robert Bork, AI, March 23, 2007. I happened to attend the same lecture (January 27, 1988) and offer an eyewitness account.

24. C. Everett Koop and Francis A. Schaeffer, *Whatever Happened to the Human Race?* rev. ed. (Westchester, Ill.: Crossway Books, 1983), 4–8; William Martin, *With God on Our Side: The Rise of the Religious Right in America,* rev. ed. (New York: Broadway Books, 2005), ch. 10.

25. John B. Judis, "An Officer and a Gentleman," *New Republic* 200 (January 23, 1989): 19–22; Koop, "AIDS and the Social Order" (TS, October 15, 1987), Koop Papers, http://profiles.nlm.nih.gov/QQ/B/C/L/X/_/qqbclv.pdf; Stephen Inrig, "A Broad Responsibility: Public Health, Private Opinion, and the Career of C. Everett Koop" (M.A. thesis, Duke University, 2004), "Koop" at p. 115.

26. Jeffrey Lord to Frank Donatelli and Frank Lavin, October 16, 1987, box 15548, Jeffrey Lord Files, RL.

27. "White House Talking Points: Judge Douglas H. Ginsburg" (TS, October 29, 1987), box 15548, Jeffrey Lord Files, RL; remarks of October 29, 1987, *PP: Ronald Reagan, 1987,* book II, 1252.

28. Bronner, *Battle for Justice,* ch. 15; Stuart Taylor Jr., "Man in the News . . . Douglas Howard Ginsburg," *NYT,* October 30, 1987 ("ultimate"); Ronald Reagan, *The Reagan Diaries,* ed. Douglas Brinkley (New York: HarperCollins, 2007), 545.

29. "White House Talking Points: Judge Anthony M. Kennedy" (TS, November 12, 1987), box 15548, Jeffrey Lord Files, RL; remarks of November 11, 1987, *PP: Ronald Reagan, 1987,* book II, 1321–1323; "Anti-Abortion Groups Divided on Kennedy Nomination," AP wire, November 16, 1987.

30. Vieira and Gross, *Supreme Court Appointments,* ch. 18.

31. Bronner, *Battle for Justice,* 342.

32. R. W. Apple Jr., "Sununu Tells How and Why He Pushed Souter for Court," *NYT,* July 25, 1990; Ann Devroy, "In the End, Souter Fit Politically," *WP,* July 25, 1990; Bush MS notes, daily file, July 23, 1990, BL. Robert Holzweiss helped me secure President Bush's permission to consult these notes, which are not currently open to the public.

33. L. Gordon Crovitz, "David Souter, Bush's UnBorkable Nominee," *WSJ,* July 25, 1990; Judy Mann, "Former Souter Girlfriend Says He's Fair-Minded," *WP,* July 27, 1990.

34. "Insider Baseball: How Sununu Sold Souter," *Harper's* 281 (November 1990): 24–27; Patrick McGuigan to John Sununu and Ed Rogers, August 3, 1990, John Sununu Files, CF 00153, BL.

35. Barrie Tron to C. Boyden Gray, August 20, 1990, C. Boyden Gray Files, 45081–13, BL; Herbert S. Parmet, *George Bush: The Life of a Lone Star Yankee* (New York: Scribner, 1997), 436 (quote); NARAL "Supreme Court Alert," July 23, 1990, Lee S. Liberman Files, 45254–004, BL; Richard L. Berke, "Souter Nomination Stirs Abortion Rights Groups," *NYT,* August 1, 1990.

36. Lyle Denniston, "Souter Confirmation Expected Despite Lingering Feminist Opposition," *Baltimore Sun,* September 25, 1990; U.S. Senate, *Nomination of David H. Souter . . . : Hearings before the Committee on the Judiciary,* 101st Cong., 2nd sess. (printed 1991), 163, 189; "Judiciary Committee Approves Souter Nomi-

nation," AP Wire, September 27, 1990; Neil A. Lewis, "Liberal Bloc in Turmoil after Souter Encounter," *NYT,* September 27, 1990.

37. Andrew Peyton Thomas, *Clarence Thomas: A Biography* (San Francisco: Encounter Books, 2001), parts 1–4.

38. Leigh Ann Metzger Pusey, AI, May 22, 2008.

39. Kate Michelman to Daniel Patrick Moynihan, September 13, 1991, box II:606, DPMP; White House news summary, July 5, 1991, Lee S. Liberman Files, 45250–018, BL.

40. Adam Clymer, *Edward M. Kennedy: A Biography* (New York: William Morrow, 1999), 495; Thomas, *Clarence Thomas,* 376.

41. Tom Squitieri, "Blacks Split on Thomas," *USA Today,* July 5, 1991; Juan Williams, "Open Season on Clarence Thomas," *WP,* October 10, 1991.

42. "Weekend Edition" transcript, October 6, 1991, box II:1949, DPMP; Thomas, *Clarence Thomas,* ch. 19.

43. U.S. Senate, *Nomination of Judge Clarence Thomas . . . : Hearings before the Committee on the Judiciary,* 102nd Cong., 1st sess. (printed 1993), part 4, p. 157.

44. Phone comment summary sheets, "racist" from October 14, 1991, John Sununu files, CF 000473, BL; Ken Foskett, *Judging Thomas: The Life and Times of Clarence Thomas* (New York: William Morrow, 2004), ch. 14; "Thomas Expected to Win Senate OK," *WT,* October 15, 1991; Robert Teeter to C. Boyden Gray, October 23, 1991, Mark Paoletta Files, 45526–012, BL.

45. Jeffrey Toobin, *The Nine: Inside the Secret World of the Supreme Court* (New York: Doubleday, 2007), 33; Clarence Thomas, *My Grandfather's Son: A Memoir* (New York: HarperCollins, 2007), 280.

46. Xan Smiley, "The Dubious Prime of Anita," *Sunday Telegraph,* April 19, 1992; Toobin, *The Nine,* 111; Thomas, *My Grandfather's Son,* 232; "The Justice Nobody Knows," *60 Minutes,* September 30, 2007.

47. *Congressional Record–Senate,* October 15, 1991, p. 26532.

48. Toobin, *The Nine,* 36; Stanley K. Henshaw and Kevin O'Reilly, "Characteristics of Abortion Patients in the United States, 1979 and 1980," *Family Planning Perspectives* 15 (January/February 1983): 6, 14.

49. Peter Occhiogrosso, *Once a Catholic: Prominent Catholics and Ex-Catholics Reveal the Influence of the Church on Their Lives and Work* (Boston: Houghton Mifflin, 1987), 288.

50. Karen Lamoree interview of Juli Loesch Wiley (TS, October 19, 1994), "get out" at p. 49; Kelly Monroe, "The Writing on the Wall," *Liberating Options* 1(Spring 1991): 3; Tom Case to Juli Loesch, August 13, 1985, all box 1, Juli Loesch Wiley Papers, WHS; James Risen and Judy L. Thomas, *Wrath of Angels: The American Abortion War* (New York: Basic Books, 1998), 64–65 (Berrigan).

51. Juli Loesch to Nat Hentoff, July 22, 1985, and Paul Marx to Juli Loesch, August 23, 1985, box 1, Juli Loesch Wiley Papers, WHS; Randall Terry, AI, August 12, 2005; chant from *With God on Our Side,* part VI (Alexandria, Va.: PBS Video, 1996).

52. Juli Loesch, "Operation Rescue," *Fidelity* 7 (July/August 1988): 17–27; Garry Wills, "Fringe Government," *NYRB* 52 (October 6, 2005): 47.

53. Dale Vree, "Christopher Lasch: A Memoir," *New Oxford Review* 61 (April 1994): 2, 4; *Lake of Fire* (THINKFilm, 2007), a documentary by Tony Kaye.

54. Randall Terry, AI, August 12, 2005; Risen and Thomas, *Wrath of Angels,* part III, Loesch at p. 296; Lamoree interview of Loesch, pp. 30–31, box 1, Juli Loesch Wiley Papers, WHS.

55. U.S. Senate, *Nomination of David H. Souter,* 699.

56. Donald T. Critchlow, *Intended Consequences: Birth Control, Abortion, and the Federal Government in Modern America* (New York: Oxford University Press, 1999), 220; Risen and Thomas, *Wrath of Angels,* 335–337.

57. Toobin, *The Nine;* Bush MS notes, daily file, July 23, 1990, BL, restrictions as noted above; Robert Bork, "Again, a Struggle for the Soul of the Court," *NYT,* July 8, 1992.

58. Jon Gottschall, "Reagan's Appointments to the U.S. Courts of Appeals: The Continuation of a Judicial Revolution," *Judicature* 70 (June–July 1986): 52; Neil A. Lewis, "Selection of Conservative Judges Guards Part of Bush's Legacy," *NYT,* July 1, 1992; Joan Biskupic, "Bush Treads Well-Worn Path in Building Federal Bench," *Congressional Quarterly* 50 (January 18, 1992): 111.

59. Theodore B. Olson, "The Thomas Hearings, Confirmations and Congressional Ethics" (TS, October 31, 1991), Mark Paoletta Files, 45526–002, BL; Charles Reich, AI, January 18, 2008.

9. LIKE BATTLING THE DEVIL

1. Herbert S. Parmet, *George Bush: The Life of a Lone Star Yankee* (New York: Scribner, 1997), 30–31 (quotations); Robert Bork, AI, March 23, 2007.

2. Parmet, *George Bush,* 107, 246; Lee Edwards, *Goldwater: The Man Who Made a Revolution* (Washington, D.C.: Regnery, 1995), 420–422; Maureen Dowd, "President Hints at a Compromise over Federal Funds for Abortion," *NYT,* October 14, 1989.

3. Robert D. Novak, *The Prince of Darkness: 50 Years Reporting in Washington* (New York: Crown Forum, 2007), 447; Richard Ben Cramer, *What It Takes: The Way to the White House* (New York: Random House, 1992), 947.

4. Craig Unger, *The Fall of the House of Bush* (New York: Scribner, 2007), 94–95; William Martin, *With God on Our Side: The Rise of the Religious Right in America,* rev. ed. (New York: Broadway Books, 2005), 262–264.

5. Doug Wead, AI, May 19, 2008.

6. Kevin Phillips, *American Theocracy: The Peril and Politics of Radical Religion, Oil, and Borrowed Money in the 21st Century* (New York: Viking, 2006), 187–188; David John Marley, *Pat Robertson: An American Life* (Lanham, Md.: Rowman & Littlefield, 2007), 113, 129, 154.

7. Marley, *Pat Robertson,* 160; Unger, *Fall of the House of Bush,* 96–97.

8. Ralph Reed, *Active Faith: How Christians Are Changing the Soul of American Politics* (New York: Free Press, 1996), ch. 1; J. Taylor Rushing, "Swing Voters Still Up for Grabs," *FTU,* December 17, 2007 ("eighty"); Dan Gilgoff, *The Jesus Machine: How James Dobson, Focus on the Family, and Evangelical America Are*

Winning the Culture War (New York: St. Martin's Press, 2007), 106–109; Michael Isikoff, "Christian Coalition Steps Boldly into Politics," *WP,* September 10, 1992.

9. Gerald F. Seib and John Harwood, "America's Race to the Middle," *WSJ,* May 10–11, 2008.

10. Geoffrey Layman, *The Great Divide: Religious and Cultural Conflict in American Party Politics* (New York: Columbia University Press, 2001), 332; Stanley G. Hilton, *Senator for Sale: The Unauthorized Biography of Senator Bob Dole* (New York: St. Martin's Press, 1995), 28 (quote).

11. Michael Dukakis, AI, December 8, 2008; Parmet, *George Bush,* ch. 18; Peter Goldman and Tom Mathews, *The Quest for the Presidency, 1988* (New York: Touchstone, 1989), 314–328.

12. Bill Clinton, *My Life* (New York: Knopf, 2004), 344; Bush acceptance speech (TS, August 18, 1988), http://bushlibrary.tamu.edu/research/pdfs/rnc.pdf, June 24, 2008.

13. Garry Wills, *Under God: Religion and American Politics* (New York: Simon and Schuster, 1990), ch. 3, quotation at p. 60; Michael Dukakis, AI, December 8, 2008.

14. Michael Dukakis, AI, December 8, 2008; "Evangelicals Riding High in GOP," *FTU,* August 21, 1988.

15. John C. Green et al., *Religion and the Culture Wars: Dispatches from the Front* (Lanham, Md.: Rowman & Littlefield, 1996), 184–185; Doug Wead to Chase Untermeyer, March 30, 1989, David Demarest Files, 01140, and Wead to President Bush, March 27, 1989, Presidential Daily Backup, CF 01791, both BL; Doug Wead, AI, May 19, 2008. "Evangelicals," as Wead used the term, referred only to white, born-again Protestants.

16. Les Csorba to Doug Wead, February 8, 1989, John Sununu Files, 01806, BL; Doug Wead memoranda of July 19, October 18, and November 1, 1989, David Demarest Files, 01140, BL.

17. Chase Untermeyer, AI, September 2, 2008; Reed, *Active Faith,* 16.

18. Doug Wead, AI, May 19, 2008.

19. Doug Wead marginal notes on Les Csorba to David Demarest, June 23, 1989; Wead to Joseph Hagin, June 13, 1989; Wead to President Bush, December 20, 1989 (quoting Decter), all David Demarest Files, 01140, BL; Phillips, *American Theocracy,* 251, 260–261.

20. Address of September 5, 1989, *PP: George Bush, 1989,* book II, 1136–1142, quotation at p. 1137; Michael Isikoff, "Drug Buy Set Up for Bush Speech," *WP,* September 22, 1989; Jofi Joseph to Bruce Reed, May 18, 1994, and attached data, box 7, DPC: Bruce Reed: Welfare Reform, WJCL; Biden speech transcript (TS, September 5, 1989), box II:979, DPMP.

21. Michael Massing, *The Fix* (New York: Simon and Schuster, 1998), ch. 15; John Machacek, "Moynihan Rips Drug Czar Bennett," Gannett news wire, June 13, 1990; Bryna Brennan, "Drug Czar Bennett Quits," *New York Daily News,* November 8, 1990; Robert Pear, "Drug Policy Debate Turns to Feud Between Moynihan and Bennett," *NYT,* June 18, 1990.

22. John Robert Greene, *The Presidency of George Bush* (Lawrence: University Press of Kansas, 2000), 72–74; Maureen Dowd, "Bennett Rejects Top G.O.P. Post . . . ," *NYT*, December 14, 1990.

23. David Mervin, *George Bush and the Guardianship Presidency* (New York: St. Martin's Press, 1996), 118; David Hansen to Ed Rogers, Teeter poll data fax, October 18, 1989, John Sununu Files, folder 01807, BL; "Washington Whispers," *U.S. News and World Report* 108 (February 12, 1990): 20.

24. Michael Kramer, "The Abortion Issue—Again," *Time* 138 (November 25, 1991): 46; George Bush, *All the Best: My Life in Letters and Other Writings* (New York: Scribner, 1999), 420; George Bush to Frank R. Dickinson, May 30, 1990, to Lynn Martin, October 30, 1989, and to Jessica Catto, November 18, 1989, subject file WE 003, nos. 152244, 094876, and 092054, BL.

25. Boniface Ramsey to John Sununu, October 24, 1989, subject file WE 003, no. 121303, and David Demarest to George Bush, January 23, 1989, Presidential Daily Backup, CF 01790, both BL; Tim Wildmon, "A Pro-Life President?" *AFA Journal* 14 (June 1990): 2.

26. Martin, *With God on Our Side*, 324; Randall Terry, AI, August 12, 2005.

27. *NYT / CBS* News poll, June 10–15, 2005, http://www.nytimes.com/pack ages/html/politics/20050617_poll/20050617_poll_results.pdf; Arthur M. Schlesinger Jr., *Journals, 1952–2000*, ed. Andrew Schlesinger and Stephen Schlesinger (New York: Penguin, 2007), 713–714; Lee Edwards, *The Conservative Revolution: The Movement that Remade America* (New York: Free Press, 1999), 289.

28. Doug Wead, AI, May 19, 2008.

29. Bill Wilder to David Demarest, August 10, 1990, Demarest Files, 03108, BL; Martin, *With God on Our Side*, ch. 12, Kilberg on p. 310. Wead denied that he was fired. Martin argues otherwise. Whatever transpired behind the scenes, Evangelicals saw the matter as a firing and angrily said so, for example, in Leigh Ann Metzger Files, 04380, BL.

30. Richard Darman, *Who's in Control? Polar Politics and the Sensible Center* (New York: Simon and Schuster, 1996), chs. 10–13, quotation at p. 278.

31. Charles Kolb, *White House Daze: The Unmaking of Domestic Policy in the Bush Years* (New York: Free Press, 1994), 15–16, 99, 266–267.

32. "1992: A Rebuke—and the End of a Record," *Manchester Union-Leader*, November 1, 2004; Greene, *Presidency of George Bush*, 168.

33. Gerald Posner, *Citizen Perot: His Life and Times* (New York: Random House, 1996), quotation at p. 293; Albert J. Menendez, *The Perot Voters and the Future of American Politics* (New York: Prometheus, 1996).

34. Andrew Rosenthal, "The 1992 Campaign," *NYT*, March 4, 1992; James A. Baker III with Steve Fiffer, *"Work Hard, Study . . . and Keep Out of Politics! Adventures and Lessons from an Unexpected Public Life* (New York: G. P. Putnam's Sons, 2006), 317–318; Martin, *With God on Our Side*, 327 (Reed).

35. Buchanan speech transcript (TS, August 17, 1992), box II:2947, DPMP.

36. Clinton, *My Life*, 426; Doug Wead, AI, May 19, 2008; Randall Terry, AI, August 12, 2005; Reed, *Active Faith*, 141; Tanya Melich, *The Republican War*

against Women: An Insider's Report from Behind the Lines, updated ed. (New York: Bantam, 1998), ch. 17.

37. Leigh Ann Metzger Pusey, AI, May 20, 2008.

38. Darman, *Who's in Control?*, 289.

39. "I'm 60 and I Hate It: Bill Clinton," Breitbart wire, August 15, 2006.

40. Carl Bernstein, *A Woman in Charge: The Life of Hillary Rodham Clinton* (New York: Vintage, 2008), ch. 1. I also draw on Clinton, *My Life,* David Maraniss, *First in His Class: The Biography of Bill Clinton* (New York: Touchstone, 1996), and John F. Harris, *The Survivor: Bill Clinton in the White House* (New York: Random House, 2005).

41. Gennifer Flowers with Jacquelyn Dapper, *Gennifer Flowers: Passion and Betrayal* (Del Mar, Calif.: Emery Dalton Books, 1995), 74–75; *People* survey (MS, December 20, 1999), http://www.clintonlibrary.gov/movie1.pdf (Bogart); Nigel Hamilton, *Bill Clinton: Mastering the Presidency* (New York: Public Affairs, 2007), 533–534.

42. Bill Clinton, "'He and I Discussed the Presidency,'" *Newsweek* 143 (June 21, 2004): 49; Joe Klein, *The Natural: The Misunderstood Presidency of Bill Clinton* (New York: Doubleday, 2002), 36.

43. Clinton, *My Life,* 365.

44. Bernstein, *Woman in Charge,* 188.

45. Clinton, *My Life,* 368–369.

46. Ibid., 391; Parmet, *George Bush,* ch. 23.

47. Jack Wills to Daniel Patrick Moynihan, July 24, 1992, box II:2947, DPMP.

48. Robert P. Casey, *Fighting for Life* (Dallas, Tex.: Word Publishing, 1996), 186.

49. Layman, *Great Divide,* 1–2; Louis Bolce and Gerald De Maio, "Our Secularist Democratic Party," *Public Interest* no. 129 (Fall, 2002): 9–10.

50. Gwen Ifill, "Clinton, in Houston Speech, Assails Bush on Crime Issue," *NYT,* July 24, 1992.

51. Robin Toner, "The 1992 Elections," *NYT,* November 4, 1992; Phillips, *American Theocracy,* 188–189; Menendez, *Perot Voters,* 175–185.

10. REFERENDUM ON THE 1960s

1. John F. Harris, *The Survivor: Bill Clinton in the White House* (New York: Random House, 2005), xxvii.

2. Bob Woodward, *The Agenda: Inside the Clinton White House* (New York: Simon and Schuster, 1994), chs. 10–11.

3. Bill Clinton, *My Life* (New York: Knopf, 2004), 384 (quote), 458–459.

4. Harris, *Survivor,* 29, 92.

5. Christopher Matthews, "Clinton Gets in Step with Public's Priorities," *WT,* January 4, 1994; Woodward, *Agenda,* 319.

6. Paul Starr, "What Happened to Health Care Reform?" *American Prospect* no. 20 (Winter 1995): 20–31; Harris, *Survivor,* chs. 9–10; Carl Bernstein, *A Woman in Charge: The Life of Hillary Rodham Clinton* (New York: Vintage, 2008), ch. 11;

David Blumenthal and James A. Morone, *The Heart of Power: Health and Politics in the Oval Office* (Berkeley: University of California Press, 2009), ch. 10; file memos, August 22, 1994, and January 9, 1995, box II:39, DPMP.

7. Kohut poll press release, April 6, 1994, box 77, DPC: Bruce Reed: Crime, WJCL.

8. Bruce Reed, "Crime—Talking Pts." (MS, n.d.), box 79, DPC: Bruce Reed: Crime, WJCL; Paul Bedard, "Clinton Happily Signs the Crime Bill," *WT,* September 14, 1994.

9. Jody Powell to George Stephanopoulos, January 14, 1994, box 76, DPC: Bruce Reed: Crime, WJCL.

10. Kristin S. Seefeldt, *Welfare Reform* (Washington, D.C.: CQ Press, 2002), ch. 1; Ian Fisher, "Albany Study Finds Fraud in Welfare," *NYT,* August 3, 1994.

11. Seefeldt, *Welfare Reform,* ch. 2.

12. *This Week with David Brinkley,* January 2, 1994, transcript excerpts in box 7, DPC: Bruce Reed: Welfare Reform, WJCL; Morton M. Kondracke, "Welfare Reform," *Roll Call,* February 24, 1994.

13. Jason DeParle, "White House Seeks a Sleight-of-Hand Strategy on Welfare Reform," *NYT,* January 5, 1994; William M. Welch, "Welfare Reform Easier Said than Done," *USA Today,* January 10, 1994.

14. Bruce Reed, undated MS notes, box 32, and Reed to Clinton, February 17, 1994, box 21, both DPC: Bruce Reed: Welfare Reform, WJCL.

15. Bruce Reed to Clinton, May 30, 1994, box 21, and Joe Goode and Stan Greenberg to Welfare Reform Group, May 20, 1994, box 29, both DPC: Bruce Reed: Welfare Reform, WJCL.

16. Lars-Erik Nelson, "The Republicans' War," *NYRB* 46 (February 4, 1999): 8; *NYT* / CBS News poll, June 10–15, 2005, http://www.nytimes.com/packages/html/politics/20050617_poll/20050617_poll_results.pdf.

17. Ralph Reed, *Active Faith: How Christians Are Changing the Soul of American Politics* (New York: Free Press, 1996), 164, 186; Dole press release, February 4, 1993, acquisition 329–95–180, box 8, DI; Clinton, *My Life,* 481–486; Greg Pierce, "Protection for Sexual Orientation Now Part of White House Policy," *WT,* December 8, 1993; Bernstein, *Woman in Charge,* 256–258.

18. David John Marley, *Pat Robertson: An American Life* (Lanham, Md.: Rowman & Littlefield, 2007), 222–223; Lou Dubose and Jan Reid, *The Hammer: Tom DeLay, God, Money, and the Rise of the Republican Congress* (New York: Public Affairs, 2004), 84–85; Reed, *Active Faith,* 187; Clinton, *My Life,* 630 (quote).

19. Tim Hames, "The US Mid-term Election of 1994," *Electoral Studies* 14 (June 1995): 222–226; Dan Goodgame, "Right Makes Might," *Time* 144 (November 21, 1994): 53; Richard Viguerie, AI, June 22, 2006; Robert D. Novak, *The Prince of Darkness: 50 Years Reporting in Washington* (New York: Crown Forum, 2007), 517.

20. Robert Dallek, *An Unfinished Life: John F. Kennedy, 1917–1963* (Boston: Little, Brown, 2003), 475–476.

21. David Brock, *The Republican Noise Machine: Right-Wing Media and How It Corrupts Democracy* (New York: Crown, 2004), ch. 14.

22. Zev Chafets, "Late-Period Limbaugh," *NYT Magazine,* July 6, 2008, pp. 30–37, 50, 53–54.

23. Cal Thomas, "A Fox in the Media Henhouse," *FTU,* November 6, 2003 (Ailes).

24. Todd Gitlin, "The Clinton-Lewinsky Obsession: How the Press Made a Scandal of Itself," *Washington Monthly* 30 (December 1998): 13–19; Richard A. Viguerie and David Franke, *America's Right Turn: How Conservatives Used New and Alternative Media to Take Power* (Chicago: Bonus Books, 2004), 277–278.

25. Clinton, *My Life,* 574, 613, 670, and Ken Gormley, *The Death of American Virtue: Clinton* vs. *Starr* (New York: Crown, 2010), 432.

26. Clinton, *My Life,* 692–693. Taylor Branch, *The Clinton Tapes: Wrestling History with the President* (New York: Simon and Schuster, 2009), 64, 71, 90, 125–126, shows that Clinton was thinking along these lines before his conversation with Simpson.

27. Bob Woodward, *Shadow: Five Presidents and the Legacy of Watergate* (New York: Simon and Schuster, 1999), 336.

28. Clinton, *My Life,* 632; Newt Gingrich, "Contracting with America," *Left, Right, and Center: Voices from across the Political Spectrum,* ed. Robert Atwan and Jon Roberts (Boston: Bedford Books, 1996), 552, 555.

29. Katharine Q. Seelye, "Gingrich's Life: The Complications and the Ideals," *NYT,* November 24, 1994; Mel Steely, *The Gentleman from Georgia: The Biography of Newt Gingrich* (Macon, Ga.: Mercer University Press, 2000); Steven M. Gillon, *The Pact: Bill Clinton, Newt Gingrich, and the Rivalry That Defined a Generation* (New York: Oxford University Press, 2008), ch. 1, "weird" at p. 6.

30. Gillon, *Pact,* 67; Randall Terry, AI, August 12, 2005.

31. Clinton, *My Life,* 635.

32. Dick Morris, *Behind the Oval Office: Winning the Presidency in the Nineties* (New York: Random House, 1997), ch. 3.

33. Clinton, *My Life,* chs. 20–22.

34. Bernstein, *Woman in Charge,* 408–409; George Stephanopoulos, *All Too Human: A Political Education* (Boston: Little, Brown, 1999), ch. 13; Nancy Soderberg, AI, October 24, 2008.

35. Lou Michael and Dan Herbeck, *American Terrorist: Timothy McVeigh and the Oklahoma City Bombing* (New York: ReganBooks, 2001).

36. Harris, *Survivor,* 179–180 (quotes); Donald T. Critchlow, *Intended Consequences: Birth Control, Abortion, and the Federal Government in Modern America* (New York: Oxford University Press, 1999), 221–222.

37. David Maraniss and Michael Weisskopf, *"Tell Newt to Shut Up!"* (New York: Touchstone, 1996), 148.

38. James A. Stimson, *Tides of Consent: How Public Opinion Shapes American Politics,* 2nd ed. (New York: Cambridge University Press, 2004), xiv.

39. Morris, *Behind the Oval Office,* 187; Earl and Merle Black, *The Rise of the Southern Republicans* (Cambridge, Mass.: Harvard University Press, 2002), 31–32; Newt Gingrich, *Lessons Learned the Hard Way: A Personal Report* (New York: HarperCollins, 1998), 49; Harris, *Survivor,* 217.

40. Stimson, *Tides of Consent,* 90–95.

41. White House press release, October 30, 1995, box 71, DPC: Bruce Reed: Crime, WJCL.

42. McCaffrey remarks, 35th Anniversary of the White House Drug Czar Conference, University of Maryland, June 17, 2006; "Fickle," *Houston Chronicle,* March 11, 1996.

43. Janet Reno and McCaffrey to Clinton, July 3, 1997, box 81, DPC: Bruce Reed: Crime, WJCL; Donna Shalala to Clinton, April 10, 1998, McCaffrey to Clinton, April 9, 1998, and McCaffrey to Bruce Reed, April 10, 1998, all box 122, DPC: Bruce Reed: Subject File, WJCL; Harris, *Survivor,* 331; Clinton interview, "The Age of AIDS," May 30 and 31, 2006, http://www.pbs.org/wgbh/pages/frontline/aids/interviews/clinton.html; and Nicolas Rasmussen, *On Speed: The Many Lives of Amphetamine* (New York: New York University Press, 2008), 256–257.

44. Moynihan file memo, May 19, 1995, box II:39, DPMP.

45. Robert Pear, "Senate Passes Welfare Measure . . . ," *NYT,* August 2, 1996; Bruce Reed and Rahm Emanuel to Chief of Staff [Panetta], December 18, 1995, box 37, DPC: Bruce Reed: Welfare Reform, WJCL; Mickey Kaus, "Preserving Welfare as We Know It," *WSJ,* March 26, 1996.

46. Harris, *Survivor,* ch. 22, "sack" at p. 238; Morris, *Behind the Oval Office,* ch. 8.

47. Michael Waldman, *POTUS Speaks: Finding the Words That Defined the Clinton Presidency* (New York: Simon and Schuster, 2000), 132; Daniel Patrick Moynihan, "Evolution of a Platform Plank," *Congressional Record—Senate,* September 18, 1996, p. 10868.

48. Robin Toner, "A Revival and a Party Transformed," *NYT,* December 27, 2000.

49. Novak, *Prince of Darkness,* 532–533; Bob Woodward, *The Choice* (New York: Simon and Schuster, 1996), 403; Morris, *Behind the Oval Office,* 267.

50. Morris, *Behind the Oval Office,* 267–268.

51. Dan Gilgoff, *The Jesus Machine: How James Dobson, Focus on the Family, and Evangelical America Are Winning the Culture War* (New York: St. Martin's Press, 2007), 103.

52. Evan Thomas et al., *Back from the Dead: How Clinton Survived the Republican Revolution* (New York: Atlantic Monthly Press, 1997), 275 (quarter); Robert Dole, AI, June 13, 2006; Harris, *Survivor,* 241 (cartoon).

53. Novak, *Prince of Darkness,* 538; Marley, *Pat Robertson,* 232.

54. Gillon, *Pact,* ch. 12; Waldman, *POTUS Speaks,* 216.

55. Clinton, *My Life,* 863. Representative letters, too numerous to cite individually, can be found in the Samuel Dash Papers, LCMD (box numbers not yet assigned) and box II:826, DPMP. Approval ratings: James L. Guth, "Clinton, Impeachment, and the Culture Wars," *The Postmodern Presidency: Bill Clinton's Legacy in U.S. Politics,* ed. Steven E. Schier (Pittsburgh: University of Pittsburgh Press, 2000), 211, 217.

56. Josh Getlin, "The Truce Behind the Culture Wars," *Los Angeles Times,* February 7, 1999 (quotes); Gillon, *Pact,* ch. 17.

57. Howard Kurtz, "Going Weak in the Knees for Clinton," *WP,* July 6, 1998 (Burleigh); Randall Terry, AI, August 12, 2005; Paul Weyrich, AI, October 24, 2007.

58. Bernstein, *Woman in Charge,* 520, 528.

59. "Voters Say Clinton Not an Issue," AP wire, November 4, 1998.

60. Gillon, *Pact,* ch. 15.

61. Gormley, *Death of American Virtue,* 5 ("resign"); Tom DeLay with Stephen Mansfield, *No Retreat, No Surrender: One American's Fight* (New York: Sentinel, 2007), 82–83, 108–110; Dubose and Reid, *The Hammer,* chs. 1, 9.

62. Bob Barr, AI, March 17, 2009, and *The Meaning of Is: The Squandered Impeachment and Wasted Legacy of William Jefferson Clinton* (Atlanta: Stroud and Hall, 2004), ch. 5; Bruce Bryant-Friedland, "Evangelicals See Issue as Moral Decay," *FTU,* December 18, 1999; "Falwell Slams Clinton," *FTU,* February 9, 1999; Peter Baker, *The Breach: Inside the Impeachment and Trial of William Jefferson Clinton* (New York: Scribner, 2000), ch. 7, and Nicol C. Rae and Colton C. Campbell, *Impeaching Clinton: Partisan Strife on Capitol Hill* (Lawrence: University Press of Kansas, 2004), chs. 3–5, Frank at p. 91.

63. David E. Kyvig, *The Age of Impeachment: American Constitutional Culture since 1960* (Lawrence: University Press of Kansas, 2008), preface, ch. 12. Clinton Rossiter, quoted p. 36, coined "rusted blunderbuss."

64. Howard Kurtz, "Dick Morris, High on the Critical List," *WP,* February 3, 1999; Caryl Rivers, "Why Women Back Clinton," *Boston Globe,* December 27, 1998; Carey Goldberg et al., "Nation through a Looking Glass . . . ," *NYT,* February 3, 1998; "Clinton Rating Near Record High," *Atlanta Journal-Constitution,* January 21, 1999.

65. Clinton, *My Life,* 824–825, 862.

11. THE ILLUSION OF CONSERVATISM

1. "'What's a Man Got to Do to Get in the Top 50,'" *Times of India,* January 24, 2007; William J. Bennett, *The Death of Outrage: Bill Clinton and the Assault on American Ideals* (New York: Free Press, 1998); Paul Weyrich, "An Open Letter to Conservatives," in *Conservatism in America since 1930: A Reader,* ed. Gregory L. Schneider (New York: New York University Press, 2003), 429.

2. Ethan Bronner, "Left and Right Are Crossing Paths," *NYT,* July 11, 1999.

3. Paul Blanshard, *Personal and Controversial: An Autobiography* (Boston: Beacon Press, 1973), 281; White House Office of Management and Budget, *Historical Tables* 7.1 and 10.1, http://www.whitehouse.gov/omb/budget/fy2009/hist .html, March 22, 2009.

4. Jeffrey Hart, *The Making of the American Conservative Mind: National Review and Its Times* (Wilmington, Del.: ISI Books, 2005); Kevin Mattson, *Rebels All! A Short History of the Conservative Mind in Postwar America* (New Brunswick, N.J.: Rutgers University Press, 2008), 1–21.

5. Charles Reich, AI, January 18, 2008.

6. Ralph Reed, *Active Faith: How Christians Are Changing the Soul of American Politics* (New York: Free Press, 1996), 5, 9, 25, 75–78, 222–223, 264–265.

7. Sam Roberts, "To Be Married Means to Be Outnumbered," *NYT,* October 15, 2006; Kate Zernike, "Why Are There So Many Single Americans?" *NYT,* January 21, 2007; "The Decline of Marriage," *Scientific American* 281 (December 1999): 36–37, with additional data from the *Statistical Abstract of the United States* (Washington, D.C.: GPO, various dates).

8. Andrew J. Cherlin, *The Marriage-Go-Round: The State of Marriage and the Family in America Today* (New York: Knopf, 2009), 3–10; W. Bradford Wilcox, "How Focused on the Family? Evangelical Protestants, the Family, and Sexuality," in *Evangelicals and Democracy in America,* vol. 1, ed. Steven Brint and Jean Reith Schroedel (New York: Russell Sage Foundation, 2009), 251–275.

9. Brooke E. Wells and Jean M. Twenge, "Changes in Young People's Sexual Behavior and Attitudes, 1943–1999: A Cross-Temporal Meta-Analysis," *Review of General Psychology* 9 (2005): 255–256; Jean M. Twenge, *Generation Me* (New York: Free Press, 2006), 161–162, 168.

10. Nina Bernstein, "Behind Fall in Pregnancy, a New Teenage Culture of Restraint," *NYT,* March 7, 2004; Twenge, *Generation Me,* 165–167; Theodore Caplow et al., *The First Measured Century: An Illustrated Guide to Trends in America, 1900–2000* (Washington, D.C.: AEI Press, 2001), 74–75.

11. *Statistical Abstract, 1972,* p. 217, and *2007,* p. 373; Caplow et al., *First Measured Century,* 40–41; Andrew Hacker, "How Are Women Doing?" *NYRB* 49 (April 11, 2002): 65; Thomas E. Ricks, *Fiasco: The American Military Adventure in Iraq* (New York: Penguin, 2006), 247.

12. John Burnham, *Bad Habits: Drinking, Smoking, Taking Drugs, Gambling, Sexual Misbehavior, and Swearing in American History* (New York: New York University Press, 1993); Eric Schlosser, *Reefer Madness: Sex, Drugs, and Cheap Labor in the American Black Market* (Boston: Houghton Mifflin, 2003); "Abortion Poll Filled with Conflicted Views," *FTU,* June 19, 2000 (homosexuals).

13. "National Gaming Industry Statistics," http://www.casino-degrees.com/statistics.php, October 17, 2008; Reed, *Active Faith,* 223; Connie Bruck, "McCain's Party," *New Yorker* 81 (May 30, 2005): 60.

14. Lawrie Mifflin, "TV Stretches Limits of Taste, to Little Outcry," *NYT,* April 6, 1998; Warren Berger, "Censorship in the Age of Anything Goes," *NYT,* September 20, 1998; Jane E. Brody, "Children, Media, and Sex," *NYT,* January 31, 2006; "Study: Violence, Sex Increase in Movies," AP wire, July 14, 2004; Peter Bart, "Pix Ratings Deserve an 'A' for Anachronistic," *Variety,* July 26, 1999.

15. *Statistical Abstract, 2007,* pp. 74, 191; Hacker, "How Are Women Doing?" 63; James Risen and Judy L. Thomas, *Wrath of Angels: The American Abortion War* (New York: Basic Books, 1998), 376–377; Kate Zernike, "30 Years after Roe . . . ," *NYT,* January 20, 2003; Andrew Lehren and John Leland, "Scant Drop Seen in Abortion Rate if Parents Are Told," *NYT,* March 6, 2006.

16. John J. Donohue III and Steven D. Levitt, "The Impact of Legalized Abortion on Crime," *Quarterly Journal of Economics* 116 (2001): 379–420; Bennett transcript, http://mediamatters.org/mmtv/200509280006, March 20, 2010. Nixon himself, in a January 23, 1973, conversation with Colson, said that legal abortion was necessary in cases of black–white pregnancies or rapes. Tape 407–18, NPMS.

17. Jeffrey Rosen, "The Day after Roe," *Atlantic Monthly* 297 (June 2006): 56–66; Sheryl Gay Stolberg, "The War Over Abortion Moves to a Smaller Stage," *NYT,* October 26, 2003; Michael Dukakis, AI, December 8, 2008.

18. George McGovern, AI, March 20, 2009.

19. Robert Wuthnow, *After the Baby Boomers: How Twenty- and Thirty-Somethings Are Shaping the Future of American Religion* (Princeton, N.J.: Princeton University Press, 2007), ch. 2; Egon Mayer and Barry Kosmin, *American Religious Identification Survey, 2001,* http://www.gc.cuny.edu/faculty/research_briefs/aris.pdf, August 4, 2009; Rodney Stark, *What Americans Really Believe: New Findings from the Baylor Surveys of Religion* (Waco, Tex.: Baylor University Press, 2008), 22.

20. Hazel Gaudet Erskine, "The Polls: Church Attendance," *Public Opinion Quarterly* 28 (1964): 672; Roger Schwietz, "Recruiting Vocations," *America* 185 (July 29, 2001): 7; D. Paul Sullins, "Empty Pews and Empty Altars: A Reconsideration of the Catholic Priest Shortage," *America* 186 (May 13, 2002): 13.

21. Richard Viguerie, AI, June 22, 2006.

22. William V. D'Antonio, "American Catholics from John Paul II to Benedict XVI," *National Catholic Reporter,* September 30, 2005; Roger Finke and Rodney Stark, *The Churching of America, 1776–1990: Winners and Losers in Our Religious Economy* (New Brunswick, N.J.: Rutgers University Press, 1992), 255–274; Rachel Zoll, "Leaders of Conservative Judaism Confront Failures of Movement," AP wire, March 10, 2005.

23. Charles Taylor, *A Secular Age* (Cambridge, Mass.: Harvard University Press, 2007), ch. 14.

24. Karen Owen, "Study Shows Facts Are Fudged in Polls on Attending Church," Knight Ridder/Tribune wire, January 15, 1999 (including Walsh); Ellen Gamerman, "When Voters Lie," *WSJ,* August 2–3, 2008 (abortion); "Church Size: It's All in the Numbers," *FTU,* June 30, 2008; Robert D. Putnam, *Bowling Alone: The Collapse and Revival of American Community* (New York: Simon and Schuster, 2000), 72.

25. *The Unchurched American . . . 10 Years Later* (Princeton, N.J.: Princeton Religion Research Center, 1988), 27, 28, 31; Alan Wolfe, "The Pursuit of Autonomy?" *NYT Magazine,* May 7, 2000, p. 54.

26. George Gallup Jr. and Sarah Jones, *100 Questions and Answers: Religion in America* (Princeton, N.J.: Princeton Research Center, 1989), 42; Wade Clark Roof and William McKinney, *American Mainline Religion: Its Changing Shape and Future* (New Brunswick, N.J.: Rutgers University Press, 1987), 97.

27. Alan Wolfe, "And the Winner Is . . . ," *Atlantic Monthly* 301 (March 2008): 60; Thomas C. Reeves, *The Empty Church: The Suicide of Liberal Christianity* (New York: Free Press, 1996), 11, 67; Mark O'Keefe, "Number of Those Who Claim No Religion Swells," *Presbyterian Outlook* 185 (December 22, 2003): 3.

28. Norman Mailer to Sal Centrano, March 28, 1999, reprinted in *The New Yorker* 84 (October 6, 2008): 63; John Paul II, *Centesimus Annus,* http://www.vatican.va/holy_father/john_paul_ii/encyclicals/documents/hf_jp-ii_enc_01051991_centesimus-annus_en.html, October 28, 2008; Benjamin Barber, "Shrunken

Sovereign: Consumerism, Globalization, and American Emptiness," http://www.worldaffairsjournal.org/articles/2008-Spring/full-Barber.html, March 20, 2010.

29. Garrison Keillor, *Homegrown Democrat: A Few Plain Thoughts from the Heart of America* (New York: Viking, 2004), 112; Thomas Frank, *What's the Matter with Kansas? How Conservatives Won the Heart of America* (New York: Metropolitan Books, 2004), 136.

30. David Garland, *The Culture of Control: Crime and Social Order in Contemporary Society* (Chicago: University of Chicago Press, 2001), 88–89; Bill Bishop with Robert G. Cushing, *The Big Sort: Why the Clustering of Like-Minded America Is Tearing Us Apart* (New York: Houghton Mifflin, 2008), 5, 8, 10, 34, 213.

31. Gary Cross, *An All-Consuming Century: Why Commercialism Won in Modern America* (New York: Columbia University Press, 2000), ch. 6, quotation at p. 219.

32. John Schwartz, "Always on the Job, Employees Pay with Health," *NYT*, September 5, 2004; Tony Judt, "Europe vs. America," *NYRB* 52 (February 10, 2005): 37; Keith Naughton, "The Long and Grinding Road," *Newsweek* 147 (May 1, 2006): 54; James J. Cramer, *Confessions of a Street Addict* (New York: Simon and Schuster, 2002), 42–43, 65; A. Roger Ekirch, "Sleep We Have Lost: Pre-Industrial Slumber in the British Isles," *American Historical Review* 106 (2001): 384; "Duke Cuts 8 A.M. Classes," AP wire, April 19, 2004.

33. Peter T. Kilborn, "The Five-Bedroom, Six-Figure Rootless Life," *NYT*, June 1, 2005; Reeves, *Empty Church*, 61 (most important reason); Putnam, *Bowling Alone*, 72, 454 n. 32.

34. Mary Leonard, "On Many College Campuses, Comforts Are Major," *Boston Globe*, September 2, 2002.

35. Joe Bageant, "A Feast of Bullshit and Spectacle," http://www.alternet.org/media/58437, March 20, 2010.

36. David Brooks, *Bobos in Paradise: The New Upper Class and How They Got There* (New York: Touchstone, 2000), 39; Andrew Hacker, "They'd Much Rather Be Rich," *NYRB* 54 (October 11, 2007): 33; Donald T. Critchlow, *Phyllis Schlafly and Grassroots Conservatism: A Woman's Crusade* (Princeton, N.J.: Princeton University Press, 2005), 14.

37. David Brooks, "'The Chosen': Getting In," *NYT*, November 6, 2005; David A. Hollinger, *Science, Jews, and Secular Culture: Studies in Mid-Twentieth-Century Intellectual History* (Princeton, N.J.: Princeton University Press, 1996), chs. 1, 7; Barack Obama, *Dreams from My Father: A Story of Race and Inheritance* (New York: Times Books, 1995), 93; Andrew Delbanco, "Colleges: An Endangered Species?" *NYRB* 52 (March 10, 2005): 20 ("miniature"); David Brooks, *On Paradise Drive* (New York: Simon and Schuster, 2004), 174.

38. "By the Numbers," *Chronicle of Higher Education*, November 24, 2006, pp. A17–A18; Ed Vulliamy, "'The Liberal Elite Hasn't Got a Clue,'" *Guardian*, November 1, 2004.

39. C. Vann Woodward, "What Became of the 1960s?" *New Republic* 171 (November 9, 1974): 23; Mark Lilla, "A Tale of Two Reactions," *NYRB* 45 (May 14, 1998): 7.

40. Daniel Patrick Moynihan, "Defining Deviancy Down," *American Scholar* 62 (Winter 1993): 17–30; Robert H. Bork, "'Thanks a Lot': Free Speech and High Schools," *National Review* 59 (April 16, 2007): 25.

41. Moynihan to Deborah A. Dawson, August 14, 1992, box II:2946, DPMP.

42. Dan Gilgoff, *The Jesus Machine: How James Dobson, Focus on the Family, and Evangelical America Are Winning the Culture War* (New York: St. Martin's Press, 2007), 110.

43. Ibid., ch. 5.

44. Paul Weyrich, AI, October 24, 2007.

45. Sylvia Ann Hewlett, *Creating a Life: Professional Women and the Quest for Children* (New York: Talk Miramax, 2002), 33, 309–310 n. 1.

46. Philip Longman, *The Empty Cradle: How Falling Birthrates Threaten World Prosperity and What to Do about It* (New York: Basic Books, 2004), 33, 73; Dennis Cauchon, "'Fertility Gap' Helps Explain Political Divide," *USA Today*, September 27, 2006; Arthur C. Brooks, "The Fertility Gap," *WSJ*, August 22, 2006; "Houston Reflects America's Changing Face," http://futurity.org/tag/stephen-klineberg/, March 20, 2010.

47. David R. Sands, "Europe's 'Baby Bust' Signals Major Change," *WT*, November 24, 2005; Michael Specter, "Population Implosion Worries a Graying Europe," *NYT*, July 10, 1998.

48. David DeCamp, "Ballot Confusion Still Simmering in Duval," *FTU*, November 22, 2000.

49. Edmund L. Andrews, "Report Finds Tax Cuts Heavily Favor the Wealthy," *NYT*, August 13, 2004.

50. Jeff Brumley, "'Moral Values' Swayed Voters to Choose Bush," *FTU*, November 4, 2004.

51. Kevin Phillips, *American Theocracy: The Peril and Politics of Radical Religion, Oil, and Borrowed Money in the 21st Century* (New York: Viking, 2006), gay marriage at p. 242.

52. David Lightman, "Bush Is the Biggest Spender since LBJ," McClatchy wire, October 24, 2007; Maris A. Vinovskis, "Federal Education Policy and Politics," in *The Columbia History of Post-World War II America*, ed. Mark C. Carnes (New York: Columbia University Press, 2007), 472; Dennis Cauchon, "Senior Benefit Costs Up 24 Percent," *USA Today*, February 14, 2008; Richard Wolf, "Growth in Federal Spending Unchecked," *USA Today*, April 3, 2006 (Flake).

53. David Kuo, *Tempting Faith: An Inside Story of Political Seduction* (New York: Free Press, 2006), 229–230 ("nuts"); David D. Kirkpatrick, "In Secretly Taped Coversations, Glimpses of the Future President," *NYT* February 20, 2005 ("kicking"); Gerald S. Seib, "Right Grumbles . . . ," *WSJ*, May 20, 2008 ("died"); Scott McClelland, *What Happened: Inside the Bush White House and Washington's Culture of Deception* (New York: Public Affairs, 2008), chs. 5–7.

54. Jeffrey Toobin, *The Nine: Inside the Secret World of the Supreme Court* (New York: Doubleday, 2007), ch. 22.

55. Daniel M. Fox, "Context Matters: The Politics of Expanding Access to Healthcare since 1932," American Association for the History of Medicine paper, Cleveland, April 24, 2009.

56. John Steele Gordon, "A Short History of the National Debt," *WSJ*, February 18, 2009; Evan Thomas et al., "Decline and Fall," *Newsweek* 148 (November 20, 2006): 65; Scott Shane, "In Washington, Contractors Play Biggest Role Ever," *NYT*, February 4, 2007; William Kristol, "Small Isn't Beautiful," *NYT*, December 8, 2008.

57. Paul Krugman, *The Great Unraveling: Losing Our Way in the New Century*, rev. ed. (New York: Norton, 2004) and *The Conscience of a Liberal* (New York: Norton, 2007).

58. Zev Chafets, "Late-Period Limbaugh," *NYT Magazine*, July 6, 2008, pp. 37, 50; Joseph Rago, "Old School," *WSJ*, November 12, 2005 (Buckley); Tom DeLay with Stephen Mansfield, *No Retreat, No Surrender: One American's Fight* (New York: Sentinel, 2007), caption opposite p. 79; Nick Gillespie, "Bush Was a Big-Government Disaster," *WSJ*, January 24, 2009 ("bizarro"); Patrick J. Buchanan, "The Crisis of the GOP," Creators Syndicate column of November 10, 2005; Dana Milbank, "At Conservative Forum on Bush, Everybody's a Critic," *WP*, March 8, 2006; Bob Barr, AI, March 17, 2009; Anthony Gregory, "What's Left of the Old Right," *American Conservative*, October 6, 2008, http://www.amconmag.com/article/2008/oct/06/00029/ (Rockwell); David Hunt, "GOP Didn't Deliver on Conservatism," *FTU*, December 6, 2008 (Huckabee).

59. James K. Galbraith, *The Predator State: How Conservatives Abandoned the Free Market and Why Liberals Should Too* (New York: Free Press, 2008), xiii.

60. "Barack Obama's Inaugural Address," *NYT*, January 20, 2009; Naftali Bendavid, "Republicans Address Values Voters in Effort to Shore Up Base," *WSJ*, September 19–20, 2009.

61. Brian Doherty, "Best of Both Worlds," *Reason* 27 (June 1995): 38; *PBS News Hour*, February 5, 2010, http://www.pbs.org/newshour/bb/business/jan-june10/makingsense_02-05.html (Stockman).

Phillip Greven planted the seed for this book. When I read *The Protestant Temperament* in 1983, I realized that his scheme of religious temperaments, updated and expanded, could help explain the Culture War going on under my nose. I have since consulted many other authorities on the subject. I trust that I will be forgiven for restricting my citations to direct quotations, key statistics, unusual or controversial details, and the most pressing of intellectual debts.

I am also indebted to the University of North Florida, which provided a research leave and generous support through the John A. Delaney Presidential Professorship. Dale Clifford and Mark Workman freed up additional time; Corrine Connally, Deb Miller, Marianne Roberts, Erin Soles, and David Wilson helped me prepare the manuscript. UNF librarians Eileen Brady, Alisa Craddock, Shirley Hallblade, and Barbara Tuck assisted my research. So did the staffs of the Bush Presidential Library, particularly John Blair, Bonnie Burlbaw, Mary Finch, Chris Pembleton, Robert Holzweiss, and Zachary Roberts; the Carter Presidential Library, particularly Albert Nason; the Clinton Presidential Library, particularly Kim Coryat, Kelly Hendren, and John Keller; the Library of Congress Manuscript Division, particularly Jeff Flannery and John Haynes; the National Archives and Records Administration, particularly Sam Rushay and Sahr Conway-Lanz; the Reagan Presidential Library, particularly Kelly Barton; the Robert Dole Institute of Politics, particularly Jean Bischoff and Jamin Dreasher; the Spencer Research Library, particularly Rebecca Schulte and donor Laird Wilcox; and the Wisconsin Historical Society Archives, particularly Harry Miller. I supplemented the interviews I found in these libraries and archives with some three dozen of my own. I have acknowledged the interviewees' contributions in the endnotes.

Nicholas Bodnar, Amanda Chapman, Carol Clark, Charlie Cold, Judy Connolly, Chris Corcoran, Jack and Stephanie Crosby, Andrew Courtwright, Chris Courtwright, Sidney Cunningham, Ramon Day, Alex Dufresne, Bob DuPont, Mark Fafard, Charlotte Gara, Amy Glover, Andrew Hartman, James Hill, Julie Ingersoll, Sam Kimball, Beth Maycumber, Shelby Miller, Carlos Monell, Patrick Nolan, Roger Sharp, Danielle Weinstein, and Zack Zoul commented on drafts. Acquisition editor Kathleen McDermott worked with me from the beginning, and Betty Pessagno, Wendy Muto, and Heather Shaff Beaver saw me through the final stages of editing and design.

Any research effort that spans a quarter century will have its share of trial balloons. I began working out my ideas in, and incorporate some language from, "Which Sides Are You On? Religion, Sexuality, and Culture-War Politics," in *The Columbia History of Post-World War II America,* ed. Mark C. Carnes (New York: Columbia University Press, 2007), 311–339, and "Morality, Religion, and Drug Use," in *Morality and Health,* ed. Allan M. Brandt and Paul Rozin (New York: Routledge, 1997), 231–250. I remain grateful to the editors for their advice and support.